VOICES

FOR FREEDOM

an Amnesty International publication

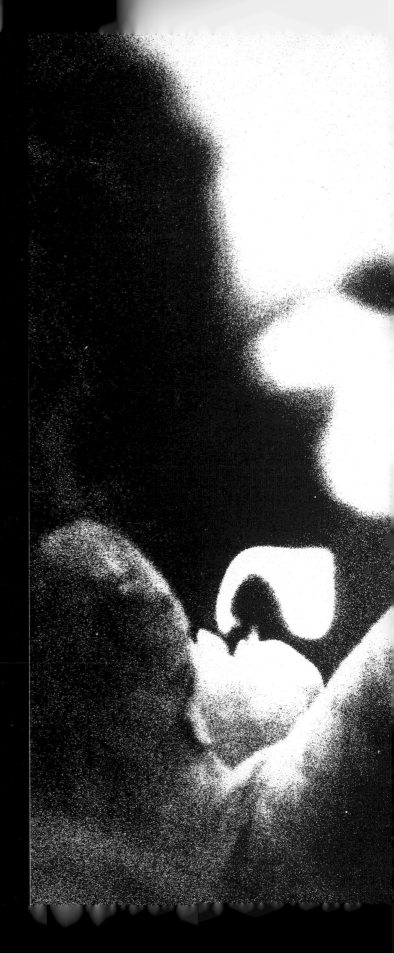

The candle burns not for us, but for all
those whom we failed to rescue from
prison, who were shot on the way to
prison, who were tortured, who were
kidnapped, who "disappeared". That's
what the candle is for...'

● <u>PETER BENENSON</u>, founder of Amnesty International

Back cover photograph: "patience, hope,
courage" ... an inscription made by
detainees out of cigarette packets. This
photograph was taken in Camp Boiro,
Conakry, Guinea, which before the
overthrow of ex-President Sekou Touré in
April 1984 housed hundreds of political
prisoners, many of whom died of torture or
thirst and hunger.

First published 1986
by Amnesty International Publications
1 Easton Street, London WC1X 8DJ
United Kingdom

© Copyright Amnesty International
Publications 1986

ISBN 0 86210 095 X
AI Index: ACT 03/04/86
Original language: English

Index compiled by: Steve Pinder
Design: John Finn
Typesetting & production: Artworkers, London
Printed by: David Green (Printers) Limited,
Kettering, Northants

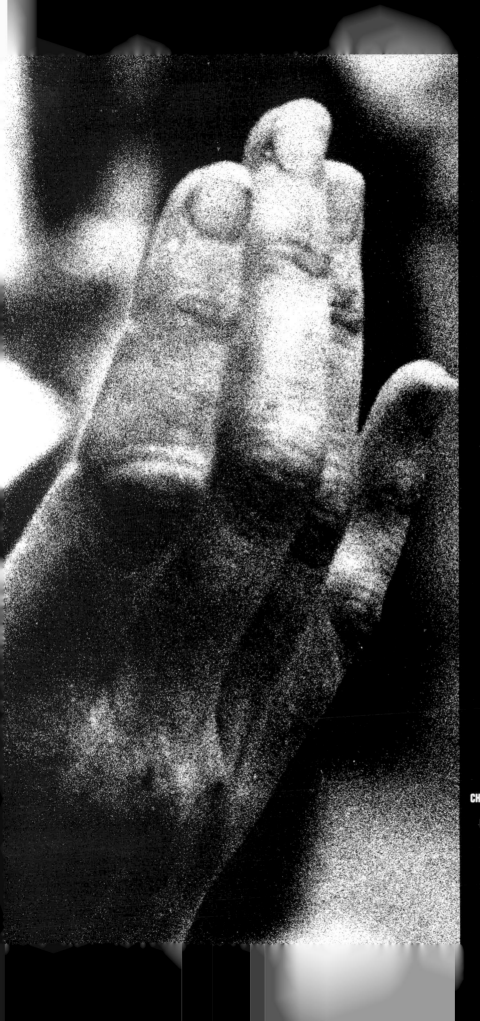

CONTENTS

INTRODUCTION

This is a book of voices. The voices of prisoners of conscience, of political prisoners held without trial, of torture victims, of people threatened with execution and 'disappearance'. Most of all this a book attesting to the countless men and women around the world who have raised their voices in defence of those who have been silenced.

Some victims have braved repression by successive governments, speaking out consistently for human rights. One such was the Iranian poet and playwright, Saeed Soltanpour.... Imprisoned many times for his writings under the Shah and then arrested by the new Islamic government and executed after accusing the authorities of torturing people and suppressing freedom. He wrote:

Upon this plain of blood roses and iron stalks
I will not stay silent ...
So hear my voice
As it sings in the slaughterhouse.

His story is one of the thousands reflected in this anthology, culled from Amnesty International's work over the years.

This book also portrays a unique movement which has brought together people from all walks of life to work in defence of human rights under all political systems.

It started with a newspaper article, 'The Forgotten Prisoners', in May 1961 calling for action to free men and women in prison because of their religious and political beliefs. These were called 'prisoners of conscience' – a new phrase had entered the vocabulary of world affairs.

Within a month more than a thousand people had offered to help – 'letters came in from all quarters by the score, and offers of help from people of all kinds' recalled an early participant. Six months later a permanent international movement had been established. 'We believe that these first six months have shown that in an increasingly cynical world there is a great latent reservoir of idealism to be tapped' declared Peter Benenson, the movement's founder.

At that time – in 1961 – trade unionists in Spain were being arrested, dissenters faced long prison terms in the German Democratic Republic, detainees in South Africa were being brutally ill-treated in custody, civil rights workers in the United States of America were being persecuted, political trials were taking place in the Soviet Union, and in many other countries people were being imprisoned, tortured or executed because their opinions were unacceptable to the ruling authorities.

The campaign has since widened in response to political arrests, torture and execution. What Amnesty International members have attempted is the seemingly impossible – one of the 'larger lunacies' as it has been described. They have battled against official silence and political persecution using as their only weapons the publicizing of awkward facts and that reservoir of idealism.

This anthology hopes to give a flavour of the movement's work and the spirit behind it. It is not intended as a history of the organization, nor as a record of its most important initiatives. Much of Amnesty International's work is not reflected in the pages that follow, for example the material support given to prisoners of conscience and their families through relief funds, or the interventions of the organization at intergovernmental arenas such as the United Nations. Rather it is a series of 'snapshots', glimpses of the prisoners and the campaigns on their behalf over a span of 25 years. Such a compilation cannot begin to be comprehensive, nor can it hope to record all the vital work carried on by ordinary men and women in the face of apathy, ignorance and executive power. The selection ranges from letters from prison and the story of a single prisoner of conscience, to extracts from a submission to a government inquiry into ill-treatment of detainees and a survey of political killings by governments. Through these brief excerpts from Amnesty International's reports, bulletins, news releases and newsletters it is hoped that the reader will gain an idea of the range of Amnesty International's concerns and a sense of the continuing challenge of political imprisonment, torture and executions.

It will be clear from the pages that follow that Amnesty International's membership, research capacity and work have grown enormously over the decades, and that with that growth has come change. However, they do show that Amnesty International has sought to abide by certain principles from its inception. Fundamental among those principles are independence and impartiality. Amnesty International is linked to no political grouping or government. It neither supports nor opposes any government or political system. It is concerned solely with the protection of the human rights involved in each case, regardless of the ideology of the government or the views of the victims. Amnesty International always seeks and remains open to dialogue with governments to get their version of the facts and to make concrete proposals for improvements. It does not grade governments according to their human rights records or try to compare one country with another. As well as political independence, Amnesty International regards financial independence as vital. Its rules about accepting donations are strict and ensure that funds received do not affect the organization's integrity, make it dependent on any donor or limit its freedom of action. It does not accept government funds for its budget. Amnesty International works on the basis of a single universal standard: the human rights proclaimed by the international community through the United Nations and other bodies.

Amnesty International plays a specific role in the international protection of human rights. It seeks the immediate and unconditional release of men and women detained anywhere because of their beliefs, colour, sex, ethnic origin, language or religious creed, provided they have not used or advocated violence. These are prisoners of conscience. It calls for fair and prompt trials for all political prisoners, and works on behalf of political prisoners detained without trial. It opposes the death penalty and torture or other cruel, inhuman and degrading treatment of all prisoners.

The organization's work towards freeing prisoners of conscience, fair trials for political prisoners and an end to torture and the death penalty leads it to oppose the forcible return of anyone to a country where they might reasonably fear becoming the victim of such human rights violations. It presents information about the risks refugees face in their countries of origin to specialized refugee organizations and to governments considering applications for political asylum.

Working with the most reliable information available to it, Amnesty International seeks effective ways of helping victims wherever it is aware that those rights it seeks to protect have been violated. The techniques it uses include long-term adoption of individual cases; campaigns on particular countries or human rights abuses; mobilizing professional occupational groups on behalf of colleagues; publicizing patterns of human rights abuses; missions to talk with government representatives; or, in cases where torture or death are feared, a network of volunteeers to send urgent telegrams signalling international concern. Each technique, or combination of methods, is used in the best interests of the prisoners, and therefore varies from country to country. For this reason, the whole range of the movement's work must be taken into account when assessing its overall impartiality – particularly in an anthology such as this when only brief extracts can be included to illustrate a quarter of a century's work.

Above all, Amnesty International remains a movement of 'ordinary' people. People who accept, as a personal responsibility, the international protection of human rights. Each is responsible for the growing strength of international public opinion. Each has become a voice that speaks on behalf of those who cannot.

Early in 1961, a British lawyer named Peter Benenson read in his morning paper of two students in Portugal who had been arrested in a restaurant and sentenced to 7 years' imprisonment for raising their glasses in a toast to freedom.

Indignant, Peter Benenson's first reaction was to go to the Portuguese Embassy in London and protest personally, but he realized that such an individual gesture would accomplish little for the students themselves.

Government repression of dissent was a problem that had long troubled Peter Benenson. During the 1950s he had attended political trials in Hungary, Cyprus, South Africa and Spain, either as a legal observer or as defence counsel. He had also written and broadcast widely about the problem.

Now he began to wonder how oppressive regimes might react to concerted worldwide protests at acts of political injustice, rather than to the individual protest he had contemplated in the case of the Portuguese students. Gradually he conceived the idea of a one-year international campaign to draw world attention to the plight of people detained throughout the world – under all political systems – for the peaceful expression of their political or religious opinions.

He discussed the idea with Eric Baker, a prominent English Quaker, and other friends. Their enthusiastic reactions led to him writing the article in *The Observer* newspaper, entitled 'The Forgotten Prisoners'. The article and a report in *Le Monde* the same day announced the launching of a one-year campaign called 'Appeal for Amnesty, 1961' whose object was to obtain an amnesty for all political and religious prisoners of conscience. Part of the campaign was the establishment of an office in London to collect information about such prisoners and to publicize individual cases.

The appeal quickly attracted international support and within a few short months the groundwork was laid for a permanent organization that eventually became known as Amnesty International.

SIX POLITICAL PRISONERS: left, Constantin Noica, the philosopher, now in a Rumanian gaol: centre, the Rev. Ashton Jones, friend of the Negroes, recently in gaol in the United States: right, Agostino Neto, Angolan poet and doctor, held without trial by the Portuguese. Their cases are described in the article below.

Left, Archbishop Beran of Prague, held in custody by the Czechs: centre, Toni Ambatielos, the Greek Communist and trade unionist prisoner, whose wife is English: right Cardinal Mindszenty, Primate of Hungary, formerly a prisoner and now a political refugee trapped in the United States Embassy, Budapest.

ON BOTH SIDES of the Iron Curtain, thousands of men and women are being held in gaol without trial because their political or religious views differ from those of their Governments. Peter Benenson, a London lawyer, conceived the idea of a world campaign, APPEAL FOR AMNESTY, 1961, to urge Governments to release these people or at least give them a fair trial. The campaign opens to-day, and "The Observer" is glad to offer it a platform.

The Forgotten Prisoners

OPEN your newspaper any day of the week and you will find a report from somewhere in the world of someone being imprisoned, tortured or executed because his opinions or religion are unacceptable to his government. There are several million such people in prison—by no means all of them behind the Iron and Bamboo Curtains—and their numbers are growing. The newspaper reader feels a sickening sense of impotence. Yet if these feelings of disgust all over the world could be united into common action, something effective could be done.

In 1945 the founder members of the United Nations approved the Universal Declaration of Human Rights:—

Article 18.—Everyone has the right to freedom of thought, conscience and religion; this right includes freedom to change his religion or belief, and freedom either alone or in company with others in public or private, to manifest his religion or belief in teaching practice, worship and observance.

Article 19.—Everyone has the right to freedom of opinion and expression; this right includes freedom to hold opinions without interference and to seek, receive and impart information and ideas through any media and regardless of frontiers.

There is at present no sure way of finding out how many countries permit their citizens to enjoy these two fundamental freedoms. What matters is not the rights that exist on paper in the Constitution, but whether they can be exercised and enforced in practice. No government, for instance, is at greater pains to emphasise its constitutional guarantees than the Spanish, but it fails to apply them.

There is a growing tendency all over the world to disguise the real grounds upon which "non-conformists" are imprisoned. In Spain, students who circulate leaflets calling for the right to hold discussions on current affairs are charged with "military rebellion." In Hungary, Catholic priests who have tried to keep their choir schools open have been charged with "homosexuality." These cover-up charges indicate that governments are by no means insensitive to the pressure of outside opinion. And when world opinion is concentrated on one weak spot, it can sometimes succeed in making a government relent. For instance, the Hungarian poet Tibor Dery was recently released after the formation of "Tibor Dery committees" in many countries; and Professor Tierno Galvan and his literary friends were acquitted in Spain this March, after the arrival of some distinguished foreign observers.

London office to gather facts

The important thing is to mobilise public opinion quickly, and widely, before a government is caught up in the vicious spiral caused by its own repression, and is faced with impending civil war. By then the situation will have become too desperate for the government to make concessions. The force of opinion, to be effective, should be broadly based, international, non-sectarian and all-party. Campaigns in favour of freedom brought by one country, or party, against another, often achieve nothing but an intensification of persecution.

That is why we have started Appeal for Amnesty, 1961. The campaign, which opens to-day, is the result of an initiative by a group of lawyers, writers and publishers in London, who share the underlying conviction expressed by Voltaire: "I detest your views, but am prepared to die for your right to express them." We have set up an office in London to collect information about the names, numbers and conditions of what we have decided to call "Prisoners of Conscience," and we define them thus: "Any person who is physically restrained (by imprisonment or otherwise) from expressing (in any form of words or symbols) any opinion which he honestly holds and which does not advocate or condone personal violence." We also exclude those who have conspired with a foreign government to overthrow their own. Our office will from time to time hold Press conferences to focus attention on Prisoners of Conscience selected impartially from different parts of the world. And it will provide factual information to any group, existing or new, in any part of the world, which decides to join in a special effort in favour of freedom of opinion or religion.

In October a Penguin Special called "Persecution 1961" will be published as part of our Amnesty campaign. In it are stories of nine men and women from different parts of the world, of varying political and religious outlook, who have been suffering imprisonment for expressing their opinions. None of them is a professional politician; all of them are professional people. The opinions which have brought them to prison are the common coinage of argument in free society.

Poet flogged in front of family

One story is of the revolting brutality with which Angola's leading poet, Agostino Neto, was treated before the present disturbances there broke out. Dr. Neto was one of the five African doctors in Angola. His efforts to improve the health services for his fellow Africans were unacceptable to the Portuguese. In June last year the Political Police marched into his house, had him flogged in front of his family and then dragged away. He has since been in prison in the Cape Verde Isles without charge or trial.

From Rumania, we shall print the story of Constantin Noica, the philosopher, who was sentenced to twenty-five years' imprisonment because, while "rusticated," his friends and pupils continued to visit him, to listen to his talk on philosophy and literature. The book will also tell of the Spanish lawyer, Antonio Amat, who tried to build a coalition of democratic groups, and has been in prison without trial since November, 1958; and of two white men persecuted by their own race for preaching that the coloured races should have equal rights—Ashton Jones, the sixty-five-year-old minister, who last year was repeatedly beaten-up and three times imprisoned in Louisiana and Texas for doing what the Freedom Riders are now doing in Alabama; and Patrick Duncan, the son of a former South African Governor-General, who, after three stays in prison, has just been served with an order forbidding him from attending or addressing any meeting for five years.

'Find out who is in gaol'

The technique of publicising the personal stories of a number of prisoners of contrasting politics is a new one. It has been adopted to avoid the fate of previous amnesty campaigns, which so often have become more concerned with publicising the political views of the imprisoned than with humanitarian purposes.

How can we discover the state of freedom in the world to-day? The American philosopher, John Dewey, once said, "If you want to establish some conception of a society, go find out who is in gaol." This is hard advice to follow, because there are few governments which welcome inquiries about the number of Prisoners of Conscience they hold in prison. But another test of freedom one can apply is whether the Press is allowed to criticise the government. Even many democratic governments are surprisingly sensitive to Press criticism. In France, General de Gaulle has intensified newspaper seizures, a policy he inherited from the Fourth Republic. In Britain and the United States occasional attempts are made to draw the sting of Press criticism by the technique of taking editors into confidence about a "security secret," as in the Blake spy case.

Within the British Commonwealth, the Government of Ceylon has launched an attack on the Press, and is threatening to take the whole industry under public control. In Pakistan the Press is at the mercy of the Martial Law administration. In Ghana, the opposition Press operates under great disabilities. In South Africa, which leaves the Commonwealth on Wednesday, the government is planning further legislation to censor publications. Outside the Commonwealth, Press freedom is especially in peril in Indonesia, the Arab world, and Latin American countries such as Cuba. In the Communist world, and in Spain and Portugal, Press criticism of the Government is rarely tolerated.

Churchill's dictum on democracy

Another test of freedom is whether the government permits a political opposition. The post-war years have seen the spread of "personal regimes" across Asia and Africa. Wherever an opposition party is prevented from putting up candidates, or from verifying the election results, much more than its own future is at stake. Multi-party elections may be cumbrous in practice, and the risk of coalitions makes for unstable government; but no other way has yet been found to guarantee freedom to minorities or safety to nonconformists. Whatever truth there may be in the old remark that democracy does not fit well with emergent nationalism, we should also remember Winston Churchill's dictum: "Democracy is a damned bad system of government, but nobody has thought of a better."

A fourth test of freedom is, whether those accused of offences against the State receive a speedy and public trial before an impartial court; whether they are allowed to call witnesses, and whether their lawyer is able to present the defence in the way he thinks best. In recent years there has been a regrettable trend in some of those countries that take pride in possessing an independent judiciary: by declaring a state of emergency and taking their opponents into "preventive detention," governments have side-stepped the need to make and prove criminal charges. At the other extreme there is the enthusiasm in Soviet countries to set up institutions which, though called courts, are really nothing of the sort. The so-called "comradely courts" in the U.S.S.R., which have power to deal with "parasites," are in essence little more than departments of the Ministry of Labour, shifting "square pegs" into empty holes in Siberia. In China the transmigration of labour by an allegedly judicial process is on a gigantic scale.

The most rapid way of bringing relief to Prisoners of Conscience is publicity, especially publicity among their fellow-citizens. With the pressure of emergent nationalism and the tensions of the Cold War, there are bound to be situations where governments are led to take emergency measures to protect their existence. It is vital that public opinion should insist that these measures should not be excessive, nor prolonged after the moment of danger. If the emergency is to last a long time, then a government should be induced to allow its opponents out of prison, to seek asylum abroad.

Frontier control more efficient

Although there are no statistics, it is likely that recent years have seen a steady decrease in the number of people reaching asylum. This is not so much due to the unwillingness of other countries to offer shelter, as to the greatly increased efficiency of frontier control, which to-day makes it harder for people to get away. Attempts to reach agreement on a workable international convention on asylum at United Nations have dragged on for many years with little result.

There is also the problem of labour restrictions on immigrants in many countries. So long as work is not available in "host" countries, the right of asylum is largely empty. Appeal for Amnesty, 1961, aims to help towards providing suitable employment for political and religious refugees. It would be good if in each "host" country a central employment office for these people could be set up with the co-operation of the employers' federations, the trade unions and the Ministry of Labour.

In Britain there are many firms willing to give out translation and correspondence work to refugees, but no machinery to link supply with demand. Those regimes that refuse to allow their nationals to seek asylum on the ground that they go abroad only to conspire, might be less reluctant if they knew that, on arrival, the refugees would not be kicking their heels in idle frustration.

The members of the Council of Europe have agreed a Convention of Human Rights, and set up a commission to secure its enforcement. Some countries have accorded to their citizens the right to approach the commission individually. But some, including Britain, have refused to accept the jurisdiction of the commission over individual complaints, and France has refused to ratify the Convention at all. Public opinion should insist on the establishment of effective supra-national machinery not only in Europe but on similar lines in other continents.

This is an especially suitable year for an Amnesty Campaign. It is the centenary of President Lincoln's inauguration, and of the beginning of the Civil War which ended with the liberation of the American slaves; it is also the centenary of the decree that emancipated the Russian serfs. A hundred years ago Mr. Gladstone's budget swept away the oppressive duties on newsprint and so enlarged the range and freedom of the Press; 1861 marked the end of the tyranny of King "Bomba" of Naples, and the creation of a united Italy; it was also the year of the death of Lacordaire, the French Dominican opponent of Bourbon and Orleanist oppression.

The success of the 1961 Amnesty Campaign depends on how sharply and powerfully it is possible to rally public opinion. It depends, too, upon the campaign being all-embracing in its composition, international in character and politically impartial in direction. Any group is welcome to take part which is prepared to condemn persecution regardless of where it occurs, who is responsible or what are the ideas suppressed. How much can be achieved when men and women of good will unite was shown during World Refugee Year. Inevitably most of the action called for by Appeal for Amnesty, 1961, can only be taken by governments. But experience shows that in matters such as these governments are prepared to follow only where public opinion leads. Pressure of opinion a hundred years ago brought about the emancipation of the slaves. It is now for man to insist upon the same freedom for his mind as he has won for his body.

PETER BENENSON

Appeal for Amnesty, 1961

THE AIMS

1. **To work impartially for the release of those imprisoned for their opinions.**
2. **To seek for them a fair and public trial.**
3. **To enlarge the Right of Asylum and help political refugees to find work.**
4. **To urge effective international machinery to guarantee freedom of opinion.**

To these ends, an office has been set up in London to collect and publish information about Prisoners of Conscience all over the world. The first Press Conference of the campaign will be held to-morrow, where speakers will include three M.P.s, John Foster, Q.C. (Con.), F. Elwyn Jones, Q.C. (Lab.), and Jeremy Thorpe (Lib.).

All offers of help and information should be sent to: Appeal for Amnesty, 1, Mitre Court Buildings, Temple, E.C.4.

FAULTS
ESH

THE OBSERVER WEEKEND REVIEW | Pages 21-40

Page
35 Architecture
29-31 Books
25 Bridge
28 Chess
34 Cookery
38 Dodos of to-morrow
27 Films
27 Galleries
38 Gardening
22, 38 LETTERS
26 Music
35 Open Air
35 Property
35 Saleroom
40 Savings
27 Sound Radio
27 Television
26 Theatres
37 Time Off
Universities
Wine List

Butlin's new image p. 36

The second of "The Observer's" picture reports on aspects of The English Summer deals with a uniquely British but paradoxically Marxian concept of escapism. It also reveals a subtle change in the technique of holiday-selling.

PINEAPPLE and l'autostop page 33

23 Saving the white rhino by **Colin Willock**
25 MOROCCAN NOTEBOOK by **Hugh Massingham**
26 The new Glyndebourne season by **Peter Heyworth**
27 TELEVISION **Maurice Richardson** on "The Village Viewers"
28 PARIS PERSPECTIVE A new monthly report by **Barbara Bray**
29 NEW FICTION by **John Davenport**
30 IN OUR TIME Sex and literary values by **John Weightman**
31 **Harold Nicolson** reviews the diary of a 16th-century medical student
32 Sportswear for the inactive by **Katharine Whitehorn**
33 A girl's best friend by **Elizabeth Gundrey**

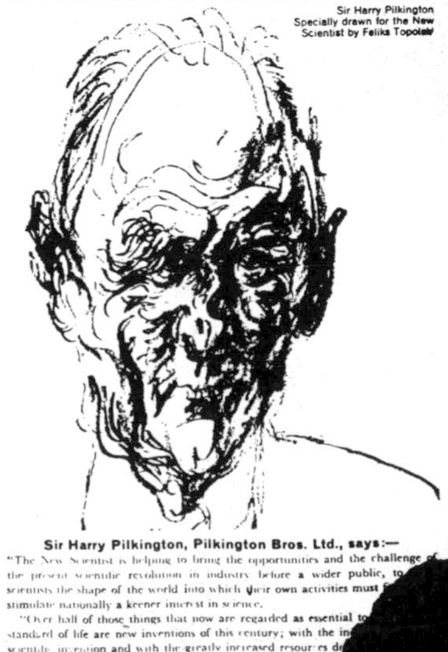

Sir Harry Pilkington Specially drawn for the New Scientist by Feliks Topolski

Sir Harry Pilkington, Pilkington Bros. Ltd., says:—

"The New Scientist is helping to bring the opportunities and the challenge of the present scientific revolution in industry before a wider public, to ... scientists the shape of the world into which their own activities must ... stimulate nationally a keener interest in science.

"Over half of those things that now are regarded as essential to ... standard of life are new inventions of this century; with the in... scientific invention and with the greatly increased resources de... and development, a further spate of new revolutionary bene... assured. Anything that quickens the appreciation of the... is of great value."

POET OF FREEDOM

Within a month of the launch of the Amnesty appeal, a fortnightly journal on political imprisonment called 'Amnesty' was being published from an office staffed by volunteers in London's legal district. Spanish poet and journalist Cristobal Vega Alvarez – imprisoned for over 20 years from the time General Franco took power at the end of the Spanish Civil War – featured in the November 1961 issue.

On 5th March, 1960, Cristobal Vega Alvarez, the Spanish poet and journalist, had already served twenty years in prison because of his liberal political views. Yet on 6th March, 1960, one day after he was due to be discharged, he was faced with a new sentence of eight years – based, apparently, on nothing more circumstantial than having been in the possession of a newspaper of 'democratic' views. For this he was sentenced by a Military Tribunal to the eight-year term which he is today working out behind the walls of the prison of Santa Maria in Cadiz.

The long story of Vega Alvarez's arrests begins in March 1939, when he was detained at the prison in Utrera. From there he was taken to Avila, where, because of his journalistic activities under the Republic, he was court-martialed and sentenced to 20 years' imprisonment. In 1941 he was transferred to Astorga, and in 1942 to a penal detachment in Guipuzcoa, where the prisoners worked for a building enterprise called 'Ferrocarriles y Construcciones ABC' (ABC Railroads and Constructions).

In 1943 he was released conditionally, and he remained a free employee of the ABC Railroads. But after a short time he crossed to France where he worked on the editorial staff of *Reconquista de España* (Reconquest of Spain), the paper of the Spanish National Union. During this period, in October 1944, he was a delegate to the Congress held in Toulouse.

At this time he was deeply interested in the activities of the 'Spanish Maquis'. He returned to Spain to live and work in this movement so that he could gain personal experience and documentation for a series of articles he was planning on the subject.

Once more he was arrested – this time in the mountains of Navarre. This time he had neither taken part in any action of violence, nor held office or command in the military units. Legally, even if tried as an ordinary soldier, he could only have been condemned to a maximum sentence of six years and a day. Nevertheless, the sentence climbed to 12 years and a day, then to 20 years and a day, until it was finally settled at 30 years' penal servitude.

Vega Alvarez is said to have been an 'exemplary' prisoner. All the reports requested by the military and prison authorities carry the same phrase: 'His conduct is exceptionally good.' Vega Alvarez always worked in prison so as to benefit from the system of 'redemptions through work' which is in operation in Spanish prisons. In spite of this and the right to conditional freedom granted, subject to good behaviour, he had been in prison for 11 years before he could claim to be discharged conditionally on 5th March, 1960. It was then that he received his last sentence of eight years.

This last trial was, it seems, based on an incident that had happened as far back as 1946, when Vega Alvarez was found with a certain newspaper, which was then confiscated. The name of the paper is not known, but it is described as a newspaper which anybody can read freely anywhere where there is a minimum of freedom, a 'democratic' paper which was not directed at any institution or any person. Vega Alvarez could have had no idea that this would be held against him let alone that it would warrant a full court-martial. Nevertheless, a Council of War was set up and decreed a period of no less than eight years' imprisonment for an 'offence' for which any ordinary tribunal might, at most, have sentenced him to two months.

The crimes of C. Vega Alvarez, for which he has paid for so many years, seem to be that he had been a journalist before the Civil War, that he had lived with the 'Maquis' to gain material for articles, and that he had been found with an unpopular newspaper.

Vega Alvarez has been described as representing the authentic liberal thought of Spanish intellectuals. He has had several works published, the last one being a book of poems. The irony is that most of his poetic output has come from behind bars, even though he is known to his admirers as 'the Poet of Freedom'.

Published November 1961

◀ A prison camp in Spain (1965).

▼ *Good news: a Christmas card sent to a prisoner of conscience in Spain is returned by the prison authorities marked 'Return to sender as consignee is free'. From 'Amnesty', January 1962.*

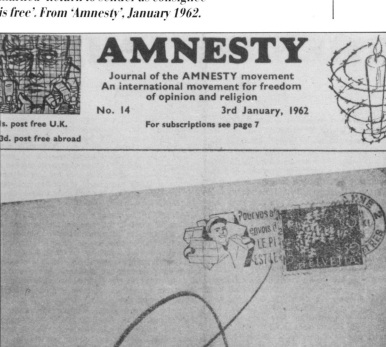

AMNESTY

Journal of the AMNESTY movement
An international movement for freedom
of opinion and religion

No. 14   3rd January, 1962

For subscriptions see page 7

s. post free U.K.
3d. post free abroad

PORTUGUESE REPORT

When two Portuguese students were sentenced to seven years' imprisonment for toasting freedom, Peter Benenson was moved to take action. Not long after, Neville Vincent, joint secretary of Amnesty International in 1962, went on a mission to Portugal to query the detention of five more people imprisoned for their political beliefs under Dr Salazar's dictatorship. This account illustrates one of Amnesty International's ways of working – sending delegates to talk to the authorities about the organization's concerns and to gather information. It was published in the first issue of the quarterly journal 'Amnesty'.

Few people who visit Lisbon will deny that it is among the most beautiful capitals of Europe. Its seven hills, the medieval fort of St. George, and the eighteenth-century city centre, built on the gridiron plan by Pombal after the great earthquake of 1755, are set off magnificently by the broad sweep of the Tagus dotted with sailing barges.

When I arrived there it was difficult to believe that such a beautiful capital could be the scene of a great deal of misery. I had gone to intercede with the authorities over five doctors who were imprisoned for their political beliefs and I did in fact find that, wherever I made inquiries for them, there was an atmosphere of fear and tension.

I started off my inquiries at the office of a man to whom I had a letter of introduction and who I thought might be able to help me with news of Dr. Julietta Gandra. This woman was a well-known physician in Luanda, the capital of Angola, until she was sentenced to a year's imprisonment because of her opposition to the régime. She has in fact served her year but has also done another three in the Caxias Fortress in Lisbon because she is considered 'a bad security risk'.

When I entered the office of the man I was to make contact with, I realized he was extremely busy and offered to telephone him later. He looked at me as though I had just made a bad joke, and assured me that he had not used the telephone in connection with matters such as we meant to talk about since 1945. I had received my first object lesson in security. I fixed a later appointment with him there and then and when I met him again he told me that fear of the PIDE, the secret police, was so great that he did not dare use the telephone for things he did not want them to hear.

While I had been provided with a list of private people to see by friends in London, one of the main purposes of my visit was to see people in official positions in the hope of getting some relief for the five doctors who were my special concern. In the event I failed, for one reason or another, to make contact with the Ministers of Justice, the Interior and External Affairs. Pressure of other engagements, I was told, or, in the case of the Minister of External Affairs, his absence from Lisbon, prevented me from seeing any of them.

I was, however, received by Cardinal Cerejeira, the head of the Portuguese hierarchy and a close friend of Dr. Salazar, with whom he co-operated in the founding of the present Portuguese régime. I was able to ask him about the fate of the African Vicar-General of the Angolan diocese of Luanda, who was arrested and brought to Lisbon during the recent African insurrection in that territory. His Eminence pointed out that a priest could exercise his ministry wherever he went and that the nine excited clergy had as many opportunities to carry out their duties in Portugal as they had had in Angola. Cardinal Cerejeira insisted throughout my talk with him that Church and State were two separate entities in Portugal, and that he did not have control over politics. When I talked with him about the case of the Bishop of Oporto, a severe critic of the régime, who has recently been given duties outside Portugal, His

Eminence repeated that he had no control over the bishop's appointment, but would convey to Dr. Salazar the anxieties of the outside world regarding the treatment of prisoners in Portugal.

Having got very little encouragement from either Church or State I returned to private individuals to whom I had introductions, in the hope of getting information on the doctors whom I was trying to help.

I sought information from one diplomat who had had contact with one of the doctors in question. The scarcely credible caution that I had witnessed in the office of my first acquaintance was repeated at one of the embassies I visited. Before starting our conversation my host unplugged the telephone, a precaution against the secret police being able to take a record of our words.

A similar precaution against possible police action was taken by a lawyer whom I visited in my search for information. Before leaving we arranged that if either of us were later questioned about the conversation we should not disclose the real purpose of my visit, but say that it was merely a social call, during which I passed a friendly message from a mutual barrister friend in London.

As a result of my inquiries, I was able to visit some of the prisoners' families. I found the wife of one, together with her family of four, living in one room in the utmost poverty. Her pleasure at realizing that an outside organization like Amnesty International was working on behalf of her husband and other prisoners, made the whole trip seem worthwhile.

In addition I made fruitless attempts to see the prisoners themselves. There was no reason, I was told, why I should not visit Dr. Gandra and her companions in Caxias. The process of getting the permission of various authorities was a lengthy business. In fact permission had not arrived before it was time for me to leave Portugal.

I left Lisbon then, without seeing Dr. Gandra, Dr. Neto or any of their companions, Dr. Maria Luiza Costa Dias Soares, another woman doctor from Mozambique, Dr. Agostino Neto, true distinguished African physician and poet, or Dr. Orlando Ramos, a cancer specialist who was arrested in July, 1960, tortured and kept in prison ever since.

As I left Lisbon, however, I learnt the news that Dr. Noshir Wadia had, after many representations from his friends in his native India, been allowed to go free. Arrested on his plane at Lisbon airport at the time of the Indian invasion of Goa, he had been finally allowed to go free after having been a political hostage for two months.

At the end of February it seems as though the PIDE were working on the principle of last in first out.

Published 1962

● **ALBERT SCHWEITZER**

An early supporter, the humanitarian Dr Albert Schweitzer, declared in 1963: 'I believe that world peace can only be achieved when there is freedom for people of all politics, religions and races to exchange their views in a continuing dialogue. For this reason I would particularly ask all those who are working in their different ways towards world peace to make their contribution, preferably by active service or, failing that, by financial contribution, to this great new endeavour called Amnesty International.'

GANDHI OF THE NORTH WEST FRONTIER

Khan Abdul Ghaffar Khan has been imprisoned in Pakistan because of his work for the rights of the Pathan people and opposition to successive governments on many occasions since 1947, most recently in 1983. An ardent admirer and close friend of Mahatma Gandhi, he persuaded his people to adopt non-violent methods of protest. The following article about him appeared in the journal 'Amnesty'.

Non-violence has its martyrs. One of them, Khan Abdul Ghaffar Khan, was chosen by Amnesty International as 'Prisoner of the Year'. His one example symbolizes the suffering of upwards of a million people all over the world who are in prison for their convictions.

Known as the 'Gandhi of the North West Frontier', Ghaffar Khan, 72 and ailing, lies in Lahore prison, detained without trial by the Pakistan Government. He has been in prison almost uninterruptedly since Pakistan became independent in 1947.

In 1911, at 21, Ghaffar Khan was founding schools for Muslims and in 1919 joined the Satyagraha (non-violent) Movement. Although a Muslim he became an ardent admirer and close friend of Gandhi, and persuaded the warlike Pathans, his own people, to adopt non-violent methods. Under his leadership, Pathans, who would normally kill on the slightest provocation, stood smiling under British lathi charges and shootings. Feeling that Pathans without arms were more dangerous than those with, the British imprisoned him for three years.

Since Pakistan independence he has been continually suspect and feared by the Government for his insistence on Pathan rights. His Party, Khudai Khidmatgar (the Servants of God, known as the Red Shirt Movement) was declared illegal. In 1948 he was sentenced to three years rigorous imprisonment, but was actually detained in prison until 1954.

A brief period of freedom followed, although he was not allowed to return to the North West Frontier. He was tried in September 1956 under Pakistan Criminal Procedure, again imprisoned and later freed, only to be re-arrested in April 1961 under the West Pakistan Maintenance of Public Order Ordinance. Despite appeals and review – the last of which took place on November 25th 1962, the old man still lies in gaol.

Miss Muriel Lester, an Englishwoman, who knew and worked with him, says: 'No one but this gentle giant, strong in his humility, could have got the Pathans, conditioned from birth to border warfare, to abandon their faith in it and come together morning by morning to learn the skills of non-violence.'

Published 1963

Khan Abdul Ghaffar Khan ▶

● 'I NEVER LOSE HOPE'

Two-and-a-half year-old Maria Luisa and her 15 month old brother Jorge scampered about without a care in the world, too young to realise why their mother had called the press conference. Blanca de Rosal was celebrating her own escape from the death squads. But she was also telling the world how her husband, Jorge, had been abducted exactly two years earlier. On 12 August, 1983, he had been followed by armed men from 7am until 5pm. They seized him for no apparent reason on a rural road near his farm in Guatemala. He 'disappeared'. The truck he was driving, his money and the cargo of eggs he was planning to deliver were never recovered.

Blanca de Rosal said, 'These things happen every day in Guatemala ... you never know why people are abducted or tortured. Sometimes it is because you don't agree with the government, but Jorge was not active in politics ... he did not want to join the army ... he loved his farm ...' She became a member of a mutual support group which included the families of over 500 others who had 'disappeared'. Together, they organised a meeting with the Head of State, General Oscar Mejia Victores, petitioned the Constituent Assembly, held non-violent demonstrations and vigils and distributed leaflets:

'Brother Guatemalans ... the days go by, the nights become interminable, and the persistent question becomes even more cruel: where are our loved ones? Help us! These are brother Guatemalans who just like you have a mother, a wife, children, a brother, a father. Offer your hand in solidarity! Alive they were taken! Alive we want them back!' The authorities were deaf to their appeals: 'Our resistance grew stronger after we met with high government officials who said that the support groups were subversive ... they warned me to leave ...'

Leading members of the group began to receive death threats. One was later found dead on the streets of Guatemala City; another was killed in a suspicious car accident together with her brother and infant son; a third fled to Mexico after armed men searched his house in his absence. Blanca de Rosal also escaped: 'I came here to preserve my life and the lives of my children ... I hope to return to Guatemala someday, but I know it cannot be soon because things will be bad for a long time ...'

She has learned that her husband has been tortured, but believes that he is only alive today because of the efforts of Amnesty International. She looked plaintively at her son and said, 'The boy has never seen his father ... but I never lose hope'.

ACTION TO HELP BOY

The group who adopted 15-year-old schoolboy Jose Silva campaigned for his release, writing to the authorities to try and obtain more information and urging them to free him unconditionally. This is still the basis of Amnesty International's work for the release of prisoners of conscience. Groups write to government and prison authorities. They also visit embassies and organize petitions and other activities to publicize the person's plight. Groups might also contact a prisoner's family and try to help with legal and medical costs.

The International Secretariat of Amnesty International announced this afternoon that it had decided to take emergency action on behalf of Jose Augusto Silva, a 15-year-old Portuguese schoolboy, who was arrested on the 21st January...

Jose Silva, a pupil at the Pedro Nunes School in Lisbon, is one of 17 schoolboys and schoolgirls arrested during student demonstrations in the last two weeks. He is the only one under the age of 16 and consequently cannot be legally held by the political police. In order to detain him the authorities have sent him to a home for juvenile delinquents at Tutoria. He is being held in a cell there; his mother is only allowed to see him once a fortnight. He has not been charged with any offence. The case is a particularly tragic one because he himself was born in prison where his mother was at the time a political prisoner. His father, an engineer, actually died in prison.

Because it has been reported that the authorities are trying to hold him in this juvenile delinquent home until his 16th birthday on the 15th August (when he can be transferred to prison) the International Secretariat decided to take immediate steps on his behalf. Jose Silva will be straight away 'adopted' by a newly formed Amnesty group in West Berlin.

News release 12 February 1965

● **'YOUR EFFORTS HAVE BORNE FRUIT OF JUSTICE'**

For thousands of people all over the world, events move with frightening speed after they are seized by the security police. In the course of a few hours, a perfectly normal life can be shattered by the personal experience of torture. For Rodolfo Romano in the Philippines, it happened on 12 February 1984 – the day he tried to find his father-in-law, Jose Laceda, who had been detained by the security police. He went to the local police headquarters, hoping for some kind of explanation ... Instead: 'They ordered me to strip ... they punched me. I cannot count the number of blows because of the number of men who hit me. They burned all parts of my body with lighted cigarettes. I begged for mercy. But they were deaf and blind to my pleas...' His nightmare treatment continued all night, until, at 10 a.m., they released him after holding a gun to his head and forcing him to sign a statement and a forged letter.

Rodolfo Romano later wrote: 'In those moments ... I was not functioning as a moral person as a result of the intense tortures I underwent. I still feel pain in my body ... I wonder how I will get back that statement ... and the letter I allegedly wrote. I am concerned about my family.' After launching urgent appeals on his behalf, Amnesty International received this letter from the office of the Bishop of Sosorgon: 'Greetings of Solidarity and Justice! We have received countless letters from different groups of Amnesty International all over the world, mostly concerning the plight of Rodolfo Romano and his father-in-law, Jose Laceda.

'It has touched us deeply that all compassionately expressed sympathy to the the victims and revulsion to the perpetrators of torture and cruelty. These gestures of commiseration we will remember forever. The barrage of letters you sent to our Minister of National Defence and the Acting Chief of Staff of the Armed Forces denouncing the brutalities done by their men has certainly hastened action on these cases. We are pleased to bring the good news that your efforts have borne fruit of justice: the fabricated case which was filed against Rodolfo Romano by his torturers was finally dismissed by the court.'

LETTERS FROM PRISONERS

Prisoners' letters to adoption groups published in Amnesty International's news sheet for groups.

Gonakudzingwa Restriction Area, Vila Salazar, P/B u 304, Bulawayo, Rhodesia. 23.12.64.

'I acquaint you that I have received your Christmas card with a great mixture of pleasure and surprise, being a young man of 24 years, who knows not much about practical life. Your Christmas card, Sir, is a 'landmark' in my life. It has remade me and remoulded my way of thinking.

When received your Christmas card, I had food for the thought, I asked myself a question 'why does this person think of us in Zimbabwe, does he know me, what does it profit him to worry about me?' This at length came to my mind that 'we are linked together by common humanity and human needs and sympathies and we are all vessels of different colours and shapes of God-given lives. In truth I have been made to think not only nationally but also internationally'. But I became more worried when I again realised that I cannot help somebody before I am able to help myself, so really you made me to think of creating an 'Harmonious wordly-community after our National Free-dom'.

Long Life. From Master Isidore Kumire to I. Hedegaard, Vejen, Denmark.'

5307 Hetchburg 24, Near Weimar, East Germany. 4th January 1965

'Dear Miss Fitzgerald, I thank you very much for your Christmas greetings. But I didn't receive your card in jail as I was released a few weeks ago. That's too, the reason that I can give you thanks.

You cannot imagine what a joy it has been for me to get so many greetings from Ireland. It is a good feeling to know to have friends after a long time of loneliness.

As I don't know the reason for my early release (I was sentenced to eight years jail and have spent only 50 months there) it is possible that Irish activity was the cause. So I'm deeply in your debt.

With the best wishes for 1965. Sincerely yours, H. Friedrich Müller.'

Tehran (Gassra Prison). January 13th 1965

'Dear Mr. Thorsen, Thank you very much for your kind and significant greeting card. I have received it, without any paper, today, here in prison. I hope also a happy year for you, and I wish you all success.

Very truly yours, Y. Sahabi, Professor of Geology in Sciences Faculty of University in Tehran.'

'I write in reference to your letter of 24th October, regarding enquiries relating to Kalin Nedyalkov Batakov.

Further to the information sent you on June 22, 1964, we are now in a position to inform you that Batakov was sentenced to five years imprisonment for anti-State actions. The Supreme court reduced this sentence to 2½ years. Later Mr. Batakov was released under an Amnesty by the Presidium of the National Assembly, on the occasion of the 20th Anniversary of the 9th September, 1944, that is to say, before 9th September this year.

We trust this information is satisfactory, and that you will now feel it unnecessary to have your letters to the press published.

Yours sincerely, (Sgd) G. Shkutov, Secretary to the Bulgarian Embassy.'

'Dearest Mrs. Levett, I replied to your wonderful letter and requested that, if you have a minute to spare you

'We know that we are not alone in our life long battle. We owe this feeling to you…' Winnie Mandela in a letter to the Oxted (UK) Amnesty International group in 1965.

should drop me a line, now and then…

We have been able to face our problems with great determination as a result of encouragement from people like you. We know that we are not alone in our life long battle. We owe this feeling to you…

Yours sincerely, Winnie Mandela.' (South Africa)

'Dear Friends, One of the most heartening things that reached me whilst in prison was your most encouraging support to Adelaide and the family. I wish to take this opportunity of thanking you from the bottom of my heart, for all that you have done.

It is actions like yours that make us feel in this bitter country, that the world still has many more good people like you, that makes our cause so noble.

It is the one of the most powerful elements, when one is under stress or strain, when an unknown helping hand stretches across the Atlantic to provide some warmth and comfort. How does one repay such kindness and understanding? I can say, your action has produced a counter-reaction – to spiritually embrace all our people of this land – black, white, coloured. We have told all our friends about you. In this way more and more people here come to accept that not all White People are bad.

Needless to say we have a small and dwindling section of white people who at a great risk still manage to introduce a spark of decency into the White (foolishly called here 'Europeans') people of this country.

It is to the honour and credit of the people of the whole of the UK particularly England that for many years they have rallied to our cause. We will never forget this. One day we hope we will all dance in the streets.

Zoya has after much difficulty started school. She was hoping that she would not be accepted and that she could be with me. After a couple of weeks Tanya has got used to me. Anand appears to be aware of my presence. He cries to be rocked to sleep. Drushka (Adelaide may not have told you, Drushka is my dog) has come back to life and he refuses to come out from under the bed at night, and my beloved Adelaide has not put on any weight. Our excitement has not yet worn off. Everybody is just radiant and I too have put on weight. In our tumbled down house life is a paradise in spite of the fact that I am still under house arrest. As for my plans I hope to get started with selling clothes from door to door. I like it. It gives me a chance to meet people, to chat, laugh and make new friends. I love life and people.

Should one day one of you wish to visit this beautiful land of ours, you can rest assured a most welcome awaits. Don't worry about accommodation, it is no problem. Just tell us when, even if it is for a short while. We will move mountains for you.

So much for the time being from me. You will learn from Adelaide very soon. Presently she is at the fort visiting another prisoner still held there.

With fondest regards to all of you, I am yours sincerely, Paul Joseph.' (South Africa)

Published February 1965

JUSTICE IN THE AMERICAN SOUTH

British lawyer Anthony Lester spent three months in the southern states of the United States of America researching persecution of civil rights activists and blacks. His findings were published as a report 'Justice in the American South', from which this is an extract.

Law has traditionally been used in the South to preserve white supremacy. The Civil Rights Movement now invokes the Federal law of the American Constitution for the right to challenge white supremacy and establish equal civil rights for every citizen. It seeks freedom of speech and assembly, universal suffrage, and equal protection of the law. In the Deep South, these demands are revolutionary, but, because of the ultimate threat of Federal intervention and a second Reconstruction, they cannot be met with overt violence by Southern State officials. The resistance is usually more subtle and depends on massive abuse of the machinery of the law. ... Some samples of the use of these laws are illuminating. Over 300 Freedom Riders arrested in Jackson, Mississippi in May and June 1961 were sentenced to $200 and four months' imprisonment for breaches of the peace, apparently only on the basis of evidence that their presence at bus and railway terminals in Jackson in racially-mixed groups put other people in a 'foul mood'. The police captain in charge neither spoke to nor arrested any people who allegedly were threatening the Freedom Riders. When the Freedom Ride cases came before a Federal court, Judge Wisdom stated in his judgment that 'we again take judicial notice that the State of Mississippi has a steel hard, inflexible, undeviating official policy of segregation. The policy is stated in its laws. It is rooted in custom. The segregation signs at the terminals in Jackson carry out that policy. The Jackson police add muscle, bone and sinew to the signs.' (*United States v. City of Jackson* 318 F.2d. 1 at pp. 5-6)

In May 1963, about 1,080 Negro students were expelled or suspended from public schools in Birmingham, Alabama, by order of the Board of Education because, during the civil rights demonstrations, they had been arrested for parading without permit. No hearings were held to determine the propriety of the dismissals. The students were simply told that not enough time remained in the school term to hold any hearings.

On World-wide Communion Sunday, in October 1963, three young women, two of whom were Negroes, were arrested for attempting to attend religious services together at a Methodist Church in Jackson, Mississippi. They never entered the church. When they reached the steps they were told that they were not welcome. A policeman gave them two minutes to move on. As they started to walk away he told them that they had taken too long, and arrested them. They were indicted for trespass and disturbing divine worship. The Police Justices' Court of Jackson sentenced them to one year's imprisonment and fined each $1,000.

On December 15th, 1961, 1,500 Negroes demonstrated in front of East Baton Rouge Parish Courthouse, Louisiana, where 23 Negroes had been sentenced to imprisonment for picketing. On April 1st, 1962, Rev. B. Elton Cox a CORE [Congress of Racial Equality] field secretary was convicted of three misdemeanours arising out of the demonstrations. He was sentenced to one year's imprisonment and a $5,000 fine for impeding the administration of justice by holding a demonstration near the courthouse, and 5 months' imprisonment and a $500 fine for obstructing the pavement.

Clyde Kennard was a Negro from Mississippi, who had served in the United States Army in Korea, and graduated from Chicago University. He returned to Mississippi, and in 1959 in spite of several attempts to dissuade him, he applied to Mississippi Southern College (which was segregated) for admission as a graduate student. Kennard's application was rejected, but he intended to re-apply. Under Mississippi law, no one convicted of felony can be admitted to a State college or university. On September 25th, 1960, Kennard was arrested and prosecuted for being an accessory to the burglary of chicken feed worth $25 (in Mississippi any accessory to any felony is deemed to be a principal). Kennard was convicted largely on the evidence of an illiterate 19-year-old Negro who admitted having actually stolen the chicken feed, and was himself placed on probation. The trial had several unusual features (See generally, the *Reporter*, November 8th, 1962, pp. 30-34). The local white jury convicted Kennard, and the judge gave him the maximum sentence of 7 years' imprisonment. When I was in Mississippi, I examined the records of sentences imposed in one county for the past 4 years. The following are typical heavy sentences: forgery, 3 years; burglary and larceny, 4 years; manslaughter, 6 years; armed robbery, 12 years; kidnapping, 5 years; rape, 2 years plus 3 years probation. Assuming that Kennard was guilty, it is hard to avoid the conclusion that the sentence against him was deliberately vindictive. Kennard served a few years, then contracted cancer, was released and died shortly thereafter.

At about 3 am on May 8th, 1963 (according to the brief of the US Department of Justice in a case now pending), unidentified white men exploded 3 fire bombs in the home of Hartman Turnbow, in Holmes County, Mississippi. Turnbow was a Negro who had previously attempted to register to vote. His house was newly decorated but not insured, and he and his family were asleep inside. When Turnbow heard the noise of the explosions, he seized his rifle and ran out of the house. One of the men allegedly shot at him and his family, and Turnbow returned the fire before they escaped. The Turnbows succeeded in putting out the fire and told a local civil rights worker what had happened. They also indirectly informed the High Sheriff. Shortly thereafter, Robert Moses, Programme Director of COFO [Council of Federated Organisations], came to the house and began to take photographs. The Deputy Sheriff then arrived, and told Moses to stop taking pictures. However, when the Sheriff himself arrived, Moses tried to take another photograph and was promptly arrested on a charge (as he was later told) of refusing to obey an officer. During that afternoon, three Negro civil rights workers, who tried to visit Moses in gaol, were arrested on suspicion of arson, and Moses was also charged with arson and impeding an investigation. Later Turnbow too was arrested and charged

with arson. In their brief, the Department of Justice described these charges as 'false and baseless' and allege that the prosecutions were brought 'for the purpose of intimidating, threatening and coercing Negro citizens of Holmes County from applying for registration and from registering to vote.' The charges of arson were subsequently dismissed against all but Turnbow himself, and he himself was not ultimately indicted by the Grand Jury. The transcripts do not indicate that there was any evidence whatever that Turnbow or the civil rights workers had committed arson.

Between June and September 1964 in Mississippi there were over a thousand arrests of civil rights workers. Many of these were for alleged traffic offences or breaches of the peace. There can be little doubt that by these tactics the local law enforcement officials hoped to weaken the spirit and financial resources of the Movement. As for the civil rights lawyers, their tactics were either to attempt to transfer the cases to a Federal court, on the ground that their clients could not expect a fair trial in a State court, or to appeal from the State court's verdict. But many such cases are transferred back to the State court, by which time the accused civil rights workers, out on bail, may be back in college in the North. The civil rights organisations cannot afford continual appeals to the State and Federal appellate courts, and, in spite of the large number of lawyers who volunteered to work for the Lawyers Constitutional Defence Committee during the Summer Project, there are not enough lawyers to deal with myriad minor cases throughout the Deep South...

Bail

Northern civil rights workers accused of crimes in the South must expect to have to raise larger sums for bail than local civil rights workers, since sterner sanctions may be necessary to secure their presence at their trials. One of the problems which the civil rights organisations have had to face is the cumulative effect of high bail. In December 1962, the cash requirements for bail bonds in the Freedom Ride cases in Jackson, Mississippi, amounted to $372,000. In June 1963, bonds for demonstrators in Danville, Virginia, exceeded $145,000. Another problem is that many civil rights workers return to Northern universities after their work in the South. If they fail to attend their trials in the South, not only will they forfeit their bail, but they will provide Southern officials with justification for increasing bail requirements in the future. On the other hand, the Northern student, after travelling several hundred miles to attend his trial, may find that it has been adjourned, that he must come again, at further expense and loss of time at university. These are problems of the legitimate use of bail, but there are still greater problems where the bail system has been deliberately used to intimidate the Movement.

A survey of 'Bail and Civil Rights' was recently carried out by Louis F. Claiborne, a staff member of the US Department of Justice, for the 1964 National Conference on Bail and Criminal Justice. It found that in some rare

cases, a civil rights worker had been accused of a felony in order to justify prohibitive bail, or a denial of bail. For example, in Americus, Georgia, four demonstrators were held without bail on the capital charge of 'insurrection' until ordered release on bail by a Federal court. Sometimes, bail problems are aggravated by the 'unnecessary multiplicity of charges instituted for a single course of conduct.' For example, in March 1964, demonstrators at a theatre in New Orleans were required to post $4,500 on 8 charges: 'trespass,' 'resisting arrest,' 'disturbing the peace,' 'refusing to move on,' 'criminal mischief,' 'blocking an entrance,' and two counts of 'contributing to the delinquency of a minor'.

Another abuse, apparently confined to Louisiana, consists of 'pyramiding'. The case of the Rev. B. Elton Cox has already been referred to. When he was arrested in December 1961, after the demonstrations in front of the East Baton Rouge Parish Courthouse, bail was originally set at $2,000. When this sum was paid, bail was increased to $4,000, then on each successive payment, to $6,000 and $8,000. Eventually, after protests by attorneys, it was settled at $6,000.

Exorbitant bail is not usually set before trial though there have been exceptional cases in the South and North. However after conviction the position is different. In Atlanta, Georgia, in one case involving a 77-year-old Californian minister, convicted of disturbing public worship, bail on appeal was set at $20,000. The Georgia Supreme Court reduced it to $5,000, but the minister spent 7 months in gaol because his tender of $5,000 in cash was refused, and he was unable to post that amount in unencumbered property, as required by the Court.

The Justice Department Survey finds that in Jackson, Mississippi, 'the bond required on appeal to the circuit court has almost invariably been set at the legal maximum:

$1,500 ($500 'cost bond' plus $1,000 'appeal bond'). Bonds of $1,000 or more pending appeal are apparently common in civil rights cases in many Southern jurisdictions. Since the sentence is often a much smaller fine, there is a great temptation to abandon the appeal … nor is the distinction between local residents and others observed. In Itta Bena, Mississippi, last June, some forty local Negroes were held on $500 or $750 bond pending trial *de novo* in the county court, on a charge of disturbing the peace, the only distinction drawn being between men and women.' There is difficulty in obtaining local property bonds, and local bonding companies are often unwilling to do business with civil rights organisations, while out-of-State companies are not accepted as qualifying locally. During the Mississippi Summer Project, it was impossible to obtain help from any of the local bonding companies.

The Survey concludes that 'in many Southern communities (and perhaps elsewhere) bail requirements in civil rights cases did much more than merely assure the defendant's appearance in court. In many instances, the net effect of bail demands was to arrest the demonstrations, by exhausting the organisation's treasury or temporarily removing the participants, or their leaders. Doubtless, that consequence was sometimes unintentional. But, in other cases, bail was obviously used, even manipulated, to achieve that end. The nature and number of the charges, the amount of the bonds, and the form of security required, in some instances were plainly intended to delay or prevent release.'…

Southern juries

In many parts of the Deep South, Negroes have traditionally been and remain systematically excluded from juries. In recent years, the US Supreme Court has reversed a number of convictions of Negroes on the ground that such racial exclusion violated their constitutional rights to equal protection of the law. It is encouraging to note that the Georgia State courts have followed this example. However, most Southern juries are still predominantly or entirely white. The role of the Southern jury in the trial of civil rights workers has already been discussed. Its effect is equally important in the trial of white persons accused of crimes against Negroes and civil rights workers.

The right to be tried by one's peers is deeply embedded in Anglo-American law. Allegations of serious Federal or State crimes are usually investigated by a grand jury drawn from the appropriate locality to determine whether there is a *prima facie* case to be tried. The trial itself is by jury. Federal juries are usually drawn from a wider area than local State juries and are better educated, but they are still selected from the State in which the offence has allegedly been committed. Naturally, the Southern jury reflects white Southern opinion and, in effect, the prosecutor is faced with the task of persuading a representative group of white Southerners to punish the accused for defending their way of life. Not surprisingly, the accused is acquitted, or, more often, never prosecuted at all. The virtual impossibility of convicting the murderer of a civil rights worker is one of the most potent sources of injustice in the Deep South. Some recent examples will illustrate the problem.

On the night of June 10th, 1963, Medgar Evers, Negro NAACP [National Association for the Advancement of Colored People] Field Secretary in Mississippi, was killed by a sniper's bullet outside his home. A few days before his death he said, in a press interview, 'If I die it will be in a good cause. I have been fighting for America just as much as the soldiers in Viet Nam.' Byron De La Beckwith, a fertiliser salesman from Greenwood, Mississippi, was arrested by FBI [Federal Bureau of Investigation] agents on June 22nd 1963, and indicted for the murder of Evers by a Grand Jury of 17 white persons and one Negro. Beckwith was well known for his racial views and had once written that a 'lot of shooting' would be required of Mississippians in the future to protect their families from bad Negroes. While Beckwith was in prison awaiting trial, he was treated as a hero and given every possible comfort. A White Citizens' Legal Defence Fund collected $15,000 on his behalf. At his first trial, in early 1964, 2 taxi-cab drivers gave evidence that Beckwith had asked 4 times for Evers' address, a few days before Evers was shot. Beckwith's car was identified by a number of witnesses as having been in the area twice before the murder and, on the night of the killing, 300 feet from Evers' house. Beckwith gave evidence that the rifle found near the scene of the crime 'could be' his, but that it was lost or stolen shortly before the murder. Beckwith had incidentally been traced by a fingerprint on the telescopic sight of the rifle found near the scene of the crime. He claimed that at the time of the murder he was 90 miles away. During the 24 hour wait for the jury's verdict,

▶ *Black women arrested after a protest demonstration in Orangeburg, South Carolina, USA, being marched from the county jail to the city jail – May 1963.*

◀ *Two black girls try to escape the police after attempting to board a bus taking white students to an all-white school. They were part of a picket line in Crawford, Georgia, USA; November 1965.*

former Governor Ross Barnett and former Major-General Edwin A. Walker were at Beckwith's side. Barnett had entered the courtroom during the trial and shaken hands with Beckwith. The all-white jury was unable to agree on its verdict, so there was a mistrial. Several police officials called the decision 'a moral victory for the state'. Beckwith was tried again in April 1964 before a second all-white jury. On April 12th, 1964, the *New York Times* reported that 'The Ku-Klux-Klan is putting on a show of force on behalf of … Beckwith … Ten crosses were burned in the Jackson area last night. Today, about 75 tough-looking men, some linked with Klan activity, showed up as spectators in court.' At the second trial, one of the taxi-cab drivers testified that Beckwith 'resembled' (rather than was) the man who had asked where Evers lived. The prosecuting District Attorney later told the press that the taxi-cab driver had been beaten since the first trial. Incidentally, during the trial, the local press in Jackson gave extensive coverage to the evidence on Beckwith's behalf, but little to that of the prosecution. For a second time the jury failed to agree, and Beckwith returned home as a hero. To many people whom I met in Mississippi, the Beckwith case was shocking because a white Mississippi jury had actually disagreed, instead of unanimously acquitting Beckwith, while Federal officials regarded this disagreement as a sign of substantial progress towards justice in the State. In theory, since the case is still pending, Beckwith could be tried for a third time, but in practice it is unlikely that this will happen.

On July 11th, 1964, Lemuel Penn, a Negro schoolteacher and Army Reserve Colonel, was killed while driving through rural North Georgia by a shotgun blast from a passing car. On August 6th, 1964, 4 Ku-Klux-Klansmen were arrested, and 2 were indicted for Penn's murder. The FBI had obtained a confession from an accomplice incriminating the 2 men. They were tried before an all-white jury in September 1964. Two witnesses gave evidence that they saw the men walk into a garage 24 miles from the scene of the crime at about 5.0 am on the morning of the murder, carrying a sawed-off shotgun. The defence attorneys urged the 'Anglo-Saxon Madison County Jury' not to 'send these here boys into those cold grey stone walls' to be electrocuted, and said that FBI agents were 'carpet-baggers … who are infiltrating our justice'. The jury acquitted the men. Federal charges of depriving Penn of his civil rights are still pending against them. If they are indicted by the Federal Grand Jury, they will be tried by a Federal jury, drawn from the State of Georgia.

On June 21st, 1964, the day the Mississippi Summer Project began, three civil rights workers, James E. Chaney, a Mississippi Negro, Michael Schwerner, and Andrew Goodman, went to Neshoba County, Mississippi, to investigate the burning of a church. That afternoon, Deputy Sheriff Cecil Price arrested the three men in Philadelphia, Mississippi, and held them in gaol for several hours on a speeding charge. Price said he released them at about 10.30pm after Chaney had paid a $20 fine. Two days later, their car was found burned in a swamp a few miles from Philadelphia. After a massive search, on August 4th, the FBI found the bodies of the men under an earthen dam 5 miles from the town. In the course of the search, they also discovered 2 half-bodies of Negro men in the Pearl River, about whom there had previously been no concern or interest. The State authorities refused to release the official autopsy report on the three civil rights workers even to the coroner's jury, and, on August 25th, the coroner's jury reported that the available information was insufficient to enable it to determine the cause of death. On September 30th, the local grand jury failed to return any indictment in the case. It publicly exonerated local law enforcement authorities, stating that they had done well to maintain law and order 'in the face of drastic provocations by outside agitators.' After their report was read, Circuit Judge O.H. Barnett told the jurors that they had 'exhibited the courage of men of the Revolutionary days of this country.'

On October 2nd, a Federal grand jury indicted Sheriff Rainey, Deputy Price, two policemen, and a former sheriff, all from Philadelphia, Mississippi, on charges of violating the rights of local Negroes by unlawfully detaining and beating them. These indictments grew out of the FBI investigation into the murders of the three civil rights workers but related to crimes allegedly committed long before the murders. On December 4th, the FBI arrested Sheriff Rainey, Deputy Price, and 19 other white men in connection with the murders. The FBI alleged that Sheriff Rainey had been involved in a conspiracy, but had not been involved in the actual killings, while Deputy Price had unlawfully arrested and detained the 3 men before giving them to a lynch mob of which he was part. Nineteen of the defendants, most of them members of the Ku-Klux-Klan, were charged under Federal law with conspiring to violate the constitutional rights of the 3 dead men. Two others were charged with failing to disclose information about the crime. It was not possible to prosecute any of the accused for murder, since murder is only a State crime, and the Mississippi State authorities apparently refused to prosecute. On December 10th, the FBI disclosed in a preliminary hearing before the US Commissioner in Meridian, Mississippi, that they had obtained a signed confession from one of the defendants. The Commissioner proceeded to rule that the FBI agent's evidence about the confession was hearsay and inadmissible, and to dismiss the charges against 19 of the defendants. A spokesman for the US Justice Department later stated that 'In the experience of the Department, the refusal by a US Commissioner to accept a law enforcement officer's report of a signed confession in a preliminary hearing is totally without precedent.' The Department decided to withdraw the charges against the remaining 2 defendants, and to refer the case to the Federal grand jury. At the time of writing, 16 of the men have been re-arrested and indicted by the Federal grand jury. They are now awaiting trial before a Federal jury in Mississippi.

Published February 1965

PRISON CONDITIONS IN SOUTH AFRICA

Three reports were published simultaneously in September 1965. They dealt with prison conditions in Portugal, South Africa and Romania. Reports followed on prison conditions in Paraguay, Rhodesia and East Germany. The 'Berliner Zeitung', an East Berlin daily newspaper, commented in 1966: '...The report on Portugal is excellent, but it is absurd to focus on East Germany, as there are no political prisoners in East Germany, anyone looking for violations of human rights in that part of the world should concentrate on West Germany...' The following extract is from 'Prison Conditions in South Africa'.

Robben Island, South Africa's maximum security prison, seven miles from Cape Town. Robben Island has been a penal settlement for 400 years and it is claimed that no one has survived the icy swim to freedom.

The treatment and conditions of a sentenced prisoner in South Africa are largely determined by the two factors of his race and his prison category.

Racial differences

The Regulations provide that whites and non-whites shall receive different clothing, diet and bedding allowances. Some privileges also depend on race; tobacco, for example, is allowed to white males, in category B but to no other races. White and non-white prisoners are at all times segregated; when possible they are kept out of view of each other. Where it is practicable, non-whites of different races are also separated, and also given separate diets, clothes and bedding; but these distinctions are often implemented only when there are a large number of Coloureds or Indians in a particular prison at any one time. No allowance, however, is made in conditions for the normal living standards of a non-white prisoner, with the result that a highly educated African accustomed to living standards higher than many Europeans receives the food and clothing laid down for so-called 'primitive Bantu'.

Robben Island 'elite'

On Robben Island, however, at the present time, it appears that a small group among the political prisoners, perhaps 5%, has been allowed slightly better conditions than the others; this 'elite' consists of those individuals thought by the authorities to constitute the 'leadership' in political terms, as opposed to the rank and file. These prisoners have small cells of their own, receive better clothing and bedding and many of them are allowed to study. They are kept apart from the other prisoners and so their influence upon them is made minimal. In this group are the 'Rivonia' trialists and other prisoners whose names are known outside South Africa.

Observation and classification

On his reception in prison, a person with a sentence of over two years spends an initial period under 'observation', as a result of which he is placed in one of the four prison categories, A,B,C & D. During his observation period, he is placed in an 'observation centre', separate from the rest of the prison and may be kept in strict isolation when this is thought necessary for classification purposes. The prisoner is kept under close surveillance by trained officials with the object of determining his 'age, health, mental condition, character traits, social background, previous conduct, ability to work and aptitude ... for the purpose of classification and training'. He is then placed in a category from which he can subsequently be 'promoted or downgraded according to progress or otherwise'. It is this classification which determines the privileges he may receive, the standard of his general living conditions, the quality of his clothing and bedding, the type of prisoner with whom he lives, (very often) the general attitude of the prison authorities towards him and, sometimes, the type of work he does. The Regulations do not lay down that a low category carries with it inferior conditions, but in practice this appears to be the case.

According to the Prisons Department, the group into which most ordinary prisoners are placed is Grade B; this allows a monthly visit by two people, two letters a month, tobacco in the case of white males, certain sporting and communal recreations, two books and magazines a week. Groups C and D, however, are allowed one three and six monthly visit respectively by one person, and a 500 word letter written and received at the same intervals; they may not smoke, or take part in any form of recreation other than reading two books which must be from the prison library and may not be sent in from outside. Study is accounted a privilege and is allowed for all grades.

Up to the present time, all persons convicted of political offences have been initially graded 'D'; a few individuals have worked their way to Grade 'C', but this has taken two or three times as long as is usual for criminal prisoners. Grade 'D' is officially stated to be for 'the type of prisoner with a previous record and/or convictions of serious crime of a daring or aggressive nature or other aggravating circumstances, such as convictions for rape, robbery or violence in one form or another, ... (he) will not hesitate to inflict serious bodily harm in order to escape or effect his criminal purposes. Initial maximum security measures or institutional safe custody, treatment and training are indicated.'

Of the 20 white male political prisoners at present serving their sentences at Pretoria Local, all began their sentences in Grade 'D', most, if not all, remain there and some are into the second year of their imprisonment; all but two are university graduates, four are university lecturers, one is a lawyer, one a teacher and one a schoolteacher.

It is reported that long term African political prisoners undergo no classification process; all are graded 'D' on their conviction and sent direct to Robben Island. For those political prisoners who are classified, the process may take up to a year, although one or two months is the usual period for other prisoners, and they report that there is no 'surveillance by trained officials'...

Clothing

The clothing worn by prisoners is determined by the Commissioner according to health and warmth requirements; it varies according to the racial group. Africans receive short trousers, a jacket, a shirt, and a sweater during winter months. They have no underwear or socks, and complaints have been received that prisoners on Robben Island have no shoes or sandals. Men performing heavy quarrying work throughout the year and living in unheated buildings with stone floors complain severely of the cold when they have to go barefoot. It also appears that the authorities' refusal to allow prisoners their sweaters except in the winter months is more of a hardship in the changeable climate of the Cape than it might be elsewhere. Indians and Coloureds have similar clothing to that of the Africans, but are allowed long trousers. Whites receive long

▲ *African and Indian women give the 'thumbs up' sign on their release from Durban prison after they were imprisoned for using 'European only' seats in government buildings.*

▲ *A group of prisoners on Robben Island building a road outside the confines of the prison. South Africa 1977.*

trousers, underwear, shirt, jacket, socks, boots, sweater and pyjamas. Prisoners on Robben Island receive clean shirts once a week. Although in Pretoria Central, in the observation centre, some prisoners had to wash their clothes themselves during their exercise period and dry them in the cells.

Toilet articles

Prisoners in Grades 'C' and 'D' are allowed no personal possessions of any sort.

According to the Regulations, each prisoner, on reception, shall be allowed a toothbrush, toothpaste, comb, shaving brush and razor blades; other toilet articles such as a hairbrush, shaving soap, nailbrush, etc., may be bought by the prisoner either from private funds or from money he has earned. Many instances have been reported from different prisons, but particularly from Robben Island, where non-white prisoners were not given a comb or a toothbrush. In these cases, unless they receive money from their families, they have no way of obtaining them unless they achieve a 'gratuity' post, which can only happen when they are in Grades B or A. Prisoners on Robben Island may spend 10/- every six weeks on toilet articles.

Punishment

Certain punishments are officially laid down for breaking the regulations, and for misdemeanours ranging from disobedience, the use of indecent words, singing, whistling, speaking without permission, to causing discontent, excitement or insubordination, or acting in any way 'contrary to good order and discipline'. If the prisoner admits the offence, the head of the prison may summarily remand him and deprive him of all privileges and gratuities for up to a month, or of one or more meals for a day. If he denies it, he is charged and tried by either a magistrate or a commissioned officer; he may have his legal adviser present. After trial by a commissioned officer, punishment may be imposed of corporal punishment of up to six strokes, solitary confinement with or without spare diet for up to six days, with or without light labour for up to 15 days of which 10 may be on a reduced diet. After trial by a magistrate, the court may impose a sentence of up to six months imprisonment or solitary confinement with or without light labour for up to 42 days, 28 of which may be on a reduced diet. There is no appeal for a prisoner against a sentence for disciplinary contravention, although appeal may be made against a sentence imposed by a magistrate for an offence under the Prisons Act. Corporal punishment may only be administered after the medical officer has examined the prisoner, the head of the prison must be present, and more than ten strokes may not be inflicted at one time. Solitary confinement may not exceed two months without a special order from the Minister of Justice, and a person in solitary confinement must receive 30 minutes exercise twice a day. A prisoner undergoing either solitary confinement or spare diet must be visited daily by the head of the prison and as often as possible by the medical officer. A prisoner on spare diet shall do no work and must receive normal diet once in every three days; spare diet is defined as 8 oz. of rice or mealie rice boiled in four pints of water without salt a day for men and 6oz. for women. A reduced diet may also be imposed, consisting of half the normal daily ration, without jam, treacle or curry.

The most usual forms of punishment imposed in practice appear to be depriving a prisoner of meals for one or two days. In practice, the times of meals make this a harder penalty than is specifically laid down. 'When punished by missing three meals, we were allowed nothing but water. Normally breakfast on Saturday is at 8.30am, lunch at 10.30am and supper at 2.00pm. So the punishment, which was always on a Sunday, meant no food from 2.00pm Saturday to 7.00am Monday.' This punishment appears to be imposed for failing to work hard enough either in the quarries or on mailbags. On one occasion a group of 175 prisoners on Robben Island had their meals withdrawn for a day for making too much noise.

Sentences of segregation or solitary confinement are also imposed. On Robben Island there is a block of single cells used as a punishment block; although built for 15, it is reported to hold up to 50 prisoners at any one time. Prisoners are kept in solitary confinement; they are made to sew mail bags and if more than a certain number (Strachan says three) are unsatisfactory, they lose their meals for a day. Prisoners are not allowed to talk, they exercise at a distance of five paces from each other, lose all privileges during their punishment and receive the lowest quality clothes. It is not known whether, or for what offences, political prisoners have been put in segregation for long periods.

Prisoners state that they have been put in isolation or deprived of meals for complaining about assaults, bad food, bad work conditions and also for reporting sick; it would also appear that punishment is imposed summarily by some warders without an enquiry being made into his alleged offence.

Searching

Searching of prisoners appears to take place in public. Prisoners are made to remove their clothes whenever they come into their section from outside. An officer examines a prisoner's body for smuggled tobacco or money with apparently little regard for the prisoner's dignity. The 'tausa' dance is still used as a method of searching; in it the prisoner is made to remove his clothes and leap into the air, turning round and bending to expose his anus. The Lansdowne Commission recommended that as soon as possible this method should be abandoned and at Leeukop criminal prisoners returning from work are now searched with an electric eye. The Regulations themselves say: 'Searching shall be conducted in a seemly manner and as far as possible without injury to self-respect ... A prisoner shall as far as possible not be stripped and searched in the presence and sight of other prisoners'. One prisoner has described searching as the 'greatest humiliation' of prison.

Published September 1965

ALLEGATIONS OF TORTURE IN ADEN

Unrest in Aden – a former British colony now part of the People's Democratic Republic of the Yemen – in the early 1960s brought British troops into action against local demonstrators. Many were detained. Controversy surrounded a 1966 Amnesty International mission that investigated allegations of torture by British interrogators in the colony. The mission concluded in its report that specific tortures had been inflicted on many of the hundreds of detainees in custody. Subsequent protests prompted the British Government to conduct its own inquiry, which recommended changes – eventually accepted by the government – to protect detainees. Extracts from the report of the mission are given here.

The military authorities in Aden have not caught many terrorists throwing handgrenades or in short duels with the military. The majority of those now detained are arrested in the following way:

The house is encircled in the early morning hours when the military are convinced that their suspects are sleeping inside. They break in the door, or a window, and enter the house, immediately arresting and taking away the man whom they are looking for and search the house, it is said, without consideration for the furniture and other belongings of the family; they often leave the house in a mess. The arrested man is allowed no contact with the outside world for an indefinite period of time. After interrogation, which in many cases has taken more than 28 days, he is moved to a detention centre and can be visited by his family and relatives. The exact number of these detainees is unknown but may lie between 200 and 300 persons, according to the Adeni sources. On July 25, 1966, Amnesty International received the names of 164 Adeni citizens who were arrested under similar conditions mentioned above...

Next comes the question of ill-treatment and torture practised as a method of interrogation. The very fact that a neutral organisation such as Amnesty International is not allowed to interview the detainees increases the suspicion of practice of torture at the interrogation centres. The ex-detainees, the relatives of the present detainees, whom I interviewed in Aden and other sources complained of the following forms of torture:

1. Undressing the detainees and making them stand naked during interrogation.

2. Keeping the detainees naked in super-cooled cells with air conditioners and fans running at the highest speed.

3. Keeping the detainees awake by irritating them until they are exhausted.

4. Offering food to hungry detainees and removing it just as they start eating.

5. Forcing the detainees to sit on poles directed towards their anus.

6. Hitting and twisting their genital organs.

7. Extinguishing cigarettes on their skin.

8. Forcing them to run in circles until they are exhausted.

9. Banning visits to lavatories so that they soil their cells with fæces and urine.

10. Keeping them in filthy toilets with the floor covered with urine and fæces.

Other forms of ill-treatment can be read in individual case reports...

Hashim Jawee:

Elected member of the Municipal Council of the City of Aden. Profession clerk. About 25 years. I spoke to this ex-detainee in a private house in Aden on July 29, 1966. He gave me some information spontaneously but I had to ask some questions in order to get a detailed record of his interrogation at Fort Morbut. He seemed to be deeply

▶ *British Army sergeant with two demonstrators in the Crater district of Aden ... April 1967.*

▼ *Demonstrators in Aden are rounded up by British soldiers during a protest against the arrival of a United Nations mission in April 1967.*

shaken by the interrogation and showed some feelings of shame for the humiliating treatment to which he had been subjected. There was no doubt about the truth of his description of his arrest and interrogation. I read to him what I had written about his case; he approved the report and had no objection to the publication of his case report by Amnesty International. Hashim Jawee spoke to me in fluent English:

Two hours after midnight July 6th, 1966, the entrance door to his house was broken, and the house searched by a number of soldiers. He was taken to Fort Morbut and thrown into an isolated cell. The iron door was banged by kicking at half-hour intervals. Later on his clothes were taken off and he was left naked for a while before the interrogation began, by British Military personnel. His buttocks and genital organs were examined in order to humiliate him. The examiner was not a physician and the examination was not a medical health examination. After this examination they asked for his address which they already knew and he was sent back to his cell and his clothes were returned. During the first three days the barrel of a gun was pointed at him through the cell window and Jawee was told that he was going to be shot within a short time. The cell had a temperature of nearly 100°F (37°C) which is not unusual in this climate. He was not allowed to take a cold shower. On the third day he was asked about a list of names which the interrogators suspected that he was in contact with. On one occasion he was drawn by his hair and on another occasion he was kicked. He was not allowed to receive visitors or to confer with a lawyer.

On several occasions he was taken out of his cell at night and ordered to run round the courtyard until he was exhausted. When asking for a glass of water he was spat upon in the face. Inventories of the cell consisted of an iron bed covered by hard brushy clothing and a dirty blanket which was soaked in sweat. The food he received was inedible. He was asked to clean the lavatories several times. He was released after nearly two weeks without a charge.

Muhammed Said Basharain:

28 years old. Born and raised in Aden. Ex-detainee. Arrested twice; in 1963 and 1964. I met this man on July 29th, 1966. He spoke English fluently. He gave an open and reliable account about his arrests. I read up his case story which he accepted and had no objection that the information which he gave to Amnesty International was published.

First arrest, 1963. Mr. Basharain was arrested together with 58 trade union leaders including Mr. Abdullah Al Asnag and people belonging to PSP (Peoples Socialist Party). They were all arrested in the early hours of the morning. This happened after the bomb incident at Aden airport on December 10, 1963, and immediately after the proclamation of the State of Emergency. All the prisoners were taken to the capital of the Fadhly Federal State and imprisoned there for 62 days. They proclaimed a hunger strike in protest at the inhuman treatment to which

they were subjected. They were released after 62 days of detention. All of them were interrogated several times and no evidence could be produced against them for their participation in the bomb incident.

Second arrest, October 1964. After the burning of a newspaper house he was arrested at noontime and taken to Fort Morbut. His clothes were removed except for underpants before he was interrogated by British Military personnel. He was left in a toilet for 12 hours lying on the floor covered by urine and faeces. He proclaimed a hunger strike which drew attention after 24 hours. He was then removed to a separate cell. After seven days of interrogation he was released for lack of evidence.

Radiya Ihsan:

Miss Radiya Ihsan is the general secretary of the Arab Women's Society in Aden. This case is taken to exemplify that people can be arrested in Aden for purely political reasons. Miss Ihsan, who is 32 years old, has been arrested twice.

First arrest: In December 1962 she was accused of participating in demonstrations against the union of Aden with the South Arabian Federation. She was kept in prison 10 weeks. During this period another charge was brought against her and she was fined a small sum of money. On one occasion she was kept in the same room with a number of psychiatric patients.

Second arrest: In December 1963, she was arrested once more, this time under the emergency laws. She spent one week in a cell at a police station followed by 8 weeks in Aden prison. The reason for this detention was, she says, to cut off her contacts with some journalists who were visiting Aden. The Arab Women's Society demonstrated in favour of Miss Ihsan. This case is well-known in Aden.

Published December 1966

● 'YOUR EFFORT AND PRAYERS SAVED MY LIFE'

Lee Shim-bom, a law student at Seoul National University in the Republic of Korea, was arrested in June 1980 and sentenced by a military court to nine years' imprisonment for organizing student demonstrations. Taken to prison, he was in great pain, attributed to the beatings inflicted on him during interrogation. He was said to be unable to move his neck and one arm. The authorities, however, denied him medical treatment on the grounds that the prison did not have the necessary facilities. In protest, Lee Shim-bom started a hunger-strike.

Amnesty International learned of his worsening condition and launched a worldwide Urgent Action appeal on his behalf. He then received only minimal medical attention in prison and was not examined or treated in an appropriate hospital. Amnesty International continued its appeals for him to receive proper medical attention throughout his term of imprisonment.

The organization campaigned for Lee Shim-bom's unconditional release on the grounds that he was a prisoner of conscience, jailed for the non-violent exercise of his human rights. Under a presidential amnesty granted for Christmas 1982, he was released – having served only two years of his nine-year sentence. He now lives in the United States where he has received medical treatment by doctors connected with Amnesty International. In February 1983 he told an Amnesty International conference in California:

'During the dismal and lonesome days, international concern and support have always encourged us greatly ... All the dictators have fantasies that they can suffocate and divide people in their own country. Under these circumstances we know what they are afraid of most is world opinion and criticism of their tyranny. Here we can see the effective role of the Amnesty International movement encouraging the oppressed.

'Your efforts and prayers saved my life and thanks to your support I can have an opportunity to live as a human being ...'

MASS CHRISTMAS CARD MAILING TO PRISONERS

By 1967, Amnesty International was working for nearly 2,000 prisoners in 63 countries. There were 550 groups in 18 countries. Hundreds responded to a Christmas card mailing organized that year for prisoners and the following news release was issued.

Amnesty International, like other charities, produces a Christmas card. Unlike others, the Amnesty card is sent not only to friends and relations but also to prisoners of conscience in gaols all over the world.

With every order of one dozen cards goes a list of 12 prisoners, giving brief details of their imprisonment and postal instructions. 36 prisoners are listed, all of whom are now paying the price for following their political or religious beliefs. They include Eleni Voulgari, a Greek girl imprisoned since last year with her baby son, because her family sheltered a communist in 1953; Vladimir Batshev, a young Soviet poet sentenced to 5 years imprisonment for being an 'idler'; and Maoulvi Mohammed Farooq, a young Kashmiri nationalist, in prison in India since 1965 and reportedly in bad health.

Already over 13,000 cards have been sold. It is hoped that 50,000 will be sold by Christmas, most of which should find their way into prisons and camps in 25 countries. Experience has shown that although it is sometimes difficult to get ordinary letters or postcards through to a prisoner, Christmas cards are often allowed. So an Amnesty card may well be the only contact some prisoners will have with the outside world this Christmas...

News release 7 November 1967

TRIAL OF THREE YOUNG WRITERS

Amnesty International asked the Soviet Attorney General if it could send an observer to the trial of three writers in 1967. No reply was received.

Vladimir Bukovsky of the USSR was one of three writers whose trial in Moscow in August 1967 aroused international protest. He spent 11 years in labour camps, jails and psychiatric hospitals and was finally exchanged by the Soviet Government in December 1977 for a Chilean communist leader. He is shown here on his arrival in London.

Amnesty International is urgently mobilizing the 800 members of its Postcards for Prisoners Campaign all over the world to send cards to protest to the Soviet Government at the trial of the young writers Vladimir Bukovsky, Vadim Delone and Yevgeny Kushev which began yesterday at Moscow City Court. As early as February of this year, when the news of the arrests was made known, Amnesty International wrote to the Soviet Attorney General saying that it would like to send an observer to this trial and asked to be informed of the date. No reply was ever received and no warning of the trial was given.

Vladimir Bukovsky is the best known of the three men. Six years ago he was detained in a mental institution for contributing to 'Phoenix 1961', a forerunner of 'Phoenix 1966', an underground literary journal which has been the core of the present trouble. On his release four years later, Bukovsky again became active in the unofficial literary world and participated in the demonstration in Moscow in December 1965 calling for a fair trial for Sinyavsky and Daniel. He was again arrested and confined to a mental institution. His case was taken up by Amnesty International and an Amnesty member called on the Director of the Serbsky Institute of Forensic Psychiatry where Bukovsky was detained. Shortly afterwards Bukovsky was released and was free until his arrest in January this year.

In the meantime the people for whom Bukovsky, Delone and Kushev organised the January demonstration are themselves in prison awaiting trial. They are Yury Galanskov, Alexei Dobrovolsky, Peter Rodzievsky and Alexander Ginsburg (who also compiled the 'White Book' on the Sinyavsky/Daniel case). Galanskov, a dedicated pacifist, is noted for the solitary demonstration which he staged in June 1965 in front of the United States Embassy in Moscow to protest against American intervention in the Dominican Republic. He was editor of 'Phoenix 1966' and the author of an article explaining his ideas on improving the working of the United Nations, thereby improving international understanding and preserving peace.

The new Paragraph 190 of the Penal Code, sections 1 and 3. The demonstration in Moscow in January 1967, apart from calling for the release of the imprisoned writers, protested against the introduction of this new law as an infringement of the rights of freedom of speech and assembly guaranteed by the Soviet Constitution. The previous month, 21 leading Soviet scientists and cultural figures, including the composer Shostakovich, had protested against this law. Briefly, section 1 of the new Paragraph forbids the writing or spreading of literature deemed to be anti-Soviet; section 3 forbids the organisation of or participation in group activities which disturb public order, i.e. any kind of unofficial demonstration or lobbying. Under this paragraph both 'Phoenix 1966' and the January demonstration were illegal and all the people involved in them are liable to up to three years detention in labour camps.

News release 31 August 1967

CONDITIONS IN A CHINESE LABOUR CAMP

From 'Amnesty International Review': an interview with a former Chinese civil servant about conditions in a Chinese labour camp. He had been sent for 're-education' to a State Farm near the Soviet border. He provided a rare glimpse into labour camp life at a time when information was difficult to obtain from China following the Cultural Revolution.

Over the last 18 months the Chinese Cultural Revolution has received wide coverage in the international press. The fact that many reporters have been expelled and others, as foreigners, have been isolated from the Chinese, has prevented detailed reporting at first-hand. News-stories have thus described only the general trends and it has been impossible to know what practical effect political events have had on the lives of individuals.

This is an interview with a former Chinese civil servant who worked in a Peking ministry until the late nineteen-fifties when he was sent to a State Farm near the Soviet border, in the north-east of Heilunkiang Province. Although the experience he describes ended some six years ago, the farm is still believed to exist.

Q. Why were you sent to this camp?

A. Because during the Hundred Flowers movement in 1957, I criticised the Chinese Communist Party during a meeting. I was accordingly declared a rightist counter-revolutionary. I was never officially arrested, but simply told that I would be sent to a camp for labour and reform (re-education). My family was told in advance and given my address … I was never officially charged or tried or sentenced, nor was I officially regarded as a prisoner.

Q. What were the general conditions of your imprisonment?

A. We were sent to a part of Manchuria that had previously been uncultivated and virtually uninhabited, and imprisoned in a State Farm to cultivate the land. The State Farms are modelled on the military pattern, each farm being equivalent to an army division. My 'company' consisted of 100 men who, like myself, had all been in government service when arrested. We were still theoretically government officials, not prisoners, and continued to receive our government salaries while we were in the camp. The conditions of our imprisonment were therefore considerably better than those of real prisoners.

We were not given bed-clothes or toilet articles, but we could bring what we needed from Peking. We could also receive necessary articles from our families or buy them in the prison shop. There was no heating whatsoever and we suffered terribly from the cold, since the temperature went down to −16°C indoors in the winter. None of us was allowed to take a bath for the first several months. The toilets consisted of simple holes in the ground, and this resulted in considerable hardships during the winter months.

Q. Did you receive an adequate diet?

A. At first it was quite good. Each prisoner received 90 catties of food a month (1 catty=1.3lb), including rice, Chinese bread, quite good meat and fish. Because our working hours were long, we received 4 or 5 meals daily. During the Great Leap Forward, however, our ration was cut progressively from 90 to 50 to 45 to 36 to 21 catties a month. We no longer received any grains, only a type of feed normally given to pigs. There was no longer any hot food, and we had only two meals a day. We all began to suffer from malnutrition, which resulted in swellings and other forms of illness. We tried to supplement the regular diet by eating leaves, dead birds and field rats that we found on the ground, etc.

Q. Were visits allowed?

A. No, our camp was too far away and visiting permission was never granted.

Q. What punishments were given to prisoners?

A. We were occasionally refused meals if other prisoners had reported us as being counter-revolutionary. We were all encouraged to spy on our fellow-prisoners and to report any suspicious remarks to the authorities. We received no corporal punishments of the type that were inflicted on 'official' prisoners.

Q. How did your treatment compare with that of criminal prisoners?

A. No real distinction is made in China between criminal and political prisoners. All crimes (including theft) are regarded as basically political (anti-government, anti-Party, etc.).

Q. Did you have any contact with 'official' prisoners?

A. No, but there was a camp fairly near ours in which political prisoners who had been officially sentenced by a court were kept. These prisoners had usually received sentences of at least ten years and some were in prison for life. They were guarded by soldiers with guns, they were flogged for various offences such as trying to escape (at night we could hear screams and shouts from their camp); and their diet was considerably worse than ours; they had no prison shop, could not receive parcels from outside, etc. These men were regarded as active counter-revolutionaries, while we were simply considered to be 'rightists', 'bad enemies' or 'historical counter-revolutionaries', i.e. as men who had worked for the Kuomintang government but who were nevertheless not responsible for current counter-revolutionary activities in China.

Q. What work did you do?

A. Mostly digging ditches to drain water. In the winter the earth was frozen three feet deep, in summer we were immersed in water as we dug. We also did some planting and harvesting soy beans, and built roads and houses. We worked between 14 and 16 hours a day. During an extremely bad period at the time of the Great Leap Forward we worked for 10 days and nights at a stretch with virtually no rest at all.

Q. Was there a 'norm' to be fulfilled?

A. No, but there was a competitive system between groups. Rewards and special titles were given to the hardest workers. We were told that this was very effective in expediting our release from the camp, that in fact it was the only way to become free. So we all worked as hard as we possibly could.

Q. Would you complain about your working conditions?

A. Yes, we were forced to work far too hard. As a result, many of us fell ill, some seriously so. Of the 100-odd people in my original group about 20 died from illnesses which resulted essentially from over-work and malnutrition. There was no adequate hospital facility for those who became ill. When I myself was released and returned to Peking, I was too weak to walk upstairs.

Published November 1967

Crowds in a Shanghai street, October 1966, listen to Red Guards publicizing points of the Cultural Revolution.

One year after the Warsaw Pact intervention in Czechoslovakia in 1968, laws restricting freedom of expression and assembly and limiting the rights of detainees were introduced. The imprisonment of Czechoslovak citizens for the non-violent exercise of their human rights was to remain an Amnesty International concern throughout the years that followed. The organization has worked for the release of numerous prisoners of conscience and published details about their prison conditions. Amnesty International delegates sent to observe trials of prisoners of conscience in Prague have been refused entry to the courts or barred from entering the country.

POLITICAL TRIAL IN GREECE

Within months of the April 1967 military coup in Greece thousands of political prisoners were detained.
Over the next seven years, Amnesty International adopted many of the victims as prisoners of conscience and its members flooded the authorities with appeals for their release.
The trial report here illustrates a frequently used technique: sending observers to political trials to establish first-hand whether internationally recognized standards for a fair trial are being met. Stelios Nestor, one of the defendants in this case, was later to become a leading member of Amnesty International.
In 1968 Amnesty International published evidence that torture was a systematic practice in Greece. A report by the European Commission of Human Rights – concluding that torture was an administrative practice of the Greek Government – was adopted in 1969 by the Committee of Ministers, setting a historic precedent for the principle of international responsibility for the protection of human rights.

Derek Page, Labour MP for Kings Lynn, attended the trial in Salonica of six lawyers and professional men charged with resistance to the Greek Government. He has given the following report to Amnesty International.

The main prosecution evidence was that the accused had printed and distributed opposition leaflets and had been in contact with Democratic Defence, the illegal Centre Union resistance organisation. The six defendants were found guilty and sentenced to terms of imprisonment ranging from 16 to 10 years.

Amnesty regards these savage sentences as quite disproportionate to the evidence brought by the Prosecution. Moreover the allegations of torture give rise to particular concern in view of the case now before the European Commission of Human Rights in Strasbourg; Sweden, Denmark and Norway have charged the Greek Government with contravening Article 6 of the European Convention on Human Rights, which categorically forbids the use of 'torture, inhuman and degrading treatment'.

Report to Amnesty International

On November 5th, I flew to Athens and thence to Salonica in order to attend the trial of six men accused of being members of the resistance organisation Democratic Defence. At Athens the passport control officer checked each person arriving against an extensive card index. At Salonica, I was met by the British Consul General, Mr Little, and taken to the Mediterranean Palace Hotel where he had booked a room for me. The Consul General and an interpreter also accompanied me to the trial which started on the morning of the 6th. About this time, I noticed two plain-clothes men taking turns in following me and this shadowing continued throughout the visit.

The trial was by court martial, although the prisoners are civilians. They were: S. Nestor (36), lecturer in law, S. Dedes (39) lawyer, P. Zannas (40), former director of the Salonica Trades Fair and film executive, N. Pyrzas (30), English teacher, A. Maltsides (31) civil engineer, and C. Sipitanos (31) businessman. Also present in court were a civilian prosecutor and one lawyer for each prisoner. Five officers were acting as judges, the President of the court being Colonel Karapanos. The charges as read out, comprised the setting up of a resistance group for treasonable purposes, the printing and publishing of subversive leaflets and the distribution of newspapers from Democratic Defence in Athens. The trial was held under Law 509.

The President initially put on a jovial, fatherly tone and said that this court was not going to be conducted in a rigid manner, that there must be a free exchange of ideas and discussion to clarify the facts. During the proceedings he repeatedly interrupted, prompted witnesses, suggested evidence to them, argued with lawyers and prisoners, sometimes in friendly, sometimes in hectoring tones. On various occasions, the court became somewhat disorganised, with people moving about and policemen smoking.

I learned that three of the prisoners had been

▼ *Stelios Nestor, a law lecturer, stood trial with five others in Thessaloníki, Greece in 1968. All of them were found guilty of being members of a resistance organization and were sentenced to prison terms ranging from 10 to 16 years. (Stelios Nestor was released in 1973. He is now a lawyer in Thessaloníki.)*

seriously maltreated and tortured, both physically and mentally, during interrogation. One had been hung up by the feet and beaten on the soles with wire mesh until his heart gave trouble. One prisoner's toe had been broken. Another was beaten heavily on the head and chest. Threats of summary execution were made with guns pointed at the man. One prisoner's fourteen-year-old son was beaten by police for attempting to smuggle *Le Monde* into the prisoners' cell. The police had threatened to bring the wife of one prisoner to him, with the statement that unless an admission was forthcoming, she would be made to suffer as he had. The six prisoners were kept together for four months in a single cell measuring three metres by three, from which they were allowed out for ten minutes per day. The cell contained no furniture and the prisoners slept on mattresses on the floor. I also learned that some thirty members of another resistance organisation, the Patriotic Front, had been particularly badly treated. Their trial is expected in the near future.

The prosecution's witnesses consisted of security officers. The first such witness, Karamitsou, made a long general statement as to the nature of the group and their activities. This evidence was largely composed of rather nebulous allegations but it soon became clear that the tactic was to link the group with the Patriotic Front in Salonica and with the Democratic Defence in Athens, with the implication that the latter were linked with the Patriotic Front. The communists, it was alleged, wanted to use the association of these prominent men to give an air of respectability to anti-government activities. One of the defence lawyers got in one good point when he asked the witness whether it was not contradictory to allege this and also that the accused had taken care to keep anonymous. This witness, together with a second security officer, Bitsios, called in corroboration, occupied all the first day.

On the second day of the trial, the first witness called was a civilian named Melpos who was both the original instigator of the group and the person who gave them away, fear being the probable motive. This man is now free. He made a large statement admitting his part in forming the group. He went on to say that the group had no contact with the Patriotic Front until he himself made a contact with them and was offered cooperation. He discussed this with the others who decided not to cooperate except to the extent of using Patriotic Front equipment such as typewriters and duplicators. It was also denied that the Salonica Democratic Defence was under the direction of their colleagues in Athens. He himself was the only one to run contacts with the Patriotic Front, the group as a whole had not. This change in tone from what must have been his previous statements to the authorities caused some acrimonious exchanges with the prosecutor and judge, but he stuck to his story as he said it in court.

During the lunch break I learned that a telegram had arrived addressed to the President of the court from Richard Burton, Elizabeth Taylor and other prominent film actors protesting at the trial.

The short final session that day was taken up by two character witnesses for the defence who said that they had been invited to join the group, had not done so, but said that they were never given the impression that the group was treasonous. When asked by a defence lawyer how the group could overthrow the regime, the President of the court interjected with a joke 'By getting tanks, of course!..', then apparently realised this this showed the ludicrous nature of the treason charge and added that their activities would provoke a spirit of resistance.

The trial was expected to go on for about two days more and I had to leave that evening to return to London.

The atmosphere frankly is much worse that I had thought possible. Prisoners' relatives, while grateful for the visit, were fearful of being seen with me. The allegations of torture are plainly well founded, but the oppression is such that proof is unlikely to be obtained in a form to suit normal courts. The people on this trial, as well as some two hundred others who are reliably reported to have been tortured and then released, are extremely cautious of even being seen with a foreigner and are unlikely to sign affidavits or present themselves as witnesses. The sight of civilians before a court martial is in itself revolting and a condemnation of the regime. In many years of travel to foreign countries, I have never seen a country where such fear of the authorities exists, with the possible exception of East Germany and even there, the blatant brutality is not to be compared.

During the time that the trial was in progress the town was doing a roaring trade outside the courtroom, due to a courtesy visit of the US Sixth Fleet. Whilst the Democrats were in no way anti-American it was felt that the acceptance of the junta in Nato military circles left a great deal to be desired.

Published November 1968

National Police force officers in Athens.

● 'A BOMBSHELL FOR THE PRISON AUTHORITIES...'

Friday 9 June 1978 remains etched into the memory of Shahid Nadeem, a Pakistani television producer and trade unionist imprisoned four times for his union work and student political activitites. It was a day of searing heat which saw one of his fellow prisoners die of heat-stroke, with eight others collapsing in the factory at the notorious Mianwali maximum security prison situated in a semi-desert region of the Punjab. It was also the day a letter brought him hope.

Shahid Nadeem, now abroad, recounts how at about 6.00 pm on 9 June 1978 a fellow prisoner arrived in his cell just before locking-up time with a piece of paper he called 'your letter from the USA'. It was a copy he had made of a letter in the possession of the prison superintendent, who was studying it, suspecting it contained a secret coded message. Addressed to Shahid Nadeem the letter said: 'You are not alone; don't lose heart. We pray for you. If there is anything you need, don't hesitate to ask.'

In spite of the intense heat, Shahid Nadeem said, 'Suddenly I felt as if the sweat drops all over my body were drops from a cool, comforting shower ... The cell was no longer dark and suffocating.' Soon the whole prison knew about his letter from an Amnesty International adoption group member in San Antonio, Texas. 'My colleagues were overjoyed and their morale was suddenly high.'

That evening the deputy-superintendent summoned him. 'He was so friendly and respectful I was shocked ... He explained his dilemma as a God-fearing jailer who had to obey orders and follow the rules ...' The head warden also began to 'behave himself'. Taking their cue the junior staff changed as well. After a week the original letter was handed over to Shahid Nadeem.

As he puts it now: 'A woman in San Antonio had written some kind and comforting words which proved to be a bombshell for the prison authorities and significantly changed the prisoners' conditions for the better.'

CALL OVER US WAR RESISTERS

In 1966 the movement's annual International Assembly (forerunner of the biennial International Council Meeting of delegates elected from Amnesty International sections which is the movement's supreme governing body) decided to give prisoner of conscience status to those who refuse to fight in specific wars, in addition to those who refuse to fight in all wars. The following appeal to the United States Government on behalf of Vietnam war resisters comes from the 'Amnesty International Review'.

Amnesty International appeals to the American Government to keep faith with its tradition of freedom of dissent by declaring an amnesty for all those imprisoned, awaiting trial, or in exile because of their refusal, on grounds of principle, to participate in the Vietnam war.

Few, if any, localised wars have provoked as much international debate and concern as the present war in Vietnam. Amnesty's concern here is not the rights and wrongs of the war as an international or political issue, but with the crisis of conscience which it has created for so many young Americans.

In the United States a unique combination of freedom to express dissent, side by side with conscription for an unpopular war and the absence of recognition of the right of selective conscientious objection (i.e. moral objection to participation in a particular war) has affected the lives of not hundreds, but thousands, of young American men between the ages of 18 and 26.

The dimension of the problem has not been fully publicised or appreciated. If all those directly affected are taken into account, including those currently indicted or in prison – as civilians or inside the army – those previously indicted or imprisoned, and the large numbers in hiding or in exile as deserters, the total figure would be in the region of 10,000 (Amnesty International is preparing a report which is to be published before the end of the year). Since the Civil War there has been no issue which has so divided the American people or resulted in imprisonment – in some cases sentences of as much as 10 years have been imposed – for so many *only* because of their moral objection to government policy.

These young men are constantly and openly told by many of the most respected and respectable members of their society: churchmen, writers, professors, doctors, ex-ambassadors, even generals, that the war in Vietnam is immoral or illegal, suicidal for their country and murderous for the Vietnamese. On the other hand they are forced by the Selective Service Law to join the armed services, where they run the risk of fighting in a war that outrages their deepest moral beliefs.

The men in gaol, or indicted and awaiting trial, are not draft-dodgers in the sense of wanting an easy evasion of an unpleasant task. Many of them have given up their student deferments. Most of them are of above average education and intelligence. Men with these advantages have excellent opportunities of avoiding the draft within the law and without social stigma.

The indicted draft-resisters and some of the deserters in exile form a reservoir of potential prisoners of conscience who may populate the gaols of America long after there is no Vietnam war unless some form of amnesty is granted. The great majority of exiles are anxious to return, but see no profit to themselves or their country in surrendering their liberty while the war continues.

Men in the army who object to the war on conscientious grounds have very little chance of release. Because they are not normally accused of any specifically

Jefferson County sheriffs drag a protesting anti-war demonstrator to a waiting jail bus. He was one of hundreds of students from the University of Colorado, USA, attacked with tear-gas and batons, 1968.

TEN YEARS ON

Extracts from the 'Amnesty International Annual Report', nearly 10 years after the movement's launch. The first is from the introduction by the Secretary General, Martin Ennals, the second is a message from Sean MacBride, Chairperson of the International Executive Committee.

political crimes, the numbers involved are difficult to ascertain but it is certain that hundreds, and probably thousands, of objectors to the war are deserters or imprisoned in military stockades.

Amnesty International has recently had reason to write to, among others, the Italian, Norwegian, Spanish and Yugoslav governments about their policy in relation to conscientious objection. We now appeal to the American government, by declaring an amnesty, to confirm its long established stand as a champion of liberty of conscience and by introducing legislation to to cover selective conscientious objection to ensure that young Americans will never again be faced with imprisonment because of their courageous decision to make a stand about what they believe, rightly or wrongly, to be an immoral policy.

Published November 1969

As Amnesty International approaches the end of its first decade it is confronted with the problems of growth both in size and recognition. The number of Amnesty groups adopting prisoners of conscience has increased from 640 to 850 and is still going up. New Amnesty committees are being established in countries in Latin America, Asia and Africa....

Inevitably Amnesty International is a controversial organisation. The publication of criticism always produces retaliation. Criticism does not always need to be public and great care is taken to avoid publicity if reasonable progress seems possible without it. But publicity is one of the few weapons in the armoury of a human rights non-governmental organisation and from time to time it is bound to be used. The extent of the publicity depends of course not on Amnesty International but on the press and television.

The political balance and committed neutrality which is the hallmark of Amnesty International's work does not mean that every action must immediately be balanced by another. Action taken must reflect the interest of the prisoners as much as the interests of the organisation. The balance must be seen and understood but it must not be contrived for effect. It is encouraging that both Soviet and American dissidents have used Amnesty International's channel of contact to the United Nations for the delivery of petitions to the Human Rights Commission....

The aims of Amnesty International are clear and limited. There is always a temptation to expand them to cover allied topics where other organisations exist and are active. To concentrate our limited resources on the areas where we are known to be specialist is a policy which the Executive and Council have maintained since the new statute was approved in 1968.

The great advantage of Amnesty International is that it is practical and provides a real programme for individuals and groups. Its specialisation is within the reach of anyone provided with the basic information about the prisoners. There is no one else with precisely the same function. It would, I believe, be ill-advised to throw away these advantages. There are many bodies who pass goodwill resolutions or who condemn governments in the field of human rights. We are unique in concentrating on practical work and therein lies much of our effectiveness.

As a voluntary international organisation Amnesty is a team of people each with a specific contribution to make. No one activity is adequate on its own. The groups who write the letters prepare the ground for the international executive who send the representatives to talk to the governments who receive the letters. It is interesting that talks with governments frequently start with discussions of the contents of cards and letters which have never been answered but are on the desk of the minister or in the hand of the ambassador who denies that he takes any notice of Amnesty correspondence.

Published 1970

Message from Sean MacBride, SC, Chairperson of the International Executive Committee

When you read of people being imprisoned for having expressed views that displease an authoritarian government or of prisoners being tortured you are shocked, but you feel helpless. You are anxious to do something to help but you do not know how. Instead of feeling helpless, you can help by supporting Amnesty International. It has the courage and ability to act for you – and to act effectively. Amnesty acts as the voice of the human conscience in these matters and can translate your sense of helplessness into concrete action that will protect Prisoners of Conscience. You can help Amnesty International by joining an Amnesty Group, or by forming one among your friends or by sending a subscription.

One hopeful feature of the present period of world history is that public opinion is now becoming more powerful. Because of the mass media of communications there is a growing awareness of world happenings. This growing awareness leads to the formation of public opinion on a world-wide basis. In turn, Governments can no longer act in secret: they are dependent on their own image both nationally and internationally and therefore must heed world public opinion. In this situation Amnesty International is becoming more potent and Governments can no longer ignore it.

We are glad to register a growing reaction against the brutality and arbitrariness which disgraces this era. Amnesty International can well take credit for having aroused world opinion on this issue. The expulsion of Greece from the Council of Europe and the world-wide exposures of tortures of prisoners in Brazil have been some of the immediate results. Many more such cases in other areas of the world will need the attention of Amnesty. We welcome in this connection the recent call made by the Christian Churches at Baden (Austria):

'No one, who respects the principles of Christianity, the sacredness of human life and the inherent dignity of the human personality, can fail to be alarmed by the mounting violence and brutality of our times. Massacres, tortures, summary executions and arbitrary imprisonments have become such common currency that the natural reaction of horror tends to be blunted. Thus a degradation of human values is taking place. This is a serious problem which demands the untiring and fearless efforts of all Christian Churches. Neither a sense of helplessness nor the violence of the age should be permitted to dull the sense of horror and indignation which acts of brutality, hostility and cruelty arouse.'

Sean MacBride

ILL-TREATMENT IN NORTHERN IRELAND

Following the introduction of internment in Northern Ireland in 1971, Amnesty International investigated allegations that suspects were being subjected to ill-treatment by security forces. A fact-finding mission concluded that the medical evidence was consistent with the claims made by former detainees interviewed. Amnesty International published its findings and made recommendations to a government inquiry. The torture techniques – which in some cases caused long-term psychological harm – were dropped. Six years later the European Court of Human Rights ruled that the interrogation methods violated Article 3 of the European Convention on Human Rights which prohibits 'cruel, inhuman or degrading treatment or punishment'. The first of the following extracts comes from Amnesty International's 1971 submission to the government inquiry into interrogation techniques (the Parker Committee). The second is from 'Torture in the Eighties' (1984) and examines the situation in Northern Ireland in the late 1970s.

It is said that the physical ill-treatment described in the Compton Report [report of a government Committee of Enquiry into allegations of ill-treatment] is less severe than the methods of ill-treatment used by other regimes in other countries. But this should not serve to disguise or blind us to the true nature of the procedures described in the Compton Report. There is a danger that even by considering the procedures at length we become anaesthetized to the degree to which they constitute an offence against the person. It is a form of torture to force a man to stand at the wall in the posture described for many hours in succession, in some cases for days on end, progressively exhausted and driven literally almost out of his mind by being subjected to continuous noise, and being deprived of food, of sleep, and even of light.

But the moral impropriety of these techniques principally derives not from their physical effects at all, but from the fact that they constitute a grave assault on the human mind. It is clear that the purpose and effects of these techniques is to disorientate and break down the mind by sensory deprivation. If we regard the physical ill-treatment as merely a means to achieve the same effect as would be achieved by the forcible injection of an hallucinatory drug or of a drug designed to break down and disorientate the mind, we begin to appreciate the true nature of the moral offence committed. It is because we regard the deliberate destruction of a man's ability to control his own mind with revulsion that we reserve a special place in our catalogue of moral crimes for techniques of thought control and brainwashing.

Case History: Patrick McKavanagh Age: 24 years

1. The Commission heard oral evidence from Mr. McKavanagh and read a medical statement by Conor J. Gilligan, MB, FRCS, Mater Infirmorum Hospital, Belfast. The case was presented by Mr. Francis Irvine, solicitor.

2. Mr. McKavanagh says that he, his brother William, and Edward Rooney, met a military patrol on Catherine Street at about 2 a.m. on 11 August 1971. They were ordered to halt but William McKavanagh turned to run, was shot and died some minutes later. Mr. Patrick McKavanagh and Mr. Rooney were placed under arrest. An army vehicle arrived at about 6.30 a.m. and they were taken to Hastings Street Barracks. The body of Mr. McKavanagh's brother was taken in the same vehicle.

Mr. McKavanagh was later taken to the Police Office on Townhall Street and charged with theft (he had taken up a rivetting tool, a pair of boots and some socks that were lying on the street during the disturbances – and kept them) and appeared in court on 12 August 1971 and was released on bail. No other charges were preferred against him. He was examined by Mr. Gilligan on 12 August.

3. Mr. McKavanagh alleges the following: He was struck in his face by a baton or a rifle butt when he entered the army vehicle. His glasses were smashed and a soldier trampled on them deliberately. Both McKavanagh and Rooney were verbally abused and they were also threatened that they would be beaten up and shot. Mr. McKavanagh

was further beaten with batons and rifle butts.

In the barracks he was made to stand spreadeagled against a wall, finger tips against the wall and legs forced back and out. He was hit repeatedly. This went on for about twenty minutes. After this he was forced to do exercises and was hit on the head and elbows. An empty sand bag was put over his head for about half an hour and he found it hard to breathe. When he was interrogated later he was tapped from behind on the back of the head. He was first given the diabetic medicine, which he should take three times a day, at about 8 p.m. on 11 August.

4. On examination, Mr. Gilligan found a bruised swelling on the bridge of the nose with the skin broken in centre. There were tender swellings close to the left ear, on the right parietal area, on the right arm and in the neck. There were several extensive areas of swelling and bruisings on the limbs. There was especially extensive bruising on the right thigh and the skin was broken, which could have been caused by an instrument or a weapon with a sharp point. there was evidence that he had been struck repeatedly over different parts of this body by a blunt weapon, used with considerable force.

In Mr. Gilligan's opinion, the injuries he observed were consistent with Mr. McKavanagh's account of how they were inflicted.

5. Conclusion: The Commission finds no major inconsistencies in Mr. McKavanagh's testimony and his account is essentially corroborated by the evidence from Mr. Rooney regarding experiences when the two were together. The Commission, having considered the evidence given by Mr. McKavanagh and Mr. Gilligan, accepts the substance of Mr. McKavanagh's allegations.

Published March 1972

'TORTURE IN THE EIGHTIES': NORTHERN IRELAND

In January 1976 the European Commission of Human Rights in Strasbourg concluded that the authorities in Northern Ireland and the British Government were responsible for practices in 1971 amounting to torture and inhuman treatment of detainees under interrogation by the police, in breach of Article 3 of the European Convention on Human Rights.[1] In the meantime, the British Government gave the British Parliament in 1972 and the European Court of Human Rights in 1977 unqualified undertakings that the most objectionable techniques of interrogation would not be used again. Yet despite this declared concern (which led the European Court to state in 1978 that it was hardly plausible that practices in breach of Article 3 would continue or recommence), complaints of assault during interrogation in early 1976 in Northern Ireland were increasing.

Castlereagh interrogation centre in Belfast, Northern Ireland, one of the places where political suspects were tortured.

The Maze prison, Belfast, Northern Ireland.

A pattern recurs

Between 1976 and 1978, one in 11 detainees arrested under emergency legislation in Northern Ireland filed official complaints of assault by the Royal Ulster Constabulary (RUC).[2] Prior to May 1977 almost all such complaints came from members of the Roman Catholic community, detained as 'Republican' suspects. Starting in May and June, with the advent and collapse of a Protestant-led strike, 'Unionist' detainees also began to file complaints.

The 443 complaints of assault during interrogation filed in 1977 represented a 101 per cent increase over 1976, although fewer suspects were detained. An Amnesty International mission to Northern Ireland in late 1977 investigated 78 cases, both 'Republican' and 'Unionist'. It found that ill-treatment by the RUC had taken place. The alleged methods included such physical and psychological abuses as beatings, bending of limbs, prolonged standing, burning with cigarettes, threats of death and threats to the suspect's family.[3]

It is important to ask why the preventive measures taken and assurances given by the British Government, following the exposure by Irish and British journalists (and by Amnesty International) of the torture of 14 detainees and the ill-treatment of hundreds more in 1971, did not prevent the assault of suspects from becoming a frequent and tolerated practice in Northern Ireland from late 1975 or early 1976 until early 1979 and to examine what steps were taken to reduce the number of complaints so significantly by 1980.

The law and interrogation

Northern Ireland security needs in 1972, in the British Government's view, dictated a review of arrest and trial procedures. The officially appointed Diplock Commission recommended changes that became law in the Northern Ireland (Emergency Provisions) Act 1973, which altered the rules of evidence for the admissibility of confessions. In English and Northern Ireland common law a judge can allow in evidence only a voluntary statement made by the accused, 'in the sense that [it has] not been obtained from him by fear of prejudice or hope of advantage, exercised or held out by a person in authority, or by oppression'.[4] The Diplock Commission concluded that this common law test was 'hampering the course of justice in the case of terrorist crimes',[5] and the 1973 Act altered the test of voluntariness. Whereas the common law test renders inadmissible confessions obtained by 'oppression', section 6 of the 1973 Act had the effect of disallowing confessions only if the accused 'was subjected to torture or to inhuman or degrading treatment'.[6] Since the 1973 Act applied only to Northern Ireland, the police in the province became exempt from restraints applying elsewhere in the country. Although the Diplock recommendations and the new act did not specifically make physical violence or psychological coercion lawful, they did imply that a confession previously disallowed by judges due to police misconduct in obtaining it might henceforth be admitted in evidence. Furthermore, Lord Diplock recommended that the law prohibit the threat of physical violence, but this prohibition was not included in the 1973 Act. The omission could only encourage the view that a degree of coercion would be tolerated.

Until late 1975 this change in law did not significantly alter police interrogation practices. Prior to this time the security strategy of the government was based either on executive internment without trial or on quasi-judicial internment regulated by commissioners. Neither system required a high level of proof to ensure a suspect's continued detention. Indeed, the purpose of these systems was to put *suspected* terrorists or their sympathizers out of action even when there was not sufficient evidence to convict them in a court of law. As internment was phased out gradually during 1975, however, evidence became essential to the conviction of terrorist suspects in the trials that Lord Diplock had recommended to replace internment. In Northern Ireland forensic evidence is difficult to obtain in hostile areas. Witnesses are subject to fear and intimidation. Intelligence information, whether from informers or detainees, until recently has rarely been used in court. Under these circumstances, the RUC came to rely almost exclusively on confessions as evidence against the accused. For example, during the first half of 1978, 75-80 per cent of all convictions for politically motivated offences were based solely or mainly on confessions.[7]

Between 1972 and 1975 there were allegations of ill-treatment during interrogation, but the numbers were few and no pattern emerged. The need to get confessions for convictions in court, however, brought changes in 1976. The RUC took over from the army in all but the most hostile neighbourhoods. New RUC crime-squads were formed to specialize in interrogation. Centralized police interrogation centres were opened or planned at Castlereagh police station in Belfast and Gough Barracks in County Armagh. In July, the new Chief Constable, Kenneth Newman, issued an internal directive that made an important distinction between the 'interview' of a suspect, which would lead to a specific criminal charge and to which common law protection of the Judges' Rules on admissibility of evidence would apply, and the 'interrogation' of suspects, which was for general questioning and gathering intelligence. By implication, because this more general questioning need not lead to a charge for a specific offence, the Judges' Rules need not apply. Since available evidence indicates that approximately two-thirds of those arrested in Northern Ireland under emergency legislation at that time were released without charge,[8] this relaxation (or implied suspension) of the Judges' Rules and of the protection they afford suspects had special significance for 'interrogations'. During 1976 complaints of assault during interrogation increased by approximately 85 per cent over 1975, whereas arrests increased by only 49 per cent.

The government's view of interrogation

Successive British governments throughout the 1970s had a common policy on interrogation: to protect police discretion to question a suspect in private for extensive periods without the intrusion of the courts, lawyers or any other independent person. One consequence of this policy was the failure to safeguard suspects' rights and physical integrity. Besides relaxing the rules governing the admissibility of confessions in court, the government gave the police new powers in 1973 to hold persons suspected of politically motivated crimes incommunicado for up to three days (increased to seven days under the Prevention of Terrorism (Temporary Provisions) Act, 1974).

A prominent factor in the rapid decline in police standards was the prolonged failure of government ministers and senior RUC officers to intervene with

interrogators, directly and forcefully, to show that assault and illegal coercion would not be tolerated. On the contrary, the increased number and seriousness of complaints in 1976 and 1977 came when the government was pressing the police for confessions to use in court. Since the 1971 Compton Committee (which actually justified the use of the interrogation techniques subsequently identified as torture by the European Commission of Human Rights), no government-initiated inquiry has specifically investigated allegations of ill-treatment in Northern Ireland. All such inquiries have dealt with legal or police procedure, not with individual allegations of brutality. No British government took any decisive action before 1979 to halt the abuses that had begun to increase three years earlier, and to this day (to Amnesty International's knowledge) no government minister having responsibility in this area has accepted that ill-treatment took place in the late 1970s.

The extension of police discretion

Nor did the RUC command intervene despite the increasing evidence of misconduct by plain-clothes detectives in the middle and lower ranks. In April 1977, a senior police surgeon wrote to one of the government authorities, complaining that although police surgeons forwarded reports on a prisoner's injuries to the appropriate police station, 'no senior officer has ever seen fit to ring up to see me or my colleagues about the injuries noted'.[9] Several police interrogators were found at fault in civil proceedings, and the Police Authority chose to settle other claims out of court. In some instances these complaints were of serious assault and the damages paid were substantial. Yet no police officer ever admitted ill-treating a suspect, and no internal disciplinary proceedings were brought against any police officer.

The RUC took the position that allegations against its officers were part of an orchestrated campaign to sully the reputation of the force throughout the community, thereby damaging its aim of gaining acceptance for its law-enforcement role, especially by the Roman Catholic community, and thus reducing its effectiveness against paramilitary groups. In the official RUC view the injuries sustained by prisoners were either self-inflicted or resulted from attacks made by the detainee on police officers, who then had to restrain the suspect. Chief Constable Newman asserted in June 1977 that the increasing number of allegations of police brutality were a sign, not of police misconduct, but of growing police success in combating terrorism. He also pointed out, correctly, that suspects had strong motives to file false complaints of assault against their interrogators. They might need to justify their confessions to their own paramilitary groups, and their only defence in court was often to claim that their confessions had been extracted under torture, or inhuman and degrading treatment. If the confession could be ruled inadmissible on that statutory ground, under section 6 of the 1973 Act, the accused would probably go free since it was usually the only evidence available.

The legislation earlier in the decade had increased police powers without providing for corresponding safeguards to protect the rights of suspects. The RUC sought (and were allowed) to increase police discretion over the interrogation process, violating the common law principle of access to a lawyer and undermining the machinery for the investigation of complaints against the police. None of the 78 people whose cases of alleged ill-treatment were examined by the Amnesty International mission in 1977 had been allowed to see a lawyer while in police custody. The majority of them had specifically requested to see a lawyer soon after arrest. The Judges' Rules state that 'every person at any stage of an investigation should be able to communicate and to consult privately with a solicitor (lawyer) … provided that in such a case no unreasonable delay or hindrance is caused to the process of investigation…', but this latter proviso was invariably interpreted by RUC officers so as to deny access to a lawyer. Detainees spent as many as seven days in incommunicado detention. It appears that the discretion assumed by RUC investigating officers to exclude lawyers was not the practice at this time elsewhere in the United Kingdom.[10]

Concerning complaints machinery, the RUC frequently pointed out, correctly, that it was more elaborate in Northern Ireland than anywhere else in the United Kingdom. However, the oversight role of the independent Police Authority does not cover complaints of criminal assault, which are referred to the Director of Public Prosecutions (DPP). Furthermore, the DPP does not have an independent investigative staff, and all complaints against the police are investigated by the RUC itself. Chief Constable Newman often argued that the DPP's decision not to prosecute a police officer was an indication that the allegations were false. In fact, the DPP himself reminded the Chief Constable in November 1977 that the failure to bring a prosecution against a police officer did not indicate that the complaint itself was untrue. In a review of 300 complaints from the first nine months of 1977, wrote the DPP, he had found some evidence of assault in about half of them, some of which were medically documented. But he had found a level of evidence high enough to make conviction possible, and therefore to warrant prosecution, in only one case.

The government-appointed Bennett Committee found that from 1972 until the end of 1978 only 19 police officers were criminally prosecuted for ill-treating terrorist suspects out of the hundreds of complaints that had been filed. Of these 19, only two were convicted, and both these convictions were set aside on appeal. In five of the cases resulting in acquittals, civil proceedings in respect of the same incidents resulted in the police paying damages to the complainants.[11]

The main reason for this low number of prosecutions was that in order to bring a prosecution, the DPP must be satisfied – beyond reasonable doubt – that the assault was committed by an identifiable police officer and can be proved in court. Nevertheless, Chief Constable Newman continued to maintain that the general lack of prosecutions cleared the RUC of allegations of misconduct. In other words, no crime had been committed because the officers responsible could not be convicted.

The judiciary

In ordinary circumstances one would expect judges in the United Kingdom to provide a measure of protection to suspects by their rulings on arrest and interrogation procedures. Given their independence as well as the degree of discretion allowed judges in English and Northern Ireland common law, it is fair to ask why cruel, inhuman and degrading treatment took place in spite of the role and authority of the Northern Ireland judiciary.

The primary role of the judiciary in the UK, according to the Judges' Rules, is to 'control the conduct of trials and the admission of evidence…; they do not control or in any way initiate or supervise police activities or conduct.' Nevertheless, the courts' decisions do influence police practices indirectly by indicating, after the fact, what kind of conduct by the police makes evidence inadmissible in court. In Northern Ireland interrogating officers attend trials of terrorist suspects regularly in order to give evidence, and they do take note of the attitude of the courts. The Bennett Report cites the evidence of an officer who testified in a civil proceeding that because the courts had accepted confessions made after 'interviewing hours on end with no sleep', he continued to interrogate prisoners in this way.[12]

One means of protecting detainees' rights during interrogation left unused by the courts is to disallow confessions obtained during incommunicado detention. Principle (c) of the Judges' Rules, cited earlier, protects the right of access to a lawyer. Although it can be argued that section 6 of the 1973 Act negated this principle in Northern Ireland, Mr Justice Bennett, citing police practice and court precedents elsewhere in the United Kindom in 1977, implied that discretion was still available to Northern Ireland judges to exclude confessions obtained after the police had denied a prisoner's request to see a lawyer. In no case in Northern Ireland involving people charged under emergency legislation did judges exercise this discretion.[13] In effect, judges did not help to ensure the detainee's right of access to a lawyer, which they could have done by disallowing evidence obtained during incommunicado detention, some of which was allegedly the result of ill-treatment.

More extreme assaults, especially if medically documented, presented judges with little difficulty in disallowing the confession of the accused. But in less clear-cut cases the Northern Ireland judiciary seemed uncertain of their authority to intervene positively. Several Northern Ireland judges attempted to interpret the degree of judicial discretion over disallowing from evidence confessions obtained by coercion that in their view was short of torture and of inhuman or degrading treatment (the language of section 6 of the 1973 Act). After reviewing some of these judgments the Bennett Committee found that 'the uncertainty, despite the standards upheld and applied by the courts, about what is permissible and what is not … may tempt police officers to see how far they can go and what they can get away with.'[14] The police interrogators appear to have interpreted the judges' too frequent silence as assent.

Pressure from the police surgeons

The most striking single action taken by any official in Northern Ireland to prevent ill-treatment was Chief Constable Newman's order on 21 April 1978 to install 'spy-holes' in the doors of interview rooms at the Gough Barracks interrogation centre so that senior officers could monitor interrogations. The suggestion came from the Senior Medical Officer (SMO) at Gough, Dr Denis Elliott, who had held a long-awaited meeting with the Chief Constable the previous night to discuss prisoners' injuries that doctors were continuing to see. During the next five months there were no complaints of assault filed by prisoners interrogated at Gough for terrorist offences.

Also in attendance at the meeting in April were Dr Charles Alexander, SMO at Castlereagh police station in Belfast, and Dr Robert Irwin, Secretary of the Forensic Medical Officers Association, who had himself seen many injured detainees from Castlereagh. Since late 1976 doctors employed by the independent Police Authority or by the government's Department of Health and Social Security (DHSS) as police surgeons had documented injuries that they were convinced could not be dismissed as self-inflicted. In March 1977 Dr Irwin's association informed the Police Authority of its concern about the increasing number of injuries to prisoners. Both individual doctors and groups of doctors kept pressing their employers and the RUC to respond to their demands. They cited the decision of the European Commission of Human Rights about the 1971 events, which was still under consideration by the European Court, as cause for doctors to play an active role in protecting prisoners from abuse and the police from false allegations.

The doctors kept their appeals within the system's administrative channels, shunning publicity. In the wake of a national television program about Castlereagh, however, having failed for months to get a personal interview with the Chief Constable, their association's executive committee stated publicly in October 1977 that they had sought a meeting with him to discuss injuries to detainees. In November, doctors at Castlereagh and Gough informed their employer that they would resign unless action were taken to stop the assaults. When taking up his post as SMO at Gough on 1 November, Dr Elliott stipulated that if there were serious police misconduct towards detainees, he would request a transfer to his previous post. The cumulative pressure of the national television program, the visit of the Amnesty International mission to the province in late November and early December 1977 and the doctors' steadfastness appears to have had an impact. Complaints of

assault during interrogation dropped from the autumn 1977 average of 40 a month to eight in December. The association's representatives noted this improvement in their discussions with the Amnesty International mission in December as an explanation of why the mission had examined released prisoners with recent but not fresh injuries.

In March 1978 the Police Authority informed the government that the doctors had noted a renewed pattern of injuries, that resignations might soon follow, and that the doctors wished their assessment of the recent decrease in injuries given in December to Amnesty International to be withdrawn. The next month Dr Irwin's association wrote formally to the Police Authority on this last point; four doctors at Gough, where Dr Elliott was SMO, wrote to the Police Authority in order to protest against the continuing injuries in custody, and Dr Elliott himself formally requested a transfer. Their pressure seems to have conveyed a sense of urgency to the government and the RUC command. The Amnesty International mission had collected considerable medical evidence, and a report would soon appear. Resignations at this time by police surgeons would have been an acute embarrassment to the government. Chief Constable Newman met Drs Alexander, Elliott and Irwin on the evening of 20 April and took decisive action the next morning. Besides the new 'spy-holes' to be installed, the meeting discussed a suggestion to install closed-circuit television in interroga-

After thorough investigation, Amnesty International declared that the British Army practised torture on political detainees in Northern Ireland. Until 1975 hundreds of people were imprisoned under very harsh conditions without being brought to trial or being sentenced. In Long Kesh camp many prisoners were detained without trial from 1971 to 1975.

tion rooms so that senior officers could monitor interrogators' conduct. The Chief Constable objected that this would be costly, to which Dr Irwin replied that it would be cheaper than having to return to the European Court.

Amnesty International published its report in June 1978. The immediate result was the government's appointment of the Bennett Committee of Inquiry into police procedures which ultimately led to the introduction of administrative safeguards to protect detainees and to a drop in the number of complaints of ill-treatment.

In August a new job description was agreed for police surgeons which formally extended their duties. SMOs would henceforth have access to any prisoner at all reasonable times, not just when the police called them in, and they would occasionally tour the police station, making use of the new 'spy-holes'.

During the remainder of 1978, while the Bennett Committee received evidence, complaints of assault declined but did not cease. Their report was published in March 1979 and their major recommendations were accepted by the government in June. But the Bennett Report did not lay the doctors' fears to rest. A few days before its publication Dr Irwin broke the doctors' long public silence and gave a nationally televised interview. He described some of the 150 injured prisoners he had personally examined – injuries he believed were not self-inflicted – during the past three years, some as recently as the month before. One week after publication of the Bennett Report, Dr Elliott resigned in protest at the 'undisciplined' treatment of prisoners at Gough and at the failure of either the government or the RUC to acknowledge that ill-treatment had occurred during the past three years. Drs Elliott and Irwin, whose actions had done so much to bring about an official inquiry, now underlined the importance of its recommendations.

The significance of an independent inquiry

The Bennett Committee addressed the balance between the efficiency of police interrogation and the protection of suspects' rights. Its terms of reference prevented an investigation of individual complaints. Nevertheless, it examined considerable medical evidence that revealed 'cases in which injuries, whatever their precise cause, were not self-inflicted and were sustained in police custody'. Nor did the government permit a general review of the emergency legislation or a specific one of section 6 of the 1973 Act. Such a review might have led to recommendations for statutory protection of prisoners. Given these restrictions, the committee recommended self-regulation by the police: for example, closed-circuit television monitoring of interrogations by senior officers; more detailed record-keeping on detainees; and the offer of a medical examination once every 24 hours. Even the recommendation for access to a lawyer after each 48 hours in custody, without exception, was to be incorporated in a revised RUC code of conduct, rather than in legislation. The report thus offers an impressive set of preventive administrative measures that, if fully implemented, would significantly reduce the likelihood of torture or ill-treatment of suspects.

Once implemented, these measures did reduce the number of allegations of assault and ill-treatment in Northern Ireland. The average number of complaints filed in the first three months of 1979 was 20 a month. This was somewhat down on the 1978 monthly average of 22, but in April 1979, the first full month after the Bennett Report appeared, the number of complaints dropped sharply to 8.[15] More significantly, the administrative measures introduced seem to have prevented the recurrence of the previous pattern of ill-treatment.

At present a very high percentage of convictions in non-jury trials in Northern Ireland are based solely or mainly on confessions. However, Amnesty International's approaches to the British Government about current police and judicial procedures used in Northern Ireland have not concerned allegations of ill-treatment. They have concerned the use of continuous, oppressive interrogation, which has resulted in a steadily high rate of confessions for which no objective corroborating evidence is presented in court. Under these conditions it is doubtful whether the 48-hour rule concerning absolute right of access to a lawyer provides adequate protection for detainees under interrogation.

There are several generalizations to be drawn from this examination of ill-treatment in Northern Ireland in the late 1970s:

1. The attitude towards the treatment of detainees shown at the top of the command structure within a security agency and by ministers responsible for their conduct affects officers' attitudes and actions right down the line.

2. Emergency legislation (or the interpretation of existing law by the courts) that extends the powers of the security forces specifically at the expense of detainees' legal guarantees may be perceived by the security forces as a signal that the law, the government and the courts will tolerate official violence towards and coercion of detainees.

3. When emergency legislation extends the powers of the executive, the judiciary must increase its vigilance on behalf of suspects and defendants if their rights are to be protected.

4. Post-facto investigations, prosecutions, civil suits and internal disciplinary proceedings may not be sufficient by themselves to stop abuses. The responsible authorities must take direct preventive actions, particularly those measures that will guarantee detainees access to individuals independent of the security forces, for example, the detainees' lawyer, doctor and relatives. This is all the more true in a legal system that does not provide for contemporaneous judicial supervision of interrogation.

5. Organized pressure from within the security system for respecting the rights of suspects is most likely to be effective when complemented by external pressures, in particular from the news media, which in some societies can

play a relatively independent watchdog role in bringing alleged abuses of authority to public attention.

6. The existence and use of inter-governmental human rights machinery, although lengthy and capable of being obstructed by a government, can act as a restraint on human rights abuses if the government fears the findings, the expense, the embarrassment or even the propaganda that may result.

1. European Commission of Human Rights, *Report of the Commission on Application No. 5310/71, Ireland against the United Kingdom of Great Britain and Northern Ireland,* adopted 26 January 1976, pp. 402 and 468. The European Court of Human Rights, in their judgment on this case in January 1978, modified the Commission's findings, omitting the word 'torture' but confirming that there had been an 'administrative practice' of inhuman and degrading treatment in breach of Article 3. For a discussion of the significance of this judgment in international law, see Chapter 2 to this report, page 15.

2. This ratio is calculated on the basis of data given in the *Report of the Committee of Inquiry into Police Interrogation Procedures in Northern Ireland* (hereafter called Bennett Report), HMSO London, Cmnd. 7497), paragraph 44 and Appendix 2. The ratio given in paragraph 313 of the Bennett Report (one in eight detainees held under emergency legislation filing complaints of assault during interrogation between 1975 and 1978) appears to be erroneous in that this calculation is based on the number of complaints by *all* detainees in Northern Ireland, not just by those held under emergency legislation.

3. Amnesty International, *Northern Ireland: Report of an Amnesty International Mission* (London, 1978), p. 4 (hereafter called Amnesty International Report on Northern Ireland).

4. *Judges' Rules and Administrative Directions to the Police,* Home Office circular No. 31/1964, principle (e). The Judges' Rules are in the form of advice to police officers on what will and will not be allowed as evidence in a trial.

5. *Report of the Commission to consider legal procedures to deal with terrorist activities in Northern Ireland* (hereafter called Diplock Report), (HMSO London, Cmnd. 5185, December 1972), paragraph 87.

6. The phrase quoted from section 6 was taken verbatim from Article 3 of the *European Convention for the Protection of Human Rights and Fundamental Freedoms.* Section 6 of the 1973 Act became section 8 in the consolidated version of this act in 1978.

7. Bennett Report, paragraph 30. The figures were prepared by the Director of Public Prosecutions for Northern Ireland and were thought by the Bennett Committee to be accurate for 1976 and 1977 as well.

8. Bennett Report, appendix 1, gives precise statistics for September 1977 until August 1978: only 35 per cent of those detained were charged.

9. Letter of 14 April 1977 from Dr Robert Irwin, Secretary of the Forensic Medical Officers Association in Northern Ireland, to Dr Terence Baird, Chief Medical Officer at the Department of Health and Social Security, Belfast. Quoted in Peter Taylor, *Beating the Terrorists?* (London, Penguin Books, 1980), p. 180. This and other details concerning pressure for improvements from within the system are available due to the research, after the events, by the well-known British journalist Peter Taylor, who conducted personal interviews with the police surgeons and authorities involved.

10. Bennett Report, paragraph 271.

11. Bennett Report, paragraphs 157 and 338. While standards of proof in civil cases may be lower than in criminal cases, a substantial number of successful civil suits should at least stimulate a serious investigation by the authorities of the allegations of ill-treatment.

12. Bennett Report, paragraph 178.

13. Bennett Report, paragraphs 271-276. Elsewhere in the United Kingdom denial of access to a lawyer is common, but only for the first 24 hours in detention.

14. Bennett Report, paragraph 84.

15. Statistics on complaints of assault during interrogation were made available by the RUC to Peter Taylor. Those given here are drawn from his book *Beating the Terrorists?* The monthly average for 1978 would be higher except for the low figures for June and July which were eight and nine respectively. It may be significant that the Amnesty International report on Northern Ireland was leaked in May and was published officially in June.

Published April 1984

● **'HOW DO THEY KNOW HIS EXACT ADDRESS...?'**

The mother of Soviet prisoner of conscience Anatoly Koplik travelled thousands of kilometres from the Ukraine to visit him in his labour camp near the Soviet-Chinese border in 1977. Before the visit began the head of the camp's 'operation unit' met her. According to a report she prepared after the meeting, the following discussion took place:

'The head of the operations unit scowled and said: "Do you know what kind of trouble is coming?"

'I asked him to explain what he meant by trouble. Some papers were lying on the table and the director of the camp, Pushkin, picked them up and showed me three pages. "Just look," he said, "this is already the second time we're getting these from Amnesty International." I asked him to read out loud what the trouble was. The director summarised what was written: "On account of his religious beliefs A. Koplik did not take the military oath and is serving his sentence in the camp. We urge that he be released and returned to his family, that he be allowed to live in peace, and that his youth be taken into account."

'Hearing this, I asked what the trouble was. The head of the operations unit raised his voice and said, "But do you know what this smells like? Just how do they know his exact address, even his detachment number? How is it that your son has contacts abroad?" I answered these questions with questions of my own: "And what are you surprised about? My son has no foreign contacts. You don't even give him the possibility to write letters home at the allotted times. Many of his letters home you don't even send on."

'The head of the operations unit said, "But do you know who leads this organisation?" I answered: "I only know one thing: my son was condemned and is suffering innocently, and this organisation concerns itself about such people." '

Anatoly Koplik was released in August 1979 on completion of his sentence.

HUMAN RIGHTS VIOLATIONS IN IRAN

In 1972 Amnesty International revealed that prisoners in Evin Prison, Tehran, Iran were being tortured and that the methods used included being burned on a heated metal table. Throughout the 1970s the organization campaigned against human rights violations perpetrated by SAVAK, the National Intelligence and Security Organization. After the overthrow of the Shah of Iran in February 1979, Amnesty International continued to investigate human rights violations and to press for protection of fundamental rights. That work continues unabated, as thousands of political prisoners remain in prison in Iran, sometimes without charge or trial or following summary trials, or even after their sentence has expired. Judicial proceedings are unpredictable and often arbitrary. Political detainees are reported to be tortured and ill-treated in hundreds of secret detention centres throughout the country. Floggings and amputations – which Amnesty International regards as forms of torture and cruel, inhuman or degrading treatment – are imposed as judicial punishment. Thousands have been executed, often after summary trials with no right of appeal.

REPORT OF AN AMNESTY INTERNATIONAL MISSION TO IRAN, 1972: VISIT TO EVIN PRISON BY MAITRE NURI ALBALA

… Despite the obstacles described in my report, L— and I were able to see Nasser Sadegh and Ali Mihandoust. We were in the company of two interpreters who introduced themselves as employees of the Ministry of Information, later declared that they were attached to the Prime Minister's office and who, in fact, represented one particular branch of the Prime Minister's office, SAVAK.

Nasser Sadegh told us that he was born in May 1945 at Tehran. He is an engineer trained in electro-mechanics. He gained his diploma in 1967, did his military service and then worked in the Pars Electrical Company; he was arrested in September 1971 and has been detained ever since. Ali Mihandoust was born in October 1947 at Qazvin. He is a mechanical engineer. He gained his diploma in 1969 and told us that since then he 'had been engaged full time in political activities'. Mihandoust was arrested in October 1971.

Mihandoust told us that before his arrest his activities were centred on Tehran, that they were secret and that he formed part of a group which was preparing for an armed struggle against the regime. He is charged with activities against the state, membership of an organisation (Peoples' Movement), and being involved in the theft of an aeroplane.

Nasser Sadegh, who was his friend, worked with him before their arrest but Sadegh swore that he was not like Mihandoust a member of a group but that he took part in the general leadership of the movement. I then put this question: 'You mention accusations brought against you. Can you tell us who brought forward these accusations?' Sadegh replied: 'SAVAK'.

Neither had seen the Military Prosecutor since about mid-January. When we asked them when they had seen the Examining Military Magistrate for the first time, they replied: 'Yesterday, 5th February.' I should add that after their arrest, in September and October respectively, they ought to have been brought before an Examining Military Magistrate within 24 hours; this is laid down by Iranian law

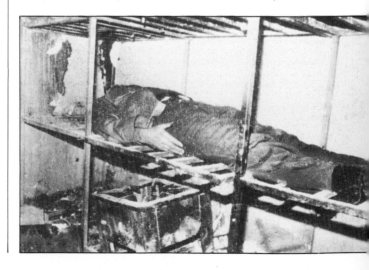

and we were reminded of it by the Military Tribunal's spokesman, Captain Gavam.

When we asked Nasser Sadegh what torture they had undergone, he made a long reply in Persian. This was shortly translated by the interpreters as: 'They were beaten the day they were arrested.' Sadegh signalled to me that this translation was incorrect, and so I repeated the question until the interpreters became bored with translating the same thing; I finally asked Sadegh: 'Were your friends beaten?' to which he replied in English: 'No, toasted'.

The interpreters told us the interview was over and that it was time to go. Sadegh indicated to me that he wanted to speak to me, and while L— spoke in French to the interpreters, who were urging us to leave, Sadegh confirmed to me that he had been beaten with the butt of a revolver and that this had caused a haemorrhage and fainting. He told me that Massoud Ahmadzadeh, Badizadeghan, Abbas Meftachi and Bazargan, amongst others, had been burned by being placed on a table which was then heated to white heat, and that Badizadeghan had since then been paralysed in the lower limbs and could move only by crawling forward using his upper arms. His last words to me were: 'Let them know that I saw Behruz Tehrani die near me in the torture room'.

I am able to confirm that the description of the metal table given by Nasser Sadegh corresponds exactly to the rectangular burn marks which I had seen that same morning on the back of Massoud Ahmadzadeh.

Published February 1972

IRAN BRIEFING 1976

The following human rights issues in Iran are of particular concern to Amnesty International:

(a) arbitrary arrest of suspected political opponents who are held incommunicado for long periods before being charged or tried;

(b) the use of torture;

(c) lack of legal safeguards and unsatisfactory trial procedures;

(d) executions and unofficial deaths.

◄ *While interviewing political prisoners in Iran in 1972, Amnesty International learned of a torture device composed of three tiers of grids with a burner underneath known as a 'toasting table'. Several such 'tables' were found in the cellar of a SAVAK centre stormed by demonstrators in 1978.*

Legal/administrative detention procedures

(a) *Arrest process.* SAVAK [the National Intelligence and Security Organization] is responsible for the internal security of the state. Its functions include repressing the activities of illegal organizations, preventing plotting against the national security and insuring against the formation of new groups which advocate policies contrary to the Constitution of 1906. To this end it is empowered to act as the sole investigator of all alleged political crimes and to initiate the bringing of charges against involved persons. SAVAK can directly order the arrest of any person suspected of political crime, and in practice no recourse to any court for approval is necessary. The Military Justice and Penal Law of 1938 does provide that where the investigator orders an arrest, the agreement of the Office of the Military Prosecutor (an entity independent of SAVAK) must be secured within 24 hours. Suspects also have the right, under article 10 of the Supplementary Constitutional Law of 8 October 1907, to be informed of the charges against them within the same 24-hour period. However, in no cases known to Amnesty International have either of these requirements been fulfilled and from what is known of SAVAK's interrogation procedures it is considered most unlikely that a suspect is actually informed of the charges against him or her until just before the case comes to court. At no stage does a suspect have access to a lawyer of his or her own choice and in all cases which have come to the attention of Amnesty International prisoners have been held incommunicado until they have been brought to trial or released. SAVAK conducts the entire investigation into each case and prepares the file which forms the entirety of the prosecutor's case at trial. As SAVAK controls the investigatory process, the accused will not stand trial until the case file is satisfactorily complete, which usually results in long periods of pre-trial detention for the accused, awaiting the successful production of evidence. There is no independent control of the way in which SAVAK obtains this evidence and it is not subject to any time limit for the preparation of a case.

(b) *Conduct of trials.* All trials of political prisoners are held before military tribunals, with attendant military counsel for the prosecution and defence. As noted above, during the investigation stage of proceedings, the accused has no right to consult with defence counsel or any other person. Upon completion of the SAVAK investigation, the accused is allowed access to defence counsel 10 days before trial. Defendants are asked to choose their defence counsel from a short list of persons presented to them by the tribunal; these are usually retired military officers who need not be learned in law. If the accused refuses to make a choice, the court directly appoints counsel for the defence. Proceedings before military tribunals are usually held *in camera*. Since March 1972 no foreign lawyers or journalists have been admitted to political trials in Iran and the information available to Amnesty International concerning the conduct of trials is based on observers' reports of trials prior to that date. The court itself is composed of four serving officers, sitting without a jury in apparent contravention of article 79 of the Supplementary Constitutional Law of 8 October 1907, which provides: 'In political and press offences, a jury must be present in the courts.'

The accused has no right to demand that witnesses against him or her be called and has no right of cross-examination. The only witnesses heard by the tribunal are the defendants themselves. The prosecutor proceeds by reading into the evidence the findings of the SAVAK investigation, including confessions, if any. Amnesty International observers have reported instances of defendants repudiating their confessions in court on the grounds that these have been obtained as a result of torture. The prosecution is not required to produce in court evidence referred to in the SAVAK files and the defence is not allowed to introduce evidence to support the defence case other than the testimony of the defendant. In practice the defendant is assumed guilty and Amnesty International knows of no case of a defendant being acquitted, although defendants who recant before the court may receive short sentences, or have their sentences reduced on appeal.

The Military Court of Appeal, to which convicted persons have recourse, has the power to confirm, reduce or increase sentences and may even impose the death penalty in cases where the tribunal of the first instance thought it unwarranted. After the Military Court of Appeal has reached its decision (usually within a few weeks of the lower court sentence) defendants' legal remedies are effectively exhausted. Appeals to the Shah for clemency sometimes result in the reduction of death sentences to life imprisonment. However, in January 1976, only one of ten people sentenced to death who appealed to the Shah had his sentence commuted. In cases where the death penalty is imposed executions usually take place within days of conviction.

(c) *Release process*. The release process in Iran is as arbitrary as that pertaining to arrest. There appears to be no possibility of remission of sentence for political prisoners and prisoners are very often kept in detention long after their sentences have expired. Amnesty International has been informed that one section of Qasr prison in Tehran is kept aside for people whose sentences have expired, but who have not been released. Amnesties are often declared to mark anniversaries and traditional celebrations, such as the birthday of the Shah and the Iranian New Year, but it is not known that political prisoners are ever included in these amnesties. Prisoners are sometimes released before trial if they agree to make a public recantation on television and recantation appears to be the only way of obtaining a reduction of sentence and early release.

International legal instruments

Iran was one of the 44 states which voted in favour of the adoption by the United Nations General Assembly of the Universal Declaration of Human Rights on 10 December 1948, and in April 1968 the Shah spoke in support of the declaration when opening the International Conference on Human Rights in Tehran. Furthermore, Iran has ratified the International Covenant on Economic, Social and Cultural Rights and the International Covenant on Civil and Political Rights which is a treaty binding upon the parties to it under international law. By ratifying the International Covenant on Civil and Political Rights, Iran has committed itself to guaranteeing the rights recognized by the covenant, which include the right to be presumed innocent until proven guilty; the right to have adequate time and facilities for the preparation of one's defence; the right to communicate with counsel of one's own choosing; the right to be tried without undue delay; the right to examine, or have examined, the witnesses against one and to obtain the attendance and examination of witnesses on one's behalf under the same conditions as witnesses against one. The right of the individual to be protected from torture or cruel, inhuman or degrading treatment is, of course, stipulated by the covenant and by the Universal Declaration of Human Rights. Iran has not ratified the Optional Protocol to the covenant, which would permit individuals to have complaints regarding violations of their human rights examined by the Human Rights Committee. Iran is presently a member of the United Nations Commission on Human Rights, represented by Manouchehr Ganji, who is also a member of the United Nations Sub-Commission on the Prevention of Discrimination and the Protection of Minorities, and has been elected to the Human Rights Committee established under the International Covenant on Civil and Political Rights.

As stated in *Iran: Trial Procedures for Political Prisoners*, an Amnesty International report published in August 1972, 'the repudiation by its domestic practice of the principles of human rights publicly espoused by Iran is unfortunately manifest.'

Published November 1976

IRAN URGED TO OBSERVE INTERNATIONAL HUMAN RIGHTS STANDARDS

Amnesty International today (Friday 9 May 1980) said it had urged the Iranian authorities to conform to internationally agreed standards for trials and the treatment of prisoners. The international human rights organization stressed that Iran is committed to these standards by international treaty.

Amnesty International, which previously condemned political imprisonment, torture and execution under the Shah, said it had sent the new government a report based on a fact-finding mission to Iran in mid-1979 and on a study of hundreds of trials before Islamic Revolutionary Tribunals.

The report found that defendants were consistently denied fair trials, including the opportunity to prepare or present an adequate defence.

Many people were sentenced to death and executed

without fair trials, AI said. In the six months following the February revolution more than 400 people were executed. AI listed 438 executions reported in local and foreign media by 12 August 1979 and it added that the list was not definitive.

The report, which covered the period up to 14 September 1979, focused on the role of the revolutionary tribunals, special courts set up after the revolution. It cited an Iranian newspaper estimate that the tribunals processed some 10,000 cases in the first four months after the overthrow of the Shah.

AI found that defendants were often not told the exact charges against them; that they were not always allowed to call defence witnesses; that they were often not permitted to question witnesses against them; that they were not allowed counsel of their choice; that many trials were closed to the public; that in practice there was no right of appeal and no effective presumption that defendants were innocent until proved guilty.

Amnesty International concluded that 'the guarantees necessary for a fair trial are effectively lacking in cases heard by the Revolutionary Tribunals'.

The only defence facility known to have been offered those about to stand trial, who sometimes learned of the charges against them just before the trial opened, was an opportunity to write a defence on a piece of paper, the report said.

It pointed out that Ayatollah Khomeini, the Iranian leader, had explicitly stated the presumption that those brought before the Tribunals were guilty. He said in a televised address on 2 April 1979, 'There should be no objection to the trial of these people because they are criminals and it is known that they are criminals. All this about a lawyer being needed ... and that their pleas should be listened to – these are not people charged with crime, they are criminals.'

The Ayatollah was reported in the British newspaper *The Guardian* on 6 April 1979 as also saying, in reference to criticism of the trials, that he was 'sorry that there was still Western sickness among us ... The defendants should have been killed on the first day instead of being held. Among them are people who are not even worthy of contempt.'

The report said the Tribunals operated independently of the Provisional Government. It noted that the Minister of Justice told the newspaper *Ayendegan* on 7 April 1979 that his ministry had 'nothing to do with the Revolutionary Court.... The conditions of these courts are like war-time trials acting under their own rules and regulations.'

A firing-squad executes nine Kurdish rebels and two former National Police officers of the Shah in August 1979, after summary trials in Iran.

The jurisdiction and procedures of the courts were not defined in law when they began operating. On 5 April 1979 regulations were promulgated, but neither the practice nor the rules offered adequate defence facilities, Amnesty International said.

Formal investigation of cases was undertaken by the official investigator or assistant prosecutor assigned to the case. After the investigation, recommendations were made to the Public Prosecutor as to whether those arrested should be prosecuted.

On the information available to it, Amnesty International concluded that the decision on whether to draw up an indictment seemed in most cases effectively to be a determination of guilt or innocence, rather than a decision on whether there was a case to be answered.

The most frequent complaints of prisoners reported to AI were that interrogations were not carried out promptly after arrest and that some prisoners were not told why they had been arrested. There was no rule limiting how long a prisoner could be held without being charged or indicted, the report said.

The Revolutionary Tribunals heard cases concerning offences that encompassed activities said by the authorities to have been directly or indirectly in support of the Shah. The Tribunals' jurisdiction was soon extended, however, to cover violent and sexual crimes and 'counter-revolutionary' offences, meaning activities said to be directed against the Islamic Republic.

AI's conclusions and recommendations were made on the basis of internationally recognized human rights standards, contained in such documents as the Universal Declaration of Human Rights and the International Covenant on Civil and Political Rights.

'There is no dispute that these standards are applicable to Iran', AI said. It noted that during a session of the United Nations Human Rights Committee on 26 April 1979, the Iranian delegate, Mr Shemirami, said that Iran, 'as a State Party to the International Covenant on Civil and Political Rights, would in due course submit a report to the Human Rights Committee in conformity with Article 40 of the Covenant'.

The AI report included detailed recommendations to the Iranian authorities, aimed at ensuring the rights of defendants. The report recommended that people should only be arrested or held on legally defined grounds, that they should be told the reasons for their arrest, be brought promptly before a judicial authority, permitted access to lawyers and relatives, and either tried or released within a reasonable time. It also recommended that medical treatment should be provided when necessary and that authority and responsibility for the treatment of those held should be clearly defined.

AI also reiterated its opposition to the death penalty and to flogging in all circumstances.

The report was based in part on an AI mission which visited Iran from 12 April to 1 May 1979, and had discussions with ministers of the Provisional Government,

personnel of a local *Komiteh* in Tehran, members of the former secular opposition to the Shah, and others. The AI delegates studied the procedures of Revolutionary Tribunals, but were unable to observe them in operation despite permission from a member of the Provisional Government. Each time the delegates went to Qasr Prison in Tehran they were told that trials had just finished or were not scheduled to take place. The delegates were given new appointments, but the result was always the same.

The report was therefore based in large part on a study of legal procedures through information available to AI on some 900 cases. (On 9 July 1979 the newspaper *Ayendegan*, published in Tehran, reported that the revolutionary courts had processed approximately 10,000 cases since the revolution.) In addition, AI studied statements attributed to government or religious spokesmen in the local press, official PARS News Agency reports, the foreign press and on Iran Radio. Such statements were revealing about such subjects as unauthorized arrests, 'on-the-spot' whippings and executions, and court practice.

The report was sent to Ayatollah Khomeini on 9 January 1980 and comments on it were invited from the Ayatollah or his advisors. AI expressed its willingness to include any official Iranian response to the contents in any future publication of the report or parts of it. At the same time, copies of the report were sent to the Iranian Foreign Minister Sadegh Ghotbzadeh and the Iranian charges

◄ *The hanged body of Habibbolah Islami, member of the People's Mojahedine Organization, executed in Tehran's Evin prison in 1981.*

► *Twenty-eight people charged with taking part in an armed attack on the town of Amol are surrounded by pictures of the victims at the trial in Evin prison, Tehran, in January 1983. Twenty-two of the 28, all members of the Union of Communists, were executed.*

d'affaires in London and Washington. On 26 February 1980 the report was sent to President Bani-Sadr, again inviting comments, and with a request to discuss the contents with him and his ministers following the parliamentary elections in Iran. No comment has yet been received by AI from the Iranian authorities.

AI welcomes the decision of the Iranian authorities, reported in *Kayhan* newspaper at the end of March, to set up a Supreme Court to hear appeals against verdicts passed by Islamic judges, but remains concerned about reports of people being arrested and held incommunicado for long periods. In some cases reported to AI the relatives of people arrested in November and December 1979 have still not been able to learn their whereabouts or the reasons for their arrest.

Appendix

Amnesty International's recommendations to the Iranian authorities were:

– no one should be deprived of his or her liberty except on such grounds and in accordance with such procedures as are established by law;

– anyone who is arrested should be informed, at the time of arrest, of the reasons for his or her arrest and should promptly be informed of any charges against him or her;

– anyone arrested or detained should be brought promptly before a judge or other officer authorized by law to exercise judicial power and should be entitled to trial within a reasonable time or to release;

– anyone who is deprived of his or her liberty by arrest or detention should be entitled to take proceedings before a court in order that the court may decide without delay on the lawfulness of the detention and order release if the detention is not lawful;

– a time limit should be fixed within which a detained person must be charged, tried or otherwise released;

– the authorities should immediately inform the family of an arrested person of the reasons for, and place of, detention and grant the family access to him or her;

– detainees should be permitted access to a lawyer and/or other representative of his or her own choice. Free legal aid should be provided in all cases where a detainee is unable to afford and/or to choose his or her own legal representation;

– detainees should be afforded medical treatment whenever necessary;

– bail, when offered, should be of a reasonable, not excessive, sum;

– the authorities should continue to seek to establish clear lines of authority and responsibility for the treatment of suspects and detainees.

News release 9 May 1980.

centers
Sao Paulo.
ison to be
al para-
.
mporary
ention of
no positive
ers' pet-

resident
rn about
s and urg-
nto the
questions

ARIA TER-
lletin), AI's
sident of
tional Dir-
OTERO.
in "excel-
is letter in-
ecretary
l expressed
ssion for
evidence

uay

EN OTH-
of Tunis.
s arrested
ived a
in 1970,
l asthma
on condi-

Othman
ement un-
health de-
d by a doc-
ed, and dir-
ation.
French cit-
nd after
finally ex-

again with
spreading
. An ob-
ugust 1974
to torture,
lled out,
. This
he skin,
excruciat-
n was sen-
at present

r his release,
Président
ce M.
ia.

Pregnant Woman Was 'Tortured to Death'

Maitre YVES BAUDELOT, a Paris lawyer who visited Teheran during the first week of November 1974 on behalf of the International Association of Democratic Lawyers and the International Association of Catholic Lawyers in order to investigate conditions of detention in Iran, has brought back fresh allegations of torture, extremely harsh prison conditions, and gross violations of internationally accepted standards of legal procedure.

In the report of his mission, Maitre Baudelot recounts his failure to obtain permission from both the Attorney General at the Military Tribunal (which is the only competent authority with regard to political offences) and the SAVAK (Iran's notorious secret police - see also November *CAT Bulletin*) to visit the Comité and the Evine prisons in Teheran, which are the main centers for pre-trial detention of political suspects.

He had requested such permission after having talked to former prisoners and relatives of prisoners, who made detailed statements to him about conditions of detention, torture, and political persecution in Iran. He was also refused interviews with the Prime Minister, the Minister of Justice, and high-ranking officials of the judiciary in Teheran.

Former political prisoners told him about the systematic practice of torture by SAVAK, which in Iran is aimed at obtaining confessions and at terrorizing the victims as well as the whole population. They described some of the methods of torture to which they and their fellow-prisoners had been subjected. These included beating with a metal whip, burning with cigarettes, electric shocks on the genitals, forcing a bottle into the rectum of a victim hung from the ceiling by the arms, and strapping the victim on a metal table which is heated. The latter device literally roasts the victim, and some of the former prisoners recounted how they could sometimes smell roasted flesh when they entered the torture room in Evine prison.

This is not the first time that this table torture has been referred to in Evine prison.

Torture is apparently also practiced on close relatives of the prisoners, in order to make them talk. One case was cited in which a 17-year-old child was whipped and given electric shocks before the eyes of the father. In another, a 4-year-old child was whipped and cut in the neck with scissors before the eyes of the mother. One of the former prisoners told that it was so unbearable to see his child being tortured that he wished he had a knife to kill the child and put an end to its suffering.

Maitre Baudelot also tried to obtain information about a few individual prisoners, but found himself confronted, just as their relatives had experienced, with a
authority. One of the cases conc
medical doctor who was arrested
five months pregnant. After hav
campaign groups at the end of O
ation became available, to act on
was informed at the end of Nove
prison, presumably as a result of
been unable to substantiate this
especially when considering the
above and in the November 197
urgent appeal to the Iranian aut
happened to Dr Salehi.

Please send courteously-word information and urging that ste tice of torture, to: His Imperial Niavaran Palace, Tehran; *and to* siri, SAVAK Headquarters, Niav

Maitre Baudelot's report will *AI* International Secretariat.

*In a bid to help end the mass executions in Iran, **AI** has asked the government to receive an **AI** mission to Tehran for talks with Iranian leaders*

Iran executions average 450 a month

More than 1,800 people were executed in Iran in the less than four-month period from 20 June 1981 to 12 October, according to figures compiled by *AI*.

In the whole of 1980 there were 1,229 known executions throughout the world, including 709 in Iran.

Since the February 1979 revolution more than 3,350 people have been executed in Iran. This figure, which is based on reports which have become known outside the country, must be regarded as a minimum. Opposition sources say the total is much higher.

The latest execution figures include 127 people described as "leftists" who were executed in various cities during the weekend of 3 to 5 October 1981. Among them was a son of Ayatollah Ali Golzadeh GHAFURI, a member of parliament. Another son of his had been executed in September 1981.

In a news release on 12 October, *AI* disclosed that it was asking the government to receive an *AI* mission to Tehran for talks with Iranian leaders in an effort to stop the mass executions in Iran. *AI* has asked the Prime Minister, Ayatollah Mohammad Reza MAHDAVI-KANI, to agree to a visit by a delegation.

AI believes that Iran's mass executions are in violation of its obligations under international law. The International Covenant on Civil and Political Rights, ratified by Iran on 24 June 1975, provides for the right of a defendant to have adequate time and facilities to prepare a defence and to be able to appeal to a higher tribunal. In Iran, however, executions appear to have taken place immediately after sentence, and in some cases without any formal trial.

The use of the death penalty in Iran is difficult to reconcile with United Nations General Assembly Resolution 35/172 on arbitrary or summary executions. This resolution urges member states "to guarantee the most careful legal procedures and the greatest possible safeguards for the accused in capital cases" and "to provide that no death sentence shall be carried out until the procedures of appeal and pardon have been terminated and, in any case, not until a reasonable time after the passing of the sentence in the court of first instance".

Although there is a high level of violence in Iran, this cannot be a reason for the suspension of fundamental human rights which Iran is required to provide its citizens under international law. Under the International Covenant on Civil and Political Rights, no derogation under any circumstances is possible from the right to freedom of thought, conscience and religion or the right of a person not to be arbitrarily deprived of life. *AI* believes that the use of the death penalty cannot be justified by a threat to the social order or by an unproved "deterrent" effect.

- **During the reign of the late Shah, before the revolution, *AI* persistently called for public pressure to halt torture, executions and other abuses of human rights in Iran. Among those whose rights it defended were people who went on to become leaders in the Islamic Republic established since the revolution□**

A member of the left-wing Mujahideen organization, hanged by the authorities in September in front of other prisoners.

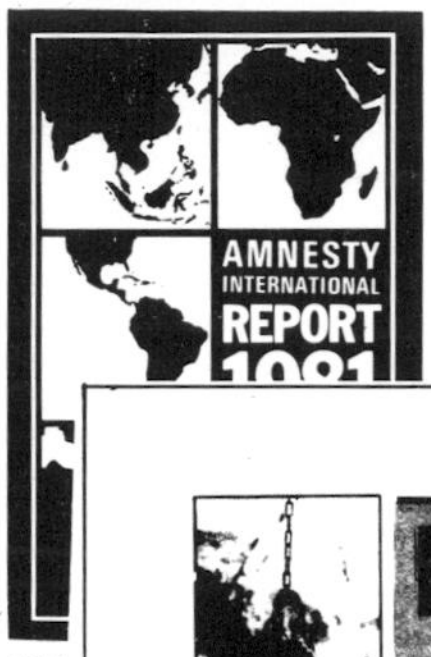

AI's l
100 c
Hum
£5.0
and a

AMNI
TION
WC2E
Britai
Way,
subsc
year.

Bangladesh Army officers are executed

The 12 army officers condemned to death by a military court for their part in the death of President Ziaur RAHMAN in last May's attempted coup were executed early on 23 September 1981 (see October *Newsletter*).

The day before, the Bangladesh Supreme Court had rejected their appeals against the military court's verdict, saying it had no jurisdiction to interfere. The court gave its ruling after a five-day hearing.

The executions are reported to have been carried out in five prisons througout Bangladesh; the families are said to have been told to collect the bodies.

Mexico
Continued from page 1

border at Arroyo Negro, department of Campeche, on 11 May 1981. They are said to be held at the Guatemalan military camp in Camojaíto, La Democracia, department of Huehuetenango□

Amnes
April 1978 Volume VI

List names 113 Dead Guatemal

A list of 113 cases of death squad killings and "c during the last quarter of 1977 was released by those killed or missing was considered to be a vi murder for financial gain, or murder in private q be part of a longstanding pattern of political mu investigations into the cases have been insubstan

More than 20,000 Guatemalans have been murdered by paramilitary groups since 1966. These groups were originally formed in response to leftwing guerrilla activity and enjoy total impunity before the law. An apparent decline in the number of killings in urban areas early in 1977 was followed by a significant increase in violence by mid-summer.

AI said that there was little indication that the Guatemalan authorities had taken any action over the past year to stop the free operation of the death squads. There was, however, considerable evidence that the highest levels of government tacitly condoned the continuing abductions and murders, especially of peasant farmers and of the urban poor□

SOVIET WORKERS DOCUMENT PSYCHIATRIC ABUSE

AI has received new documentation from Moscow issued by the unofficial Association of Free Trade Unions of Workers in the USSR, whose formation was announced in Moscow by a group of workers in January 1978.

AI has delivered their appeal for recognition as a trade union, dated 1 February, to the International Labour Organization.

The documents list dozens of cases of workers who it states have been confined to psychiatric hospitals in recent years for protesting too vigorously about poor working conditions and for persistently lodging complaints against their work superiors. One of the documents, an open letter signed by 43 workers, details 14 such cases since January 1977.

Between December 1977 and the end of February 1978, ten of the workers who signed these documents had been detained by police. Four of these have been confined to psychiatric hospitals. Seven of the detained members were "missing" or known to be in psychiatric hospitals on 27 February. From the workers' documents, *samizdat* and emigré sources, it appears that a number of these workers have been acting collectively in support of their complaints since 1976□

FAIR TRIALS DENIED IN IRAN

On 28 February, English barrister Brian WROBEL testified to the United States Congressional Sub-Committee on International Organizations, that despite recent amendments to the law, trial procedures for political prisoners in Iran "were such as to deny defendants any possibility of a fair trial".

Mr Wrobel, who gave his testimony on *AI*'s behalf, had attended a political trial in Tehran, Iran's capital, in April 1977. He stressed that fair trials are not afforded to those people charged with offences over which the military tribunal has jurisdiction. He pointed out that as long as defendants are not permitted to call formal evidence that a confession has been improperly extracted, denials of ill-treatment during interrogation may not command a great deal of respect.

AI publicized Mr Wrobel's testimony and a detailed analysis of the procedure governing military tribunals which was submitted to the Shah of Iran in November 1977. This submission summarized the major areas of *AI*'s concern about trial procedures:

- no legal advice is permitted on arrest;
- no legal advice is permitted during lengthy pre-trial detention;
- preliminary investigations before the examining magistrate are conducted in secret by the National Intelligence and Security Organization (SAVAK). No legal advice or representation is permitted;
- defence counsel, who are military officers or civilians whose "competence" has been endorsed by the authorities, are not permitted to meet their clients freely *before* trial. The defence is allowed only 15 days to study the file at the bureau of the court, depending on "sufficiency of time" but is not given its own copy of the file. There is no procedure by which defence counsel may ask to appear before the tribunal to make preliminary applications;

Continued on page 3, column 3

In Georgia, Gary Lee HAWES remains under a death sentence imposed in 1976 when, aged 15, he was convicted of murder.

In its appeal to Governor Busbee *AI* pointed out that article 6 of the United Nations International Covenant on Civil and Political Rights, signed by President CARTER on 5 October 1977, states: "Sentences of death shall not be imposed for crimes committed by persons below the 18 years of age. . . ."

- In February and March *AI* appealed to President Carter and to Governor James B. Hunt of North Carolina on behalf of adopted prisoners James GRANT, Charles PARKER and T J REDDY, known as the "Charlotte Three".

AI acted in support of a petition for a pardon of innocence submitted to Governor Hunt by the three black political activists who were convicted of arson in April 1972.

In the letter to President Carter, *AI* stressed that, despite the charges, *AI* "is convinced that the real reason for their imprisonment was their political activities and ethnic origin"□

AI REPORTS ON BANGLADESH

On 27 February *AI* released the report of its mission to Bangladesh which expresses concern at the wide jurisdiction given to martial law courts to try civilians as well as members of the armed forces.

AI drew attention to at least 130 and perhaps several hundred summary executions of military personnel which followed the abortive military uprisings in September and October 1977. These executions were carried out after summary trial by military tribunals and continued at least until December. "We are gravely disturbed at these executions, particularly in view of the absence of legal safeguards in military trial procedures where trials are held *in camera* without appeal to a legal authority," *AI* stated.

The report also expresses concern at the

Continued on next page, column 1

6
Ir
E

The
ann
Iran
197
repo
mon
exe
pub

are
in T
Mar
on
Peo
Iran
wer
and
repo
Mar
wee
visi

refe
800
Feb
new
desc
pen
eve
figu
for
ann

con
oth
the
Iran

Iran

Political detainees in Iran are reported to be detention centres throughout the country. purpose by the SAVAK secret police during the received information that more are now in use or *Pasdaran* (Revolutionary Guards). The prem schools — Amnesty International has receive

The number of reports of torture and ill-tre persistence and consistency make it clear that widespread and, in some places, systematic.

Amnesty International has not been able t Since then it has repeatedly raised its conce revolution — and has on a number of occasion the country, most recently in September 1984.

The following material is based on a wide v over the years with scores of former political

Detainees at mercy of their captors

Political detainees are reported to be tortured immediately after arrest, during incommunicado detention in *komiteh* or *Pasdaran* centres and afterwards in prison.

The torture may begin as soon as they arrive at the centres — although by then some of them are reported to have been ill-treated already, beaten up in the vehicles delivering them.

Once at the centres they appear to be completely at the mercy of their captors and may be held incommunicado for periods of up to several months without charge or trial.

Torture may continue even after their transfer to recognized prisons, where *Pasdaran* also serve as guards.

There is no limit to how long detainees may be held without charge or trial. They have no access to lawyers — or doctors — nor is there any way they can challenge their detention in the courts.

Their isolation — and their sense of it — is increased by the knowledge that their families may not have been told where they are and may indeed have been warned not to make inquiries about them for a number of months — relatives have in fact been threatened with arrest themselves if they ignored this "advice". Amnesty International has also learned of relatives having been tortured in order

'I heard th back were

The scarred bac arrested in Although he h Iran's educatio not a membe movement. He national that du

"They (Pasd my head and

... toll over 4,400 ... shot in secret

...cially ...xecuted in ...f February ...00 but ...e that many ...to death in ...been made

...ecutions ...carried out ...12 and 26 ...a statement ...fice of the ...ization of ...dly executed ...rsity student, ...75 people ...cuted on 12 ...n given a ...e on tele-

...*Le Matin* ...rts of some ...and 11 ...reached the ...isons; it ...tally inde-...els". How-..."Such ...vestigated, ...r

...e for *AI* to ...unts from ...embers of ...p of exiled ...*indépe...*

dant des avocats iraniens "en exil" – confirm that people are being executed secretly in Iran and that in many cases the families are not informed until well after the executions.

Many executions appear to have taken place without trial or when no death sentence has been passed:

- Omid **Gharib**, a former student in France, was arrested on 9 June 1980 after a letter of his to a friend in France had been intercepted by the authorities. His indictment stated that he had been "westernized, brought up in a westernized family . . . had been too long in Europe for his studies. . . smoked Winston cigarettes and. . . displayed a tendency to the left". At his trial he was sentenced to three years' imprisonment but on 2 February 1982 his parents learned that he had been executed two days earlier.
- Ebrahim **Eshghani** is reported to have been secretly executed in November 1981 in Chah Bahar Prison in Baluchistan, after having been sentenced to life imprisonment.

AI is still seeking information about 11 Baha'is who were arrested in August 1980 and have not been seen or heard of since. Nineteen Baha'is have been executed in Iran during 1982, bringing the total number of adherents executed since the 1979 revolution to more than 100☐

El Salvador

Human rights worker killed, two 'disappear'

Three more human rights workers are reported to have become victims of "disappearance" and political killing in El Salvador in recent months.

Two of them, María Jesús **Echeverría** and Juana **Lara**, are reported to have "disappeared" in April, together with several children. The two women are members of the *Comité de Madres y Familiares de Presos, Desaparecidos y Asesinados Políticos*, Committee of Mothers and Relatives of Political Prisoners, the "Disappeared" and Victims of Political Killings. *AI* has no further details on their case.

A third human rights worker, Tomás Antonio **Leiva**, is reported to have been killed by a paramilitary group in Morazán Province in late April or early May. He was a journalist and member of the *Comisión de Derechos Humanos de El Salvador*, El Salvador Human Rights Commission, an independent human rights monitoring group.

- In early October 1980 María Magdalena **Enríquez**, the commission's press secretary, was found dead in a shallow grave about 20 miles from San Salvador. She had been abducted on 3 October 1980. Another representative of the commission, Ramón **Valladares** Pérez, was killed on 26 October 1980 by unidentified gunmen. In December 1981 three more members of the commission were arrested: Carlos Eduardo **Vides**, aged 20, a medical student; Norberto **Huezo** Martínez, aged 25, a dental student; and Francisco Antonio **Barraza**, aged 2... school ... in a cav... been ta... ment. I... latest ir... are still... charges...

VIETN...

AI has ... being d... Khuat ... They w... are bei... who we... and Jar... of the ... Decem... suppler...

cervical vertebrae and lumbar vertebrae; headaches, in the occipital and frontal regions; disturbed sleep with frequent nightmares; loss of concentration, with intrusive flashbacks of his prison experiences; chest pains.

Amnesty International doctors in Europe have examined a number of torture victims from Iran, often many months after their torture was alleged to have taken place. Photographs of scars on two such victims appear on page 1 and page 3. In these cases, as in others, the doctors concluded that the condition of physical scarring sustained was consistent with both the kinds of torture alleged and when it was alleged to have been inflicted.

WHAT YOU CAN DO

Amnesty International has issued a 12-point program of practical measures for the prevention of torture. In view of the detailed and recurrent reports of torture in Iran over the years, the organization believes the Iranian Government should implement the 12-point program as a sign of its commitment to stop torture and uphold human rights. The following 10 points are especially relevant:

- **The highest authorities of Iran should issue clear public instructions to the Revolutionary Guards and all other officials involved in the custody, interrogation or treatment of prisoners that torture will not be tolerated under any circumstances.**
- **The government should ensure that all detainees are brought before a judicial authority promptly after being taken into custody and that relatives, lawyers and doctors have prompt and regular access to them.**
- **Relatives and lawyers should be informed promptly of the whereabouts of detainees. No one should be held in secret or unacknowledged detention.**
- **There should be regular, independent visits of inspection to places of detention to ensure that torture does not take place.**
- **The Iranian Government should establish an impartial body to investigate all complaints and reports of torture. Its findings and methods of investigation should be made public.**
- **Steps should be taken to ensure that confessions or other evidence obtained through torture may never be invoked in legal proceedings.**
- **All acts of torture should be made punishable offences under the criminal law.**
- **Where it is proved that an act of torture has been committed by or at the instigation of a public official, criminal proceedings should be instituted against the alleged offender.**
- **It should be made clear during the training of all officials who are involved in the custody, interrogation or treatment of prisoners that torture is a criminal act. They should be instructed that they are obliged to refuse to obey any order to torture. The United Nations Code of Conduct for Law Enforcement Officials and the Standard Minimum Rules for the Treatment of Prisoners should be widely distributed.**
- **Victims of torture and their dependants should be afforded redress and compensation for their material and moral sufferings, without prejudice to any other civil or criminal proceedings.**

Please write courteous letters urging the Iranian authorities to take effective measures for the prevention of torture in Iran, as indicated above.

Send your letters to: Ali Akbar Nateq Nouri / Minister of Interior / Tehran / Islamic Republic of Iran; and to: Hojjatoleslam Ali Akbar Hashani Rafsanjani / Speaker of the Majlis / Tehran / Islamic Republic of Iran. Send copies of your letters to Iran's Ambassador in your own country.

Investigation ordered

In December 1980 Iran's revolutionary leader, Ayatollah Ruhollah Khomeini, ordered an investigation into allegations of torture. On 17 May 1981 the Torture Probe Commission reported, among other things, that some of the complaints of torture related to injuries sustained in armed street clashes; others related to *ta'zir* punishments which could not be described as constituting torture; some of the physical scars had been self-inflicted; but "some persons' claims were found to be reasonable and those who were accused of having committed torture are being held now and their faults will be dealt with by [the] competent legal authorities."

Amnesty International believes that a new investigation into allegations of torture and ill-treatment in Iran is overdue. It has called on the authorities to initiate a thorough and impartial investigation, and to make public both the findings and the procedures followed in conducting such an investigation.

Iran's obligations

Iran's obligations under international instruments before the 1979 revolution prohibiting the use of torture remain in force today.

On 8 February 1978, the Iranian Government made a unilateral declaration against torture, thereby reaffirming its support for the United Nations Declaration on the Protection of All Persons from being Subjected to Torture and Other Cruel, Inhuman or Degrading Treatment or Punishment, which was adopted by the General Assembly on 9 December 1975.

On 24 June 1975 Iran ratified the International Covenant on Civil and Political Rights, of which Article 7 states: "No one shall be subjected to torture or to cruel, inhuman or degrading treatment or punishment . . ."

While certain individual Iranian Government representatives have indicated that they consider provisions contained in United Nations instruments related to human rights to be incompatible with Islam, and that they therefore disagree with them, the government itself has taken no formal steps to revoke its commitment to the international agreements mentioned above.

Moreover, on 3 December 1984 Iran's representative introduced a draft resolution (A/C.3/39/L.68) to the Third Committee of the United Nations which would have reaffirmed the importance of the United Nations Declaration against Torture. It would have recognized that new techniques and machinery for torture "are detrimental to the fate of the individual and of the society as a whole," and it would have condemned all acts of torture and deplored and called for the prohibition of all means of torture, as well as their development, production or storage.

Although this draft resolution was subsequently withdrawn, it was a clear and positive indication that the Islamic Republic of Iran does not challenge the international legal obligation to prevent and prohibit the practice of torture.

...RTURE
...y international

...l-treated in hundreds of secret ...laces were used for the same ...e, but Amnesty International has ...by the local *komiteh* (committee) ...de office buildings, houses and ...ne of them was a theatre.

...by Amnesty International, their ...of human rights are continuing,

...e just after the 1979 revolution. ...horities — as it had before the ...owed to send another mission to

...s, including personal interviews ...outside Iran.

...hip and I felt as though my ...huge knife'...

cloth around my mouth . . . first of all they punched me hard and repeatedly in the face. Then they removed my shirt and told me to lie face down on a bench. I heard the crack of a whip and I felt as though my back were being cut by a huge knife.

"They gave me six lashes and then asked me questions . . . the pain was so bad that, had I been able to, I would have committed suicide. I was punched and kicked and thrown . . . against the wall. One of them jumped on my chest.

"This same treatment, beating and kicks, then five or six lashes, then questions, was repeated over and over for about two hours. They didn't believe me when I said I didn't belong to any organization."

In May 1984 this prisoner was examined in London by an Amnesty International doctor, who stated in his medical report that he had counted 18 distinct marks up to 30cms long on the man's back "consistent with whipping". There were also very small scars on each leg, "probably caused by kicks".

to induce prisoners to make confessions or provide information.

Vital safeguards lacking

Vital basic safeguards against torture are therefore lacking — limits on incommunicado detention, prompt appearance of the detainees before a judicial authority and prompt and regular access to lawyers, doctors and relatives; detention only in publicly recognized places (not secret centres); and regular governmental review of procedures for detention and interrogation.

Purpose of torture

Torture in Iran is usually inflicted on prisoners in order to extract confessions about political activities, names and addresses of political activists and safe houses.

Another motive for torture is to induce prisoners to agree to appear on television to recant their political or religious beliefs or activities. Bahais have been tortured in order to force them to recant their faith, to give televised confessions that they are spies, or to give names of and information about other Bahais.

Amnesty International believes that confessions extracted by torture should never be invoked in legal proceedings and indeed such practice is in clear contravention of Article 38 of Iran's Constitution, which states: "Any form of torture for the purpose of extracting confessions or gaining information is forbidden. It is not permissible to compel individuals to give testimony, make confessions or swear oaths, and any testimony, confession or oath obtained in this fashion is worthless and invalid. Punishments for the infringement of these principles will be determined by law".

Amnesty International knows of no specific cases where individuals have been charged or tried for the infliction of torture on or ill-treatment of prisoners.

Methods

The methods of torture most widely and consistently reported are beating and whipping — the latter may also be inflicted as an Islamic judicial punishment *(ta'zir)*, and in practice it may be difficult to distinguish between the two.

Human Rights Committee set up under the International Covenant on Civil and Political Rights has held in General Comment 7(16) on Article 7 of the Covenant, which Iran has ratified, that ". . . the prohibition (of torture and cruel, inhuman or degrading treatment or punishment) must extend to corporal punishment, including excessive chastisement as an educational or disciplinary measure."

...punched and kicked.

According to one former detainee: "This 'football' game is often used on people who have just been arrested. It breaks down the resistance, and can make one feel lonely and unstable."

In other forms of beating, the interrogators concentrate on particular parts of the body, especially the soles of the feet or the back, for prolonged periods. Prisoners are always blindfold during such beatings and usually have their hands and sometimes their feet bound together; they may also be tied to a bed. The thrashings may be administered with genuine whips or else cables of varying thicknesses may be used, ranging from telephone cable to heavy wire cable whose strands open into a claw at one end which rips the flesh.

Tabriz prison

"X", a member of the People's Mojahedine Organization, who was held in Tabriz Central Prison between February 1981 and September 1983, told Amnesty International in an interview that detainees there were beaten systematically with a claw-like steel cable on their backs, sides and chests. To increase the pain water was then poured over the wounds. The swollen wounds would then again be beaten or kicked, resulting in severe bleeding.

Detainees usually wore their underclothes at the time, he said, and shreds of cloth would get into the cut flesh. Because of inadequate sanitary and hygienic facilities and lack of medical care, the result would be infected, painful and malodorous wounds.

'When they stopped my feet were bleeding . . .

"Y", a woman student aged 26, detained at Evin Prison in Tehran between September 1981 and March 1982, described her first beating to Amnesty International:

have lunch and left me sitting on a chair, but I was shaking so violently I couldn't even stay on it, yet they wouldn't let me lie on the floor.

"All I wanted to do then was to drink water, and when I went to the lavatory I found there was blood in my urine."

Sexual abuse

Other forms of physical torture reported to Amnesty International since 1980 by former victims include being hung up for hours at a time, sometimes with the body contorted by having one arm stretched over the shoulder and tied behind the back to the opposite ankle; burning with electricity and cigarettes; and various forms of sexual abuse, including rape of both men and women prisoners.

A 23 year-old woman volunteer social worker, who was not a member of any political movement, gave Amnesty International the following account of her torture and ill-treatment. She was arrested twice by *Pasdaran* in Tehran. The second time, in late 1982, she was kept isolated in a *komiteh* building for five weeks, during which time she was repeatedly questioned about her presumed political affiliations and asked to name her friends. On one occasion she was forced to undress and submit to oral and anal sex. She was a virgin . . .

"I had never been close to a man before. I didn't understand what was happening to me, I was terrified. I'd heard that if women were raped in prison they would never be released. When it was over I kept vomiting, and couldn't stop crying . . ."

She was released a week later, but was unable to speak of her ordeal until she was able to leave the country over a year later.

She said she was independent, self-confident and "afraid of nothing" before her imprisonment. Now, she said, she was afraid of everyone and had

them I had nothing to say. They told me to write my will, but I said I had nothing to write. Suddenly they fired shots all around me, or so I realized later. At the time I was so shocked I thought I was actually being executed. They repeated the mock execution twice more that evening trying to get me to confess, then beat, kicked and punched me, and pushed and shoved me violently against the trunks of trees until daylight."

Threats to relatives

Many former prisoners interviewed by Amnesty International have reported receiving threats of the arrest or execution of relatives if they continued to refuse to confess.

A member of the Baha'i faith, imprisoned at Shiraz in early 1983, told Amnesty International of a young woman prisoner there at the same time who was informed by prison guards that her husband had been severely tortured but that this would come to an end if she agreed to recant her faith. When she refused she was taken to see him and was shocked at his condition. He had lost weight drastically, had bleeding, running sores on his back and his toe-nails had been removed. Husband and wife were later executed.

Forced to watch executions

Other former prisoners have reported on the psychological effects of being forced to watch the execution of fellow prisoners, or even having to collect the bodies after executions.

"X" (the former prisoner in Tabriz Central Prison) told Amnesty International that about 60 of his cellmates were taken away for execution during the 32 months he spent there.

"When you're in a cell with other political prisoners you share an inti-

ON TORTURE

The photograph s... of a member of th... Party who was arr... He told Amnesty... was repeatedly ... punched while tie... bed. *Pasdaran* me... bare feet and the... barefoot in the co... forced to lie, tied t... block which he e... kilos on his back f... was examined in ... an Amnesty Inter... concluded that the... with the ex-pris... torture.

mate, special r... With time I g... prisoners and ... time they woul... to be execut... prisoners came... to know them ... the same thin... times.

"In the end ... painful, that I ... I'd be the nex... apart from th... emotional and ... was terrible . ... executions, we... onto a lorry, ... limb missing f... it three times, ... bags and loadi...

"Sometimes ... executed toget... would be exec... they would be... meeting. My ... execution yard... these meeting... followed the e...

The female ... Amnesty Interna... other women pri... were led blindfol... she heard crying ... told them their ... removed, but tha... to the side, but ... they did so, the... young man hangi... tree:

". . . The han... the elbow, and...

TORTURE IN BRAZIL

Amnesty International's 1972 'Report on Allegations of Torture in Brazil' recorded evidence in 1,081 torture cases and criticized a battery of legislation, including secret decrees, that suppressed human rights. The report described the emergence of clandestine 'death squads', operating with the covert acquiescence of the official security forces. The government reacted by banning all references to Amnesty International's statements on Brazil in the country's news media. The two letters that follow were published in the report: one was written to Pope Paul VI and the other to the judge of the military tribunal in charge of the case.

▶ *Cemetery gates: Maracipu, Brazil. This photograph was taken in the early 1970s when allegations of killings by 'death squads' were frequent.*

Marcos Arruda, a young geologist, son of an American mother, and Marlene Soccas, painter and dentist, had known each other for a short time and arranged to meet for dinner. Their meeting was the beginning of an agonizing tragedy. Marcos Arruda is at present at liberty and abroad. Marlene Soccas wrote an open letter from her prison cell in Tiradentes to the judge of the military tribunal which is to try her.

Here is the letter which Marcos Settamini Pena de Arruda sent to the Vatican on 4 February 1971:

Please find herewith an account of all that happened to me during almost nine months imprisonment ... I was arrested on 11 May 1970 in São Paulo on my way to dinner with a young lady that I had recently met. I learnt afterwards that she belonged to a political organization. She had been arrested several days previously, violently tortured and taken to *Operação Bandeirantes* [OBAN].

I was picked up even before I reached the meeting place and taken off in a car (the licence plate was not an official one) by four armed policemen. We went to OBAN headquarters. During the journey the leader of the group ordered the young lady to show me her hands so that 'I could have an idea of what awaited me'. She lifted her hands, which were handcuffed, and I saw that they were greatly swollen and were covered with dark purple hematomes. I learned that she had been badly beaten with a type of *palmatoria*. Once the car stopped in the OBAN courtyard, they began immediately to punch and kick me in the presence of some people seated on benches in front of the main building. I was beaten as I went up the steps to a room on the top floor where they continued to slap me, hit me about the head and bang my ears with cupped hands (telephone torture); they took the handcuffs off and continued to hit me with their truncheons whilst questioning me.

They ordered me to strip completely; I obeyed. They made me sit down on the ground and tied my hands with a thick rope. One of the six or seven policemen present put his foot on the rope in order to tighten it as much as possible. I lost all feeling in my hands. They put my knees up to my elbows so that my bound hands were on a level with my ankles. They then placed an iron bar about eight centimetres wide between my knees and elbows and suspended me by resting the two ends of the iron bar on a wooden stand so that the top part of my body and my head were on one side and my buttocks and legs on the other, about three feet from the floor. After punching me and clubbing me, they placed a wire on the little toe of my left foot and placed the other end between my testicles and my leg. The wires were attached to a camp telephone so that the current increased or decreased according to the speed at which the handle was turned. They began to give me electric shocks using this equipment and continued to beat me brutally both with their hands and with a *palmatoria* – a plaque full of holes – which left a completely black haematome, larger in size than an outstretched palm, on one of my buttocks. The electric shocks and the beatings continued for several hours. I had arrived at about 14.30 and it was beginning to get dark when I practically lost consciousness. Each time that I fainted, they threw water over me to increase my sensitivity to the electric shocks. They then took the wire from my testicles and began to apply it to my face and head, giving me terrible shocks on my face, in my ears, eyes, mouth and nostrils. One of the policemen remarked 'Look, he is letting off sparks. Put it in his ear now'…

The torture was so serious and long-lasting that I thought I would die. I began to feel completely drained; my body was covered in a cold sweat; I could not move my eyelids; I was swallowing my tongue and could only breathe with difficulty; I could no longer speak. I tried throughout this time to think of great men who had suffered horrible things for a noble ideal. This encouraged me to fight on and not give way to despair. I felt that my hands would become gangrenous because circulation was blocked for some hours. I moaned 'my hands, my hands!' and they continued to beat my hands with their clubs. I think I eventually lost consciousness. When I came to, they had lowered the bar and laid me out on the ground. They tried to revive me with ammonia but I didn't respond. They struck me on the testicles with the end of the stick; they burnt my shoulders with cigarette stubs; they put the barrel of a revolver into my

mouth saying they would kill me. They threatened me with sexual abuse. Suddenly, my whole body began to tremble and I began to writhe as if shaken by an earthquake. The policemen were alarmed and called for a doctor from the first-aid post. They said I was a soldier who was feeling ill. They gave me an injection and refused to give me water although my body was completely dehydrated. They left me to sleep in the same room in which I had been tortured.

The following morning I was shaken violently by the shoulders. I realized that I was still shaking, my eyelids were shut, my tongue was paralysed and I felt strange muscular contractions on the right side of my face. My left leg was like a piece of wood, the foot turned downwards and the toes had contracted and would not move. The small toe was totally black. After enduring many insults, I was carried to the general military hospital of São Paulo. The sole of my left foot was again forcibly struck in order to try and return it to its normal position and to make it fit into my shoe. Despite shooting pains, the foot would not move. The torturers took me by the arms and legs and brought me like a sack to the courtyard where I was thrown into the back of the van.

I later learned that at the hospital they gave me only two hours to live. The military chaplain came to hear my confession. I asked the soldiers who were on guard in my

room to leave us alone but they refused. In these circumstances, the priest could only give absolution *in extremis* in case I should die. For several days I was subjected to interrogation at the hospital despite the fact that my condition had not improved. The fifth day after I was admitted to hospital two policemen opened up the door to my room saying 'now that you are alone we are going to get rid of you. You are going to die...' and one of them began to hit me about the face and body. I tried to protect myself and to cry out but I was still shaking and could hardly move. In addition, my twisted tongue prevented me from crying out loudly. I could not see them well because my eyelids still would not move. The policeman continued to say 'no one can hold out against S— A—, you are going to die...' He went out for a moment with the other to see if anyone was coming and then returned to continue. Eventually, I managed to cry out loudly. They were frightened and left me...

I remained in the general hospital for about a month and a half. During this time I was visited several times for questioning. My family had been trying to help me and for over a month had been trying unsuccessfully to find me. I finally received a note which told me that they had discovered where I was. But I remained incommunicado without permission to see my family for five more months, and I received no visit from a lawyer throughout the duration of my detention.

When I was released from the hospital, my right eyelid was still paralysed (it remained so until the month of December) and I had a slight but constant shake in the shoulders, the left arm and leg; the latter, half paralysed, could not support any weight and I was obliged to use a broom stick for a walking stick.

I was sent back to OBAN, put in a cell, and told to write out a statement ... I finished this in three days, at the end of which time I was brought face to face with the young woman whom I had been on my way to meet at the time of my arrest. It was six o'clock when I was carried into the room where she was kept. They wanted me to admit the name of the organization to which they believed I belonged and to give names of supposed comrades. They began to carry the young woman off into another room and gave her a strong electric shock in order to make me talk (they were afraid to torture me again in view of my poor physical condition). I heard the cries of the girl being tortured and when they brought her back into my room she was shaking and totally distraught. I was paralysed with fear at witnessing such cruelty and even more terrified when they threatened to do the same to members of my family if I didn't tell them what they wanted to know. They repeated the electric shock treatment to the girl and, seeing that they were not achieving anything, decided to call the doctor to examine me physically to see if I was fit to undergo more torture. The doctor ordered certain tablets and said that I should not be given food. They brought me back to my cell and were to return for me later. Having seen that they were ready to torture the young woman again, and possibly members of my family as well, I decided to try and protect these people and I agreed to write out another deposition.

I was carried into the room of a certain Captain, who, along with another officer, offered me coffee and cigarettes and advised me in a friendly way to cooperate with them. I began by saying that I did not want to cooperate with them since they represented the institutions of force and violence to which we are subjected and because they used such inhuman treatment when dealing with people against whom they had no proof. They were irritated and began to torture the young woman once again in order to make me talk. Finally, they used violence on me again, along with insults and moral attacks, threats concerning members of my family and even attempts to strangle me. They blindfolded me and pushed a revolver against my forehead – all to the same end. After several hours, they carried the young girl and me back to our cells....

The following evening when they came for me I was again suffering from contractions, my right side was paralysed, I dribbled, my body twitched constantly...

The next morning I was carried into court. My condition had considerably worsened and my seizures were continual and more visible. I was photographed, my fingerprints were taken and I was then brought into a room on the same floor as the torture room. A sergeant in a military police uniform, with his name band covered with a sash, interrogated me calmly for 45 minutes. He threatened me alternately with torture and death if I refused to confess. Later, he told me that he was a doctor and knew that I would die if he permitted me to be tortured again. In the end, he gave me an injection for my spasms and told me that I ought to be taken back to the hospital. Throughout the night, I was locked up in a bathroom and was then taken to a doctor, Primo Alfredo, who had recently been arrested. Throughout the night, we heard as usual the terrible screams of people being tortured. The following morning I was once again brought to the military hospital.

Two days later my condition began to worsen and I lost consciousness and became delirious – this condition lasted more than 10 days. I learnt afterwards what had happened during that period...

...It is clear that my case is not exceptional as such events have become commonplace during the last few years in Brazil.

...I thank Your Holiness for your interest and the action taken in an attempt to secure my release. I beg you to do the same for the other thousands of men and women who suffer the same treatment in Brazil and in other countries ... unfortunate human beings who continue to be tortured...

Signed: Marcos Pena Settamini de Arruda

Letter from Marlene de Souza Soccas to the 'auditor' judge of the military tribunal

Marlene de Souza Soccas saw Marcos Pena Settamini de

Arruda while both were undergoing torture and she mentions it in her letter:

... As I have been under arrest for two years, I have vast and unhappy knowledge of Brazilian justice. In May 1970 I was arrested by OBAN. I was prevented from contacting my lawyer or even from informing my family.

I remained incommunicado for two months, 12 days of which were spent in OBAN headquarters – here I suffered all sorts of physical and mental torture. Brutally stripped by policemen I was put on the 'dragon chair' (a kind of metallic plate) with my hands connected to electric wires and the various parts of my body including the tongue, ears, eyes, wrists, breasts and sex organs also connected. I was then suspended from the *pau de arara*, an iron bar which is placed on two stands, and passed under the knees. The wrists and ankles are tied together and the whole body hangs downwards in a defenceless position. I was given electric shocks and was beaten about the kidneys and the vertebral column; I was burnt with cigarettes, I was tortured in the presence of naked political detainees, men and women, and suffered the insults of the policemen who threatened me with revolvers.

Two months after my arrest, when I was in Tiradentes prison, I was brought back to OBAN again. My torturers believed that I was in contact with the geologist Marcos Settamini Pena de Arruda, who had been tortured for the last month. I was carried into the torture room and one of the torturers, an army captain, said to me 'get ready to see Frankenstein come in'. I saw a man come into the room, walking slowly and hesitantly, leaning on a stick, one eyelid half closed, his mouth twisted, his stomach muscles twitching continuously, unable to form words. He had been admitted to hospital between life and death after traumatic experiences undergone during violent torture. They said to me 'encourage him to talk, if not the 'gestapo' will have no more patience and if one of you doesn't speak we will kill him and the responsibility for his death will lie with you.' We did not speak, not because we were heroic, but simply because we had nothing to say. Thanks to his family, who have relations abroad, Marcos Arruda was able to avoid being placed on the list of those 'killed in shoot-outs' and one year later he was acquitted.

I am a painter and when I was arrested, the police took 18 paintings, an easel, and cases full of clothes, shoes, books etc. The stolen paintings are all dated and could be used in my favour at my trial since the dates prove that I was absent from São Paulo at the time in question. I was painting at Laguna (in the state of Santa Catarina), where I was born, and was completely cut off from any political activity. All of these possessions were taken by OBAN and none have yet been returned to me. What words can one use to describe such actions?

I am awaiting my trial in a building built in 1854, which served in the past for the buying and selling of slaves who laboured in the cultivation of São Paulo's coffee. It is a historical monument with an unhappy past, a place where much suffering and death have occurred. The strange irony is that it bears the most significant name of Brazilian history, that of one of the martyrs for liberty – *Tiradentes*. Here both political and common law prisoners are housed. After what I have seen and lived through, I am now better able to know what a 'democratic and Christian' society signifies. All that I learnt at school and throughout my life about human dignity has been obliterated by my experiences inside these high and insurmountable walls.

I very often heard, from beneath my cell, the deafening noise made by *correcionais* (common law) prisoners detained here illegally by the police, who are piled up for months at a time on cold cement without mattresses or coverings. There were terrible scenes each time a young newcomer arrived in the cell for there was no lack of sexual perverts there. The youth was obliged to submit, in view of the silent complaisance of the prison employees, and was not left alone until he was covered in blood ... I have often asked that something be done about these inhuman conditions which provide a lugubrious amusement for the jailers and police.

... Returning from the DOPS [Department for Political and Social Order] one day and crossing the courtyard on the men's side, I witnessed a sad spectacle which would not have been allowed even in a Nazi concentration camp: three *correcionais* detainees were thrown into a well, with water reaching to shoulder level; they were surrounded by the military police and jailers with clubs and sticks in their hands. They held the heads of the three men under the water with their feet; it was winter and the unfortunate victims were trembling convulsively, eyes wide open staring, fixed, appealing, their faces skeletal due to the freezing water.

... I have reported here, your honour, the experiences that I have undergone. They are not relevant just for me but also for the millions of people who have followed the same path. When I was a young girl, I was taught to love Brazil, respect its flag, to do my best for its people, to dedicate to my country my brains, my work, and, if necessary, my life. These sentiments have not changed, the small girl is still inside me, but I know that the illusions died an abrupt death when I was tortured under Brazil's flag and the portrait of the Duke of Caxias.

In conclusion, just a brief remark: the world is changing daily. I am not the person who will make it change any quicker, nor can I prevent it from changing, because it is whole peoples who make history. Nothing will prevent these people, once they learn of their lot, from taking into their own hands the control of their destiny and constructing a world of justice and solidarity. Even death will not prevent this because those who die for the ideals of justice become symbols of a new life and serve as an inspiration for others to continue the struggle.'

Presidio Tiradentes, Women's Prison, March 1972.
Signed: Marlene de Souza Soccas

Published September 1972

● THE 'UNKNOWN PERSON' RETURNS...

After three years in one of Haiti's most dreaded prisons, Marc Romulus was reunited with his son, Patrice. The 34-year-old teacher had been arrested on suspicion of opposing the government. An Amnesty International group in the Federal Republic of Germany was put to work on the case. The government said he was one of a number of 'unknown persons', but the Amnesty International campaign continued. It took two years for the government to admit he was in detention, although he was then described as an 'unrepentant terrorist'. Amnesty International continued to work on Marc Romulus' behalf. In September 1977 he was included in an amnesty for political prisoners. The man who the government at one stage said did not exist was at last reunited with his family.

CAMPAIGN TO ABOLISH TORTURE

1972 saw the launch of Amnesty International's first worldwide campaign to abolish torture and end the widespread official practice of torturing prisoners and detainees to stifle political dissent. The following extracts appeared in 'Epidemic Torture' published as part of the continuing campaign.

'Incredible as it is, 2370 years after Socrates drank hemlock, 1970 years after the crucifixion of Christ, 435 years after Thomas More was beheaded and 370 years after Giordano Bruno was burnt at the stake, hundreds, thousands of men and women waste away their days in prison for their opinions. But opinions should be free. Let the violent man be guarded, but the man who utters what he thinks must be free, and if he is behind bars it is not he but those who keep him there who are dishonoured.'
Salvador de Madariaga

Where torture is being practised, by Carola Stern

I speak about torture today. The average citizen encounters it most often as entertainment, as 'spice' in a television thriller, gangster film or Western, as a story without basis in reality, which shows the armchair reader how pain can be inflicted on other people and how it can be justified. When he hears about torture as a factual news item, he hardly reacts. Through entertainment, he is psychologically conditioned and his mind has been blunted by the almost daily reports about other acts of violence, terror and mass killings. Or he unintentionally reacts in the way intended by the torturers: he does not believe the reports. The lack of credibility of an unimaginable crime is still its best camouflage.

The torture of political prisoners is at present spreading like an epidemic throughout the world and even more terrible, just because of this, it seems to become more and more difficult to rouse people against it.

Since Amnesty International came into being, we have received proof of torture and maltreatment of thousands of political prisoners. This year alone, we have had such reports from 32 countries.

The sites where torture is carried out are called by various names: Con Son in Vietnam; Korydallos Prison in Athens; Public Security Headquarters, Sao Paulo; Psychiatric Clinic, Chernyakhovsk in the USSR; Savak office in Iran. The often harmless-sounding descriptions of the methods also vary: 'parrot perch', 'dragon chair' and 'telephones' (Brazil), 'bicycle', 'record player' (Spain), etc. Yet the methods are alarmingly similar. Partly they go back to the Middle Ages, were adopted by the Gestapo and GPU, while newer methods, such as torture by electric shocks, were tried out by the French during the war in Algeria. Amnesty International is in possession of reports about electric shock torture – where joints, sensory organs and genitals are connected to electrically-charged wires – being practised in South Africa, Turkey, Indonesia, Brazil, Iran, South Vietnam and Greece, to name only a few instances.

Governments co-operate by exchanging information about instruments of torture and their effects. Relevant schools and courses have been set up. In 1959, for instance, a French priest reported after returning from Algeria, where he had been a reserve officer, that he had been forced to attend a course on so-called humane torture. Exactly ten years later, in October 1969, a course on torture was held in

A former political prisoner from Brazil shows reporters how victims were tied to a pole in the 'pau de arará' (parrot's perch), which in the late 1960s and early 1970s was a common form of torture in Brazil.

Rio de Janeiro for Brazilian army personnel. Techniques were explained, advice given on the use of different instruments, and the effect on the prisoner was demonstrated – partly by lantern slides, but also on living objects: political prisoners. American soldiers, back from Vietnam, told how they were trained by their sergeants and officers in interrogation and torture techniques of enemy prisoners. Amnesty International also knows that there are international torture training programmes where torturers are trained in the latest medical and psychological techniques by instructors from different countries.

That which Herbert Marcuse describes as 'the aggressiveness of present-day industrial society' in the average person, and what he calls technological aggression, also affects torture in a perverse way. In the 'modern' methods of physical torture, the destruction of a person is not brought about directly by another person but by technical tools whose use does not require physical force, but only the pressing of a button. Electric shock torture, for instance, has a two-fold advantage for the torturer. It inflicts pain without leaving any traces, and it reduces the sense of guilt in the perpetrator by giving him the illusion that it was not he personally who had inflicted the pain, but the wires.

It is mainly in the USSR that a 'modern' form of psychological torture has been practised since the early 1960s: the committal of dissidents to mental hospitals, where they are detained together with seriously ill patients; and on the pretext that they need medical treatment, they are given overdoses of Aminasyn and Sulphasyn, which cause shock effects and serious physical disturbances.

According to the information available to Amnesty International, political prisoners are tortured most severely immediately after their arrest, while still at police stations, in the offices of the security police, and while under preliminary detention – in the first place to make them reveal the names and hiding-places of their friends; and then to extort from them an extensive confession and declaration of remorse while their trial is being prepared, if there is to be a trial at all. The verdict is not being entrusted to independent judges; the outcome of the trial is decided in the torture chamber.

To attack the use of torture does not mean the defence of guerrilla warfare and political terror. But it must be agreed that there can be no justification whatever for torture. Even the other side's political terror does not supply the torturers with a justification. The torturers know much better than we do how many innocent and uninvolved people they have worn down, how many false confessions are filed in their archives – false confessions made in desperation. At the same time, they know how often, in spite of all, the victims have refused to speak. And they know how many people were induced only by torture to declare themselves for violent, merciless war.

Extortion of information and confessions, intimidation of the political opponent, deterrence – these are often the ostensible reasons for using torture. But on the basis of their investigations into the nature of sadism and cruelty, scientists have taught us that there is a further purpose.

Those who practise torture maintain that their victims do not belong to human society.

Criticised for the persecution of the political opposition in the USSR, Soviet officials declared that opposition in their country was a kind of schizophrenia. As allegedly mentally sick people, dissidents are deemed to be of unsound mind and therefore denied the status of a political opposition.

In Iran, the security police, the Savak, is particularly anxious to make political prisoners incriminate themselves with high treason under torture. Would not the patriotic public be prepared to exclude the traitor from the community?

The intention is always the same: to label the political opponent as the enemy, to expel him from society, to depict him as a beast. This is how the torturer is to see him, even before he tortures. This is how the tortured person is to see himself after being tortured.

'The purpose of torture is not only the extortion of confessions, of betrayal; the victim must disgrace himself, by his screams and his submission, like a human animal.' (Sartre).

THREE CASES

Brazil: Vera Silva Araujo Magalhaes

Vera Silva Araujo Magalhaes was a 24-year-old student of economics in Rio de Janeiro when she was arrested by the military police in March 1970 for 'distributing leaflets.'

Her torture began twenty days after her arrest at the army police headquarters where she was first suspended for more than seven hours on the 'Pau de arara' (Parrot's Perch, where a prisoner's wrists and ankles are tied together and the whole body suspended from an iron bar under the knees, leaving the naked body doubled over and defenceless). While in this position she was subjected to different voltages of electric shocks, water was forced into her mouth and nose and she was beaten with a truncheon and whip all over the body, including her genital area.

Miss Magalhaes later reported that since she was very weak the attending doctor advised that the session be shortened and the torturers followed this order. She was then transferred to the infirmary and then to the military hospital.

In the military hospital, according to Miss Magalhaes' sworn statement, she received no medical care. Instead the doctors administered sedatives which weakened her psychologically. In general, she reported, medical practitioners attached to the military headquarters are in attendance only to control the amount of torture to which a patient may be submitted or to prescribe sedatives to aid in interrogation.

Dental treatment consisted solely of pulling out teeth to avoid further decay. There were rats and mice in the cells and infirmaries. She only saw her family three times in three months because, she said, the authorities wished to prevent them from seeing her physical condition.

Miss Magalhaes was first brought before a judge in the military tribunal after a month and a half of detention – her trial was already underway. Her case is exceptional: generally in Brazil the detained person is not brought before a judge until he has served approximately one year's detention.

The case against her was dismissed and she was released on the 15th June, 1970, more than three months after her arrest. She now lives in exile, confined to a wheelchair, her body paralysed from the waist down.

USSR: Pyotr Grigorenko

Pyotr Gregorevich Grigorenko, now aged 66, is a much-decorated former Major-General in the Red Army and permanently disabled from wounds he suffered during World War II. A devoted campaigner for human rights, he took up the cause of the Crimean Tartars deported to central Asia during the War. In May 1969, he was arrested for anti-Soviet activities; ten months later he was brought to trial, found guilty of crimes committed while of unsound mind and sentenced to an indefinite period of detention in a psychiatric hospital until his recovery.

While awaiting trial in a prison in Tashkent in June 1969 Grigorenko began a hunger strike in protest against his treatment. He was force-fed and deliberately beaten on his wounded leg. He wrote in his prison diary: 'I long to die, calculating that my death will serve to expose this tyranny.' But his captors frequently told him: 'You are utterly at our mercy, even after death.'

His physical pains were compounded by psychological pressures: his sick wife and disabled son were deprived of their pensions, he was allowed no contact with them at all or with his defence counsel before the trial, and his complaints were totally ignored.

'Only now have I realised the special horror of the fate which overtook those unfortunate people who perished by the million in the torture chambers of Stalin's regime,' Grigorenko wrote. 'It wasn't the physical suffering – that's bearable. But they deprived people of any hope whatsoever; they reiterated to them the omnipotence of their tyranny, the absence of any way out. And that is unbearable.'

In the psychiatric hospital to which Grigorenko was sent, he has been confined to a cell of six square metres containing two people: himself and a cell-mate who stabbed his own wife to death and is in a constant state of delirium.

There is room to take only two steps. Despite the acute pains in his crippled leg, he is allotted only two hours exercise each day, the rest of the time being spent in his locked cell.

Every six months he is brought before a commission and questioned on a simple question and answer basis designed, according to Grigorenko, to reveal the inconsistency of his views and to prove that he is mad.

'When will you renounce your convictions?' he is asked.

Grigorenko is reported to have replied: 'Principles are not like gloves, they are not easy to change.'

▼ *Vera Magalhaes*　　　　▼ *General Pyotr Grigorenko*

Desmond Francis

South Africa: Desmond Francis

Desmond Francis is a South African Indian schoolteacher now aged 34 and living in Zambia. He was arrested in January 1968 by Rhodesian security police when he crossed the border, allegedly because of his involvement with a magazine printed by the banned African National Congress.

He was taken first to Bulawayo in Rhodesia where he spent 17 days in an infested cell, chained by leg irons and severely beaten. His head was held under water to make him confess to corrupting African detectives and when he refused to comply, he was smothered by a canvas bag and beaten on his testicles with a copper finger-printing pad.

'All this took place in a centre office to hide screams,' reported Francis who, on the fifth day of this interrogation, tried to commit suicide by plunging a broken bottle into his chest. The police prevented his attempt and renewed their efforts to break him.

While still in Rhodesia, Francis was burnt repeatedly with a hot iron on the thigh and lighted matches held against his body. His pubic hair was singed off in this manner. To relieve the pain he was given two aspirins and placed in solitary confinement.

On the 18th of January, 1968, he was taken by car to South Africa. 'I pleaded not to be sent to South Africa,' stated Francis in a subsequent affidavit. 'I was told I would be a mental wreck by the time I reached Robben Island.'

For the next 13 months, he was held in solitary confinement in Pretoria Central Prison where, he said: 'I was beaten all over with fists and an inch-thick cane; one blow broke my right cheek-bone. I was then handcuffed and blindfolded with a wet cloth. I had to sit with a stick under my knees and over my arms. Electric terminals were applied to my ears and the current was turned on. This was a terrible experience. My whole body shook and my head seemed full of vibrations. My teeth chattered so that my tongue was cut to ribbons.'

It took over two weeks to extract a statement from Francis. The torture was kept up by rotating shifts of police using every conceivable method. Eventually he signed a statement – with a rough canvas tool bag over his head and his nerves shattered by the fire-crackers the police were throwing at him. A week later, Francis was finally granted medical attention. He had been vomiting and excreting blood almost without stop. The prison doctor's diagnosis was bleeding piles.

He was released unexpectedly without a trial 475 days after his arrest and granted an exit visa to Zambia. Speaking of the others who remain in detention, he said: 'We are confined to a silent concrete grave, a living death, painful and complete.'

A sense of loss, by Jean-Pierre Clavel

'Sadism,' wrote Erich Fromm, 'is the passion for gaining absolute control over another being.' This passion to 'break' another being is the mainspring of the act of torture: the violation of a human will by the systematic infliction of suffering.

Whether or not anyone can presume to judge all torturers as sadists, the fact remains that the act itself of deliberate and sustained cruelty is universally recognised as a crime against humanity.

As such, it is not only held to be morally indefensible, it is an indictable offence under international law.

This principle was first established in the definition of Crimes against Humanity set down in the Nuremberg Charter, 1950:

'Murder, extermination, enslavement, deportation and other inhumane acts done against any civilian population or persecutions on political, racial or religious grounds, when such acts are done or such persecutions are carried out in execution of or in connection with any crime against peace or any war crime.'

It was the Universal Declaration of Human Rights, however, and the subsequent UN Covenant on Civil and Political Rights that made explicit the international injunction against all acts of torture:

'No one shall be subjected to torture, or to cruel, inhuman or degrading treatment or punishment.'

Despite arguments advanced by strategists to justify use of controlled third and fourth degree methods in urgent intelligence operations, no government or international body has since been able to openly sanction any form of torture. In fact, a consistent and consolidated effort has been made in recent years to bring torture under strict international legal control.

Nowhere can this be seen more clearly than in the fact that at no time in the history of international law in the years since the Second World War has any provision been made to admit the legality of torture even in wartime. The Geneva Conventions Relative to the Treatment of Prisoners of War and on the Protection of Civilians in Wartime are specific and unequivocal in prohibiting the cruel treatment and torture of captives.

This refusal to provide legal sanctions for torture under any circumstances has not, of course, prohibited its practice. Sartre's warning at the height of the Algerian War is even more true today: 'Disavowed – sometimes very quietly – but systematically practised behind a facade of democratic legality, torture has now acquired the status of a semi-clandestine institution.'

But the slowness of international law to halt the spread of torture does not repudiate the fundamental moral principles upon which that law is based.

Those principles are implicit in the idea of a fundamental 'humanity', unique in each individual, yet common to all.

Historically, the idea of this humanity has been primarily rooted in the belief in a basic, inalienable freedom; 'There can be nothing more dreadful,' wrote the philosopher Immanuel Kant, 'than that the actions of a man should be subject to the will of another.'

Not surprisingly, it is the history of Black Emancipation that most clearly documents the essential character of human freedom. It has always been liberty which distinguished the citizen from the slave, the man from the sub-man. 'The slave is not a man,' wrote Angela Davis shortly before her arrest in 1970, 'for if he were a man, he should certainly be free.'

But of all forms of direct and indirect oppression, it is the practice of torture which most relentlessly seeks to disintegrate the fundamental freedom of human personality; firstly, by naked assault and degradation and secondly, by attempts to gain 'absolute control' over the victim's will.

'The purpose of torture,' argued Sartre 'is not only the extortion of confessions, of betrayal: the victim must disgrace himself, by his screams and his submission, like a human animal. In the eyes of everybody and in his own eyes. He who yields under torture is not only to be made to talk, but is also to be marked as sub-human.'

Contrary to the belief that torture is only used to prevent the spread of violent insurgence, current evidence points alarmingly to its use as an instrument of social intimidation similar to the interrogations unleashed by the KGB [Committee of State Security] during the Stalinist purges.

Whether it be Iran, Greece, Brazil, Turkey, Vietnam or South Africa, the victim usually finds himself arrested without a warrant, cut off from anyone he knows, denied even minimal legal rights: 'The rules aren't made for the police,' reply his captors. He is simply seized on suspicion and dragged out of his daily life.

Suddenly without protection he may be forced to strip naked, compelled to urinate over his own body, strapped onto a bench already sticky with the vomit of those who went before. He insists there must be some mistake. He is beaten until a punctured lung forces him to cough blood through his nose and mouth. Through spells of dizziness and nausea he hears himself sworn at and laughed at.

All this before the questioning begins. When Andreas Frangias, a civil engineer, was arrested two years ago in Greece, he found himself surrounded by seven or eight shouting men who beat him repeatedly on his head, chest, stomach and belly. In his testimony to the Appeal Court he recalled the question put to him before he lost consciousness:

'Their stereotype shouted question was, 'Tell us why we have brought you here!' and at the same time they threatened me that, if I wanted to leave the place alive and see my wife and daughter again, then I must reply at once to this question.'

'But isn't this the only language people like that understand?' asks an urbane man in the cafe.

People like what? People like Henri Alleg – the Algerian editor? People like Pyotr Grigorenko – the Soviet Civil Rights advocate? People like Marcos de Arruda – the Brazilian geologist? People like Immam Abdullah Haroun – the South African Muslim leader?

'But, of course,' says the urbane gentleman, 'mistakes occur. The police do their best to protect society from violence and sometimes, in emergencies, they have to use violence.'

Unfortunately, this gentleman reads only the news-papers where torture is printed in inverted commas. To him, 'torture' is always an exaggeration unless, of course, the circumstances are desperate; then it becomes a necessary evil which the victim brings upon himself.

But torture once tolerated as a 'last resort' becomes epidemic. When, in 1955, M Willaume, a Senior French Civil Servant sent by the French government to investigate allegations of torture in Algeria, did not unambiguously condemn the use of torture, it should be noted that from that time until the end of the Algerian war in 1962 the use of torture by the authorities was not only endemic in Algeria but spread to Metropolitan France itself.

In its study of current torture practice and training, Amnesty International this year received testimony from a score of nations – in most cases, the torture was alleged to be routine and appeared to be used solely for the systematic silencing and intimidation of political opposition. The evidence points to the establishment of torture as an institution in itself – outside the constitutional political process and completely outside the legal framework.

'Once all our army did was add a touch of colour to national festivals; now it has turned into a corps of executioners, holding 4,000 to 5,000 political prisoners at its mercy. A body of fewer than 15,000 men is enforcing a reign of terror over 2½ million people.'

This statement emerges from testimony brought out of Uruguay by the noted French religious leader, Georges Casalis. Professor Casalis, of the French Protestant Federation, was one of the four authors of the celebrated document *The Church and the Powers*, published in 1972. During a subsequent visit to eight Latin American nations, he amassed first hand evidence of what he has termed an 'abyss of horror' – often from men and women who have been torture victims themselves.

'In just a few years,' he wrote, 'a heavy yoke has

descended; the streets are constantly patrolled ... men disappear without trace, families are divided against themselves.... People grow anxious if someone is half an hour late.... If a father has a meeting he takes two of his children along with him...'

Casalis' report fits all too clearly into the cumulative evidence that an identifiable pattern of repression may now be emerging on a global scale. His findings are, unhappily, merely exemplary.

'It is taken for granted that the first stage in all interrogations is torture,' he wrote. 'A science of repressive techniques is developing. Arrests are frequently carried out on Friday evenings so that prisoners are subjected to three days of torture before being handed over to the police. In several recent cases the prisoner never was handed over; he died first.'

The accelerating violence is senseless: once developed into a method of operation it is used indiscriminately and the confessions extracted by it are usually fabrications or lies.

Studies conducted in the post-Korean War period proved that latent anxieties can be so intensified by isolation, sensory deprivation, systematic exhaustion and the administration of hallucinogenic chemicals that a 'subject' will begin to exhibit 'transient psychotic symptoms' and become highly receptive to suggestions, threats and enticements and submission can be achieved without tell-tale burn marks.

This supposed refinement serves merely to expose what has been described as the 'latent Satanism of torture': the passion to possess a human soul.

In a memorandum submitted to the United Kingdom government at the time of an official enquiry into alleged sensory deprivation torture in Northern Ireland, Amnesty International eloquently defined the fundamental character of psychological torture:

'It is because we regard the deliberate destruction of a man's ability to control his own mind with revulsion that we reserve a special place in our catalogue of moral crimes for techniques of thought control and brainwashing. Any interrogation procedure which has the purpose or effect of causing a malfunction or breakdown of a man's mental processes constitutes as grave an assault on the inherent dignity of the human person as more traditional techniques of physical torture.'

Whether a man 'goes out of his mind' from the pain of needles under his finger-nails or from an electronically induced delirium, the final effect remains that of an unbearable sense of loss, not only of control but ultimately of identity. He becomes, in Sartre's words, 'detached from his real self'. Perhaps nowhere has the suffering of this collapse been more graphically conveyed outside of literary masterpieces such as Kafka's *The Trial* or Shakespeare's *King Lear* than in Paulo Schilling's *Theory and Practice of Torture in Brazil*. In his description of the experience of electrical torture, he wrote:

'The torturer's abundant imagination determines where the shocks will be applied to the victim's body. The simplest way is to stick the contacts between the fingers or toes and then turn the crank. The electrical discharge causes a sensation which is difficult to describe; a physical and psychological commotion filled with electric sparks which, together with convulsive shaking and loss of muscular control, gives the victim a sense of loss, of unavoidable attraction for that turbulating electric trituration.

'The shock causes a stimulation in the muscle identical to the stimulation of the nerve fibres ... causing disorderly, uncontrollable movements similar to epileptic convulsions.

'The tortured victim shouts with all his might, grasping for a footing, somewhere to stand in the midst of that chaos of convulsions, shaking and sparks. He cannot loose himself or turn his attention away from that desperate sensation. For him in that moment any other form of combined torture – paddling, for example – would be a relief, for it would allow him to divert his attention, touch ground and his own body which feels like it is escaping his grasp. Pain saves him, beatings come to his rescue. He tries to cause himself pain by beating his head repeatedly on the ground. But generally he is tied, hanging on the 'parrot's perch' and not even that resource is available to him.'

In a letter smuggled out of a Greek prison two years ago, a victim of the Greek repression tried to account for torture such as this which he and his comrades suffered:

'The headhunters have locked us up in this narrow place in order to make us shrink, like those hideous human scalps which are their trophies.'

It is in this utter diminishment of humanity that torture reveals its final moral blasphemy – the secret repudiation not only of human freedom, but of humanity itself.

The victim, by George Mangakis

'I have experienced the fate of a victim. I have seen the torturer's face at close quarters. It was in a worse condition than my own bleeding, livid face. The torturer's face was distorted by a kind of twitching that had nothing human about it. He was in such a state of tension that he had an expression very similar to those we see on Chinese masks; I am not exaggerating. It is not an easy thing to torture people. It requires inner participation. In this situation, I turned out to be the lucky one. I was humiliated. I did not humiliate others. I was simply bearing a profoundly unhappy humanity in my aching entrails. Whereas the men who humiliate you must first humiliate the notion of humanity within themselves. Never mind if they strut around in their uniforms, swollen with the knowledge that they can control the suffering, sleeplessness, hunger and despair of their fellow human being, intoxicated with the power in their hands. Their intoxication is nothing other than the degradation of humanity. The ultimate degradation. They have had to pay very dearly for my torments. I wasn't the one in the worse position. I was simply a man who moaned because he was in great pain. I prefer that. At this moment I am deprived of the joy of seeing children going to school or playing in the parks. Whereas they have to look their own children in the face.' (Letter to Europeans, 1971)

Medical and psychological aspects

Pain is a signal that the body is being damaged or destroyed. To stay alive is undoubtedly one of our basic drives although death may eventually be counted as a merciful release. But few people can view with equanimity the prospect of living as a damaged body or mind. A 'mind' needs a complete 'body' for complete self expression. It needs intact genitalia for fulfilment of social ambitions such as marriage, for expression of sexual drives; intact hands for constructive and aggressive instincts; vision, speech and hearing for relating to other body/minds. A healthy body is seen as 'good', a disfigured one is 'bad' and therefore the victim sees himself as becoming regarded as a 'bad' person, a 'mind' to be shunned and therefore condemned like the wandering Jew to the continuous torture of eternal loneliness.

The most senseless of all tortures is physical trauma to the brain. If a man's skull is struck, the brain may be shaken up (concussed), bruised (contused) or torn (lacerated). Brain cells die, blood vessels get torn, cerebral haemorrhage and further destruction of brain tissue occurs. Some brain cells, if damaged, recover: but dead cells are never replaced. To damage the organ of a healthy mind can serve no purpose, further no cause. Like picking the wings off a butterfly or the burning of the ancient library of Alexandria it produces an irreparable loss. Death, coma or a

Women inmates of Tan Hiep national prison, South Vietnam, undergoing treatment for acid burns at Cho Ray Hospital in Saigon. They alleged they received these burns when the prison authorities forcibly suppressed a prisoner demonstration for better conditions.

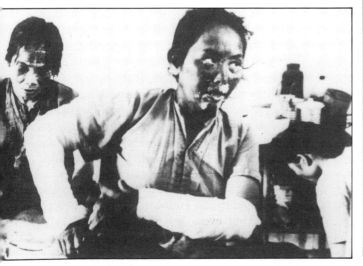

mindless 'vegetable' is a result with no suffering for the victim; but to be left aware that one's mind is damaged or distorted, deficient in its memory, its intellectual skills or its control is a terrible sentence. A profound depression often ensues; one may be subject to convulsions, or outbursts of rage, unable to work or to adjust to society.

Interrogation methods employing sensory deprivation techniques also have traumatic effects. Anxiety, hypochondria and hysteria are the most frequent in clinical situations; phobias, depressions, emotional fatigue and the obsessive-compulsive reactions are rarer. In addition to its subjective results, anxiety can lead to stomach, heart and genito-urinary symptoms as well as tremors and sleep disturbance.

The induction of convulsions by passing an electric shock through the brain is, like the use of sensory deprivation, a perverted application of medical practice. Therapy using electrical shock in this way (Electro-convulsant therapy) is widely used for alleviating depressive illnesses. Even in medical use when it is given twice a week, it may induce mild confusion and memory impairment for a short period. When repeated many times in a day it causes such cerebral disturbance as to render men demented and incontinent and is analogous to a severe head injury.

Psychiatric cases encountered after the use of electrical torture in Algeria included instances of localised or generalised cenesthopathies in which 'the patients felt 'pins and needles' throughout their bodies; their hands seemed to be torn off, their heads seemed to be bursting and their tongues felt as if they were being swallowed';[1] instances of apathy, aboulia and electricity phobia were also evident, the former two in patients who were 'inert' and the latter in patients who feared touching a switch, turning on the radio or using the telephone.

Just as severe damage to our physical system may leave a scar, so may mental stress have long term sequelae. If during the process of torture, our psychological defences are eroded and the mental systems with which we cope with stress become so overloaded that they are destroyed, we may find on return to our normal environment that we no longer have an adequate system for coping with any life problems. A survey of psychiatric casualties of World War I revealed that almost all were unable to return to normal life after discharge from the Army and were unable to work in their former capacity, if at all. Their minds became preoccupied with grief or bitterness over their misfortunes, or a permanent state of anxiety arose.

Distressing dreams and memories can occur many years after the severe stress, being re-awakened by another severe stress, and similarly a pattern of behaviour (such as a state of abject terror) acquired during torture, may suddenly reappear.

Within this context of breakdown through manipulated stress, physical abuse is also employed. The function of beatings, burnings, gaggings, finger irons and needles is clearly exhausting, demoralising and disorienting. In his study of the results of tortures of this order Frantz Fanon reported cases of agitated nervous depressions, patients

Specialist help for torture victims is provided by medical teams around the world. Like the Danish team pictured above, they work to help patients overcome the trauma of mental and physical abuse.

who were sad and depressed, who shunned contact and were liable to show signs of very violent agitation without obvious cause. Perhaps the most serious problems were encountered in patients who, after torture, exhibited a phobia against all forms of physical contact with other people. Nurses who came near the patient and tried to touch him, to take his hand, for example, were at once pushed stiffly away. It was not possible to carry out artificial feeding or even to administer medicine.[2] It is perhaps cases such as this that best reveal the meaning of Jean Amery's statement: 'Torture is the most terrible event remaining in man's memory.'

1. F. Fanon, *The Wretched of the Earth*, Penguin, 1970, Chapter 5.
2. Ibid.

Published September 1983

EQUATORIAL GUINEA: 'AN IMMENSE TORTURE CENTRE'

'A thick wall of silence, a silence of terror and of the grave, surrounds everything that goes on there.' This is how two escaped political prisoners from Equatorial Guinea describe their country in a detailed testimony recently received by Amnesty International. In retelling their prison ordeal, the two men charge that Guinean President Macias Nguema – during whose nine-year rule a quarter of the country's population has gone into exile – has made Equatorial Guinea into 'an immense torture centre' where 'the way out is the way to the cemetery'.

Amnesty International considers the report significant in that, for the first time, it provides detailed corroboration of the numerous allegations received over nine years, of brutal murders, torture and inhuman prison conditions in Equatorial Guinea.

The testimony gives names and circumstances of death of 12 prisoners who died after torture in Bata Prison. Two allegedly died after having their eyes torn out by Guinean National Guards. Others died after beatings and bizarre humiliations were inflicted during forced labour. For example, two men were forced to re-enact the crucifixion of Christ, participating in a savage 'way of the Cross' accompanied by a group of other prisoners. After their fellow-prisoners were crucified, the remaining group was forced to celebrate a mock-mass over the dying men. The present government of Equatorial Guinea is hostile to the Roman Catholic faith of a minority of the population.

President Nguema himself is mentioned as figuring in one murder, and as having knowledge of another. In the first case President Nguema allegedly ordered a prisoner brought to Bata's airport to hunt rats. When the man failed to catch more than four, the rats and the prisoner were burned alive. In the second case the President referred in a public speech to a statistician whose fingers had been cut off 'because he could not count'. The actual fate of the statistician – according to witnesses quoted in the report – was even more horrible. The man's fingers, hands, feet and ears were cut off before he died.

In the testimony, general conditions for all inmates at Bata Prison, and especially for the political prisoners, are said to be bad. Up to 18 prisoners can be kept in cells measuring either one metre square, or 2 by 3 metres. Under the harsh regime of prison director Salvador Ela and his deputy Francisco Edu, male and female prisoners work for long hours without any food or drink. Their only food is provided by their families, and those without families can starve to death.

The testimony goes on: 'The National Guard invented the most incredible methods of torture, such as the 'injection' method, where they beat a prisoner on the ribs and testicles, while forcing him to swallow water. Women had thorns and other objects thrust up their vaginas, and then they were raped. If the guards got bored with this, they might tie up a prisoner with wire, pour petrol over him, and burn him alive in the prison courtyard, in front of everyone...

'This method must have seemed too quick to them, for they discovered another method: hanging a man from his hands and feet by nylon cords from a pole parallel to the ground. After a while the weight of the prisoner's body would make the cords cut to the bone. Others would be beaten with clubs until their flesh swelled and wounds appeared. Then the wounds would be sprayed with petrol. The guards would not set the prisoners alight, but allowed the petrol to dry out their wounds in the heat of the sun, splitting the flesh open. People would die, literally split open. Antonio Ndo was one of many who died this way'. A list of 490 names of civil servants who have died under the regime was published by the Guinean exile community at the end of 1976, but even this cannot be regarded as complete.

AI Newsletter March 1978

INDONESIA: STRUGGLE OF PRISONERS' FAMILIES

Human rights in Indonesia have been of particular public interest in the Netherlands because of the country's history as a Dutch colony. In 1973 the Dutch Section of Amnesty International published 'Indonesia Special' in collaboration with the movement's International Secretariat. This presented the situation of more than 55,000 untried political prisoners, many of them 'prisoners of accident or victims of circumstance, arrested by mistake or military inefficiency, and subsequently unable to challenge their detention.' The report also described the plight of their families:

Indonesian society has always been known for its sense of social cohesion, its ability to care for those stranded by misfortune or left without a breadwinner. There is no social security system, but the traditional social cohesion has in the past managed to deal with problems which, in a welfare state, would become the responsibility of the State. Since 1965, this fine tradition has been shattered; large numbers of people have found themselves without communal sympathy and protection because of the pervading anti-communist atmosphere. They are the families of political prisoners, the wives and children of prisoners, and children deprived of parents since 1965 through imprisonment or death.

This is not simply a matter of coping with economic problems and educating children; it extends to a kind of social ostracism that has destroyed friendships, broken fraternal blood relationships and made good-neighbourliness a rare exception rather than an accepted mode of behaviour towards those related to political prisoners. It is almost as though these families suffer from a contagious disease and no one who can possibly avoid it wants to become contaminated.

How then do the wives and children of political prisoners survive? Some wives have cut their relations with their imprisoned husbands altogether. They have been unable to bear the strain of prolonged separation with no prospects of reunion. Life is not easy for a woman without her husband in Indonesian society, and many prisoners' wives have fallen prey to pressures exerted upon them by military officers. Their fear for their children's security has made them particularly vulnerable.

The vast majority of wives, however, have not succumbed to this type of pressure, and a very large number of them live on the brink of starvation. Few of them can find regular jobs, not only because of a lack of skill or qualifications, but also because most employers demand a 'declaration of non-involvement in the 1965 coup' which detainees' wives are not able to get, unless they have money to bribe local officials. Some people have been able to purchase these declarations for prices varying from two to several hundred dollars, a thing that is not uncommon in a society where corruption has become almost a way of life.

Neither is it an easy matter for the children of detainees to continue their education. A major difficulty is finance; school fees are high, even for primary schools, and transportation to and from school may require even more money than the fees. Moreover, children require 'non-involvement declarations' to take examinations or enter university; this applies even to children who were little more than infants at the time of the coup. In 1971, the press reported that children entering secondary school at the age of 14 had to produce one of these declarations, yet they were only eight years old at the time of the coup!

Many wives try to make a living from dressmaking or baking cakes which they hawk on the streets. Mrs. Pramudya Ananta Tur, wife of Indonesia's foremost writer who is now detained on Buru Island, sells cakes to try and make ends meet. She suffers from a pulmonary ailment and requires regular medical treatment. Another woman, who once ran a prosperous building firm, is now herself living in a bamboo shed in one of Jakarta's poorest districts; her husband was arrested as a member of a left-wing trade union, and she is now supported by her son who bought a 'non-involvement declaration' in order to get a job as a barman in a Jakarta hotel. Her youngest son died two years ago because she could not afford to pay for necessary medical treatment. There are numerous other examples of human tragedy that have occurred among these neglected families.

The difficulties they face are not only caused by an absence of assistance from official sources. In many cases, the families are actively harassed by local military units who force them out of their homes and deprive them of their belongings. They are defenceless against such harassment and cannot even contemplate taking legal action unless they have financial aid for the lengthy court proceedings.

Another constant worry is that of finding out about the whereabouts of a detained husband. Wives who have lost trace of their husbands, either immediately after his arrest or as a result of transfer from one place of detention to another, are often treated in a very humiliating way when they make enquiries at any military unit.

The only source of succour for these families in distress is a small number of private organisations, mainly the Christian churches, which, in some places, have started relief programmes for the families of political prisoners. One diocese of the Roman Catholic Church took steps to bring prisoners' wives together to share their problems and to try and solve them through communal effort. A chaplain took the initiative and worked out a plan of action; it included fund-raising by selling hand-made products, simultaneously providing the women with some form of employment. The money was intended to pay school-fees for their children. But, inevitably, such endeavours run into difficulties and this one was suspected of providing a cover for political activities. When the women participating in this particular scheme met together at Christmas 1971 for a small celebration, one of them rose to thank the organisers on behalf of all the wives. A few days later, she was summoned to a military office, held for a whole day and questioned about the speech she had made. She was later released but the incident disturbed many women who had found some comfort in the regular get-togethers and common effort, and they decided to stay away in future.

Relief projects are in progress in several major towns in Indonesia but they are still very limited in scope and can help only a very small fraction of those in need.

Perhaps the best way to conclude the above account is with the true story of one particular child who, for the purposes of this story, we shall call Narto:

'Mrs. S. had been under detention for several years because of her associations with the left-wing women's organisation, Gerwani. Her husband had been murdered in an incident in Jakarta shortly after the coup attempt and, ironically for her, had been buried at the Heroes' cemetery in Jakarta because his death was thought to have been the result of an attack by communist youths. When she was arrested, she took one small child with her to prison and left her other children with relatives. The relatives never visited her and she had no news of her children.

One day some years after her arrest, she, together with several other women prisoners, was carrying garbage out of the prison where she was being held in Jakarta when, glancing towards the crowded streets, she suddenly began to scream: 'Narto! Narto'. The prison commander who was guarding the women prisoners on garbage duty asked her why she was shouting.

'That's my son,' she cried. 'Narto, my son, over there, picking up fag-ends.'

The commander saw the boy to whom she was pointing, and began to run after him. The boy, seeing a soldier running after him, took to his heels and fled. Many startled bystanders joined in the chase; the boy was soon caught and the commander dragged him back to the prison. Only then did the child realise that his own mother had been calling him.

He was dressed in rags and filthy from head to foot. His mother embraced him and carried him into the prison. By the time they entered the prison compound, everyone had rushed out to see what was happening, political prisoners and their military guards, criminal prisoners in the nearby blocks and the civil administrators of that part of the prison. It was a heart-rending scene, and everyone, guards as well as prisoners, wept as they watched the mother and child. The mother was torn between joy at finding her child after years of separation and anger at seeing him in such a wretched condition. Nothing could more poignantly have depicted the tragedy of so many families torn asunder by political events for which they are not responsible.

After bathing and dressing Narto in her own clothes, the mother discovered that he had been staying with an uncle who had found the responsibility of looking after him too burdensome and had made his life a misery. Narto could not stand the life and ran away. He had been living on the streets for weeks, begging, collecting fag ends and sleeping under railway carriages in sidings.

For some months he remained in prison with his mother, but the prison commander realised that the child must be found a home outside. With the help of the visiting Catholic priest, a place was found for him with a Catholic family and he was soon able to start going to school again after having missed several years of schooling.'

Narto was saved from misery by a lucky coincidence. How many children live on as he once lived, with no escape from the wretchedness of life in a society that cares nothing – or is too afraid to care – for the children of political prisoners?

Published March 1973

POLITICAL PRISONERS IN SOUTH VIETNAM

Despite the cease-fire in the war in Viet Nam in January 1973, Amnesty International received dozens of reports that civilians were still suffering in detention in the south. The organization continued to campaign for the release and rehabilitation of civilians detained in Indo-China as a result of war until the cessation of hostilities in April 1975. In 1973 it published *'Political Prisoners in South Vietnam'* focusing on the plight of these detainees, explaining who they were, why many who did not support either of the warring sides were still detained, the conditions of their imprisonment and allegations of torture.

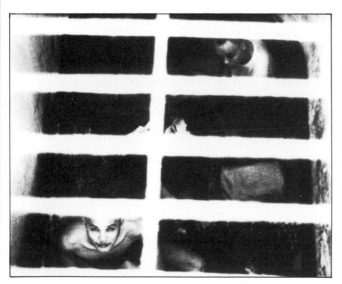

The infamous South Vietnamese 'tiger cage' prison on Con Son Island attracted public attention in 1970 with the exposure of cramped underfloor cages. The prison was used mostly to house political prisoners, many of whom were permanently crippled as a result of their imprisonment in the cages.

In November 1972 Amnesty International presented a draft Protocol to all the parties to the conflicts in Indochina. The Protocol was concerned with the release and rehabilitation in the event of a ceasefire of all the civilians detained in Indochina as a result of war. At the time this was a massive problem needing the most urgent attention, especially in South Vietnam. Since then a Ceasefire in Vietnam has come and gone; and the problem is just as urgent today.

Like most wars, the conflict in Vietnam created two sorts of prisoner: prisoners of war – that is, military personnel involved in the war – and detained civilians. Contrary to what many people think, the January 1973 Ceasefire and Peace Agreement only dealt properly with prisoners of war. It left the question of civilian prisoners largely unanswered.

As a result of the Agreement, all captured and detained military personnel (as well as foreign civilians) were released by the end of March; the Americans among them received most public attention. They were nearly 600 in all, less than the Pentagon may have hoped, but in any case only a fraction of the total number of civilian and military detainees throughout Indochina. Most of them were released by the DRVN [Democratic Republic of Vietnam], a few by the PRG [Provisional Revolutionary Government] and a handful by the pro-Communist Pathet Lao in Laos. At the same time, but with much less publicity, some 31,000 Vietnamese prisoners of war were exchanged by the PRG and GRVN [Government of the Republic of Vietnam] in the South.

The Peace Agreement also stipulated that the two South Vietnamese parties should discuss the issue of civilian detainees and try to come to an agreement by 27 April 1973, ninety days after the Ceasefire. This deadline is now long past and next to nothing has happened. This means that upwards of 100,000 civilians remain in detention throughout South Vietnam, many of them in appalling conditions, the vast majority of them held as a result of the fourteen-year-old conflict.

One of the hazards of discussing South Vietnamese civilian prisoners is the imbalance of information available. Accounts of conditions in GRVN prisons, as well as some visual material, regularly filter out; on the other hand reliable information about the condition of prisoners held by the PRG is hard to come by, even though released Americans have had their experiences to relate.

In spite of this disparity, Amnesty International feels there can be no excuse for failing to describe the appalling conditions, chaotic administration and widespread disregard for basic legal and human rights which many GRVN civilian prisoners have to endure. For this reason, while it contains a section on PRG prisoners, the greater part of this report is given to GRVN civilian detainees, with the proviso that it cannot be exhaustive.

No consideration is given here to the DRVN. This is not because Amnesty International is not concerned with North Vietnam – on the contrary, it has North Vietnamese Prisoners of Conscience in its files. However, the January

Peace Agreement on Vietnam is concerned only with civilians detained in South Vietnam, and in the present instance we are confining ourselves to these terms of reference.

The aim of this report is to publicise the plight of South Vietnamese civilian prisoners, and to stress the fact that no progress is being made towards their release. Amnesty International wishes to draw this state of affairs to the urgent attention of the International Commission for Control and Supervision of the Ceasefire in South Vietnam; to the participants of the Paris Conference on Vietnam last February; and to all interested Governments and parties, in the hope that they will prevail on the GRVN and the PRG to take concerted action and set free South Vietnamese civilian prisoners.

The peace agreement

The provisions made for civilian internees in 1954, when the French and Ho Chi Minh's People's Army signed a ceasefire, were much better than those made by the Peace Agreement this year. According to the 1954 Settlement, 'All civilian internees of Vietnamese, French and other nationalities captured since the beginning of hostilities in Vietnam during military operations or any other circumstances of war … shall be liberated within a period of thirty days after the ceasefire'.

The Settlement went on to define the term 'civilian internee' as meaning 'any persons who, having in any way contributed to the political and armed struggle between the two parties, have been arrested for that reason and have been kept in detention by either party during the period of hostilities'.

Nineteen years later, the provisions for a far more complicated situation are far less comprehensive. The January 1973 Peace Agreement should have provided for the immediate release of all civilians detained as a result of the war. Instead it just told the two South Vietnamese parties to 'do their utmost' to resolve the problem within ninety days of the Ceasefire. When this deadline was reached at the end of April, the two parties had only succeeded in agreeing to exchange a total of 1,387 civilian detainees, a tiny percentage of the total number held. Since then, negotiations on the civilian prisoner issue have ground to a halt[1].

The Peace Agreement also used the same definition of 'civilian internee' as the French and Vietminh agreed on in 1954. Even in 1954 this definition was not really satisfactory. How broadly was the phrase 'contributing in any way to the political struggle' to be interpreted, for example?

But at least there had been a fairly clearcut political and military struggle between the French on one side and the Vietminh on the other. In 1973, on the other hand, the prisons of President Thieu are filled not just with members of the NLF [National Liberation Front], but also with thousands of non-Communist opponents of his Administration. These people have 'contributed to the political and armed struggle between the two parties' – that is, the GRVN and PRG – only insofar as they have supported neither of them. They are in jail for opposing President Thieu on their own, or for supporting movements other than the NLF. It is clear that the terms of the January Peace Agreement are not broad enough to include this large section of the GRVN's prison population, and that the GRVN has no intention of setting them free on any other grounds[2].

Even if it eventually releases its NLF prisoners, there are several reasons why the GRVN may find it expedient to keep its non-Communist political opponents behind bars. These people are 'neutralists', members of the political third force, possible mediators between Communist and non-Communist in South Vietnam. If they were released and allowed to become politically active, they could well jeopardise the staunchly anti-Communist position of the GRVN. This position, which identifies neutralism with pro-Communism, is perhaps the most effective *raison d'être* of GRVN.

The pivotal role of the third force is reflected in the proposed structure of the body known as the National Council for National Reconciliation and Concord, at least as it was originally conceived. According to the Peace Agreement, this Council is designed to organise general elections throughout South Vietnam, and a lot of negotiations went on before the signing of the Agreement about the Council's precise nature. Washington and Saigon apparently wanted to reduce its potential as much as possible, while Hanoi and the PRG conceived of it as an 'administrative structure' with considerable independent power. The Council is to consist of three segments. In the January Peace Agreement it was not specified how these would be made up; but earlier it had been clear that they were to be one part GRVN, one part PRG and one part third force.

Both before and after the January Ceasefire, however, the GRVN has done all it can to discredit the idea of the third force. In a letter to President Nixon last November, for example, President Thieu denied its existence. The GRVN has also taken steps to silence claims that it is holding a large number of non-Communist political prisoners.

[1] As a first step in the negotiations on civilian detainees, the GRVN and PRG exchanged lists of civilian prisoners they considered eligible for release under the terms of the Peace Agreement. The GRVN's list consisted of 5,081 'Communist civilian detainees', while the PRG's number 137. Each side claimed the other's list fell far short of the true number, and there was an impasse until three days before the deadline on 27 April. Then, in a surprise move, the GRVN agreed to exchange 750 prisoners for 637 PRG prisoners. Since then, there have been petty disputes about venues, and about protection for the Control Commission teams who are supposed to be on hand to observe exchanges. As a result, only a few hundred civilian detainees have actually been exchanged.

[2] The PRG has claimed their release under Article 11 of the Peace Agreement, which is concerned with 'freedom of belief' and other democratic liberties.

Published July 1973

'RE-EDUCATION' IN VIET NAM

After the fall of the government of South Vietnam and the reunification of Viet Nam, thousands of former members of the armed forces and administration of South Vietnam were detained without charge or trial for 're-education'. Many of those detained were soon released, but Amnesty International became increasingly worried in 1977 and 1978 about the long-term detention without trial of the thousands remaining in 're-education' camps. This extract comes from the report of an Amnesty International mission to the Socialist Republic of Viet Nam in December 1979.

The fact that large numbers of people remain in detention without charge or trial nearly five years after the end of the war has been the cause of growing concern to Amnesty International. Article 9 of Policy Statement No. 02/CS/76 states that category (c) people 'must attend collective re-education courses for three years starting from the day they enter a camp'. The statement continues: 'those who have committed many crimes against the people and dangerous evil-doers who have incurred many blood debts to their compatriots' (Article 9), 'those who were in the ranks of the resistance and betrayed the country' (Article 10), and 'those who have not submitted to the revolutionary administration, who refuse to report to the administration for re-education courses' will be brought to trial in due course (Article 11). Policy Statement No. 02/CS/76 is therefore quite clear that 're-education' will last three years and that those individuals who would be charged with criminal acts will be tried.

In its discussions with the Vietnamese authorities and legal representatives, the Amnesty International delegation was therefore keen to establish why the Vietnamese Government continues to detain large numbers of people without charge or trial for far in excess of the three-year period. Amnesty International was informed that since the unification of Vietnam on 2 July 1976, the law of what was formerly the Democratic Republic of Vietnam (North Vietnam) now applies to the whole country. Although decrees of the Provisional Revolutionary Government were still valid, the existing law of the Democratic Republic of Vietnam was paramount. In particular, the Vietnamese authorities referred the Amnesty International delegation to Resolution 49-NQ/TVQH of the National Assembly of 1961. This resolution provides for 're-education' for two categories of people: (a) 'obstinate counter-revolutionary elements who threaten public security' and (b) 'all professional scoundrels'. There are no provisions in Resolution 49 of 1961 that those individuals sent for 're-education' be brought before a court or sentenced. Although the period of 're-education' mentioned is three years, the resolution also allows for the period of detention to be extended – something for which the Provisional Revolutionary Government Policy Statement of May 1976 did not provide. Amnesty International is concerned therefore that the Vietnamese Government now states that Resolution 49 of 1961 applies to those individuals held after the cessation of hostilities in 1975.

The Amnesty International delegation was informed that the Provisional Revolutionary Government of South Vietnam faced in May 1975 the problem of disarming a hostile armed force of 1,300,000 and that the policy of 're-education' in these circumstances was introduced in an attempt to achieve national reconciliation instead of seeking vengeance. Whatever the original intention behind the policy, the continued detention of large numbers of people in 're-education' camps in 1980, long beyond the three-year period earlier set, has since become akin to administrative detention without trial.

Although the system of detention in 're-education' camps in Viet Nam may not have been conceived of as administrative detention without trial, it appears that the element of 're-education' has now receded considerably. The Amnesty International delegation was told during its visit that new and unexpected security considerations have arisen during the past two years which have made it impossible to release all detainees in 're-education' camps within the time period first envisaged; in particular reference was made to the situation in Kampuchea and to Viet Nam's relations with the People's Republic of China. Grounds for the continued detention of these people, therefore, seems to have shifted from past misdeeds and present behaviour to the external situation, namely national security. These prisoners are therefore being held in what is usually termed administrative detention without trial.

The effect of this new policy is that thousands of people who had expected to be released after three years are still kept in detention without charge or trial and without knowing when they will be released, which results in severe hardship for them and their families.

Published June 1981

CHILE: AFTER THE COUP

The world was shocked by the violence that followed the overthrow of the civilian government of Chile in September 1973. Here is a chronology of Amnesty International's response to these events, from 'Chile: an Amnesty International report', published one year after the coup. The report examined in detail the detention of political prisoners, the numerous executions, deaths and 'disappearances' since the coup, the systematic use of torture and the flouting of recognized legal procedures. The second extract from the report highlights one of the problems Amnesty International frequently faces in its work, that of reliably estimating statistics.

AMNESTY INTERNATIONAL AND CHILE – A CHRONOLOGY

1973

11 September Chilean Armed Forces overthrow the government of Dr Salvador Allende.

15 September Amnesty International and International Commission of Jurists issue statement calling for UN intervention on threats to civilian lives and to refugees in Chile.

16 September AI's International Council, meeting in Vienna, calls on the new Chilean government to stop executions, arrests and threatened deportations.

October At the UN in New York, AI Secretary General Martin Ennals is given assurances by the Chilean Foreign Minister, Admiral Ismael Huerta Diaz, that 'torture is against the principles of the Chilean Government' and that all prisoners will be given a fair trial and the right to appeal against sentence. Admiral Huerta Diaz invites Amnesty International to visit Chile and assures Mr Ennals that a mission will be free to carry out investigations.

1-8 November AI mission visits Chile. The delegates are: Professor Frank Newman, professor of law at the University of California, Judge Bruce W. Sumner, presiding judge of the Supreme Court of Orange County, California, and Roger Plant, Researcher in the Latin American Department of AI's International Secretariat.

The mission's terms of reference are to:

○ make representations to the Chilean Government regarding executions.

○ report upon procedures of interrogation, detention, charge and trial.

○ inquire into allegations of torture.

○ meet with defence lawyers and to advise on financial and other assistance to prisoners and their families.

7 December Professor Frank Newman gives testimony on the findings of the mission to members of the Committee on Foreign Affairs of the United States House of Representatives.

11 December At AI's Conference for the Abolition of Torture, Chairman Sean MacBride criticizes torture in Chile. AI sends cable protesting against long prison sentences and death sentences.

31 December Report of mission is sent to the Chilean Government. In a letter to General Pinochet, Martin Ennals urges that:

○ all executions cease and lists of those already executed be published.

○ 'immediate steps be taken and proclaimed to establish tribunals of inquiry into allegations of torture and that international observers be invited to participate'.

○ lists of detainees be published to 'assuage the fears of people who do not know where relatives and friends are detained, or even whether they are detained'.

○ the decision to try former members of the Allende government be rescinded because legislation that creates a crime retroactively 'is an affront to any system of justice'.

○ prisoners against whom charges are not filed, preparatory to trial, should be released immediately.

○ the Chilean government 'renew its assurances to respect the right of asylum'.

1974

19 January The Chilean government issues a public statement rejecting the report in its entirety without commenting on the substance of the report.

The President of the Supreme Court publicly attacks AI in his opening annual address.

28 January Martin Ennals replies to the criticisms of the report in a letter to General Pinochet.

February-March Professor Frank Newman gives testimony to the UN Human Rights Commission.

May Judge Horst Woesner of the West German Federal Court represents AI in Chile. His brief is to investigate judicial procedures in Santiago and the provinces and to observe the air force and other trials in Santiago and the provinces.

3 June Judge Woesner reports that defence procedures in Santiago are wholly inadequate, that torture continues and that death sentences have been passed on two men in Valdivia. These sentences were subsequently commuted after widespread expression of concern from both AI sections and other organizations.

30 July Death sentences are passed on three members of the Chilean armed forces and one civilian on charges of treason. Martin Ennals, in a letter to General Pinochet, appeals for the sentences to be commuted. As a result of widespread international pressure, the four death sentences were commuted to 30 years' imprisonment on 6 August.

Throughout 1974, Amnesty International has briefed several missions to Chile, to observe trials, meet with defence lawyers, investigate torture and make arrangements for the channelling of aid to the families of political prisoners.

Considerable aid has been given to refugees from Chile and some fares have been paid from Latin America to European countries by AI national sections, especially by the sections in Germany, Sweden, Holland, Mexico and France.

By August 1974, individual AI groups are working for the release of approximately 140 Chilean prisoners.

Published September 1974

MAJOR AMNESTY INTERNATIONAL REPORT DOCUMENTS REPRESSION OF HUMAN RIGHTS BY JUNTA IN CHILE

'The infringement and repression of human rights in Chile have continued unabated' in the year since a military coup overthrew the democratically-elected government of President Salvador Allende, according to a major Amnesty International report published tomorrow (September 11), the anniversary of the coup.

The 80-page illustrated publication, 'Chile: an Amnesty International report', documents the unending

A young boy in Santiago, Chile, cries as a police vehicle takes his father away.

campaign waged against supporters of the Allende regime and other elements by the military junta that seized power on September 11 1973.

'The death roll of victims is unprecedented in recent Latin American history, and there is little indication that the situation is improving or that a return to normality is intended,' Amnesty International Secretary General Martin Ennals says in his preface to the report.

'Twelve months after the coup, despite the Government's apparent absolute control over the country, the junta still deems Chile to be in a 'state of war and a state of siege','Mr Ennals says.

The report is based on information collected from both Chileans and independent foreign observers, including Amnesty International's own team of investigators which visited Santiago last year. Much of the evidence was submitted to Amnesty International in confidence by ex-prisoners and their families.

After weighing the junta's stated justification for the coup, the report examines in detail the detention of political prisoners, the numerous executions, other deaths and disappearances of people since the coup, the junta's systematic use of torture, its flouting of all recognized legal procedures, and the fate of the thousands of foreigners who sought refuge under Allende. An appendix cites 19 typical cases of individual repression.

'In publishing this report, Amnesty International hopes that it will provide a factual basis for a continuing program of assistance to the victims of the coup and, what is equally urgent, for a renewed campaign of international pressure upon the Chilean Government to restore human rights in Chile,' Mr Ennals says.

Although the precise number of persons still detained without trial in Chile for political reasons is unknown, the report says estimates from reliable sources indicate that there are probably between 6,000 and 10,000 held in the many detention centres dotted throughout the country. They represent every sector of the population – from former Allende ministers, other politicians, doctors, lawyers, journalists and trade unionists to actors, academics, students, agricultural experts and even members of the armed forces. Only a small percentage have ever been brought to trial, although trials are pending for the Allende ministers.

The report expresses alarm at the fact that although most detainees are now held in public prisons and improvised detention centres, many more are held by units of the armed forces in military barracks where they have no recourse to legal protection of any kind. A detailed examination of prison conditions and interrogation procedures since the coup shows the brutality practised from the outset by the military against detainees.

Although the Allende ministers have now been transferred from the harsh climate of Dawson Island back to Santiago, many other prisoners are still detained in remote Chacabuco (over 1,000 kilometres from Santiago) whose very distance, 'by cutting off all possibility for legal protection, gives military intelligence *carte blanche* to study the prisoners' dossiers at random: to release some, to bring others to trial whensoever they wish, and to keep the remainder in preventive detention'.

Thousands of people in Chile have lost their lives since the coup through summary or near summary execution, being allegedly 'shot while trying to escape' or as a consequence of torture received during interrogation, the report says.

Although many of the deaths took place in the first few months after the coup, the report cites a number of cases of people who lost their lives this year. They include former Interior Minister Jose Toha, who died in mysterious circumstances in a military hospital in Santiago in March. The junta's official explanation of suicide is widely discounted.

'While the military intelligence services continue their random arrests, interrogations and assaults on private citizens, there can be no real guarantees for the protection of human life in Chile,' the report says.

In a long chapter entitled 'Chile and the rule of law', the report examines the abuse of legal procedures and international conventions by the junta.

'Since the declaration of the 'state of siege' as applied in time of war, in September 1973, civil courts and lawyers have been virtually powerless in Chile, while citizens and lawyers alike have been deprived of their fundamental legal rights. Citizens have been arrested without charges and without recourse to a lawyer; lawyers have been unable to demand access to prisoners, or even to know the charges against them until shortly before the commencement of a trial. The majority of trials have been held in secret, with the defence lawyer often excluded from the court martial proceedings. All trials have been conducted by military courts in accordance with the Code of Military Justice in Time of War ... Moreover, there is now ample evidence that the military junta has failed to fulfil many of the legal guarantees that have been published in the Chilean press or made to foreign observers.'

Defendants in the recent air force trials in Chile were repeatedly tortured in an effort to extract confessions from them. The courts however refuse to admit defence allegations of torture. Some well-known international lawyers who observed the air force trials were unanimous in asserting that the prisoners had no chance of a fair trial.

The report says Amnesty International's own mission saw marks of severe torture on the bodies of some men and women whom they questioned. Other independent observers saw marks of torture inflicted by specially-imported Brazilian interrogators during the early phase of the coup.

Although brutality appeared at first to be random, 'within a few weeks of the coup, torture appears to have become an official policy of the Chilean Government'. The report lists 16 major military centres and military schools (in addition to the well-known sites like the National Stadium) where torture is known to have taken place. It says Amnesty International is still receiving reports regularly of the continuing use of beatings, electric shocks and psychological torture.

The junta also violated Chile's own international undertakings in its xenophobic persecution of the thousands of foreign refugees caught up in the coup. Although most refugees have now left Chile, the report criticizes the manner in which the junta has continued to flout international conventions by sealing off foreign embassies in Santiago with armed guards and denying the right of political asylum.

News release 10 September 1974

NUMBERS: THE PROBLEMS OF STATISTICS

Although it has always been impossible to know the true number of political prisoners since the coup, it is certain that the figure is far greater than the junta has admitted at any given moment. In the first weeks after the coup, Church sources in Chile estimated the number of political prisoners as between 45,000-50,000 (excluding those prisoners who were detained for a period of 24 hours or less). The figure given by the junta was less than a quarter of that amount. By spring 1974, official figures were between 3,000 and 4,000, while Church estimates were approximately 10,000.

In April 1974 the International Commission of Jurists reported that approximately 6,000 to 7,000 political prisoners could be accounted for (the junta had raised the official figure to approximately 6,000) while 'there may be as many as a further 3,000 people under arrest at any one time who are being held for questioning in military barracks, police stations or other interrogation centres'.

The problem of obtaining accurate statistics was made clear to the Amnesty International mission in November 1973. We attempted to secure lists of prisoners from several sources and several ministries. We were informed by officials of the Ministry of the Interior that lists of detainees existed, but were 'secret'. According to Admiral Ismael Huerta Diaz, the Foreign Minister, approximately 10,900 persons had been in custody up to the latter part of October, though many had been released. After repeated requests for statistical lists, the Foreign Minister showed the Amnesty International mission a carefully compiled book which accounted for these 10,900 persons, but marked the majority as 'released'.

The inadequacy of such statistics was amply revealed by our independent inquiries. International organizations had reported that there were as many as 7,000 political prisoners in the National Stadium of Santiago alone at the end of September. By the end of October the figure was 1,948 (20 October) and 1,800 (31 October).

The Amnesty International delegation received reliable information shortly before it left that the numbers of prisoners recorded at various times in October in only a few places of detention were as follows:

Prison	Number
Rancagua Prison	496
La Serena Prison	449
San Antonio Prison	101
Puente Alto Regiment	334
Pudeto Regiment (in Punta Arenas)	129
Dawson Island (approximate)	100
Concepción Stadium	589
Quiriquina Island	552
Temuco Prison	341

These few statistics account for 9,990 prisoners (including the initial figures in the National Stadium in Santiago) in only *ten* places of detention. Church sources have accounted for no less than 30 places in the Province of Santiago alone where political prisoners have been detained since the coup.

We give these few scattered statistics only to illustrate the immense problems in accurate reporting. In the last weeks of October, thousands of fearful Chileans waited outside the National Stadium, hoping for some indication that their relatives were alive. Many months later, Church leaders issued a writ of *habeas corpus* on behalf of 131 Chileans who had disappeared since their last date of arrest. Hundreds of persons are still unaccounted for, while the death of many others can now be presumed. Recent information indicates that up to 2,000 Chileans may have been executed after secret military trials (or have been killed in detention without even the semblance of a trial) up to the end of December 1973.

At the present moment, it is still impossible to secure accurate statistics. The National Executive Secretariat for Prisoners (SENDET), which is officially responsible for controlling statistical information concerning political prisoners, is itself unable to secure information concerning all those detained in military barracks. Even now, statistics have to be compiled from the oral reports of ex-prisoners recently released from the many places of detention. Until the junta cooperates by publishing lists of all detainees, there will be no reason to doubt that the number of political prisoners remains as high as 7,000 or even more.

Published September 1974

Santiago, Chile, the day of the coup – 11 September 1973. Soldiers round up staff of the overthrown President, Salvador Allende.

INDIA: DETENTIONS WITHOUT TRIAL

The large-scale detention without trial of prisoners detained for 'extremist' activities in India since the early 1970s increasingly concerned Amnesty International. Most of the prisoners, held particularly in West Bengal and Andhra Pradesh, were said to be Naxalites – members of the Communist Party of India (Marxist-Leninist). The first extract here is from a news release issued in September 1974 which announced the issuing of a report. The second is taken from a report of a mission to India in 1979 and describes the case of a woman apparently detained only because of police suspicions that some of her relatives were Naxalites.

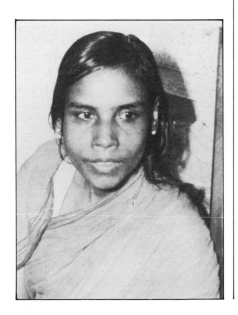

Archana Guha in 1978 when she was paralysed from the waist down.

Thousands of political prisoners in the Indian state of West Bengal have been detained without trial in grossly overcrowded conditions since 1971 and some have been kept fettered day and night for up to two years, according to an Amnesty International report issued today (Tuesday September 17).

The nine-page report says serious allegations of torture have been levelled against warders and police in West Bengal by many of the estimated 15,000-20,000 so-called Naxalites detained there. Some prisoners who have been tried and found not guilty have immediately been re-arrested and detained on other charges without trial.

'Naxalite' is the name given to the alleged members and supporters of the Marxist-Leninist Communist Party of India, whose ideology advocates armed struggle as a means to bring about social and political change. Members of the movement have, particularly during 1970-1971, committed acts of violence. Amnesty International has not adopted any of these as Prisoners of Conscience.

Most were arrested under preventive detention laws introduced after a state of emergency was declared on December 3 1971 at the time of the Bangladesh War, but are now held under clauses of the Indian Penal Code; others have been held for nearly 5 years.

The report was prepared by Amnesty International's research department after 46 prisoners in West Bengal went on hunger strike in support of demands for better prison conditions – conditions which the report says violate the United Nations' Standard Minimum Rules for the Treatment of Prisoners.

In June, Amnesty International Secretary General Martin Ennals sent the report to India's Prime Minister, Mrs. Indira Gandhi and to the Chief Minister of Bengal, S.S. Ray, with a series of recommendations. Neither has replied, nor has the Indian Government replied to several previous approaches by Amnesty International about the conditions of detainees. Amnesty International, therefore, has now decided to update and publish the report.

Some of the report's main conclusions:

– 'Prisoners tried and not found guilty on one charge are often immediately re-arrested on different charges', and even if prisoners are cleared of all charges and released, they must report regularly to the police and are restricted in their movements and political activities.

– Prisoners are kept in unsanitary, overcrowded conditions, with often only one watertap for hundreds of them and poor medical facilities.

– Bar fetters are used on prisoners regarded as dangerous or as security risks and some in Hazaribagh Jail (Bihar) have been chained day and night for up to two years.

– Legal sources as well as prisoners themselves report the use of torture against both men and women who have allegedly been beaten, hung upside down and had pins and nails inserted into their nails and sensitive organs, and been subjected to electric shocks and burning with cigarettes.

– According to official figures 88 prisoners were killed in 12 jail incidents during the period December 1970 to June 1972 alone in West Bengal and Bihar.

– Prisoners have been denied legal rights guaranteed by India's Constitution.

News release 17 September 1974

The case of Archana Guha

Miss Archana Guha, 35 years old, is totally paralysed from the waist down, as a result of treatment she received during police interrogation. At the time of her arrest, she was headmistress of Kolorah Girls' Junior High School, in Howrah, Calcutta. So far as Amnesty International is aware, Miss Guha had no involvement in politics, but was presumably arrested because the police suspected some of her relations to be involved in the Naxalite movement.

Archana Guha was arrested about 1.30 am on 18 July 1974, together with her sister-in-law, Mrs Latika Guha, and Miss Gouri Chatterjee, a friend. They were arrested by police officers who had searched the house and they were never shown a warrant of arrest. They were first taken to Cossipore Police Station and then transferred to Lal Bazar Police Station, Calcutta, where they were taken to the special cell of the detective department, on the first floor. 'The special cell' consisted of three rooms arranged like an 'L', the middle room being the office of N., and the back room being the one where, according to Miss Guha, 'tortures are being carried out'. On 18 July, at 10 am, Gouri Chatterjee was taken for interrogation and Archana Guha was forced to witness the treatment given to Miss Chatterjee. Afterwards, Archana Guha was brought in and given similar treatment: her hands and feet were tied to a pole placed behind her knees. The pole was rested on two chairs and the prisoner hung with her head down. She was hit on the soles of her feet by Inspector S. Inspector N. extinguished burning cigarettes on the soles of her feet and on her elbows, of which marks were still visible at the time of the interview. She was kicked with boots and the nails of her toes and fingers were burned. She fell unconscious. At 2 pm the three women were taken back to Lal Bazar lock-up and at 4 pm brought back for interrogation. She was again hung from a pole as before and drops of water were slowly dripped onto her forehead; she was burned on her feet and elbows and also again beaten on her feet and kicked. The next day, on 19 July 1974, the three women were taken to the Sealdah magistrates' court, but never brought before a magistrate. They were charged under various sections of the West Bengal Maintenance of Order Act and the Defence of India Rules. That same afternoon the three women were brought to the special cell for further interrogation, where Archana Guha was beaten on the head ('physical brainwashing') and forced to sign a printed paper, the contents of which she could not read but which she believed would implicate her in political actions. The same day Police Officer A.B. beat her on the head and threatened her with execution if she would not 'confess'. Inspector K.K. during interrogation pulled her by the hair and several times threw her against the wall. Her hair was pulled out

from her forehead and she was pulled up from the floor by her hair and, while she was hanging in this position, she was kicked and burned. The same methods were applied the following day, 20 July, when Archana Guha was also threatened with rape and hit on the head with a rope. She was unable to walk to her cell. From 22 July to 1 August 1974, almost every day the women were brought to the special cell. All three women prisoners remained in the police lock-up from 18 July to 13 August 1974 and never saw a lawyer.

On 13 August 1974, Archana Guha was taken to Presidency Jail, Calcutta, as an 'under trial' prisoner and, on 30 September, served with an order of detention under the MISA [Maintenance of Internal Security Act]. Her physical condition deteriorated rapidly, she often fell unconscious, but was not given adequate medical treatment and her legs became disabled. On the insistence of other women prisoners, specialist doctors were finally called in and it was not until 22 December 1975 that Archana Guha, by then completely paralysed from the waist down, was taken to hospital for a minor operation on a gland. On 24 January 1976 she was returned to prison on a stretcher and only on 9 February did the jail authorities arrange for her transfer to Medical College, Calcutta, as a 'life-saving case'. She stayed in the hospital until 17 November 1976, when she was released on parole. The detention order against her was not revoked until 3 May 1977.

Published January 1979

'Now I can walk!…'

Archana Guha, now 38 years old, was completely paralysed from the waist down as a result of torture during police interrogation in Calcutta, India, in 1974.

… Archana Guha was suffering from a lesion of the lower part of the spinal cord. After unsuccessful attempts to treat her in Calcutta lasting more than a year, her case came to the attention of an Amnesty International mission visiting India. The mission interviewed her and described her plight in its report.

Amnesty International's Danish Medical Group arranged for her to be taken to Copenhagen in January 1980 for intensive diagnosis and treatment.

After two months of care she was able to rise from bed, steady herself and walk short distances without assistance.

On 1 May 1980 she wrote from Calcutta: 'My friends and relatives are simply astonished to see me walk again! … now I can walk and move! … The secretary and colleagues of my school are waiting eagerly (for the day) when I'll be able to join the school. I have improved much in walking and climbing the staircase … You have given me a new life – you have caused rebirth to me!'

Published 1981

POLITICAL TRIALS IN THE USSR

In 1975 Amnesty International published a detailed 154-page report on the treatment and conditions of prisoners of conscience held in Soviet prisons and labour camps.

On trial in Moscow for publishing 'anti-Soviet' works in the West: Andrei Sinyavsky (bearded) and Yuli Daniel. Their four-day trial, in 1966, caught the attention of writers and intellectuals worldwide. Andrei Sinyavsky was sentenced to seven years' imprisonment, Yuli Daniel to five.

There has never in Amnesty International's experience been an acquittal of a political defendant in the USSR. No Soviet court trying a person charged for his political activity has rejected the prosecution's case on grounds of procedural violations committed during the investigation period or on grounds of insufficient evidence.

That such cases once begun always end in a conviction indicates that criteria other than criminal culpability are decisive. The counter-argument might be that the investigative organs do their job so thoroughly that there is no chance of mistake. However if the investigators are always correct, then the courts' decisions are irrelevant except in determination of sentence. Furthermore, the 'infallibility' of investigative organs applies apparently only to 'political' cases. There is a very significant incidence of acquittal in criminal cases. It is clear that in political cases the procuracy, officially the watchdog for observance of legality, steps aside on behalf of 'higher' (political) considerations.

To ensure that the predetermined 'guilty' verdict is arrived at in political cases, Soviet courts regularly make rulings which directly contravene the procedural norms laid down in Soviet law.

Article 111 of the Soviet Constitution states that the examination of all cases in all courts shall be open insofar as the law does not provide for exceptions. Many political trials, in fact, constitute the exceptions to this rule. Proceedings are often held effectively *in camera*, and sometimes close relatives and friends of the accused are not admitted into the courtroom – on various pretexts such as that 'the public benches are fully occupied'. The trial of the Ukrainian historian Valentyn Moroz was held formally *in camera* without the presence of even a specially selected audience and with no formal justification.[53]

Quite often the place, date and time of a trial are changed at the very last minute, or even after proceedings have begun. Relatives of the accused have lodged protests at what appears to be a deliberate failure to inform them. Since the creation of the unofficial Moscow Human Rights Committee[54] led by Academician Sakharov, there have been attempts by its members – chiefly Academician Sakharov – to attend political trials, but the authorities have rarely allowed them entry. Demonstrators outside court buildings at trials of dissenters are frequently handled roughly by court officials and KGB personnel, or indeed detained for hours or even days.

Inside the courtroom, the 'general public', sometimes in uniform and brought in by coach, have often interrupted the proceedings with hostile comments and jeers, or, at Jewish trials, with anti-semitic remarks, or with calls for a harsher sentence. Transcripts of political trials often find their way into *samizdat*, and show that on many occasions numerous articles of the Code of Criminal Procedure have been violated.[55] Almost invariably in such trials the evidence accepted by the court has been incomplete and unfairly weighted to the disadvantage of the defendant. In many cases defence witnesses have not been allowed to give evidence. Often defence witnesses who have been called have been prevented from giving evidence other than that elicited by the prosecution. Frequently contradictions and patent falsehoods in evidence given by prosecution witnesses have been accepted by courts without challenge. In cases where the prosecution has brought in an 'expert psychiatric diagnosis' recommending confinement of political defendants to a mental institution, the courts have invariably accepted such recommendations in spite of their unacceptability as objective evidence.[56]

Officially authorized publicity of political trials is extremely rare and, when it does occur, is so one-sided in presentation of the matter that one must conclude that such publicity is aimed at making propaganda rather than at elucidation of fact. For example, the trial of Sinyavsky and Daniel in 1966, the trial of Ginzburg and Galanskov in 1968, and, more recently, that of Pyotr Yakir and Victor Krasin in August 1973 were officially reported by the Soviet media in a tendentious fashion aimed at discrediting the accused men in the eyes of public opinion at home and abroad by linking them with various anti-Soviet or emigré organizations. After the trial of Yakir and Krasin, a news conference was even staged, partly for the benefit of foreign correspondents. The convicted men were officially presented, and they delivered prepared statements admitting their guilt. The event occasioned an official propaganda campaign against Western correspondents in Moscow and against the human rights movement in the USSR. *Izvestiya*, for example, quoted Mr Yakir as saying that what is often called the 'democratic movement' in the USSR was only executing a program and tactics brought into the country by an 'anti-Soviet' emigré organization.[57]

There are no known instances of officially-published Soviet newspapers or journals criticizing or challenging a 'guilty' sentence in a political case. This is in marked contrast to the Soviet press record on non-political criminal cases, about which Soviet publications do occasionally write in defence of convicted persons on various grounds.[58] This contrast again underlines the fact that in Soviet legal practice political defendants are, to their disadvantage, treated as a separate category of 'offenders'.

53. *A Chronicle of Current Events*, Number 17, pages 41-43.
54. The Committee of Human Rights for the USSR was formed in Moscow in November 1970. Its founding members were Academician Andrei D. Sakharov, Andrei H. Tverdokhlebov and Valery N. Chalidze, all physicists. Its goals and statutes are described in *A Chronicle of Current Events*, Number 17, pages 45-47.
55. A catalogue of such procedural violations can be found in Pavel Litvinov, *The Trial of the Four* (Penguin Books, London, 1972).
56. See below, Chapter VII. 'Compulsory Detention in Psychiatric Hospitals'.
57. *Izvestiya*, (Moscow) 31 August 1973.
58. See Alois Hastrich, 'Juristischer Alltag in der Sowjetunion', *Osteuropa* (Berlin and Stuttgart), Number 10, October 1973, pages 791-806.

Published November 1975

● A FAMILY REUNITED

Rodolfo Begnardi, his wife Nora and their son Emiliano were finally reunited in Baltimore, USA, in 1983 after spending eight years apart in Argentinian prisons. The couple were arrested in November 1975 in Campana, Argentina, and held in preventive detention without charge or trial. Nora, a primary school teacher, was not connected with any political or trade union activities. However, it is believed she and her husband were arrested because of his work as a trade union official.

Both were adopted as prisoners of conscience by Amnesty International and their cases were allocated to a group in Maryland, USA. The group corresponded regularly with Nora's mother in Campana and with Emiliano who was being looked after by his grandparents. In 1980 Nora was released, reunited with her son and exiled to the United States. She joined the Amnesty International group in Baltimore and continued campaigning for Rodolfo's release.

Finally, in May 1982, Rodolfo was released into 'restricted liberty' and returned to Campana. Eight months later the three were reunited in Baltimore where they now live.

TORTURE IN SPAIN

After the death in November 1975 of General Francisco Franco, who had ruled Spain for 36 years, the new government committed itself publicly to the restoration of civil and political liberties. However, Amnesty International continued to receive reports that detainees were being tortured. 'Torture in Spain 1976', composed of extracts of documents from Spain, contained previously unpublished testimonies and statements and photographs indicating the continuing use of torture in Spain.

'Words and phrases, unfortunately, are overshadowed by facts, the terrible facts corroborated by hundreds of testimonies and even by formal denunciations which might be consigned to oblivion in the legal bureaucracy.

'There is fear, panic. People hardly dare give their names. Threats of retaliation if people speak out are a daily matter. In spite of this, we can relate the cases of more than 100 victims of torture during the last months.'

On 27 June 1976, the Catholic Justice and Peace National Commission of Spain published a dossier entitled 'No a la tortura'. The above quotation is taken from the dossier. The names of 115 torture victims and descriptions of tortures were listed following this statement.

'It is the *Guardia Civil* which has been responsible for directing the majority of these operations. They have used all means of unimaginable tortures and have even introduced new ones. The most common ones are:

bañera (the bath: the victim is undressed, wrapped in a blanket, tied and plunged into a tub of filthy water containing the urine and vomit of other victims)

quirofano (the operating table: the victim is stretched and tied on a table for beatings with hammers and truncheons; pins are inserted under the nails and fingers and testicles are beaten)

hanging by the wrists (the weight of the suspended body causes great pain around the wrists)

electric shocks...'

Extract from a document issued by a group of Basque lawyers in May 1976 which cited allegations of more than 60 cases of torture during the months of April and May 1976.

'Our colleague arrived at the prison with his thorax bandaged and complaining of acute pains in his chest and spine. During the cross examination on 15 May by the military judge assigned to his case, he stated that the reason for his physical condition was a consequence of the treatment he had received in the barracks of the District Command of the Civil Guard. He also said that he had been forced to sign a statement prior to his transfer to the Provincial Prison, affirming that his injuries had been caused the day before his arrest (8 May) while he was playing pelota (a traditional Basque ball game). However, his family say that he left his house at 9 o'clock on the morning of [the] 8th, two hours before his arrest, in perfect health.'

Extract from the petition signed by the members of the Medical College of Guipúzcoa, appealing for an inquiry into the circumstances of the arrest and detention of their colleague, Dr Justo Aristain Gorosabel. He was detained while at work in the Provincial Hospital of Guipúzcoa on 8 May and taken to the *Guardia Civil* barracks in Avda. de Zamalacárregui (San Sebastian) where he was held incommunicado until 14 May 1976 when he was transferred to the Provincial Prison.

'The road which seemed to be opening towards a freer,

more just and peaceful society, is once again obstructed by violence, the violence which many hoped had been finally overcome … Repression has been hardened to the point where maltreatment and various forms of torture are considered a legitimate means to extract information or force confessions of criminal acts.'

Extract from the pastoral letter dated 29 May 1976 by Mgr. Jacinto Argaya, Bishop of San Sebastian and Mgr. José Maria Setién, Auxiliary Bishop, published in the Catholic weekly of Madrid, *Ecclesia*, on 12 June 1976.

'The growing number of arrests, massive and indiscriminate, has brought home the fact (of torture) to the general population … We are in a situation where detentions do not seem to pursue offences, but rather to create a climate of terror in an indiscriminate way.'

Statement by the Basque People's Commissions for an amnesty for political prisoners *(Asociaciones Pro-Amnistía de Euskadi)*, presented to the King of Spain by the Basque-Navarra Association of Architects on 5 June 1976.

'In short the impression created by the interrogators is of sheer terror. They are fanatics, sadists, enemies of everything Basque. Enemies of democracy, of all committed religion, of the Basque clergy, of certain lawyers, of the *ikastasolas* (Basque schools), that is to say, of the people…'

Extract from the testimony of Father Jesus Lasa, arrested in Tolosa on 10 May 1976. He was held at the *Guardia Civil* HQ in San Sebastian for 10 days where he was tortured by the *bañera* and beaten over a period of six days until the intervention of his bishop produced an improvement in his treatment.

Elia Martinez-Cava, a 23-year-old poultry farmer, pregnant, was arrested with seven other persons in Madrid on 16 April 1976:

'They beat me all over, on the shoulders, back, arms, thighs … strong continuous blows on the ears … they grasped my hair with fury and pushed me around like a ball … I was interrogated 12 times in five days, once for seven hours. I told them I was pregnant, but that did not stop them. I saw my husband … he was in a terrible state … he could not stand up … They beat him in front of me and told him: 'We have made her abort, we are going to kill her, you know; then we will say it was an accident.'

A group of leading Madrid lawyers issued a denunciation concerning the case of all 8 people arrested at the same time as Elia Martinez-Cava. In their statement before the court they attested:

'We have been able to see their injuries … wounds in the wrists and on the soles of the feet … bald patches on the scalp, swollen testicles and legs, torn nails…'

A petition about this case with 2,700 signatures was sent to the Minister of Interior. It includes the following statement:

'Today, when the whole of Spanish society and the country's leading political figures are calling for an amnesty and democratic liberties, police maltreatment is an impudent affront to a society which wishes to live together peacefully.'

Father Lluis Maria Xirinachs is a Catholic priest who was nominated for the 1975 Nobel Peace Prize. He has been conducting a sit-in in front of *La Modelo* prison (Barcelona) since December 1975 to request the restoration of civil liberties and the release of all political prisoners. On 1 May 1976 Father Xirinachs was arrested and taken to the Police HQ in the Via Layetana where he was severely beaten and abused:

Police Inspector: 'Why do you get into trouble?' Fr. Xirinachs: 'It's a question of conscience.'

One of the police began to pull hair out of his beard, another from his moustache; another seized his hair and shook him, pulling hairs out. The armed policeman tells them:

'Leave him, he's aleady been taken care of.'

'Pray to God for salvation.'

Another policeman says sarcastically:

'Father, forgive them for they know not what they do.'

A red flag was brought in and wrapped around Father Xirinachs. A newspaper was placed on his knees (to look like a surplice) to the accompaniment of laughter and shouts: 'Red priest, you're alright now; you're in your element…'

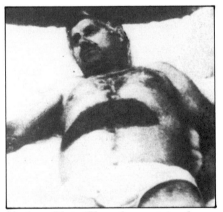

Mariano Plata 'Then the captain, the sergeant on duty and three plainclothes men started to beat him with a baseball bat, kicking him all over the body. They did this for about an hour, at short intervals. Then they tied him to a chair and two members of the Brigada Politico-Social beat him with clubs and even attempted to burn him with a lighter… 'If you denounce maltreatment, we'll kill you around any corner,' he was told.'

Extract from a report of Pax Christi, Barcelona, concerning the case of factory worker, Mariano Plata, arrested on 29 March 1976, near Barcelona. A medical certificate corroborates the injuries.

'I have observed a hematome on the right eye extended over the entire periorbital region ... a hematome of the size of a 50 peseta coin in the area of the larynx ... several hematomes in the rightside clavicular area ... serious contusions over the thorax, the abdomen ... The patient, as a result of these injuries, remained for many hours in a traumatic state ...'

– Extract from the medical certificate of Victoriano Rodriguez Casado, trade union official detained on 28 April 1976 in Aranjuez.

'... a large group of armed police were waiting at the entrance (to the church) ... at that moment inspectors from the *Brigada de Investigación Social* and the officer in charge of the forces appeared ... 'Are you Father Casasola?' 'Yes, I am.' Immediately three members of the BIS and a corporal cornered him in the left of the church against the confessional, and while two of them held him by the arms the others punched him with a glove covered with metal rings and hit him with an iron bar in the stomach.'

Extract of the testimony given by Father José António Casasola describing the raid on his church Ntra. Sra. del Reposa, La Corza, Sevilla on 1 April 1976. Report issued by the Justice and Peace National Commission, June 1976.

'We ask you to pray for the soul of the worker António González Ramos, who died in Santa Cruz de Tenerife after having been beaten all over his body for 45 minutes by the chief of the *Brigada Politica-Social* (BPS). Receive him into your kingdom and forgive him his sins in consideration of his sufferings.

'We ask you to illuminate the conscience of the policeman, José Matute Fernandez, who is believed to be responsible for the death of António, in order that he may merit your pardon.'

Extract from a prayer contained in a leaflet denouncing torture and appealing for divine help for the torturers and forgiveness for the victims. This leaflet was handed out by Gonzalo Arias Bonet, a pacifist and conscientious objector who had been adopted as a prisoner of conscience by Amnesty International. He and three other conscientious objectors were arrested on the streets on 27 June 1976 in San Sebastian while carrying out a peaceful protest.

'While asking me questions to which I said I knew nothing, they continued submerging my head in that filthy liquid and I felt more and more asphyxiated. Two others beat me on the back until I felt my stomach was going to burst, and another tickled me on the soles of my feet. When they took my head out of the water all I did was to vomit up everything I had swallowed. They continued submerging me in the filth. 'We'll leave you as we did Amparito (María Amparo Arangoa)', they told me.'

Testimony of Itziar Izaguirre Goya, a 16-year-old girl arrested on 9 May 1976 and tortured at the *Guardia Civil* barracks in San Sebastián, Guipuzcoa.

Published 1976

● **DECLARATION OF STOCKHOLM**
11 December 1977

The Stockholm Conference on the Abolition of the Death Penalty, composed of more than 200 delegates and participants from Africa, Asia, Europe, the Middle East, North and South America and the Caribbean region,
recalls that:
– The death penalty is the ultimate cruel, inhuman and degrading punishment and violates the right to life.
considers that:
– The death penalty is frequently used as an instrument of repression against opposition, racial, ethnic, religious and underprivileged groups,
– Execution is an act of violence, and violence tends to provoke violence,
– The imposition and infliction of the death penalty is brutalizing to all who are involved in the process,
– The death penalty has never been shown to have a special deterrent effect,
– The death penalty is increasingly taking the form of unexplained disappearances, extra-judicial executions and political murders,
– Execution is irrevocable and can be inflicted on the innocent.
affirms that:
– It is the duty of the state to protect the life of all persons within its jurisdiction without exception,
– Executions for the purposes of political coercion, whether by government agencies or others, are equally unacceptable,
– Abolition of the death penalty is imperative for the achievement of declared international standards.
declares:
– Its total and unconditional opposition to the death penalty,
– Its condemnation of all executions, in whatever form, committed or condoned by governments,
– Its commitment to work for the universal abolition of the death penalty.
calls upon:
– Non-governmental organizations, both national and international, to work collectively and individually to provide public information materials directed towards the abolition of the death penalty,
– All governments to bring about the immediate and total abolition of the death penalty,
– The United Nations unambiguously to declare that the death penalty is contrary to international law.

AGAINST THE DEATH PENALTY

Since its early days the movement has opposed all forms of cruel, inhuman and degrading treatment inflicted on prisoners. Several of the earliest Amnesty International missions were sent to countries where political prisoners faced imminent execution. Today, total opposition to torture and the death penalty is a central part of the organization's global human rights work. In 1977 Amnesty International held a conference on the abolition of the death penalty from which emerged the declaration opposite. In September 1979 it published a 206-page report on the use of the death penalty throughout the world – reproduced here is a Newsletter article presenting highlights from the report.

Every execution, whether it takes place on the gallows or in the street, whether it results from a decision taken publicly by a court or clandestinely by conspirators, is an irreversible and totally unacceptable abuse of power. Each killing, whether by the State or by its enemies, is shameful and senseless.

As a means of promoting a political cause or as a means of repressing political opposition, the use of the death penalty is abhorrent. It degrades the entire political process in the community of nations.

As a means of punishing individuals found guilty of serious crimes, the use of the death penalty constitutes an act of irreversible and extreme revenge carried out by the State. Decided upon according to fallible processes of law by fallible human beings, it can be – and actually has been – inflicted upon people innocent of any offence.

As a means of deterring individuals from crime, the use of the death penalty has nowhere been shown to have a special deterrent effect.

As a judicial punishment the death penalty is unequal, and unjust. Historically the principal victims have almost everywhere been the poor and members of minorities and oppressed groups within the population.

The cruelty of the punishment is evident.

The methods by which executions are carried out can involve physical torture. Hanging, electrocution, the gas chamber and the firing squad may not kill instantaneously.

Both hanging and garotting, which are meant to cause death at once by breaking the neck, may instead kill by strangulation.

Electrocution has on occasion caused extensive burns and needed more than one application of electric current to kill the victim.

In many instances executions and killings take place secretly or in countries closed to observers. The full count of victims – especially of those killed for political reasons – is therefore likely to be higher than that presented in the Amnesty International report.

Mass killings and 'disappearances' are alleged in the report to have taken place in Argentina (up to 15,000 reported missing), Equatorial Guinea (an estimated one out of every 500 citizens killed under the Macias Nguema government, most without charge or trial), Ethiopia (up to 30,000 killings reported), Guatemala (up to 20,000 killings reported), Kampuchea (at least 200,000 people reported killed under the Pol Pot government, possibly far more), Uganda (between 50,000 and 300,000 reported killed under the Idi Amin government).

Together with such 'extrajudicial' killings, executions carried out after court sentencing are now taking place almost every day in countries around the world.

In those nations where the judicial death penalty is in force for political crimes, the offences for which it may be imposed are frequently defined in such a way that virtually any activity inconsistent with government policy becomes a capital offence.

In a variety of countries large numbers of executions

have followed changes of government or acts of political violence during the years covered by the Amnesty International report.

All African countries now provide for the use of the death penalty, although the frequency with which it is imposed and inflicted varies considerably from country to country. It is used to punish a wide variety of offences. It is commonly imposed for violent offences such as murder or rape but, according to the social and political circumstances prevailing in a particular country, it may be introduced for certain 'economic crimes', such as hoarding grain or consumer goods, embezzlement, fraud, and illegal currency dealings.

One of the most disturbing features of the use of the death penalty in Africa is the frequency with which people charged with political offences are tried and executed after the most summary of judicial hearings. In a number of African countries, particularly those under military regimes, summary executions have followed periods of national crisis. Countries where such executions have taken place include Nigeria, the Sudan and Ethiopia (and, in 1979, Ghana).

Legal provision for the death penalty exists in every Asian country. In several countries it has been used against political dissenters who have been executed either for explicit political offences or for criminal acts arising from their political beliefs. In several cases known to Amnesty International, political offenders have been executed in the People's Republic of China immediately after sentencing.

Several Asian countries, including Singapore, Malaysia, Indonesia, Burma, Taiwan, and the Philippines, have passed laws providing the death penalty for a variety of drug offences.

A few countries impose the death penalty for economic offences; these include the People's Republic of China and Indonesia (hoarding).

In each of the countries of Europe (with the possible exception of Albania) which retains the death penalty, it may be passed and carried out only on a person convicted of an offence punishable in law by the death penalty. Several reports from Albania allege that summary executions are still widespread but it is difficult to verify these reports.

In recent years, states such as the USSR, Romania, Bulgaria, Albania, Turkey and Greece, have passed death sentences for offences not resulting in death – such as theft or acts of political violence. Within the Council of Europe, however, there have been significant trends towards complete abolition of the death penalty.

During the past 10 years the death penalty has been completely abolished in Denmark, Finland, Luxembourg, Norway, Portugal, Sweden and abolished for peace time offences in Malta, Spain and Switzerland. To Amnesty International's knowledge the death penalty has not been re-introduced in any country of Western Europe except Belgium where the number of offences punishable by death has been increased. The practice of executions in Western Europe shows a similar downward trend and is now limited to only three countries: France, Greece and Turkey.

Many Latin American countries abolished the death penalty in the 19th or early 20th century. Recently, however, there has been a tendency towards re-introduction of the death penalty in times of political upheaval, particularly following a military coup.

Extrajudicial executions

The death penalty in Latin America cannot be seen only in terms of sentences which are judicially imposed. Paramilitary groups, the existence of which are condoned or actively supported by the authorities, as well as units of official security forces, carry out murders of petty criminals and political activists in a number of Latin American countries.

Large numbers of people – many of them active in opposition political groups – are made to 'disappear' as a result of illegal arrests and detentions conducted by paramilitary groups or members of security forces acting outside the framework of the law but with apparent consent

▲ *Execution by firing-squad in Guatemala.*

▲ *In an ingenious move, two Death Row inmates in Texas, USA, play a game of checkers on a board made of card and held by string. The prisoners can see the board but not each other.*

of the responsible authorities. Such victims are believed to have been either kept for years in secret camps or killed.

In North America, the death penalty for acts of murder, treason and piracy was abolished in Canada in July 1976. However, a number of capital offences remain under the National Defence Act in time of war.

In the United States of America, there is a trend towards re-introduction of the death penalty. Thirty-five of the 50 US states had laws providing for the death penalty as of 1 May 1979. The first involuntary execution in 12 years in the USA took place on 25 May 1979 (July *Newsletter*).

All countries in the English-speaking Caribbean have a mandatory death sentence for murder. In addition, some have a mandatory death sentence for treason, mutiny or for assisting the enemy.

None of the countries of the Middle East has abolished the death penalty. In almost all of them there is legislation providing for the death penalty for certain categories of murder and specific offences against the internal and external security of the State, such as treason,

Three condemned prisoners in Lagos, Nigeria, receive the last rites before their execution.

espionage, plotting to overthrow the government and political acts of sabotage. Executions of people convicted of political offences are known to have taken place in Iran, Iraq, Libya, Syria and South Yemen. By the middle of 1979 more than 160 people had gone before firing squads in Iran following the February revolution.

In some countries in the region, drug smuggling also is a capital offence, while in others, offences are considered to be crimes against the State and are punishable by death.

A 'special case' is sometimes made for the retention of the death penalty as a justifiable punishment for and possible deterrent to acts of terrorism or political violence.

Amnesty International is aware of no evidence that the use of the death penalty has deterred would-be terrorists. Psychiatrists who have conducted studies on the question of hijacking recommend strongly that the death penalty not be exacted in such cases precisely because it makes the crime appear more spectacular and draws greater attention to the perpetrators.

Amnesty International deplores kidnapping, torture and murder for political motives whether such acts are committed by government or opposition groups. Similarly, Amnesty International defends the right of all individuals to stand trial according to internationally-recognized norms and be protected from torture and execution. These human rights standards apply to all people, including those accused or convicted of politically-motivated crimes.

Political violence

The conflicts which have led to the eruption of political violence, now and in the past, have not been and cannot be resolved by the execution of individual prisoners. Nor, as a matter of principle, should the horror of the crimes committed be used to justify a resort to ill-treatment and extreme punishment.

Amnesty International believes that humane standards for the treatment of prisoners must be respected by all governments, political movements and citizens throughout the world.

The historical record is clear: the value of human life is progressively lessened once a state, even in attempting to defend itself and its citizens, resorts to cruel, inhuman or degrading methods.

Amnesty International rejects the view that the cruel treatment of prisoners, of which the death penalty is an extreme case, can be justified as a fitting response to violent and repugnant crimes. Even less is there justification for the argument that there are special circumstances under which prisoners may be subjected to cruel treatment, including the taking of life, because of their beliefs or their participation in political movements.

It is not only contradictory, but a threat to humane values, for any society to proclaim that the taking of life is the most intolerable of crimes and, at the same time, to countenance any form of execution carried out as an act of retribution in the name of society itself.

AI Newsletter October 1979

GREEK TORTURERS ON TRIAL

'"We are a poor but decent family ...", said his father, a farmer, "and now I see him in the dock as a torturer. I want to ask the court to examine how a boy who everyone said was a 'diamond' became a torturer. Who morally destroyed my family and my home?"

'So spoke the father of one of the soldiers among the 32 Greek officers and soldiers who faced trial in August 1975 before the Athens Permanent Court Martial on charges of torture carried out during the seven years of dictatorship under the Junta of Colonels from 1967 to 1974.

'Amnesty International presents a detailed analysis of this historic trial, one of the few contemporary examples of the possibility of submitting accused torturers to due process of law.

'The trial was important not only as proof that torture occurred in Greece on a systematic basis under the Colonels' rule but also, from the the point of view of all those working towards the ultimate abolition of torture in all countries, it offers a rare and disturbing insight into part of the inner clockwork of a torture state.'

This is the back cover text of 'Torture in Greece, The First Torturers Trial'. The following extracts explain the context of the trial and describe the pattern of torture that emerged.

At the time of the April 1967 military coup in Greece, the number of political prisoners in Greek prisons was relatively small. Several of these people were long-term prisoners from the days of the Civil War (1946-49), and early in 1967 there was reason to believe that these and other prisoners sentenced under long-standing emergency legislation would be released before the expiry of their sentences. The coup changed this situation drastically, and within a few months there were about 6,000 people held in deportation camps on the Greek islands. During the next half-year this figure dropped considerably, but in late January 1968 there were still 2,777 deportees held without trial in the island detention centres on Yaros and Leros as well as an unknown number of detainees in police stations and prisons throughout the country.

Among these deportees and prisoners were some who were old and infirm, having been arrested on the basis of security files prepared during the Civil War 20 years earlier. Many deportees remained in the island detention camps solely because they refused to sign a 'Declaration of Loyalty' to the government. This declaration required the renunciation of any connection with the Communist Party of Greece (KKE) or 'its variously named organisations' and the acknowledgement that, among other things, such activities sought 'the mutilation and enslavement of the country to the Slavo-Communist camp and the removal of the Greek people from Helleno-Christian ideals'.[1]

From the first day of the Junta's rule, torture was an integral part of the state machinery for suppressing opposition. It should be stressed, however, that during the seven years of dictatorship it was used for different purposes at different periods. During the period 1967-71 the purposes of torture were to extract information about resistance activities and to deter the population from political activity. Torture was conducted by trained officers of middle rank from the gendarmerie, the civilian security police (*Asfaleia*), the navy, and the military police (ESA). The policy was to avoid leaving marks, or at least not to allow detainees any contact with the outside until such marks had disappeared. During the period 1971-74, however, the purpose of torture increasingly became intimidation and terrorisation, with the specific aim of destroying the student movement. To a large extent torture was conducted by military police conscripts who were encouraged by their officers to leave marks on the victims. During these years the military police would arrest and detain people almost at random, subject them to ill-treatment and torture and often release them after a relatively short period of time, without ever having brought formal charges against them.

Although torture was used from the beginning of the Junta's rule in April 1967, it was not until November 1967 that reliable reports began to reach the world outside Greece. In response Amnesty International dispatched American lawyer James Becket and British lawyer Anthony Marreco to Greece in late December 1967 to investigate the torture allegations as well as to determine the extent and implementation of a much publicised Christmas amnesty for political prisoners. The beneficence of the amnesty proved almost entirely illusory, and the situation regarding torture confirmed Amnesty International's worst fears. Necessarily restricting themselves to Athens alone, the Amnesty International delegates interviewed 16 released victims of torture and obtained evidence about 32 other cases. Twenty-two methods of torture were documented, including sexual abuse, psychological pressure, electric shock and, most commonly, *falanga* (beating on the soles of the feet), which in almost every case was the initial form of torture. Major Theodoros Theofiloyannakos, a defendant at the first ESA trial in 1975, which is the specific subject of this report, was named as a torturer in the January 1968 Amnesty International report. The report of a second Amnesty International mission, published in April 1968, confirmed the findings of the first.

The two Amnesty International mission reports affected the deliberations concerning the status of Greece within the Council of Europe. The governments of Sweden, Denmark and the Netherlands had already filed applications in September 1967 to the European Commission of Human Rights, charging the Greek regime with violating eight articles of the European Human Rights Convention. This application did not include Article 3, the one prohibiting torture, but after the 1968 Amnesty International reports and other evidence, the sponsors amended their application to include Article 3. A sub-commission then heard the evidence of witnesses, and unlike the Amnesty International mission, the sub-commission was able to gather evidence concerning the police stations outside the capital. This process and the writing of their well-documented, four-volume report lasted until the middle of 1969. In December of that year, after intense diplomatic negotiations and in the face of certain expulsion from the Council of Europe, the Greek government withdrew in order to avoid diplomatic defeat. Subsequent publication of the Commission's report left no doubt that torture and ill-treatment were regular and 'officially tolerated' activities inside the Junta's police stations in Athens and throughout the country,[2] but torture continued as usual despite these limited diplomatic efforts.

The severity of Greek torture is further borne out in the specific court-martial that is the subject of this report. As the first of the so-called 'torture trials' in Greece, it deserves attention. In addition, this trial conformed to high legal standards, and after both the prosecution and the defence had been given ample time to argue their cases, the tribunal was able to sort out individual responsibility and to apportion blame for certain of the acts of torture during the Junta years. Although the trial did not pursue some of the broader questions concerning responsibility for torture, Amnesty International welcomes the precedent of this trial and commends the military court prosecutor for ordering an investigation and prosecution of the accused torturers.

Unfortunately, the standards of this first trial were not sustained in later trials. As a consequence, this first trial of some military police torturers stands as a better precedent in itself than the whole of the procedure by which some and not other torturers have been brought to trial. Therefore, we have decided to trace the background, development and findings of the first torture trial and to assess its significance and value as a judicial precedent for bringing to justice the violent excesses of oppressive regimes.

The trial began on 7 August 1975, when 14 officers and 18 soldiers of non-commissioned rank were brought before the Athens Permanent Court Martial on charges arising from torture during interrogation. Although all Greek Constitutions since the first in 1822 (including those of 1968 and 1973 promulgated by the Junta) contain general prohibitions against torture, there is no specific prohibition in the Greek Penal Code, which would have to provide the precise implementing law. Therefore, only indirect charges could be preferred against the 32 ESA defendants. These charges were *repeated abuse of authority, violence against a superior officer, unconstitutional detention, ordinary and serious physical injury, repeated insults to a superior,* and *recurrent moral responsibility for ordinary or serious physical injury.* The defendants faced various permutations of these charges, but the only defendant to plead guilty to all charges against him was Sergeant Michail Petrou, a former jailor at the Athens headquarters of ESA who had returned from abroad to face the charges.

The court-martial was conducted according to Military Penal Procedure, which is a combination of the Penal Code and the Military Penal Code. Evidence called on behalf of the prosecution fell into five distinct categories: first, the evidence of retired officers as to their arrest and treatment from 1969 onwards; second, the evidence of students arrested after the Law School demonstrations in early 1973; third, the evidence of naval officers arrested after the unsuccessful naval mutiny in May 1973; fourth, the evidence of students and others arrested after the Athens Polytechnic events in November 1973; finally, the evidence of former ESA soldiers who described the processes of dehumanisation to which they had been subjected.

Like subsequent torture trials, the prosecution of these 32 ESA defendants was prompted by the cumulative pressure of private civil suits brought by several former prisoners against their torturers in the absence of public prosecutions. The prosecutor of the military court ordered a preliminary investigation which was facilitated by a deposition from Sergeant Petrou. Statements were taken before a military examining magistrate, and several of the accused were remanded in custody. Brigadier Digenopoulos was appointed chairman of the court-martial, with the remainder of the tribunal consisting of three colonels from the army legal branch and two active service officers. The prosecutor, Major Michail Zouvelos, was a member of the army legal service. The defendants were represented by counsel; many of the defendants, however, carried out some cross-examination themselves.

The defendants were all members of the Junta's

military police (ESA, *Elliniki Stratiotiki Astynomia*) who had served in the Special Interrogation Section in Athens (EAT, *Eidikon Anakritikon Tmima*),[3] at its training centre (KESA, *Kentron Ekpaidevseos Stratiotikis Astynomias*), at its Piraeus section or at the military prison in Boyati. Toward the end of 1968 ESA was endowed with nearly absolute powers of arrest, detention and interrogation. The object of its attention was anyone suspected of being an opponent or potential opponent of the regime – whether civilian or military personnel – in short, anyone, whether communist or conservative democrat, who did not completely support the dictatorship. 'Some of the defendants,' said the prosecutor in his closing speech at the end of the trial, 'wanted to present EAT/ESA not as a place of torture but as a national reformatory. Modestly reserving to themselves infallibility of judgement, they have tried to follow in the footsteps of the Holy Inquisition.'

Many of the more senior intelligence officers were described in the trial as being guided by a fanatical anti-communism which they worked hard to instil in their command. Indeed, it was to be the defence of almost all the soldier defendants that they were merely obeying orders and were acting in a situation of compulsion and duress.

[1] The text of this declaration was analogous to the forced recantations under torture that were extorted 30 years before, during the near-fascist dictatorship of Ioannis Metaxas, 1936–41. It is important to note that although torture was used in Greece before the Junta (specifically, during the Metaxas dictatorship, in the island concentration camps during the 1946–49 Civil War, and within the air force in a particular incident in the early 1950s), it was never an endemic part of Greek political life, as some apologists for the Junta have argued.

[2] Council of Europe, European Commission of Human Rights, *The Greek Case: Report of the Commission*, 1969.

[3] EAT literally translated is the 'Special Interrogation Section'. However, in colloquial usage EAT meant the place where the special unit operated, namely, ESA's Athens headquarters.

The pattern of torture

Arrests appear to have been carried out usually at night, without a warrant, by a car-load of ESA men under the command of an officer from the Prosecution Section and were often accompanied by a beating. On arrival at headquarters, the detainee would usually be taken to the commanding officer and verbally threatened with imminent and severe violence. In order to intimidate him, he might be shut into a guardroom where there were clubs, whips and canes hanging on the wall. He would soon be locked in a cell and told to write a statement of confession which would then be taken by the jailor to the interrogator who was responsible and then finally passed on to the commanding officer. The precise interrogation technique would be decided upon usually in conference between the commanding officer and the interrogator. The appropriate instructions were then issued to the duty officer, the jailor and the guards.

Threats of violence would be repeated to the new prisoner. He would be told in detail how powerless was his position and what was about to happen to both himself and his family. 'You're in our hands. This is ESA. You will vomit blood...', Theofiloyannakos told the taxi driver Dimitrios Kotsakis. 'You know', Ioannidis told Wing-Commander Minis, 'it is possible that some parts of your body might be destroyed.' '... Either you won't come out or you will leave a cripple,' Michail Sabatakakis, a dentistry student, was informed. 'Theofiloyannakos said he would arrest my wife and the whole lot. He said he would draw my teeth one by one....' said General Pantelis Kalamakis, the former head of the National Security Service. 'I remained worried for a fortnight,' he continued, 'that they had arrested my brother-in-law who had no connection with the case. Then Hajizisis promised to release him and play-acted in front of me, pretending to telephone.... It was a sad spectacle for a Greek officer....'

According to the testimony, shortly after the initial threats, guards – normally in a group – would enter the cell and beat the prisoners with either clubs or their fists; this type of beating was known as a 'tea-party'. There were four large cells which were used for beatings. At EAT/ESA there were two types of blows, Sergeant Petrou explained in evidence:

'"General" blows were those administered when prisoners were being taken to the punishment block. "Special" blows were administered during the ordeal. At this time there would always be two guards in the cell. The blows were administered on the buttocks and the shanks so that blood should start to collect in the lower extremities and cause pain. The blows on the buttocks were with clubs, alternatively vertical and horizontal. These caused a particular type of swelling....'

At the outset of the ESA torture routine, prisoners would be deprived of both food and drink. They would be told to remain standing in the corner of their cell, sometimes on one foot but usually at attention. This ordeal would last several days. It would often be interspersed with more beatings – standings and beatings together known as a 'tea party with toast'. If the prisoner fell down, he would be made to resume his standing position. Sometimes prisoners would be taken to the training centre, KESA, where the escorting guards would pass on to a non-commissioned officer, Nikolaos Kainich, the orders from headquarters as to who was to receive further beatings.

'They wanted to give us the sensation that we were forgotten,' said Mrs Virginia Tsouderou, a member of the present Greek Parliament who had been arrested in March 1973, 'and that there was no-one to care for us.... Antonopoulos hinted to me that ... all my friends had been arrested ... the Security had taken my children's identity cards [the same day] and in this way I would not know what had happened to them.'

After standing upright for a few days and being deprived of refreshment, the victim would normally begin to experience hallucinations. Ioannis Koronaios, a United States citizen who was arrested on 3 October 1970, said: 'I began to see that I had two faces, one in front and one behind. I was delirious. I began to insult the government and everyone there.... Then I tried to separate my soul from my body so that I could leave my body to be tortured.'

Michail Vardanis, a lawyer who was arrested in June

1973, had the following experience:

'On the walls I saw sad family faces. I saw the wall open and a gap for possible escape. I began to feel for the gap, to find the right point. Then my fingers touched the wall and I was disappointed.... The same evening, I saw a refrigerator on the wall. I said to the guard, "Why don't you open it and give me a Coca Cola?" My mouth was parched....'

Eventually, the standing ordeal would end, and the prisoner would receive some food and drink. Sometimes, it was reported, the water might contain soap, or, to increase the thirst, the food might be heavily laced with salt. Some former prisoners suspect that they were fed hallucinatory drugs.

At intervals, a prisoner might receive a visit from the former army doctor at ESA, Dr Dimitrios Kofas, also a defendant at the trial. He would advise when their condition made it dangerous for the ordeal to continue. He was said to have acted as the 'traffic controller' for torture, although he disputed the degree of control that he was alleged to have had. But Michail Vardanis gave an example in evidence of such 'traffic control': '...a man arrived who was introduced to me as Dr Kofas. He took my pulse and asked Petrou how many days I had been there. When Petrou told him it was the fourth day, he said: "All right". He then left and I continued having to stand upright.'

Many witnesses claimed that Dr Kofas promised to return 'in a minute' or 'tomorrow' with medication, but in fact did not re-appear for several days or even weeks. To one prisoner who was experiencing symptoms of heart failure, he sent aspirin after four days. When Squadron-Leader Stapas began to suffer from blood in his urine, Dr Kofas recommended orange juice and rest. Because he prescribed orange juice as though it were the panacea for many serious ailments and injuries, he became known among prisoners as 'the orange juice doctor'.

For about the first 20 days of the routine, prisoners would not be permitted to wash, change clothes or smoke. Some even had to relieve themselves in their cells during the standing ordeal. In such an atmosphere, the smallest kindess was remembered by the prisoners with disproportionate gratitude. Foivos Koutsikas, for example, a lawyer who was arrested in November 1970, recalled the following experience during his evidence:

'At 11 pm they took me back to the cell.... a soldier came to the window, very disturbed, almost in tears, and asked me anxiously: 'Are you still holding out, Sir?' I was overwrought. I told him I could hold out for once more but that the third time I would succumb. I will always remember the behaviour of this soldier. I told him to come and see me when we were both free.... The previous evening a soldier came, very scared, and gave me a piece of cake.... Another time, ... a soldier brought me a packet of cigarettes and a box of matches.'

'What have we come to?' the prosecutor subsequently asked the court-martial. 'A light for a cigarette is regarded as a benefaction.' If a guard attempted to help a prisoner, he too would be punished. One guard, Dionysios Charalambopoulos, who was a prosecution witness, was locked in a cell and beaten by Major Spanos with a club for helping several arrested students; he was subsequently transferred as a punitive measure to the 513th Infantry Battalion at Komotini. Another guard, one Papandreopoulos, dis-

◀ *Major Theodore Theophyloyannakos who commanded the Military Police Interrogation Centre (ESA) where political prisoners in Greece were systematically tortured.*

▼ *Yiaros island prison, 62 miles from Athens, which housed many political prisoners during the rule of the Greek military junta.*

appeared after allegedly helping a prisoner.

One effect of the torture routine on the victims, according to a number of prosecution witnesses, was their desire to commit suicide. Admiral Konstantinos Engolfopoulos, a former commander-in-chief of the Navy who was in compulsory retirement at the time of his arrest in May 1973, said: 'I decided to commit suicide. I tried to find a way. I was desperate. I had seen an electric razor in a dirty lavatory we used. I asked to go to the lavatory. I took the razor but there was no blade. In that way they were well organised. Then I looked for a pin to tear my veins but I failed.' Commander Iliopoulos, who was arrested in May 1973 and who was handed over to ESA by Naval HQ, confessed that he was 'under great psychological strain. I was an object and not a person. I thought of suicide but could find nothing in my cell to do it with.' Lieutenant-General Nikolaos Papanikolaou, arrested in June 1969, had been even more desperate:

'I had hallucinations from thirst and standing upright. At one moment my cell was left open. I tried to escape. I ran in the direction of the US Embassy, but they caught up with me. Then they beat me for two hours.... I woke up in a cell and my feet were swollen. Blood and liquid were running from my wounds and I had a terrible pain in my chest. I wanted to kill myself.... Sometimes I drank my own urine.... On 3 September I suffered a crisis and tried to kill myself.'

Ioannis Sergopoulos, a law student who had been arrested in May 1973 and taken to KESA, made a similar decision about suicide but changed his mind: 'Kainich beat me daily. Before beating me, he would sadistically show me the size of his fist and a monogrammed ring which he wore and which made his blows much more painful. I began to cough up blood.... Kainich also used me for training the ESA men, to show them how to beat. I was the sandbag and he was the boxer.... One morning he threw me onto a pile of bricks and began to hit me with them and kick me, preferably in the genitals. That day I decided to kill myself. I could stand no more and I didn't know how much further things might go.... The worst torture at KESA was waiting to be tortured.... The beating began at 9 am and I knew they would reach my cell at midday.... As my turn approached, I wished I could have been in the first cell to have got it over. This was a daily routine.... I was obsessed with the idea of suicide. But I suddenly came to my senses and rejected the idea. I thought my death would only help the dictatorship. I swore an oath: "I am coming out of here alive. I shall live. It is my duty to live."'

Published April 1977

● **TOGETHER AGAIN**

Much of the information Amnesty International receives can be grim and depressing, but there are also heartening moments when a life is saved or a prisoner of conscence is released. Zheng Chaolin was 78 years of age when this picture was taken. First imprisoned in the 1930s under the Chinese nationalists, he was later detained under Chairman Mao in a series of arrests of Trotskyist leaders. He was imprisoned in Shanghai in 1952 and ended up spending 27 years in prison. He was adopted by Amnesty International as a prisoner of conscience.

Little was known about his fate until in May 1979 when, not knowing whether he was alive or dead, Amnesty International launched a special campaign on his behalf. Whether it was by coincidence or not, he and his wife, Wu Jingru, were released the next month. This photo, taken in China, shows the couple together again.

AFRICAN NATIONALISTS INTERNED

Thousands of African nationalists were interned under the illegal government of Ian Smith before Rhodesia gained independence in April 1980 and became Zimbabwe. Amnesty International's concerns were set out in a report issued in 1976 from which the following extracts are taken.

Amnesty International is particularly concerned by the following human rights problems in Rhodesia:

(i) the use of preventive detention, imposed without charge or trial for periods of indefinite duration. Those detained include nationalist leaders belonging to banned political parties and rank and file members of political organizations, like the African National Council, which have not yet been proscribed;

(ii) the physical restriction of released prisoners and political detainees;

(iii) the holding of trials and detention review tribunals *in camera*;

(iv) the use of the death penalty, in some cases on a mandatory basis, for a wide range of offences, and the execution, in secret, of condemned prisoners;

(v) the torture of political prisoners;

(vi) the government's refusal to establish an independent inquiry into allegations of atrocities committed by the Rhodesian security forces;

(vii) the forced settlement of large numbers of rural Africans in so-called 'protected villages' as part of the government's counter-insurgency policy...

Since 1965 the United Kingdom has theoretically retained sole power to legislate for Rhodesia and all legislative enactments, executive actions and judicial procedures of the Rhodesian Front government have been regarded internationally as of no effect. However, in practice, the British government has been unable to exercise its legitimate authority.

The constitutional legality of the Rhodesian regime has also been tested in the courts. In 1968, the highest court of appeal for Rhodesian questions, the Judicial Committee of the Privy Council in London, ruled that the detention order served on Daniel Madzimbamuto, a political prisoner, in November 1965 was invalid since it had been issued by a 'rebel' administration. The Privy Council ordered Mr Madzimbamuto's immediate release.

This appeal was widely regarded outside Rhodesia as a test case to determine the illegality of the Rhodesian Front government, but despite initial hopes that the ruling would have effect in Salisbury, it was rejected by both judiciary and administration and Mr Madzimbamuto remained in detention. The Rhodesian government's right to implement the death penalty has been challenged internationally on similar legal grounds, and similarly upheld in Rhodesia.

Since UDI [Unilateral Declaration of Independence], the government has remained intransigent in the face of increasing pressures for African majority rule. Attempts at a constitutional settlement were made in direct negotiations between the British and Rhodesian governments in 1966, 1968 and 1971-72, and between the Rhodesian government and Rhodesia's African nationalist leaders on two occasions in 1974. These negotiations broke down because of the regime's unwillingness to make major concessions to African aspirations...

Almost without exception, Rhodesia's political prisoners are Africans who actively support the nationalist struggle for majority rule on the basis of universal adult suffrage. They may differ as to political affiliation or strategy, but they are united by their desire to see an end to the social, economic and political domination of Rhodesia by the white minority population. Until recently, almost all African nationalist leaders were in detention in Rhodesia or were political exiles abroad. Both Joshua Nkomo, the former ZAPU [Zimbabwe African Peoples' Union] leader, and Reverend Ndabaningi Sithole, the former ZANU [Zimbabwe African National Union] leader, were detained almost continuously from the time that their political parties were banned in the early 1960s until December 1974.

Since the development of African nationalism as a mass movement in the 1950s, successive governments have used political imprisonment and detention as a means of controlling African political opposition. When the various African political organizations were proscribed in turn, usually within a short time of their formation, their leaders were restricted, detained or driven into exile...

Prison conditions

Under the discriminatory system operated by the Rhodesian prison authorities, a prisoner is graded upon entry into prison according to the authorities' estimation of his or her standard of living. The grades stipulate the kind of food, clothing and cell equipment to be supplied. In practice Europeans are normally placed on scale I and receive the best treatment, Asians and Coloureds (people of mixed race) are put on scale II, and Africans on scale III, although better educated or more prosperous Africans may be placed on scale II.

Most political prisoners, including untried detainees, are classified on scale III. As such, they receive a diet consisting largely of *sadza*, a maize-meal porridge, but without items like bread and sugar which form a normal part of the diet of urban Africans. They wear shorts and singlets, but are barefoot. They are only given sisal sleeping mats and three or four blankets as bedding.

Although graded in the same way as convicted prisoners, political detainees have certain privileges not shared by other prisoners. They are allowed more frequent visits and mail, they do not have to work while in prison and they may purchase additional foodstuffs to supplement their prison diet with money sent to them from outside. Detainees are normally kept separate from convicted prisoners.

Despite these advantages, political detainees have complained many times about the harsh treatment they receive. In August 1972, 34 detainees at Salisbury Remand Prison smuggled out a letter to Amnesty International and the International Committee of the Red Cross detailing instances of bad treatment. Similarly detainees complained that the deaths in detention of Leopold Takawira in June 1970 and Kenneth Chisango in January 1974 were directly attributable to poor conditions and inadequate medical attention. The Rhodesian authorities deny these claims.

Torture allegations

There have been consistent allegations of torture since the introduction of the Law and Order (Maintenance) Act in 1960, but recent reports indicate that it is now employed almost as routine practice by both police and security forces. It is particularly acute in northeast Rhodesia where nationalist guerrillas are active. Many hundreds of Africans in that area are reported to have been detained for short periods by the security forces and subjected to interrogation and torture on the assumption that they possess information about guerrilla activities.

Various methods of torture are allegedly used. They include beating on the body with fists and sticks, beating on the soles of the feet with sticks, and the application of electric shocks by means of electrodes or cattle goads. In addition torture victims have been threatened with castration or immersed head first in barrels of water until unconscious.

Since 1974, church leaders and African parliamentarians have called repeatedly for the establishment of an independent inquiry into allegations of torture and atrocities committed by the security forces. All such calls have been rejected by the Minister for Law and Order on the grounds that any inquiry would undermine the morale of the armed forces. The minister has also stated that several allegations investigated by his department were found to be false. Nevertheless, when several torture victims brought actions for damages in the High Court in 1975, the government introduced the Indemnity and Compensation Act. This act effectively indemnifies members of the security forces against prosecution for any actions carried out since 1 December 1972 while on active service in the war zone. The act also gave the minister authority to terminate actions for damages which were before the High Court – an authority that the minister exercised immediately to forestall several outstanding suits. In effect, the Indemnity and Compensation Act gives the security forces absolute discretion as to the methods they employ against suspected guerrillas even if such methods include killings among the civilian population. Consequently no inquiry has been held into reported civilian killings at Kandeya Tribal Trust Land in the Mount Darwin area on 12 June 1975.

Capital punishment

The death penalty is very widely used not only for criminal offences such as murder or rape, but also for those convicted of certain political offences under the Law and Order (Maintenance) Act. This act, which has been amended many times since 1965 so as to provide for increasingly severe sentences, created a number of offences which *may* incur a capital sentence and also specified offences which carry a *mandatory* death penalty. Possession of arms of war, commission of acts of terrorism or harbouring of guerrillas fall within the former category, in

A Rhodesian trooper holds a gun in front of a line of prisoners as they are interrogated near Kikidoo, Rhodesia, September 1977. The prisoners were forced to hold their position in the heat of the midday sun while the trooper repeatedly clicked his pistol in their faces.

which a judge may exercise discretion in deciding whether to impose the death penalty. The latter category includes offences involving arson, the use of explosives or the recruitment of guerrillas. In these cases the judges have no discretion in sentencing and must impose the death penalty whatever the particular circumstances. Only pregnant women and children under 16 years of age are excluded from execution while youths aged between 16 and 19 may either be executed or sentenced to life imprisonment.

Since 1965 more than 60 people are believed to have been hanged. The first executions were carried out in 1968 amidst a storm of international protest, and immediately led the United Nations to impose comprehensive and mandatory economic sanctions against Rhodesia. Before any executions took place the British government had reiterated the view that the Rhodesian Front regime could not lawfully carry out executions. Queen Elizabeth II, whose position as Rhodesian head of state had not at that time been challenged, exercised the royal prerogative of mercy to commute the sentences of the first three men due to be executed. Nevertheless, the three men were hanged on 6 March 1968 after the Rhodesian Chief Justice ruled that the Rhodesian Front regime had *de facto* authority to carry out executions.

Published March 1976

LONG-TERM PRISONERS IN CUBA

In March 1978 a memorandum was sent to the Cuban Government following a visit by members of Amnesty International. The memorandum outlined issues of continuing concern, which included the long-term detention of political prisoners as illustrated by the following extract.

We appreciate that the number of political prisoners has decreased very substantially in the course of the 1970s. We nevertheless remain concerned at the number of people who remain in prison, on political charges or for politically motivated offences. It was explained to us in Havana that these persons were detained and sentenced for such offences as sabotage, arson or armed uprising. But it also appears that many were sentenced not for specific acts, but for membership of the numerous political organisations which opposed the Revolutionary Government in the early 1960s. From the information available to us, we understand that members of these political movements did regularly resort to violence and armed sabotage. We do not therefore claim that these people can necessarily be considered Prisoners of Conscience. We are nevertheless concerned by the following issues:

(1) From the information currently available to us, it does seem that certain individuals may have been arrested

One of Cuba's long-term prisoners was Huber Matos pictured (left) before his imprisonment in 1959 and (below) after his release in 1979. He was adopted by Amnesty International as a prisoner of conscience. He had been one of Fidel Castro's top commanders during the Cuban Revolution, but was accused of plotting and of crimes against state security after breaking with Castro politically.

and sentenced to long terms of imprisonment more because of their ideological opposition to the Revolutionary Government than on account of any specific offence. If the Cuban government does not accept this viewpoint, we believe that it should explain the precise charges against these persons, together with the evidence to substantiate these charges.

(2) In the early years of the Revolution, procedures before the Revolutionary Tribunals have been criticised as summary with certain restrictions on the rights of legal consultation and defence: sentences passed by these tribunals were in many cases extremely severe, and were arguably out of proportion to the alleged offence.

We are acutely aware that a substantial number of Cuban prisoners are now among the longest term political prisoners to be found anywhere in the world of today. We were informed by Cuban officials of the reasons against a general amnesty at this time. These included the continuation of externally based acts of terrorism, with particular reference to the sabotage of the *Cubaña* airline in Barbados in October 1976. We deplore these acts of terrorism. Yet we very strongly doubt that there could be any causal connection between an amnesty and the continuation of such terrorist acts.

Leaving aside the question of a general amnesty, we were informed on several occasions by both governmental and judicial officials that in accordance with Law 993 of 1961, and in accordance with the overall principles of the 'Progressive Plan', those prisoners who obey the existing prison regulations and whose conduct is deemed satisfactory may be granted conditional freedom after serving at least one quarter of their sentences. While noting the release of several hundred political prisoners from both within and outside the 'Progressive Plan' over the course of the past year, we were concerned to see that there are still 3,000 in prison *within* the 'Progressive Plan', many of them long term prisoners who have served very much more than one quarter of their sentences. We would therefore like to know more of the exact procedures by which conditional release is given or denied to people in this category.

We are also concerned that precise statistics of the number of political prisoners or 'counter-revolutionary offenders' should be readily available. It was stated by numerous officials that numbers have been grossly exaggerated outside Cuba. It was suggested by more than one official that these exaggerations should be rectified, and the true picture presented. But the Cuban government has not, as far as we know, given out precise statistical information concerning the number of prisoners, their sentences and places of detention. The several public references over the past year have only given very general information. In Havana we were informed that the number of 'counter-revolutionary offenders' was slightly in excess of 3000.... We would appreciate it if on our next visit we could be provided with precise statistics on those still in prison.

Published November 1978

● **'SINCE I AM FREE NOW EVERYTHING CAN BE FACED'**

'At last I can write to you from home. I am now a free man!', wrote Sidgi Awad Kaballo, after his release from prison in the Sudan. He had been arrested as a suspected Communist in July 1979 under the National Security Law and was detained without trial in Kober Prison, Khartoum, until he was released in December 1983.

While in prison, he was divorced from his wife. Despite the fact that he faced other personal difficulties, his sense of optimism as he set about rebuilding his life was undiminished – this is shown clearly in the letter he wrote to a member of the Amnesty International group which had campaigned for his release: 'I am now a free man ... and will continue my work on the thesis I began four years ago. ... All my problems will not make me lose hope. I look hopefully to the future. Since I am free now, everything can be faced. Life in a country like ours needs fighting and struggle on different fronts: political and personal ...

'I cannot find words to express my thanks to you in Amnesty International, for your solidarity, your sympathy and your struggle for my release. Without your help, without the feeling that other people in the world are defending our freedom and helping us and our people, life would have been so hard and difficult. Please convey my thanks and best wishes to your friends ...'

HUMAN RIGHTS VIOLATIONS IN UGANDA

While Uganda was ruled by President Idi Amin, from 1971 to 1979, tens of thousands of people were killed and Amnesty International received frequent reports of atrocities being carried out by the security forces. In 1977 it submitted its concerns to the UN Commission on Human Rights and urged that they be studied. The following year it released a report 'Human Rights in Uganda' from which this extract comes.

Amnesty International is extremely concerned about the human rights situation in Uganda. Since the military government of President Idi Amin came to power by coup d'état in 1971, there has developed a consistent pattern of gross human rights violations which is still continuing. Amnesty International's main concerns are as follows:

1. the overthrow of the rule of law;

2. The extensive practice of murder by government security officers, which often reaches massacre proportions;

3. the institutionalized use of torture;

4. the denial of fundamental human rights guaranteed in the Universal Declaration of Human Rights;

5. the regime's constant disregard for the extreme concern expressed by international opinion and international organizations such as the United Nations, which results in the impression that gross human rights violations may be committed with impunity.

These aspects of repression in Uganda are documented here in outline. This statement centres on the human rights issues within the mandate of Amnesty International's statutory concerns, and details of other political, economic and historical events and trends are mentioned only where they are relevant to this purpose. The focus is on events during 1977 and the first part of 1978. Events up to 1977 have been well documented by the International Commission of Jurists and are not generally included here, though some earlier events are briefly mentioned in order to show clearly the structure of human rights violations.

The aim of this report is not simply to deliver another condemnation of one man at the centre of this terrible structure, who has been instrumental in creating and perpetuating it: what Amnesty International considers more important is to describe the whole structure, which involves many other individuals and which penetrates all areas of Ugandan society from the severely diminished urban elite to the poorest rural peasant. The effect of this structure of repression can be said without fear of exaggeration to have transformed the whole society in a short period of time into a ruthless military dictatorship marked by arbitrary arrest, torture, murder, the removal of virtually all fundamental human rights, the terrorization of the population, and the turning of tens of thousands of Ugandans into refugees.

International concern about human rights violations in Uganda has been voiced on many occasions from many different sources. The International Commission of Jurists made important submissions on Uganda to the United Nations Commission on Human Rights in 1974 and 1976. The Commission took no action in 1975 and President Amin announced that he had been exonerated from what he called a 'smear campaign'. He falsely claimed that 'the accusations, inspired by an imperialist conspiracy, were found baseless'.[1] On 25 August 1976 the Sub-Commission on Prevention of Discrimination and Protection of Minorities recommended that the Commission should undertake a thorough study of human rights violations in

Uganda. By 1977 Uganda had secured a seat on this Commission. When the Commission met again in February and March 1977, the Commission decided again to take no action but merely to keep the situation under review. An open statement on human rights violations in Uganda was made by Amnesty International at the commencement of the Commission's session, and there were strong international protests at the atrocities and massacres which were perpetrated by Ugandan security officers at the very time the Commission was in session. In May 1977 Amnesty International made a lengthy communication to the Commission, under its confidential procedures, on human rights in Uganda. In March 1978 the Commission took an undisclosed decision on Uganda, announced by the Chairman, Mr. Keba M'Baye, after considering the case in confidential session.

[1] Uganda Radio, 18 January 1977.

Published May 1978

▶ *Naked under his canvas apron, an alleged 'guerrilla' contemplates his last few minutes before execution in public at Mbale, Uganda. A soldier in President Amin's army stands nearby with the black bag which will be put over his head. 13 February 1973*

▼ *A Tanzanian soldier looks at bodies outside the State Research Bureau in Kampala, Uganda where thousands died during the rule of President Amin from 1971 to 1979.*

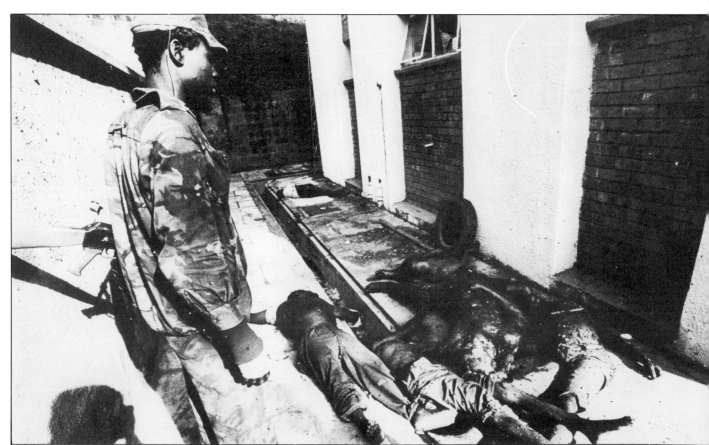

UGANDA: EVIDENCE OF TORTURE

Having overthrown Milton Obote to take power, Idi Amin was himself overthrown in 1979 and after elections the following year Milton Obote became president once again. Human rights abuses continued, however, and Amnesty International continued its appeals to the President to take action to end them. In 1985 a further report 'Uganda: Evidence of Torture', from which this extract comes, received wide international publicity and drew a public response from the Ugandan Government. Shortly afterwards, Milton Obote's government was again overthrown.

From the testimonies of many former detainees Amnesty International has been able to compile a detailed picture of conditions and the use of torture within military barracks. Many reports refer to Makindye barracks in Kampala as the most notorious of these, but conditions in other places of military detention are reported to be similar.

On arrival at Makindye it is reported that detainees are normally taken to a section just inside the main gate known as the 'quarter guard'. One former detainee describes how there were a large number of prisoners in the four cells of the 'quarter guard' and that they had to sleep in squatting positions one behind the other. In or outside the 'quarter guard' new prisoners are usually beaten with iron bars, cable, pieces of wood into which nails have been driven, rifle butts, *pangas* (machetes) or hammers. In some cases prisoners are alleged to have died as a result.

After the 'quarter guard', prisoners are taken to other sections of Makindye. The largest section, which figures in many former detainees' accounts, is known as the 'go-down'. This is a long concrete building with a corrugated iron roof, a former store. It has an iron door and no windows, but a few ventilation holes. The numbers held there reportedly vary but are sometimes more than 100. According to all accounts the turnover of prisoners is rapid.

Prisoners held in the 'go-down' at Makindye barracks are reported to be fed infrequently, perhaps twice a week, and also rarely given water. According to one former prisoner: 'People often begged for your urine because they had gone so long without water.' This claim is repeated by a number of former prisoners. Food, when it is available, consists of poorly cooked *posho* (maize meal porridge), often with maggots in it. Some prisoners are apparently able to bribe guards to let them have food provided by their families.

One woman described to Amnesty International how she was served with food in Muhoti barracks in Fort Portal. She said that prisoners were often given a hot, watery bean stew which was poured into their cupped hands. It was often too hot for them to hold. At the same time *posho* was thrown into the cell. It was impossible to catch both before they landed on the floor, which was covered with dirt and excreta.

Toilet facilities in the 'go-down' at Makindye and in most places of military detention consist of an oil drum or

► *This woman told Amnesty International that she had burns all over her upper body after being strapped to a chair placed beneath a burning car tyre.*

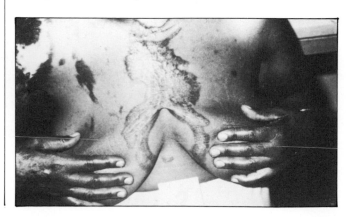

bucket in the room where prisoners are held, which the prisoners can only empty infrequently, often as rarely as once a month. Some former detainees report that the floor of the 'go-down' was covered with water. No bedding is provided.

It is reported that many prisoners die in the 'go-down', either from starvation or as a result of their beatings. Their bodies may not be removed for up to two weeks. Similarly, a detainee who was held for two months in Kireka barracks in 1984 alleges that approximately five people died there each day as a result of starvation or torture.

When dead bodies are removed, this is done by prisoners. One former prisoner has described being told to remove the 'meat and bones'. Prisoners were beaten as they moved corpses.

Other former prisoners report having regularly been taken out at night to load bodies onto lorries or Land Rovers. The bodies are reportedly driven out of the barracks and dumped in mass graves. In 1984 an Australian television crew filmed an open mass grave within a few hundred yards of an army barracks. Interviewed by the television reporter, a Ugandan Government representative said that he did not know who was responsible.

Amnesty International has received reports of mass graves in the Luwero area to the north-west of Kampala. Former Ugandan security personnel, as well as former detainees, allege that they drove lorryloads of bodies from military barracks in Kampala to dump on the edge of forests near the city.

Beatings

For many prisoners, the frequent beatings continue throughout their time in Makindye or other military barracks. In a few instances it is reported that prisoners are not beaten after being transferred from the 'quarter guard', possibly because they are from wealthy families and the soldiers guarding them hope to receive a ransom. There is a section in Makindye referred to by some former detainees as the 'paying wing'. Among those former detainees interviewed by Amnesty International, by far the largest number had bribed their way out of prison.

The victims of beatings appear to be selected at random, for example when food is brought. One former prisoner describes being regularly beaten at the same time each morning and this being described as 'breakfast'. Another gives a similar account, except that in his case it was described as 'coffee'. Sometimes prisoners are reportedly taken out of the cell for interrogation and beaten. It does not appear, however, that the main purpose of this ill-treatment is to gather information since most accounts indicate that the questioning which takes place is cursory. Those interrogated in Nile Mansions or in 'safe houses' are more likely to be thoroughly interrogated, though the methods of torture reportedly differ little.

On a number of occasions, prisoners are known to have been taken from their cells and apparently deliberately beaten to death. One former prisoner described how an inmate was beaten with an axe on his head and another had his arm cut off. Both died. He himself was beaten with an iron bar and left for dead outside the barracks.

Another former Makindye prisoner described one man being killed by having his head hit against a wall while another was killed by being hit hard on top of his head with a rifle butt.

Burns

Although beating is the most common form of torture, other methods are reported. One which is described in a number of accounts consists of tying the victim down, with a car tyre suspended over him or her. This is then set alight and the molten rubber drips onto the victim, causing serious burns. This is reportedly done for many hours, often until the victim is dead.

One prisoner who suffered such torture was detained in Makindye in 1982. She described what happened to Amnesty International:

'They tied my legs and hands and tied me onto a metal chair. Then they started asking me where the guerrillas were and which government I was supporting. They told me that we wanted to bring back the Kabaka [the former king of Buganda] and Lule as president. They accused me of being DP [Democratic Party] and Catholic and Muganda and therefore very dangerous.

'After questioning me the soldiers came and tied an old tyre over my head, lit it and then left me there. There were so many people there, men and women prisoners. The practice was that they started beating them and tied them up and then lit the tyre…

'The hot rubber droplets were made to fall on my head, my face, my right hand and on the right side of my chest. The hot rubber droplets fell and spread all over my upper body causing untold suffering to me. All along they were asking me to tell them where my sons were and insisting that my sons had joined the guerrillas in the bush and that I must know where they were operating from. I told them that my sons were not guerrillas and that I did not know whether they were engaged in guerrilla activities or not. Apart from my sons, the soldiers were asking me to tell them where Idi Amin's soldiers were operating from and who were the people supporting Yusufu Lule.

'The melting hot rubber burned the skin off my face, chest and arms and the pain is just indescribable. I spent the whole day from about 8.30 am in this position and at about midnight I prayed to the Virgin Mary with my rosary around my chest.'

She was helped to escape. She received some medical treatment inside Uganda and then fled the country. She later had a number of operations to graft skin from her thighs onto her face and right arm. She still feels considerable pain in her head, breasts, hip, back, legs and arms, as well as suffering from headaches and high blood pressure.

Published June 1985

DECLARATION OF CONSCIENCE

Issued by Amnesty International for Human Rights Day 1978.

I

Three decades after the proclamation of the Universal Declaration of Human Rights, countless men and women are in prison for their beliefs.

They are being held as prisoners of conscience in scores of countries throughout the world, in crowded jails, in labour camps, and in remote prisons.

Thousands are held under administrative orders, often by military rulers, and are denied any possibility of trial or appeal. Others are in hospitals for the insane or hidden in secret detention camps. Many are forced to endure relentless, systematic torture.

Increasingly, political leaders and ordinary citizens are becoming the victims of abductions, disappearances and killings carried out both by government and opposition.

These acts are an affront to human society. They degrade the entire political process within the community of nations.

II

Nowhere in the principles which govern the conduct of nations is there justification for arbitrary arrest, detention, torture and murder.

The Charter of the United Nations has established the individual and collective commitment of its members to the rights and fundamental freedoms of all people.

The violation of those rights and freedoms is an insult to all people and a threat to international peace and stability.

There has been progress. The International Bill of Human Rights has finally entered into force and 52 governments have ratified the covenants which form part of it. All governments within the United Nations have unanimously declared that under no circumstances is there justification for torture. They have adopted the Standard Minimum Rules for the Treatment of Prisoners.

The United Nations, the International Labour Organisation and UNESCO have established mechanisms to hear complaints of human rights violations.

Proposals are now before the United Nations for an international code of conduct for law enforcement officials and for principles to protect the human rights of all persons subjected to any form of detention or imprisonment.

The American Convention on Human Rights has now entered into force, the Council of Europe has dealt with numerous cases before its human rights commission and the creation of regional mechanisms for the protection of human rights elsewhere has been endorsed by governments in the United Nations.

This progress is of vital importance. The setting of international human rights standards and the creation of possibilities for the protection of those rights reinforce the vision of the Universal Declaration of Human Rights.

Thirty years ago, it was that declaration which elevated respect for the inalienable rights of all people above the distinctions of race, nation and belief. It proclaimed respect for the dignity of the human person as the foundation of freedom, justice and peace in the world.

III

That commitment to human dignity has not been honoured: freedom, justice and peace have become the broken promises of our time.

The victims of economic, social and political injustices have been denied even the right to defend their rights. Prisoners of conscience are known to be in detention in at least 71 countries. In at least 50 countries detention without trial is permitted or is taking place. Numbers of political prisoners are being kept in prolonged detention awaiting trial. From more than a quarter of the countries whose governments have voted for the protection of human rights, torture has been reported. Almost all retain the death penalty and in a score of nations, disappearances and summary killings have become commonplace.

The 30th Anniversary of the Universal Declaration of Human Rights is not an occasion for celebration.

This Anniversary should be a commemoration of all those who have met their deaths and who have been silenced in the streets and in the prisons, death cells, camps and torture chambers. Each killing has been senseless and shameful. Each act of torture has disfigured our common humanity. Every voice which has been silenced has diminished us all.

IV

We, the members of Amnesty International, are determined that this commemoration of the victims who have suffered and who continue to suffer despite the Universal Declaration of Human Rights shall be a signal for change:

We call for the immediate and unconditional release of all prisoners of conscience wherever they are held.

We call for the cessation of all acts of torture and cruelty inflicted upon prisoners.

We demand that all political prisoners held without charge and without trial be given a fair and public hearing by a competent, independent and impartial court with full rights of defence.

We reaffirm our total opposition to the imposition and infliction of the death penalty.

We are determined that these principles be respected by all governments, political movements and citizens.

It is only the strength of informed, popular opinion which will finally put an end to the international hypocrisy about human rights.

To this end we are totally committed.

PRISONERS OF CONSCIENCE IN CHINA

Concern about political imprisonment in the People's Republic of China led Amnesty International to publish a report in 1978. 'Political Imprisonment in the People's Republic of China' described the major aspects of imprisonment for political reasons – the laws, the judicial process and prison conditions. The Constitution and the law provided that people of a certain class origin or political background could be deprived of their political rights, as illustrated by the case of Deng Qingshan in this extract.

Class background becomes particularly important during the mass 'mobilization' campaigns which are launched periodically in China. Such campaigns are used for many purposes: to deter crime, corruption, waste and black marketeering; for the political and economic mobilization of the population; and for political purification. During a campaign, increased emphasis is given to the class struggle and the search for 'class enemies' is more intense than usual. Whatever the purpose of the campaign, people who have a 'bad' class status or origin are generally the first to be scrutinized in the process.

A Chinese language review published in Hong Kong, *Huang He*, recently gave the example of one case where class status was an important factor in arrest during the 1970 'one-strike three-anti' (*yida sanfan*) campaign. This purification campaign was carried out while Lin Biao (Lin Piao) was still in power as Vice-Chairman of the Party. It had both a political and an economic purpose: 'one-strike' meant to strike against 'counter-revolutionaries according to present activities', 'three-anti' meant to struggle against corruption, waste and the black market. According to the review *Huang He*, a 26-year-old man named Deng Qingshan was arrested in a rural production brigade during this campaign and falsely accused of slandering Chairman Mao.

Deng Qingshan had lost his mother while he was still very young and his father had died after the Land Reform. Deng's father had 'poor peasant' status and had been an active 'red element' during the Land Reform. After his death, the head of the family was Deng's older brother, who had fought in the Korean War and through this had gained the prestige of the 'revolutionary fighters'. Because of this good background, Deng's childhood was protected. He was able to attend middle-school classes and in 1963 he was preparing to enter university. However, an important event affected his brother at that time. After his return from the Korean War, Deng's brother had differences of opinion with the cadres of the production brigade and his relationship with them soon became very tense. In 1963, during a campaign to 'afforest the country', the cadres seized the pretext that the brother had gone to chop wood to accuse him of 'undermining' this campaign and labelled him a 'bad element'. Deng's life was immediately affected by his brother's fate. He was not admitted to university and returned to work as a primary school teacher in his original production brigade (village). Because of his brother's 'bad' status, Deng was dismissed from this post after a few months and was assigned to labour as an ordinary peasant in the production brigade...

In 1970, shortly after the 'one-strike, three-anti' campaign began in his production brigade, Deng Qingshan was made the 'target' of the campaign because of his 'bad' background. This decision was taken by the brigade's cadres and was not made public. It was the outcome of three days of meetings between the following people:

the brigade's Party members
members of the 'Security Protection Committee'

the production teams' leaders (rural brigades are subdivided into production teams)

members of the Youth League (the youth organization of the Communist Party)

the brigade's political propagandist (*Maozidong fudaoyuan*).

After these meetings, an investigation team was formed in the brigade, comprising the Party Secretary, the head of the Security Protection Committee, the head of the militia, some members of the 'team in charge of carrying out the class struggle' (*douchadui*) and some people responsible for taking notes.

They all settled in Deng's production team for a few days. Members of the team first talked to individual 'poor peasants' and 'activists' about the class·struggle and the need to find class enemies. Soon their actions and speeches created a tense atmosphere in the production team. People did not know exactly who was going to be the 'victim' but understood clearly that it was a serious affair. The team then displayed several slogans: 'We should drag out the class enemies' … 'You had better confess now' … 'Confession deserves clemency, resistance deserves severity' … and 'mobilization' continued in various ways. Two or three days later, a big meeting was organized for all members of the production team. They were told that there was a 'counter-revolutionary' among them whom everyone should denounce, but the name of the counter-revolutionary was not disclosed. People were frightened and started thinking of what they could report about others. They were asked to write down whatever they knew which seemed wrong to them. Those who could not write well were given help. The meeting lasted a long time because many people who presented their papers to the Party Secretary were told that they were not 'good enough' and had to be rewritten.

Finally, 81 denunciation papers were collected; most of them unimportant. However, some of them concerned several young people in the village who, in one of the papers, were accused of having once stolen a fish and were said to be often in Deng's company.

These young men were taken to the brigade's headquarters by the investigation team and a 'study class' was organized for them. They were urged to confess their 'illicit relationship' with a 'counter-revolutionary'. As they were unable to say anything, Deng's name was then mentioned and they were asked to say what they knew of him.

Meanwhile, some members of the investigation team went back to the production team to ask the peasants to denounce these young men. The previous process was repeated and in the new denunciations the investigators found accusations against two of the young men. One was denounced for having had an 'illicit sexual relationship' with a woman and the other for telling a story to some peasants about the Emperor of the Zhou dynasty and his concubine, from which it was deduced that he compared Mao Tsetung with the tyrannical Emperor and Mao's wife with the cruel concubine.

Once this information was brought back to the brigade, these two young men were taken aside by the investigators. The first was threatened with being labelled a 'bad element' unless he made up for his crime by 'exposing' Deng. Frightened, he testified that Deng had once told him that Mao had been transformed from a snake into a man, and, every year, had to go swimming at the time when the skin changed. To a Chinese mind, this would sound more like a peasant's story than one told by an educated youth and it seems unlikely that Deng was its author. Nevertheless the statement was written down, signed and finger-printed by the young man. The other young man was in his turn threatened with being branded a 'counter-revolutionary' for slandering Chairman Mao with the story of the Zhou Emperor. He then accused Deng of having told the story and he, too, signed and finger-printed a statement. The two of them were then allowed to go home. The other young men who had been taken with them to the brigade were then asked to confirm the charges, which they did, for fear of being kept longer in the 'study class'. Their testimony was also written down and their finger-prints taken.

This completed the first part of the preliminary investigation; the evidence of two 'crimes' committed by Deng plus witnesses had been found. The second part began with the return of the investigation team to Deng's production team, where the 'masses' were again mobilized. Twelve 'poor peasants' were found to confirm the charges against Deng and to give additional details. They also made statements which they signed and finger-printed and a first dossier (*shumian zuixing railiao*, was written, including the following information:

1. Deng's background and class origin
2. his two 'crimes'
3. the places and times at which the 'crimes' were committed
4. the witnesses to each of the 'crimes'
5. Deng's acceptance or rejection of the above facts.

Deng was then arrested by the militia, taken to the brigade for interrogation and told to confess. He did not yet know precisely what he was accused of. The cadres gave him the dossier to read. Under point 5, he could write either 'conforms with the facts' (*shushi*) and 'I admit my crimes' (*renzui*) or 'does not conform with the facts' (*bu shushi*). Deng was urged to write something. He had, in fact, little choice, because refuting evidence given by 12 'poor peasants' was an impossible challenge and the only other alternative – admitting the crimes – would make him a 'counter-revolutionary'. At first, therefore, he refused to say or write anything.

A 'struggle meeting' was then called – the whole brigade stopped working for an entire day to attend it. Deng was confronted with the young men and the 12 'poor peasants' who had denounced him and who, more than anybody else, were adamant that he should admit the crimes. In this situation nobody would dare to speak in his defence. Deng was pushed, insulted, even beaten and yet did not confess. Finally, the brigade's Party Secretary threatened to write on the dossier that Deng had 'resisted to the very end' – a powerful threat in China as the official policy of 'leniency to those who confess, severity to those who resist' is well known to everyone. At that point, Deng had no choice but to sign the statement and he wrote '*renzui*' ('I admit my crimes').

A 'recommendation for arrest' was then written by the brigade cadres and sent with the dossier to the commune's 'Security Defence Group'. At the same time Deng was sent to the commune and his case was no longer the responsibility of the brigade cadres.

This was the starting-point of a process of reinvestigation which was carried out in three stages. Investigators from the commune were sent to Deng's production team to interrogate the witnesses, especially about factual inconsistencies in the dossier. The commune's investigators, however, began their investigation by assuring the peasants repeatedly that they were 'confident in the masses and in the Party's grass-roots' – a guarantee of protection for the witnesses who confirmed their statements. The dossier on Deng which was finally compiled by the commune contained fewer inconsistencies than the brigade's dossier.

The commune in turn sent its own dossier of recommendations to the county Public Security authorities who, after again investigating the case along the same lines, issued an 'arrest warrant'. Deng meanwhile had been transferred to the county's detention centre and was now formally 'arrested'. As the case was considered important, the county authorities handed the dossier to the higher authorities in the district (*zhuanqu*).

The third reinvestigation was therefore made by officials from the district Public Security Bureau. This time a more detailed investigation was made. However, in order not to intimidate the witnesses, the district investigators explained again to the peasants that 'they were confident in the masses, in the Party's grass-roots and were standing at their side'. New details about the crimes were therefore discovered which made the final dossier better and fuller. It was sent by the district to Deng's production brigade for approval. The brigade's Party Secretary and the member responsible for Public Security signed it. The district's dossier did not include the original dossiers prepared by the brigade, commune and county, which were never seen again.

Several months later, preparations were made for passing judgment on Deng. Some officials from the district came to the production brigade for 'consultations with the masses', and copies of Deng's dossier were distributed to the production teams. In addition to information about the case, some space was reserved in the dossier for the 'opinions of the masses' and for the 'opinion of the Party's grass-roots'. A meeting was organized for this purpose, but people did not quite know what to say and proposed all sorts of things; some shouted 'execution'. The brigade's Party Secretary, on the other hand, seemed to feel some remorse and wrote on the dossier: '[Deng] admitted his crimes,

▲ *Bound prisoners are publicly displayed in Wuhan, China. The placards around their necks state their names and crimes.*
▼ *The arrest of a prisoner of conscience in China: Ren Wanding is arrested at the 'democracy wall' for putting up a poster criticizing the authorities' March 1979 ban on wall posters considered to be 'opposed to socialism'. He was imprisoned apparently without trial from April 1979 to April 1981.*

cooperative attitude, [he] deserves clemency'.

The district officials left the brigade after having collected the 'opinions of the masses' and judgment was decided upon outside the brigade. In November 1970, a district Public Security Bureau public notice announced sentences passed on a number of offenders. Deng was on the list. He had been sentenced to 15 years' imprisonment with three years' deprivation of civil rights after release, for slandering Chairman Mao on several occasions between 1967 and 1969. He is reported to have been sent to a labour camp. His present fate is unknown.

Published November 1978

AI: NOT A DO-GOODER FOR ALL CAUSES

By 1978 Amnesty International had grown to 2,173 adoption groups in 33 countries, with more than 200,000 individual members and supporters around the world. The preface to the 'Amnesty International Report 1978' reflects upon this growth and sets down some of the guiding principles of the movement's approach.

A demonstration called by Amnesty International to draw attention to 'disappearances'.

Amnesty International is a dynamic movement. Within less than two decades it has grown into a worldwide organization with members in more than a hundred countries. During the last two to three years especially there has been considerable growth, both in membership and activities. The movement meets with great sympathy from the public in many countries; it has been honoured by awards and prizes of high reputation.

This fame has created problems. There is a tendency to weave a myth around Amnesty International. The organization is expected to act in almost all countries on almost all violations. We are sometimes treated with a respect which we do not deserve and are faced with expectations which we cannot fulfil. It is now more important than ever for us to explain who we are and what we do: not because we want to defend ourselves, but to ensure results in our future work.

Amnesty International is not a do-gooder for all possible causes; it has a restricted mandate. It works for the release of prisoners of conscience and against torture and executions, but is not involved in work against unemployment, starvation or other social diseases. Our platform is the Universal Declaration of Human Rights, adopted thirty years ago by the nations of the world. Within that frame Amnesty International concentrates its resources on particular basic civil and political rights.

We do not cover a broader spectrum. This is not because we ignore the importance of all the other rights, but because we recognize that we can only achieve concrete results within set limits.

In fact, we believe that there is a close relation between different rights. When exploited people cannot make their voices heard, both political and socio-economic rights are violated. Very often there is an inter-relationship between the two – the most obvious example being when trade unionists are imprisoned. Amnesty International neither understands nor accepts the attempts sometimes made to create a conflict or a contradiction between these two sets of rights.

Nor do we accept a contradiction between the rights of peoples or nations on the one hand and the human rights of individuals on the other. Human rights have many times been violated in the name of so-called higher interests, such as the 'nation', the 'party' or the 'struggle'. But experience shows that these causes undermine themselves if they need the support of terror. Basic human rights must stand above all other political ambitions and should be respected under all circumstances and in all situations. And again, in the long run, civil and political rights are the basis of the other rights, and also of those of a collective nature.

This is how Amnesty International understands its role in the field of human rights: a limited mandate but an appreciation of the close relationship between the rights it defends and all other human rights.

Another of our characteristics is impartiality. Amnesty International does not take a stand for or against any religion, political party, ideology or economic system. Here again, we restrict ourselves to the narrow scope of political life which deals with specific basic rights. Of course we realize that there is a link between general politics and the rights we try to defend; changes of government often result in arrests or releases. But this fact does not make us change our approach. We simply take facts into account, without hiding some of them or emphasizing others, according to régime or ideology.

Our impartiality is not always appreciated or even understood by governments. This is not surprising: the questions Amnesty International deals with are highly sensitive 'political dynamite' in several countries. The very rights we defend are often one of the main issues in national political battles. Therefore, our reports are sometimes seen as support for the opposition. We are criticized for 'interference', branded as 'agents' for particular nefarious interests. Our purpose, of course, is not to help any side in political power struggles, but we cannot be silent about grave violations just because the facts we know could influence the reputation of certain politicians, for better or worse. Our impartiality could never mean neutrality on human rights, not even in the most politically tense moments.

Our basic approach to governments is always the same: we seek a dialogue. We are willing to talk as long as this might help our aims. We are not negotiating – we have nothing to 'sell' – but we want discussions within our mandate and opportunities to present our facts and recommendations. This means that we do not fight governments as such. Neither do we propose boycotts or cuts in aid. That kind of economic pressure is not within our mandate and is not our way of working.

Even non-governmental organizations and individuals sometimes have difficulty in understanding our efforts to safeguard impartiality and independence. We are restricted when it comes to cooperation with other organizations and we scrutinize each proposed donation according to rigid rules before accepting it. This, again, is for the sake of maintaining independence and being seen to do so.

To be impartial it is important to be correct. Amnesty International spends much of its limited resources on checking facts, to make sure that its reports do not contain distortions, false information or misunderstandings. Mistakes have been made – fortunately, very seldom – but they have been corrected. Amnesty International is always willing to put right errors of fact.

In fact, Amnesty International is less often attacked for what it publishes than for what it does not report. We are sometimes criticized for being unbalanced, for reporting too little or too much on a certain country or group of countries.

Balance for the sake of balance would be artificial. We work with realities. If there were gross violations of human rights in one group of countries and only minor infringements in another, we would *not* spend fifty per cent of our resources on each. But as the world is today, a human rights organization with an impartial and serious approach must work on all continents and in countries with the most differing political systems. This, too, is a reality and has created a need for work that is geographically 'balanced'.

That balance is not easy to establish. There are still some few countries where the authorities refuse to have any communication with Amnesty International: they will not admit observers or representatives and our letters and cables receive no reply. These same régimes have a restrictive approach to the international media and little, if any, detailed information on the human rights situation in their countries therefore exists. Our movement has made great efforts to break through such situations; the result for the past year can be seen in this *Report*.

During the past year human rights have been a major issue in international politics within United Nations bodies and regional organizations such as the European Conference for Security and Cooperation and the Organization of American States as well as in bilateral relations between governments.

This increasing interest in human rights is welcome, even if the declarations from some quarters have not always sounded genuine. It is important that so many governments now accept that human rights are an international concern. Formally, this has been so ever since the Universal Declaration was adopted. Still, many governments have for years talked about 'interference' when human rights violations have been observed. The new awareness should give bodies such as the UN Commission on Human Rights more room for forceful action.

Published 1979

The marchers wear placards round their necks, each bearing the name of a missing victim.

KILLINGS: THE YOUNGEST VICTIMS

Revelations of the killing and merciless ill-treatment of school children in the Central African Empire in 1979 provoked a world outcry against Emperor Jean-Bedel Bokassa. First reports of the deaths were verified by Amnesty International and published in early May 1979. The following account comes from 'Children', a report on human rights violations perpetrated against children.

The Central African Empire briefly became the focus of world attention during 1979 after Amnesty International condemned the killing and merciless treatment of hundreds of school children who were arrested in April.

The children, aged between 8 and 16, had originally protested in January against new regulations compelling them to purchase and wear government uniforms. At the time the students had not been paid their study grants and many of the school children's fathers who were employed by the government had not received their wages for several months.

The protest about the uniforms therefore grew into a broader protest against the government's management of the country's economy. Students and school children also began demanding the restoration of the Republic (the Central African Empire was the Central African Republic until Jean-Bedel Bokassa made himself Emperor in December 1976).

The January demonstrations in the capital city, Bangui, were followed by protests in the provinces, and by numerous arrests. The arrest of four students in early April resulted in a students' and school childen's strike on 9 April.

By mid-April young people began stoning government cars, including that of the Emperor. On 18, 19 and 20 April the Imperial Guard, which functions under the personal command of the Emperor, searched homes for children involved in the protests and took large numbers into custody.

More than a hundred children are known to have been taken on 18 April to Bangui's central Ngaragba Prison where they were held in such crowded conditions that in one cell alone between 12 and 28 of them were reported to have suffocated to death.

Other children were reported to have been stoned by members of the Imperial Guard to punish them for throwing stones at the Emperor's car. Some were bayonetted or beaten to death with sharpened sticks and whips. One boy was reported by a survivor to have been killed with the pocket knife he was carrying in his pocket when he was seized by the Imperial Guard.

Amnesty International has received reliable reports that between 50 and 100 children were killed in prison. One witness said he had counted the bodies of 62 dead children.

Several days later Emperor Bokassa described himself at a public function in Bangui as 'the father and protector of children' and said that the remaining children in prison would be released. As international protests grew over the reports of the killings, he denied that any such deaths had occurred but later admitted that some 'grown-up youths' had been killed.

High-level confirmation of the killings came from an unexpected source. General Sylvestre Bangui, Ambassador in France and the United Kingdom for the Central African Empire, called a news conference at his embassy in Paris on 22 May to announce his resignation as ambassador and to reveal eye-witness descriptions of the killings.

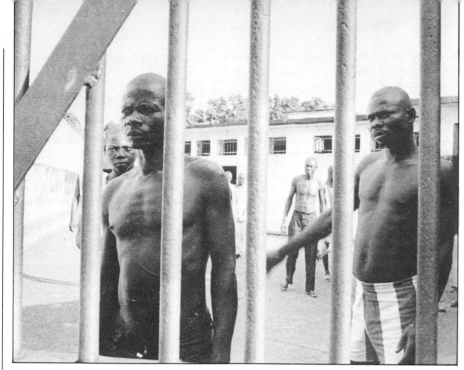

Political prisoners detained by former Emperor Bokassa of the Central African Empire (now Republic) await their imminent release after a change of government. Bangui, 26 September 1979.

Students and children in Ethiopia have, for several years, been victims of political arrest, torture and killing under the country's Provisional Military Government, the *Derg*, which came to power in 1974. Students in Ethiopia have a tradition of radical political protest, developed in opposition to the government of Emperor Haile Selassie under which they were frequently subjected to arbitrary arrest and torture. Many have also opposed the policies of the Provisional Military Government, and have met a similar fate.

One of the worst incidents known to Amnesty International took place on 29 April 1977 when soldiers and paramilitary guards in Addis Ababa attacked gatherings of students and other young people at night on suspicion that they were preparing a May Day demonstration against the *Derg*. It is estimated that about 500 young people were killed that night. The Secretary General of the Swedish Save the Children Fund, Håkan Landelius, reported: 'One thousand children have been massacred in Addis Ababa and their bodies, lying in the streets, are ravaged by roving hyenas ... The bodies of murdered children, mostly aged from 11 to 13 years, can be seen heaped on the roadside when one leaves Addis Ababa'.

In November 1977 Lieutenant Colonel Mengistu Haile Mariam, the chairman of the *Derg*, ordered that 'Red Terror' should be inflicted on 'counter-revolutionaries' in response to assassinations which the *Derg* claimed had taken the lives of many government officials since October 1976. The 'Red Terror' campaign lasted from November 1977 to June 1978. It involved mass arrests of students and young people as well as the systematic use of torture and the summary execution of large numbers of these young people. Summary executions frequently took place in public places at night, with the victims' bodies being displayed with placards warning, 'This was a counter-revolutionary', 'The Red Terror will flourish'. Victims'

relatives were ordered, at times, to join in public condemnation of those killed. At other times they were permitted to purchase the bodies for burial – 'paying for the bullet', as it was called.

It has been estimated that about 5,000 young people aged between 12 and 25 years were killed in Addis Ababa during the 'Red Terror', particularly between December 1977 and February 1978, when killings and imprisonment reached a peak, and when about 100 or more were reported killed each night. In early 1978 the campaign spread to other towns and rural areas too, although by May bodies were rarely seen exposed in the streets of the capital and many of those arrested had been released. In June 1978 the government ended its reference to 'Red Terror', but similar practices have been reported in Ethiopia since then.

Just prior to the January 1979 Conference of Latin American Bishops San Salvador's Archbishop Oscar Romero issued a decree in which he suspended all religious services in his country following the killing of young catechists by security forces.

On the weekend of 20 January a Roman Catholic priest, Father Octaviano Ortiz Luna, had gathered together some 40 young people between the ages of 12 and 19 for a Christian study program. Security forces broke into their meeting house at dawn and carried out arrests and killings. Father Octaviano and David Alberto Caballero, Jorge Alberto Gómez, Roberto Orellana and Angel Morales – all boys – were shot dead.

The government-controlled press published photographs of the dead, announcing the liquidation of a nest of guerrillas.

The remaining young people were charged with preparing subversive material and with opposing authority. Following widespread protests, they were released from custody.

Published October 1979

CHILDREN

Every October Amnesty International organizes a week-long publicity campaign highlighting prisoners of conscience. The theme of the campaign in 1979 was Children. This extract from the report 'Children' shows that the treatment meted out to children was often little different from that imposed on adults.

This photograph, taken secretly in Alexanderplatz, East Berlin, shows the arrest in 1977 of the Gerdes family who had, minutes before, unfurled a homemade banner in support of their request to be allowed to leave the German Democratic Republic. Prior to demonstrating in public they had submitted 10 unsuccessful applications for permission to leave the country. In February 1978, the parents were sentenced to 18 months' imprisonment. Their children, Claudia and Ralf, were aged 12 and 13 at the time of the arrest. They were held in a children's home until their parents were released and allowed to travel to West Berlin.

Children are subject to arrest and detention, not only because they may have been taken to prison with their parents, but also because they have been imprisoned for their own beliefs – or what the authorities believe to be their beliefs.

Some are put into prison for no reason at all.

A child of 11, Veneque Duclairon, was among the peasants of Plaine de Cul-de-Sac, Haiti, who were arrested in 1969 following protests against deteriorating economic conditions. All were imprisoned without charge or trial.

Under the conditions which have applied to detainees in Haiti, the child found himself completely isolated from the outside world and without any chance of obtaining the assistance of a lawyer. If he is still alive today, he is 21 years old. But those who have tried desperately to obtain information about him now fear that he may have died in prison.

A former Haitian political prisoner has reported that Veneque Duclairon died in 1973 in the national penitentiary. This information cannot be confirmed; however, he was not among the group of 104 Haitian political prisoners released by a presidential decree in September 1977.

On the other side of the world, a 14-year-old schoolgirl, Sumilah, was arrested in October 1965 at the time of the attempted coup in Indonesia. Amnesty International has no reason to believe that she was involved in the attempted coup, or in the violence which followed.

She was detained in various camps but was never taken before a court or given the right to contact a lawyer. After 14 years in detention she was released in April 1979.

Among Indonesia's thousands of political prisoners are many who, like Sumilah, are now in their 20s. Among them are youths who were arrested in 1965 at a government paramilitary training centre for young people at Halim airport, just outside Jakarta, which served as a military airbase. During the events surrounding the attempted coup in 1965, all those at the young people's training centre at Halim airport were arrested, regardless of whether they were airforce personnel or trainees. Most of those arrested have never been charged or tried. As a consequence young

people whose sole offence was that on 30 September 1965 they were at the Halim centre have spent the past 14 years (in many cases this is more than half their lives thus far) in prison.

In South Africa in recent years children have been detained without trial under the Terrorism Act and other security laws. They do not appear to be given different treatment to adults detained under the same laws: they are subject to interrogation and brutal treatment by security police and are frequently kept incommunicado and in solitary confinement.

Although the South African authorities have admitted that a large number of children are in detention, they have refused to give details about their ages. On 21 February 1979 the Minister of Justice stated in Parliament that 252 young people under the age of 18 had been detained under the Terrorism or Internal Security Acts during 1978. Twenty-five of these were girls.

The South African authorities are not obliged to give information to the parents of children detained incommunicado under the Terrorism Act. The parents are not allowed to visit the children and cannot demand *habeas corpus* or any form of effective legal protection for the children.

Children are also subject to prosecution and imprisonment for political offences on the same basis as adults. In answer to a question in Parliament in June 1978 the Minister of Justice admitted that six children, one of 14 and five of 15 years of age, were imprisoned on Robben Island, the prison island off the Cape Town coast – the maximum security prison for black prisoners.

Carlos Patricio Fariña Oyarce

Carlos Patricio was 13 years of age when he was detained on 13 October 1973 in his home in Santiago, Chile.

A few days before his arrest, he had been taken by his mother to a juvenile court after an accident in which another child playing with Carlos Patricio was wounded by a pistol shot.

The judge sent him to a reformatory from which he escaped, claiming he had been threatened and sexually assaulted by older boys. His mother wanted to return him to the court but the boy was ill with a fever. He remained in bed until the morning of 13 October when a group of soldiers and policemen surrounded the house. Two policemen, four soldiers and two civilians broke into the house and demanded that his mother hand over the boy. Without accepting the mother's explanations, the two policemen pulled the child out of bed. One of them hit him in the chest with the butt of his rifle, knocking him to the ground. The boy was then taken to the Santiago National Football Stadium where he was placed with the political prisoners who had already been taken there after the coup.

His mother's pleas were in vain. Carlos Patricio was last seen in the prison camp of the Mounted Infantry Regiment No. 3 of Sen Filipe. But a search of the camp proved useless, as did inquiries about the boy at police stations and military regiments. No trace of the boy's whereabouts could be obtained despite repeated appeals by his mother to the authorities from 13 October 1973 to 6 September 1976. On that day the Chilean Government informed the United Nations Human Rights Commission that the person in question 'had no legal existence'.

Señora Oyarce died of cancer on 22 November 1977 without further news of her son.

Published October 1979

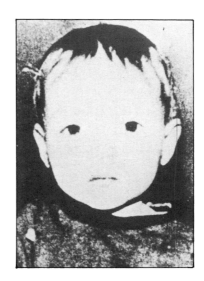

This is Carla Rutilo Artes from Bolivia. Her mother, Graciela, is Argentinian but has lived in Bolivia since she was nine years of age.

On 2 April 1976 both mother and daughter were arrested by the Bolivian Police, taken to the capital city, La Paz, and separated. The mother was held in the Ministry of the Interior where it is alleged that she was subjected to torture. Her daughter Carla was sent to an orphanage where she was registered under a false name.

On 26 August 1976 Carla was removed from the orphanage and three days later both mother and child were handed over to Argentinian authorities at the border of the two countries. There had been no formal extradition order.

Relatives of the family state that the mother had no known political affiliation. The sole motive for the arrest would appear to be her support, as a representative of a students' organization, for the Bolivian tin miners' strike.

Carla was found in August 1985 when a man wanted in connection with crimes attributed to an Argentinian 'death squad' was arrested. She had been living as his adopted daughter since 1977 when he had adopted her and changed her name. Carla was returned to the care of her maternal grandmother after a federal judge was presented with evidence confirming her identity. However, to date there has been no news of her mother.

PRISONER TESTIMONY FROM NORTH KOREA

Ali Lameda, a Venezuelan poet, worked as a translator for the North Korean Government. He had contacted the North Koreans in 1965 when they were recruiting translators and editors and was invited to work in the capital, Pyongyang, where he arrived in mid-1966. Two years later, after being accused of sabotage and spying, he was sentenced to 20 years' imprisonment; he was released in 1974. Ali Lameda was adopted as a prisoner of conscience. Here is the account he wrote of his arrest, trial and imprisonment.

Ali Lameda, a Venezuelan poet imprisoned in North Korea while working as a translator.

To understand fully my experiences in detention in North Korea, it is necessary first to explain a little why I was in Korea and the prevailing atmosphere in the country from the point of view of a foreigner. This will perhaps explain some of the limitations of my experience and knowledge.

During the time I was working in Korea, at the invitation of the North Korean government, I was almost totally isolated from Korean people generally. I dealt only with certain individuals, who were responsible for my work and worked directly with me. No other personal contact was possible. Apart from the Koreans who worked in the Department of Foreign Publications in Pyongyang who supervised my work, I did not have regular communication with functionaries of the governing North Korean Communist Party...

However much my sympathy lay with the great work of national construction of the Korean people, I could never communicate directly with them and learn more about the workings of Korean society, but constantly felt the barrier which had been erected around me.

Briefly, my work in North Korea involved translation into the Spanish language of certain materials, such as the collected works of Kim Il Sung and the promotion of these texts throughout the Spanish-speaking world. I worked at the Government Department of Foreign Publications, with other foreigners engaged on similar projects also at the invitation of the North Korean government...

First arrest and detention in an internal security prison

My arrest came as a complete surprise. Only three days earlier, I had been present at a big dinner given by the Director of the Department of Foreign Publications (who was, I believe, later arrested and imprisoned in connection with the charges against me), and I was not aware of any undue tension. Not long previously I had expressed some uncertainty about my work, as did my colleague Sedillot; we both felt that the exaggerated claims that were being made by the North Korean authorities regarding the progress made in their country would be considered too blatant propaganda in the societies we were trying to reach through our translations, but such reservations had been voiced only privately in the Department.

Nine people came to my apartment to arrest me. Two of them were in the uniform of the police, the others were agents of what is called Public Security. I was told I was being arrested as an enemy of the Democratic People's Republic of Korea, having violated Korean law. Nothing more specific was said to me, and they were not willing to discuss the laws or charges related to my arrest.

I was taken to a prison cell and interrogated by the authorities. It was demanded that I 'confess'. I was denied food, on occasions taken out of my cell at 12 noon and not allowed to return until midnight, during which time I was continuously interrogated. There were many ways in which they would apply pressure. The usual pattern of the interview would be that I was ordered to 'confess'. To this I would reply 'To what do I have to confess?' I would then be told: 'You know what there is to confess. Talk'. I would insist: 'But if it is you who are accusing me, you tell me'. So it went on, always. They sit a man down and try to convince him he has committed crimes, they insult him and demand a 'confession'.

Hunger was used as a control. No more than 300 grams of food per day was given to each prisoner. The conditions of the prison were appalling. No change of clothes in years, nor of food plates. The place lacked proper sanitary facilities. And then there was the isolation of prisoners. Young prison guards newly assigned to the camp often expressed their amazement at such conditions.

The food provided in the prison was fit only for animals. For months a prisoner is deprived of adequate food. In my opinion, it is preferable to be beaten, as it is possible to grit one's teeth and withstand physical beating. To be continually starving is worse. They didn't beat or torture me like they did the others. However, once the guard gave me a beating and kicked me with his boots, also hitting me on my bare feet which were badly swollen. He kicked and punched me just for not having saluted him or something like that. No, I was not tortured, if by this one means the systematic infliction of pain but, if terrible hunger and continual nastiness come under this definition, then I was.

In fact, beating was also used as a means of persuasion during interrogation. Whilst in my cell, I could hear the cries of other prisoners. You can soon learn to distinguish whether a man is crying from fear, or pain or from madness in such a place. I could not change my clothing at all, and a prisoner is soon covered in dirt, living in those filthy cells. The cells are also damp, and I should say that for eight months during my first period in detention I was sick with fever. I believe at times I lost consciousness.

It is impossible for me to say how many people were at that prison. It could certainly have been more than a thousand. The cells are extremely small, perhaps two metres long by one metre wide, and three metres high. There are no rights for the prisoner, no visits, parcels of cigarettes or food or opportunity to read a book or newspaper, or write. The process of 'rehabilitation', as they call it, must start straightaway, the 'self-examination' of the crimes that the prisoner has reportedly committed, to purify the self.

Apart from the noise of people crying out and screaming which could be heard at times, I also knew of people who coughed blood. There was very little medical attention; if the doctor did visit it was only to prescribe something for the fever from which all prisoners suffered. I once spoke to such a doctor, who did in fact tell me that he was unhappy with the work he was detailed to do by the Ministry of Security, since his medical practice consisted of dispensing palliatives for fever and diarrhoea. As far as I know, the only medicines used to treat the prisoners were Terramycin and edible oil.

Prison regimen was always the same: the prisoner sat for 16 hours a day looking at the warders and the prison bars. The cell had bars from the ceiling to the floor, and in the middle was a passage where the guards patrolled. Prisoners must stay awake throughout the day, the official explanation went, since how could a prisoner continually ponder his guilt if he slept?

We were given food rations three times a day: at seven o'clock, one o'clock and then again at seven o'clock. The meal consisted of a piece of dirty bread, weighing about 250 grams, and a bowl of soup, which was water with a few pieces of vegetable in it. The metal dishes the food was served from were always filthy, the same ones the prisoners had been using for years.

Release and second arrest

I was held prisoner by the Ministry of the Interior for a year. In the meantime, my companion had remained living in our apartment. When I was released a year later, I was in a terrible physical condition due to the treatment I had received in prison. I was led to believe that, after going through a period of house arrest of two months, I was to be released unconditionally, that I could not leave the country with my companion, but let her set off first. I was allowed to accompany her to the airport, and I returned to the apartment to pack my bags.

Then, at about five or six o'clock in the evening, the police returned. They seized all my belongings in the apartment and told me to make a note of everything I had there, my books and so on. The behaviour of the arresting officers was much more brutal and abrupt than it had been at the time of my first arrest. I asked why I was being arrested a second time, and was given the answer: 'You know why'. They told me that I had failed to keep my word, and had made certain denunciations, again resorted to propaganda against Korea, resuming my role as an imperialist spy. Presumably, they had installed a microphone in our apartment and recorded my conversation with my companion. What did they expect me to say to her, when I returned from a year's detention in such a bad physical condition, having lost 22 kilograms in weight, my body covered in sores and suffering haemorrhages. I was a very sick man, and it was obvious to my companion what treatment I had suffered in detention without my having to spell out what I had undergone. My literary work had been confiscated on the orders of the Party Central Committee; it was described as 'bourgeois filth', and the authorities wanted me to tell my companion that on my own orders it was to be burnt. It was unbelievable that I should tell her any such thing about my work, my life's work. Certainly, this period when I was re-arrested, after believing I was at last to be released, was one of the worst moments I was forced to endure.

Trial

Again I was interrogated, and this time the conditions, the food ration, were even worse. However, I was brought to trial before a tribunal, if it is possible to call what happened a trial. The tribunal was under the direction of the Ministry of Internal Security and, apart from members of the tribunal, there was a representative from what they call the High Court who acted as the judge and a prosecutor; I was provided with a so-called defence counsel. The only people present apart from members of the tribunal were two uniformed policemen and a young man who acted as interpreter. The trial lasted for one day, from nine o'clock in the morning till five o'clock in the afternoon. I was suffering from fever and did not eat all day. It was stressed throughout the trial that I had committed a political offence, which was considered far worse than offences by common criminals.

The pattern of my trial followed the interrogations I had undergone. It was demanded that I confess my guilt. The tribunal did not make any specific accusations – there were no formal charges – but the accused has to accuse himself before the tribunal. Thus there was no necessity for the tribunal to produce any evidence. I had no right to defend myself, I could only admit guilt. The basis for the tribunal's condemnations is the confession of the prisoner and the prosecutor told me that I should speak out and confess everything, to rid myself of my crimes. I insisted that I had committed no crimes, that I had only come to Korea as a servant of the government. During the trial, I asked for a lawyer of my choice and that the tribunal should be made open, but such demands were dismissed as bourgeois. When I tried to ask questions, I was abruptly interrupted and told that I had no rights in defending myself. The prosecutor eventually informed me that I had been in Korea to sabotage, spy and introduce infiltrators. To this I could only reply that I had been invited to Korea by the government and that allegations that I was under the control of the CIA were absurd. The prosecutor read a small extract from the Penal Code, which emphasized the gravity of my crime. As a political offender, I had committed a crime against the basis of the Korean state. In summing up, the prosecutor demanded the maximum penalty for the crimes I had committed. The so-called defence counsel, whom I had seen for just half an hour, made a lengthy eulogy of Kim Il Sung, and in lodging my plea, asked for 20 years' imprisonment. The tribunal retired for just five minutes and then returned to sentence me, to 20 years' imprisonment with forced labour.

Imprisonment

Ten minutes after I had been sentenced, I was brought a bowl of soup, since I had been before the tribunal all day without even drinking a glass of water. I was told that I would be sent to a prison camp, for rehabilitation, where I was to learn an occupation, thus rehabilitating myself through work. At the end of my trial, I asked if I would be allowed to receive letters from my family and friends whilst in detention at the camp, and I was assured that this would be so by members of the tribunal. However, I received absolutely nothing during my terms of imprisonment, in spite of the numerous parcels and letters that were apparently sent by my family and friends in Europe. I appealed to the camp authorities several times during the

Border guard, North Korea

early period of my detention, that I should be allowed to write to my family to ask for a small amount of money with which to buy some sugar, for example, but my requests were continually refused. They never gave me the chance to learn a trade as they had claimed. They may have decided not to let a foreigner such as myself mix with hundreds of Koreans in the camp or in the workshop.

I was transferred to the concentration camp by van, handcuffed to the bars of the van. The temperature outside was very much below freezing point. Opposite me in the van, sitting on a chair, was the guard, who throughout the journey spent his time loading and unloading his gun in a threatening manner. The roads along which we travelled were dirt tracks. Outside, the howls of wolves could be heard. The journey lasted about three hours, and by the time I arrived at the camp, I was in such a poor condition that the captain who initially received me immediately sent for medicines. I was then pushed into a filthy hole, where I slept on the bare floor, with no blanket or mattress, in freezing temperatures. This was, however, only a temporary cell, where I remained constantly handcuffed for the three weeks that I was there, so that I felt my wrists would break with the strain.

Following this, I was transferred to the main camp, only a couple of kilometres away. This was done at about ten o'clock at night, still in the middle of winter. The cell I was then taken to again had no heating, except for a pipe running through it which became warm for approximately five minutes each night. The windows were iced up and my feet froze. My feet remained in this condition for a month and a half, my toes were swollen with frostbite. I can still feel the effects of this to the present day. Some doctors did eventually come to see me, but by then my toenails had all dropped off and my feet were covered in sores.

I later learned that the name of the camp was Suriwon, after the nearby town, and that I had been put in a punishment cell, which should not really have happened, but since I was a foreigner, and it was the first time a foreigner had ever been held at the camp, there was no isolated cell in which to hold me. As a foreigner, I was not to be allowed to come into contact with the other prisoners who had not been sentenced or with those who had disobeyed camp regulations, wilfully damaging a machine during work or some such offence. The periods these prisoners spent in the punishment cells, however, were comparatively short, since every prisoner in isolation there was not available for work, and no prisoner is permitted to remain idle during detention in this camp.

There were some 6,000 or more people held at the camp, according to information gleaned from the guards or orderlies. Some of the guards and orderlies would communicate with the prisoners. Apparently, the camp was a huge circular place, with an enormous courtyard. One doctor told me that there were about 1,200 people sick in the camp, who were kept in a special part, so with that large number sick, I calculated, using all the information I could gather, that the total number of prisoners would be no lower than 6,000 to 8,000 people. The prisoners were forced to work for 12 hours a day, mechanical work, making jeeps for example, which was, of course, unpaid. There was no agricultural work done at this camp. But outside the camp there were several farms worked by political prisoners, and potatoes, root vegetables, pumpkins and 'ahuyama' were grown there…

Women were also held at the camp. One day, when I had been in the punishment cell, in isolation, I observed by chance a group of about 200 women arriving at the camp. Later, I discovered that some of them were imprisoned for theft, for example, and one of them, I was told, was imprisoned because of her habit of smoking cigarettes. Apparently she was the wife of an employee of the Ministry of Commerce, about 33 years old or so, and had two daughters. The woman had had to keep the fact that she smoked secret even from her husband, and would smoke only in the toilet of their apartment. It was whilst at the office where she worked that she was accused, by a colleague, of smoking, since the colleague could smell stale cigarette smoke about her person. The woman was summoned by the party cell to which she belonged and was what they call 'sent down to production', which meant being sent to work in either the iron or mining industry. She spent two years doing this harsh labour, separated from her husband and family.

Sometimes conditions in the camp were made even worse. During my third year of imprisonment, the food ration, meagre as it was, was suddenly decreased and in addition the work targets set for the prisoners were raised. This sort of treatment reduced grown men to weeping over the food they were given…

A periodical was produced at the camp, which was aimed at assisting the prisoners in rehabilitation. It was entitled *Marching Forward* and gave news of the great deeds being performed by Kim Il Sung, to spur on the prisoners to greater efforts. In fact, it was possible for a prisoner to have his sentence reduced through maintaining good work performance. Thus a prisoner might serve only 12 years out of a 15-year sentence. But my experience, of serving only seven years out of 20 would not happen to a Korean prisoner. In this I was privileged.

Published February 1979

● WITHOUT YOUR HELP…

After two and a half years' detention in El Salvador, this mother and her son are finally back together again. In prison she received letters from all over the world bringing her emotional and moral encouragement. Without the help of Amnesty International, she says, "our conditions would have been disastrous".

Vida Cuadra Hernández was working as a journalist in El Salvador when she and her colleagues were arrested in January 1981. Their office was ransacked by uniformed members of the National Police and Vida and seven others were taken to the Central Headquarters. For a month they were continuously interrogated, given rotting food and held in atrocious conditions. In February 1981 Vida was transferred to Ilopango's women's prison where there was no medical care and the women were forced to look after emergencies themselves.

The prisoners eventually staged a series of hunger-strikes as a result of which they managed to win about 70 per cent of their demands. The food improved and they were allowed to cook it themselves. There were also improvements in the medical conditions of prisoners and family visits were permitted. Throughout her imprisonment, Vida's son, Alfonso, aged five, was looked after by his grandparents. But they wouldn't let him go out of doors for two and a half years because of the risk from the death squads. Alfonso is so happy to be free he now says he wants to kiss everybody he meets.

ILL-TREATMENT BY ISRAELI AUTHORITIES

Persistent allegations of ill-treatment of prisoners in Israel and the territories occupied by it after the 1967 war prompted a mission to discuss Amnesty International's concerns with the government. The following extracts come from the 'Report and Recommendations of an Amnesty International Mission to the Government of the State of Israel, 3-7 June 1979, including the Government's response and Amnesty International's comments'.

The following is a recent testimony of ill-treatment which is representative of allegations made in recent years as regards the type of ill-treatment and the circumstances surrounding arrest and detention. Dates and places have been changed at the requests of the individual involved. The words themselves constitute a paraphrase of the testimonies as they were received by Amnesty International.

'I was arrested in early 1978, at my home, while asleep. There were soldiers with guns all around, my mother was crying and my younger brothers were in terror. I was told to get dressed and then was put into a jeep and made to lie on the floor of the jeep. My shirt was taken off me and used to blindfold me. While I was lying on the floor of the jeep, the soldiers beat me on the head with their iron helmets, and kicked me.

'I was taken to the Moskobiya (a detention centre in Jerusalem) and here I was beaten by about five people, in the stomach, in the back of the head, and on the genitals. I lost consciousness.

'After breakfast the next day, I was taken to the interrogation room which had one table and two chairs. The interrogator asked me to speak and I answered, 'I did nothing.' He said, 'Now I will force you to speak.'

'I was sitting on the chair in front of the desk and now he came and sat on the front of the desk, near me. He placed one of his feet on my genitals and pressed down on them whenever he felt like it. With the other foot he periodically kicked me in the face. The pressure on my genitals increased – it became very painful. At the same time he began to threaten me that my brother would be dismissed from his job. This treatment lasted for about two hours.

'Then my dossier arrived, and now the interrogator saw that I had been under interrogation several times before. I think the job of the first interrogator was just to throw fear into me. Now two other people were brought in to interrogate me. My hands were tied behind my back, to the chair. They began to beat me on the head and arms. One of them was beating me with a rope. This lasted about five hours. When I was sent back to my cell, my nose was bleeding, there was blood all over the inside of my mouth, and my genitals were blue.

'On the second day, I was again tied to the chair and a thick cloth sack was put over my head. But now I was not beaten. After some time, they took me into the courtyard and tied me to a pipe there so that I couldn't sit down, only stand. They left me this way for 48 hours, standing, with no food, no cigarettes, no sleeping, no going to the toilet. I urinated in my clothes at least twice. After this, I was sent back to my cell, where I rested for about two hours.

'Then I was taken for interrogation again. Now they began to throw information at me, that I had been a member of the Democratic Front for the Liberation of Palestine. They weren't beating me at all. Some of this information was correct and some of it was wrong. I admitted nothing, and they sent me back to the cell. I slept like a dead man. When I woke up, I did some exercises, since you have to be

Prisoners in Nablus jail, Israel.

strong to withstand this kind of treatment.

'The next day, they brought before me a man who said that I had recruited him to the Democratic Front for the Liberation of Palestine. This man, whom I knew, looked like he had lost 15 kilos in weight. I admitted I had done this. Then they asked me how I got my orders. I told them nothing. Now a new torture began. I was again tied to the chair, but he had tied a rope to my penis and began to pull on the rope in time to the music on the radio he had turned on. The interrogator was laughing, dancing, and pulling on the rope. He was not even asking me questions. This lasted for several hours.

'And after this, I was again brought into the courtyard, tied to a pipe, and left standing for 48 hours.

'This kind of treatment continued for 29 days.

'It was only after 20 days that I first saw my lawyer. I was never seen by the Red Cross since my identity card is from East Jerusalem and the ICRC only visits prisoners from the West Bank.

'After this treatment, I was moved to another prison for about a month, where I was not interrogated. Then I was tried – I had confessed to membership and recruiting – and I was sentenced to eight months. After two months of this sentence, I was again brought to the Moskobiya for the same kind of treatment again. Now the treatment was even worse, because some other people had confessed and named me in their confession. Here I was under interrogation for 17 days but I said nothing since I knew I would be free in several months. But I saw the others who had named me, and they were in very bad shape.

'It is hard to avoid talking, but being prepared for the experience is the most important thing. Then you know that it is better not to talk at all – if you tell them something they will always want more, and they will hurt you any way to get it. You can never give them enough to satisfy them.'....

Conclusions

1. Amnesty International reaffirms its view stated on several occasions since 1970 that there is sufficient *prima facie* evidence of ill-treatment of security suspects in the Occupied Territories by interrogators and detaining officials to warrant the establishment of a public inquiry into this matter.

2. Amnesty International is concerned that the present administrative procedures do not enable the Israeli authorities to bring forward conclusive evidence to refute allegations of ill-treatment.

3. The lack of such conclusive evidence is directly related, in Amnesty International's view, to the extended period of incommunicado detention permitted and often practised under the procedures now in effect in the Occupied Territories. During this period the arrested person is in the company only of interrogators and prison officials, may be denied visits from family, lawyer or personal doctor, and may not be brought speedily before the courts.

4. It is Amnesty International's view that certain legal provisions and practices enhance the possibility of ill-treatment of security suspects. These legal provisions and practices include:

(a) restrictions on the role of defence counsel in preparing the defence;

(b) security trials by military courts which are commonly composed of judges sometimes all of whom are career army officers and most of whom do not have formal legal training. Amnesty International questions whether sufficient weight is being given to that provision of Article 66 of the Fourth Geneva Convention which specifies that military courts are to be 'non-political';

(c) the frequent reliance in security cases on

uncorroborated confessions given to police officers as the effective basis for conviction;

(d) the absence of effective opportunities for judicial appeal for those convicted of security offences.

5. The evidence available to Amnesty International suggests that the machinery for investigating complaints of ill-treatment by interrogating and detaining officials is inadequate.

Recommendations

Amnesty International, therefore, recommends that:

1. For reasons relating to the protection of suspects and security officials alike, a public and impartial committee of inquiry should be established to investigate the allegations of ill-treatment in their totality and the administrative and legal procedures and practices relevant to the arrest, confinement, interrogation and trial of security suspects. The committee's findings, conclusions and recommendations should be made public.

2. The terms of reference of this inquiry should include consideration of the interrogation process and the procedures permitting incommunicado detention. This committee of inquiry should examine:

(a) the rules relating to notification of arrest;

(b) the procedures governing visits to detainees by family and lawyer;

(c) methods both to improve the medical document-ation available for assessing the treatment of arrested suspects and to facilitate the examination of suspects by private medical doctors;

(d) guidelines governing proper interrogation methods.

3. The terms of reference of this inquiry should also include examination of the legal rules and practices which may encourage ill-treatment. The committee should therefore consider:

(a) the composition of the military courts;

(b) ways to expand the role of defence counsel in preparing the accused's defence;

(c) providing legal rules whereby a conviction cannot be based effectively on an uncorroborated confession made in the presence only of police officers or other security personnel;

(d) the establishment of the right of judicial appeal for convicted security offenders.

4. The terms of reference of this inquiry should also include an investigation into the effectiveness of existing machinery for investigating complaints of ill-treatment.

5. Pending the establishment and reporting of such an inquiry, Amnesty International recommends that im-mediate steps be taken to ensure that security suspects under interrogation are protected against possible ill-treatment. Measures to this end should include access to family, lawyer and independent medical doctor promptly after arrest and at regular, brief intervals thereafter.

Published September 1980

AMNESTY INTERNATIONAL IN THE EIGHTIES

Amnesty International in the Eighties by Martin Ennals, Secretary General, from the 'Amnesty International Report 1980'.

In 1970 the international budget of Amnesty International was £28,741. The International Secretariat employed 19 people. There were 27 national sections and 850 groups. The idea of releasing prisoners of conscience by writing letters to governments seemed a little pretentious, but reflected proof of determination and concern. In 1980 the budget is £1,666,280; the International Secretariat has a staff of 150; there are 39 national sections and 2,200 groups. In 1970 the idea of the growth of Amnesty International into the type of structure or institution which exists in 1980 was unthinkable, or at least unthought.

The development of Amnesty International in the seventies was based on membership, research and action. The growth of membership enabled the recruitment of more researchers and then more support staff. The action program grew with experience and with increasing demands being placed on the International Secretariat by a membership hungry for work and eager to respond to ideas and facts. The novelty of the Amnesty International idea was replaced in the mind of the press and the public by an awareness of the accuracy of Amnesty International information. In the seventies Amnesty International became the first organization in the field of human rights to collect, systematically and impartially, information about the violation of a very limited number of human rights.

The Amnesty International mandate has been frequently debated but there is little doubt that it is largely because of its strict limitations that Amnesty International was able to develop effectively both its membership and its action program. Opposition to imprisonment of prisoners of conscience, to torture and to the death penalty is a program which unites people of all political and geographical backgrounds. Every society is capable of providing and does provide examples of violations of the rights which its constitution guarantees.

All nations have contradictions within their systems which create the tensions which lead to human rights abuses. Amnesty International has made no attempt to offer solutions to economic or political problems – solutions which are hard to find and which would divide the membership. On the other hand it has tried as an organization to establish through its work within the United Nations and in other governmental and non-governmental arenas, standards of conduct and laws which would make the violation of human rights more difficult in any political system and would make the exposure of human rights violations more simple.

Above all, however, Amnesty International in the seventies built up a reputation based on careful use of factual information collected and applied with the same impartiality. Governments still use the allegations of human rights violations as a weapon against their supposed enemies and governments still defend their supposed friends, despite their apparent violations of human rights. International trading, arming and aiding between nations has been little influenced by the internal repression which remained rampant throughout the decade.

On the other hand there were clear indications throughout the seventies that governments and, more especially, peoples were beginning to accept that human rights and their defence is a matter of international responsibility. The confirmation of the international standards of human rights spelled out first in the Universal Declaration of Human Rights and later in the conventions and international covenants which came into effect in the latter half of the decade confirmed Amnesty International's absolute belief that despite differences of environment, human rights are universal. In the definition of human rights there cannot be enemies and friends, rich or poor: only people.

As Amnesty International enters the eighties, therefore, it is a different organization in its capacities. But it is the same organization in its purposes. The challenge in 1970 was to develop the organization into a recognized instrument for the protection of human rights in a definite field. Amnesty International had to still the doubts of those who saw it as a tool of right or left; as an emanation of a western liberal ethic, or as a well meaning body of amateurs playing at international do-goodism. The critics of Amnesty International will always use such arguments; but the pattern of the criticism and of the movement's program is today so well recognized that Amnesty International no longer has to defend its existence: only its standards of accuracy and impartiality.

The challenge of the eighties is more complex and more daunting. To create and grow on an incoming tide of enthusiasm and recognition is delicate but exciting. To stabilize, structure and build with patience in a world where governments often seem inured against, if not immune to, criticism is probably more difficult but equally exciting. The stabilization has to start at the centre. The central component of personnel at the International Secretariat cannot and should not increase as in the past. The balance between the centre and the membership requires a strengthening in national structures and an expansion of the membership into new areas both of geography and participation. New techniques have to be developed which will enable better and more rapid use of information received and evaluated at the centre. The growth at the centre must be as a result of increased efficiency, not achieved by a substantial increase in staff. The growth, however, must be maintained: stagnation would lead to decline in capacities and use of resources.

New and better techniques must be evolved to harness the skills of the membership without losing the common language and style of the movement. It is indeed this very complexity of relating languages, styles and political and economic circumstances which is the challenge. Discipline within a voluntary and universal organization is difficult to apply and maintain. Finance is essential but the financial resources within the membership vary considerably. It is not the present complexity which is the problem. The problem we face comprises: the need to increase the complexities by adding new membership in areas hitherto unapproached; the need for new financial methods which will permit, without irritation, the coexistence within a democratic decision-making organization of those who pay and those who cannot; the need to develop new techniques which will enable a much wider use of Amnesty International knowledge and research, without the almost familial links which have until now existed within the membership.

In the seventies the centre struggled to keep up with the growth of members. But the organization remained very much rooted in the wealthy countries of the North with only tentacles slowly reaching the South.

The North/South dilemma is as much one for Amnesty International as for the rest of the world. The solutions may be as far reaching and, within the tiny context of Amnesty International, as revolutionary.

The first need within Amnesty International is to grow in areas where no Amnesty International movement yet exists. In the last decade Amnesty International has paid attention to development outside the capitalist and largely European countries where it first was born and later grew. Insufficient attention, however, was probably paid to the real dimensions of development. Amnesty International could not be identified and harnessed in Third World countries in the same fashion and with the same methods as in the highly developed economies of the West. It was a point of principle to have sections in Asia, Latin America and Africa, but the differences of culture, finance, attitude towards non-governmental organizations and means of expression were not always appreciated in either practical or conceptual terms. At the same time it became accepted that there were countries where Amnesty International could develop and countries where it would be impractical or ill-advised for political or human rights reasons. This dimension and limitation on development will need to be examined and probably challenged in the eighties.

The fundamental and central aspects of Amnesty International which need to be protected in any scheme of widespread development into new areas and therefore new styles can be summarized as:

– the impartiality of the work for the release of prisoners of conscience everywhere;

– the total opposition to the use of torture or the death penalty;

– the right to fair trial for political prisoners without undue delay in accordance with international standards;

– the collection and use of accurate information within the areas of Amnesty International's mandate;

– the fact that members do not work for prisoners in their own countries;

– the fact that research is the responsibility of the central bodies of the organization;

– the control of the movement by its participating membership;

– the protection of sources of information;

– the legal and overt nature of Amnesty International's activities.

– the significance attached by Amnesty International to the application by governments of international agreements, conventions, standards and commitments;

– the independent and self-generated financing of the movement as a whole.

The question to be answered is how, with these essential features preserved, can Amnesty International establish contact with, become recognized and active in, countries where there is little tradition of non-governmental activity, countries where the political bias of human rights activists is mistrusted, where tension and deprivation result from the low level of economic and social rights, where a one-party state prevails or where the regime is run by a dictator. In all communities there are people deeply committed to the protection of human rights. Too often, indeed, the first stage in repression of a population is a governmental attack on the fundamental rights of freedom of speech and religion. In such circumstances Amnesty International has the problem of explaining to governments and to potential members of Amnesty International that participation in the movement is related to the protection of human rights elsewhere and that it is the role of the members in other countries to exercise and express concern about violations in the country in question. This is a difficult educational task.

In itself, however, the task is important because it carries with it the idea that the first line of defence of human rights is the knowledge that those rights exist, yet everywhere people are deprived of them. Amnesty International has yet to establish its priority in the field of human rights education. Its role has been seen as a catalyst to the role of others but there is no other organization which has the information on violations of human rights, the committed membership and the mandate to work in this field. Always education is low on the list of priorities and the importance of education in active protection of human rights is often overlooked.

The United Nations and Specialized Agencies have failed to promote serious teaching programs about existing international mechanisms for the protection of human rights. Governments and national organizations have failed to include human rights teaching programs as part of their support activities for the international organizations to which they belong. By supporting the development of international human rights education policies, Amnesty International can further protect those human rights with which it is concerned and encourage an interest in the work of the organization itself. Such support may also serve to reassure governments that Amnesty International's program coincides with policies already endorsed by the governments themselves. A major program of explanation to governments about the true nature of Amnesty International's activities and mandate is thus imperative if this target of universality of Amnesty International membership and activity is to be achieved.

It is not only governments, however, that are

concerned. Efforts are needed to work with national organizations in countries where no Amnesty International membership is yet assured. National organizations in many parts of the world are close to governments in personnel and policies. To involve and collaborate with trade unions and professional bodies is to go a long way towards explaining to governments that Amnesty International's activities are impartial, motivated only by internationally accepted objectives and totally independent of any outside control other than its membership, which is open to all who accept the Statute.

The active participation in Amnesty International activities by interested organizations and individuals in Eastern Europe, China, USSR, Vietnam and Cuba is long overdue. There is a danger that unless Amnesty International makes a conscious effort to avoid it, the support for Amnesty International will come in some countries only from movements sometimes called 'dissident'. There are, however, many within the government framework who are concerned about human rights issues and who would willingly work internationally to help forward the objectives of Amnesty International if this distinction could be conveyed: that Amnesty International members are not responsible for Amnesty International activities in their own countries and that the organization applies the same impartial standards of information gathering and evaluation everywhere.

The same principles must be applied when exploring growth in areas where the need to develop in accordance with economic and social rights is used as a justification for the suppression of civil and political rights. The member states of the United Nations have repeatedly passed resolutions stating that all human rights are interrelated and of equal importance. There is sometimes a tendency in the West to excuse violations in some areas because of the economic deprivation which creates the contrasts and apparent conflicts in priorities between civil and political rights and economic and social rights. Amnesty International in trying to strengthen human rights activities, human rights awareness and the protection of human rights, must be ready to confront these arguments and extend its membership in the process.

Amnesty International has already acquired some experience in this field but is probably still too rigid, seeking a style and structure which may pose difficulties in countries of Africa, Asia, the Middle East and Latin America. Membership possibilities in the Middle East have so far been little explored by Amnesty International, apart from early contacts in Beirut and a committee not yet formalized in Egypt. Like Latin America there is an immense population with a common language but Amnesty International has not yet faced the challenge of large-scale membership action from countries with educational and economic development problems. In Latin America there are sections of Amnesty International in Mexico, Peru, Venezuela, Ecuador and Costa Rica. Yet much remains to be achieved in seeking and finding the type of Amnesty

International activities to help prisoners which can best be carried out from these areas. Africa has no common language; ex-colonial languages are spread widely but to a limited proportion of the population. Similarly, in parts of Asia, the use of a common language results not in unity, but in a division of the population into those who can and those who cannot speak the second language of national and international communication.

The third category of countries where Amnesty International has yet to develop satisfactorily is those with consistently poor records of human rights violations. The risk of members in such countries becoming hostages to government has to be appreciated, but the challenge of the eighties includes finding the means of safely and effectively recruiting Amnesty International activists in countries whose governments by and large until now have been responsible for the violations of human rights which Amnesty International has tried to combat.

The purpose of extending activity in this way is to extend the protection of the rights which fall within the Amnesty International mandate. This is not an attempt to extend growth for the sake of size or wider representation. The purpose must be to extend respect for human rights and to involve more and more people in that objective. It does not matter if Amnesty International information is used by others, as long as it is used to help prisoners of conscience. It does not matter if others are selective in the use to which the information is put. What matters is that the information which Amnesty International gathers is well used and well understood. What also matters is that the reputation and standing of Amnesty International with regard to the impartiality and accuracy of its information should be maintained and respected. Growth in the eighties will come from greater efficiency in information techniques at the centre and widely differing action techniques in these new areas into which Amnesty International develops.

The problems of such an extension are considerable. There may be a need to look yet again at the movement's structure in order to regulate the separation of functions between and within research and membership activities, or to protect sources. It may be necessary to look at other international bodies with similar problems – the Red Cross (with its tripartite structure) and other bodies which cross the boundaries of ideologies, cultures and continents. More investment is needed to communicate the meaning of Amnesty International activities in many languages. Massive efforts must be made to convince even the most repressive of regimes that Amnesty International is what it claims to be and that Amnesty International membership is acceptable and not subversive, supportive of human rights and not hostile to governments, independent and yet disciplined in its attitudes and in its program. Most of all, it must be shown that Amnesty International members are not involved in or responsible for Amnesty International activities in response to human rights violations in their own countries. As with education, this process of convincing governments can in itself increase protection of human rights. The more governments accept that Amnesty International is impartial, independent and universal, the easier it will be for them to accept Amnesty International standards and respond to Amnesty International criticisms.

Amnesty International is and must remain activist, effective and restricted in its mandate but not its membership. To achieve this will be difficult. It is a daunting prospect to try to convince governments that their critics are not only sincere but right. The finances of Amnesty International will require new examination and inventiveness to find the means of involving more people to meet the new thresholds of expenditure to finance research and travel.

The *Amnesty International Report 1980* concentrates on the work of Amnesty International for its objectives through central research and the actions undertaken by the International Executive Committee and the membership. The report is intended for unrestricted circulation and is addressed as much to the international public as to the Amnesty International membership. It should, however, be read with a view to analysing where more and better things could be done: not only by Amnesty International but also by others acting individually or collectively, as organizations or as governments.

To summarize the challenge:

Amnesty International must:

– improve at all levels the gathering and using of information about prisoners whose cases fall within Amnesty International's mandate;

– find the ways whereby Amnesty International members, associates and supporters, individually or collectively from all parts of the world, of all political persuasions and regardless of economic resources can work on behalf of those prisoners;

– find ways to convince governments and peoples that human rights are universal and that their protection demands a universally shared responsibility;

– find ways to raise the level of awareness of the very existence of human rights to the point where knowledge is positive and mobile between agencies and peoples.

When Amnesty International meets the nineties it should be universally active both in working for prisoners and identifying prisoners to be assisted. The sophistication of impartiality must be accepted and appreciated by governments and opposition movements. Amnesty International is not and should not be a movement of dissidents or opposition elements in national internal affairs. Instead it should be working for the recognition that dissidents have rights and governments and peoples have the duty to protect their societies against abuses that result or may result in imprisonment, torture or death. To convince governments of this fact, which in principle they accept and to which they have in public committed themselves, is an amazing ambition. But so was Peter Benenson's contention that prisoners of conscience could be released by writing letters to governments.

Published 1980

Whether writing letters on behalf of prisoners of conscience or staging protests such as this one, Amnesty International members around the world campaign tirelessly for human rights. Here Amnesty International members in Belgium demonstrate on behalf of those who have 'disappeared': they have been taken into custody but all knowledge of their detention and whereabouts have been denied by the authorities. Many are never seen again.

PSYCHIATRIC DETENTION

The revised and updated report 'Prisoners of Conscience in the USSR: their Treatment and Conditions' said that since its first report in 1975, Amnesty International had documented 400 new cases of people imprisoned in the USSR for exercising fundamental human rights. The organization believed there were many more such cases. Many prisoners of conscience were forcibly confined in psychiatric hospitals.

Amnesty International knows of more than 100 people who were forcibly confined to psychiatric hospitals for exercising their human rights rather than for authentic medical reasons between 1 June 1975 and 31 May 1979. This figure does not include the many known prisoners of conscience who were put into psychiatric hospitals prior to 1 June 1975 and who in many cases remained confined after that date. Nor does this figure include cases on which Amnesty International regards the available information as inadequate for categorizing the confined person as a prisoner of conscience.

A great deal of new evidence on political abuse of psychiatry in the USSR has become available since 1975. A number of victims have emigrated, been met by foreign psychiatrists and other individuals and given detailed accounts of their treatment. Other victims have been released from psychiatric hospitals and their accounts of their treatment have circulated in *samizdat*. Several psychiatrists have emigrated from the USSR and been able to add information about their professional experience to what is known of the abuses.

Most important, the work of human rights activists inside the country in chronicling cases and practices of political abuse of psychiatry has become more efficient and better informed...

Formal procedures for compulsory confinement

There are three formal procedures for forcibly confining people to psychiatric hospitals: (1) the civil procedure, applicable to those not accused of a criminal offence prior to being confined to a psychiatric hospital; (2) the criminal procedure, applicable to those accused of a criminal offence; (3) the procedure whereby individuals convicted of a criminal offence are transferred from their place of imprisonment to a psychiatric hospital.

Both the civil and the criminal procedures provide inadequate protection against wrongful confinement to a psychiatric hospital. In particular, they facilitate the arbitrary subjection of dissenters to psychiatric measures and make difficult the defence of such people through legal means.

However, in one important respect the established procedures offer a protection which, if respected by the authorities, would at least make wrongful confinement of political and religious dissenters and others rare. Under both the civil procedure and the criminal procedure even if individuals are diagnosed as mentally ill they may be confined to a psychiatric hospital only if they are shown to be dangerous to themselves or others.

In hundreds of cases of forcible confinement of dissenters to psychiatric hospitals there has been no suggestion, even by the authorities, that the subjects were physically violent or dangerous to themselves or others. In their persistent denials of political abuses of psychiatry Soviet officials, propagandists and spokesmen for the psychiatric profession have not addressed themselves to this most elementary principle of psychiatric practice, insisting invariably that well-known dissenters who had been confined were mentally ill, but rarely attempting to show that they were in any way 'violent' or 'dangerous'.

The following is a sampling of the types of actions which the authorities have used as grounds for confining people to psychiatric hospitals: giving song recitals in one's own flat (Pyotr Starchik, 1976); criticizing the government in the presence of workmates and other private citizens (Vladimir Rozhdestvov, 1978); trying to cross the border to another country without official permission (the brothers Alexander and Mikhail Shatravka, in the mid-1970s); persistently making religious craft articles (Valeriya Makeyeva, 1978); bringing personal complaints to high government offices in Moscow (Nadezhda Gaidar, 1976); publicizing one's demand to emigrate by carrying a placard in front of the Bolshoi Ballet (Valentin Ivanov, 1977) or a foreign embassy (Anatoly Uvarov, 1976); hanging up pictures of dissenters over one's sleeping place in a hostel (Mikhail Kukobaka, 1977); persistently seeking official permission to emigrate (Anatoly Glukhov in 1978 as well as twice previously); surreptitiously taking down Soviet flags in Lithuania on the anniversary of the October Revolution (Egidius Ionaitis, 1977); distributing leaflets containing 'anti-Soviet slander' (Vyacheslav Zaitsev, 1978); writing complaints to government authorities (Anatoly Ponomaryov, 1977); trying to meet with a foreign correspondent (Vasily Zhigalkin, 1976).

The fact that the authorities have systematically confined non-violent individuals to psychiatric hospitals against their will is itself clear evidence that psychiatry has been abused for political purposes.

Criminal procedure for compulsory psychiatric confinement

... Under the criminal procedure, the accused loses virtually all of his or her procedural rights, and is left only with the passive right to an honest psychiatric examination and a fair court hearing, a right which in practice is unenforceable.

It is the investigator who decides whether the accused should be subjected to a psychiatric examination. When the investigator comes to such a decision, the accused is examined by a forensic psychiatric commission, usually in a psychiatric hospital or institution but sometimes also or instead in the investigation prison.

The investigator need not even inform the accused that such an examination is to be carried out 'if his mental state makes this impossible'. The accused also has no right to be told the results of the psychiatric examination or the recommendations made by the psychiatrists. Furthermore, the accused loses the right to be informed of any fresh charges against him or her, to be told of the results of the criminal investigation of the case or to be shown the materials compiled in the investigation. The law does not grant any special right to such people to have visits from their families. Normally dissenters subjected to psychiatric examination have no visits from their families until after their cases have been heard in court. Hearings usually

Valeria Makeyeva, a Russian Orthodox nun: in 1978 she was arrested for selling religious crafts without permission and later forcibly confined in a Soviet psychiatric hospital. Forcible drug treatment reportedly paralysed her left arm. She was released in 1981.

Anatoly Ponomaryov, a Leningrad engineer who since 1971 has spent over 11 years forcibly confined in a Soviet psychiatric hospital for 'writing complaints to government authorities'. His most recent confinement began in 1978, after he applied for permission to emigrate.

occur between six and 12 months after the arrest.

In one of the very few procedural guarantees for accused whose mental health is called in question, the law states that participation of defence counsel is 'mandatory' at court hearings in such cases.

However, this provision of the law is as grossly violated in such cases as in other cases involving prisoners of conscience.

Commonly prisoners of conscience subjected to psychiatric diagnosis, and their families, have not been permitted to meet their lawyers or have any say in their selection…

If the psychiatric commission conducting the forensic expert examination finds that for reasons of mental illness the suspect is 'not accountable' (a term sometimes translated as 'non-responsible') for his or her offence, this finding is submitted to a court together with a recommendation as to what medical measures should be applied to the subject. Instead of a trial there is a court hearing on the case in which the court decides: a) whether the accused committed a socially dangerous action (i.e. committed an act defined as criminal by the criminal code), b) whether to accept the expert psychiatric commission's findings as to the subject's accountability and c) what measures to apply to him or her…

According to Article 407 of the RSFSR Criminal Code, it is left to the court to decide whether to permit the accused to attend the hearing of his or her case. In very few cases have prisoners of conscience been permitted to attend the court hearings which ruled on whether or not they were accountable. Furthermore, the accused does not have any legal right to send a written statement to the court…

Earlier in this report it was pointed out that Soviet courts invariably convict dissenters brought to trial for political or religious reasons. Dissenters diagnosed as mentally ill fare little better. The courts have heard such cases without taking remedial action against flagrant violations of legality by the investigation organs and psychiatrists. The Ukrainian cyberneticist Leonid Plyushch, for example, was held in detention for one year before his case came to court, in direct violation of Article 34 of the USSR Fundamentals of Criminal Procedure. During the whole of this period, and for six months thereafter, he was not allowed to meet his wife or a lawyer.

Furthermore, the courts themselves have frequently added their own procedural violations to those committed by the investigating officials. Often such court hearings are held *in camera*. In Plyushch's case, Judge Dyshel classified as a state secret the court hearing on Plyushch's state of mind and ordered that the hearing be held *in camera*, although the case did not fall into the categories where this might be lawful.

Judge Dyshel also refused to allow court witnesses to give evidence in favour of the defendant. Finally, the judge did not allow Plyushch's legal representative (his wife) to participate in the hearing. Consequently:

The courtroom was empty; neither the accused, nor his legal representative, nor a psychiatric expert, nor the accused's relatives were present. So great was the isolation of the hearing from the outside world that the police detachment guarding the empty hall refused (with threats of arrest) to allow on to the steps of the court building the citizens wishing to attend the hearing. It was only after many requests that the accused's wife and sister were allowed (on account of the severe cold) to await the end of the hearing in the vestibule.

When in June 1978 the Donetsk regional court ordered that the coal miner and labour rights activist, Vladimir Klebanov, be confined to a special psychiatric hospital, neither he nor his relatives were informed in advance of the court hearing.

The most important criticism that can be made of court hearings of such cases is their uncritical attitude towards the psychiatric diagnoses submitted. The psychiatric diagnoses cited below, and others, are at the very least questionable as recommendations for court action. One course of action which is available to courts presented with unclear, incomplete or contested diagnoses is to call for a second psychiatric opinion. This is rarely done, and when courts do ask for a second opinion it is always from officially-appointed psychiatrists, never psychiatrists nominated by the accused or their families. Soviet courts in political cases almost invariably accept not only the findings of forensic psychiatric commissions, but also their recommendations as to what should be done with the accused.

If, as normally happens, the court accepts the psychiatric commission's diagnosis and recommendations, it must then release the accused from criminal responsibility or punishment and order measures that are both conducive to the individual's medical recovery and protective of society.

The court has three options: it may order that the accused be placed in the care of relatives or a guardian; confined for an indefinite period to an ordinary psychiatric hospital; or confined indefinitely to a special psychiatric hospital.

Putting the accused in the care of relatives or a guardian does not entail incarceration. In no known political case has a court exercised this option.

If the court, advised by a forensic psychiatric commission, decides that the accused requires compulsory in-patient medical treatment, it orders that he or she be confined either to an ordinary or a special psychiatric hospital for an indefinite period. According to the RSFSR Criminal Code, ordinary psychiatric hospitals are intended for those who have not committed especially serious crimes; the special institutions are designed for people who 'represent a special danger to society'…

It has been common for courts to order that dissenters be confined to special psychiatric hospitals in the absence of any record of violence on their part, let alone any effort on the part of psychiatrists or the courts to show that they represented a 'special danger' to other people or to society…

In some cases courts have ordered that dissenters be sent for forensic psychiatric examination even though forensic psychiatrists had already examined the subject and concluded that he or she was 'accountable'. For example, this happened in March 1979 to Vladislav Bebko, who was charged with 'malicious hooliganism' for tearing down an official poster celebrating the anniversary of the October Revolution and 'anti-Soviet slander' for making 'oral propaganda' and distributing documents of the Czechoslovak human rights group Charter 77. Bebko was subsequently ruled 'accountable' again and sentenced to 3 years' imprisonment for 'anti-Soviet slander'.

Civil procedures for forcible commitment

Under the *civil commitment procedure* (sometimes referred to as the 'administrative' procedure) people who have not committed criminal offences but who are diagnosed as mentally ill and likely to commit socially dangerous acts may be forcibly confined for treatment on the authority of a psychiatrist and with the subsequent agreement of a commission of three psychiatrists. Those committed under this civil procedure are normally confined in ordinary psychiatric hospitals.

The civil commitment procedure is laid down in a directive ('On Emergency Confinement of Mentally Ill Persons Who Represent a Social Danger') issued on 26 August 1971 by the Ministry of Health in agreement with the Procurator General and the MVD [Ministry of Internal Affairs]. The text of this directive is not published in any easily available Soviet publication and it is virtually a secret document.

The directive states that mentally ill people may be confined to a psychiatric hospital without their permission or that of the family if they are an 'evident danger' to themselves or those around them. To guide psychiatric practitioners and law enforcement agencies, the directive lists a number of symptoms which are to serve as criteria for application of this measure. The list has been criticized by human rights activists and foreign psychiatrists because of the obscurity and lack of medical precision of the symptoms listed. The terms used are so broad as to cover almost any dissident or nonconformist behaviour: for example, among the symptoms listed are 'a hypochondriac delusion, causing an abnormal aggressive attitude in the ill person towards individuals, organizations and institutions' and 'a systematic syndrome of delusions with chronic deterioration if it results in behaviour dangerous to society'. The directive does not give even a rough explanation of what is meant by 'social danger'.

As if deliberately to invite the forcible confinement of peaceful citizens, the directive states that any of the enumerated conditions of 'mental illness' ... 'may be accompanied by externally correct behaviour and dissimulation'.

The directive states that emergency confinement may be effected by medical personnel, and that the police must render assistance if there is a 'possibility' that the subject will resist or if he or she shows aggressive behaviour or hides, or if the subject's family refuses or resists his or her being taken away.

The doctor who first orders the person's confinement must submit to the psychiatric hospital a report justifying this, and within one day of being confined the subject must be examined by a commission of three psychiatrists who are to decide whether the forcible confinement was justified and if there is a need for further confinement. The subject must be re-examined by a commission of three psychiatrists at least once a month. The commission must order the subject's release 'upon improvement of the patient's mental condition or such change of the picture of the illness that he is no longer a danger to society'. In discharging a person from confinement, the psychiatric hospital must inform the local psychiatric dispensary at his or her place of residence, and the released person must be placed on a 'special list' and receive 'systematic preventive treatment'.

The directive does not provide for any involvement of a court or other judicial agencies. The regulations do not indicate any right of the confined person to have access to a lawyer; Amnesty International knows of no case where a dissenter confined in this way has been permitted to see a lawyer. The only agency outside the psychiatric service which is given a formal role under these procedures is the police, which is administered by the MVD [Ministry of Internal Affairs]. In practice, the KGB [Committee of State Security] has in many cases played a major part at various stages between confinement and release.

Dissenters have been forcibly confined to psychiatric hospitals in a great variety of circumstances, a common feature being the direct link between the dissenters' exercise of their human rights and the official decision to have them confined to a psychiatric hospital. It is quite common for dissenters to be forcibly confined without having been seen first by a psychiatrist.

Dissenters have been picked up and taken directly to psychiatric hospitals from work, school, home, or off the streets. The abruptness of the procedure is illustrated by the case of Valeria Novodvorskaya, a linguist, who was detained at her place of work in a Moscow library on 24 November 1978, less than a month after she was publicly involved in the formation of an independent trade union group. According to a *samizdat* account of her detention:

At 5.45 pm on the day of her hospitalization a man came into the room where she was working and asked her to help him take away some books. She took a package of books, went out and did not return. A colleague who was working with her in the same room waited for a long time and then became apprehensive and raised the alarm. After lengthy searching her friends found her in Psychiatric Hospital Number 15 (telephone number 114-53-89).

In a number of instances dissenters have been summoned on some pretext to a hospital, militia headquarters or other public building, where, to their surprise, they were taken to a psychiatrist who had them committed to a psychiatric hospital. For example, in July 1976

Alexander Argentov, a participant in a religious seminar in Moscow which had been labelled 'anti-Soviet' by state security officials, was unexpectedly summoned to a local Military Commission, a body which deals with military conscription. The Military Commission told him that he must report to a district psychiatric clinic to obtain a medical certificate. Although Argentov had never been under psychiatric treatment or observation, the clinic already had a file card about him. Two doctors there questioned him (mainly about his religious views) and had him immediately committed to Moscow Psychiatric Hospital Number 14.

A number of people have been detained and forcibly confined to psychiatric hospitals when they brought personal complaints to the highest organs of government. A startling indication of the extent to which this happens came in October 1976, when the Moscow Helsinki monitoring group reported:

Every day the police sends to the duty psychiatrists approximately 12 people from the reception room of the USSR Supreme Soviet alone; besides these, another two or three of those people who try to get into an embassy; still others who are picked up from other places, including directly off the streets. Of these about half are subsequently hospitalized...

People who are forcibly confined for submitting complaints are commonly diagnosed as suffering from a 'mania for litigation'.

Violations of the regulations laid down in the 1971 directive governing civil confinement have been common. Frequently the relatives of the confined person have not been informed within 24 hours of what has happened, as is required by the directive. Often the subjects have been examined by a psychiatrist only after they were forcibly confined to a psychiatric hospital. In many cases dissenters have not been examined by a psychiatric commission within one day of being detained, as is required by the directive, but only days or weeks later; and in a number of cases confined dissenters have not had any psychiatric examination at all...

Diagnosis

Under both the criminal and civil procedure the psychiatric diagnosis is invariably carried out by officially-appointed psychiatrists. Dissenters have never been able to obtain the appointment of psychiatrists of their own choice to the psychiatric commissions that decide whether or not they should be hospitalized. In a number of cases officially-appointed psychiatrists are known to have concealed their names from the people they were diagnosing.

Under both procedures diagnoses are generally perfunctory and even in formal terms are based on inadequate examination of the subject. Dissenters who have been sent under the criminal procedure to the Serbsky Institute of Forensic Psychiatry in Moscow, officially regarded as the country's leading centre for forensic psychiatric diagnosis, have reported that their diagnosis has

Vladimir Klebanov, a coal miner, formed an unofficial free trade union in 1978. He was ordered to be forcibly confined in a Soviet special psychiatric hospital by the Donetsk regional court in the Ukraine, despite not being present at the court hearing. Amnesty International does not know if he has been released.

Sergei Purtov, a Leningrad engineer, forcibly confined in a Soviet mental hospital since 1971 for 'anti-Soviet agitation and propaganda'. With his brother and six others he had started an unofficial group advocating a return to what they called 'pure Leninist principles'.

consisted of several conversations with a psychiatrist assigned to their case and then a few minutes (as a rule '10 or 15 minutes', according to Alexander Podrabinek) in front of the psychiatric commission whose task it is to establish whether the subjects are accountable and to recommend on the measures to be applied to them. Both in the Serbsky Institute and elsewhere, psychiatrists base their diagnoses almost exclusively on 'subjective' observations (from conversations with the subjects, from visual observation of their behaviour, and from their record) and make little use of objective testing methods. As mentioned above, sometimes dissenters have been confined to psychiatric hospitals under the civil procedure without any psychiatric diagnosis at all.

The following features are common to those cases of confinement of dissenters to psychiatric hospitals mentioned in this report:

(1) In each case the subject had exercised his or her human rights in a manner which was not approved of by the authorities and which has often been punished in other cases by imprisonment under criminal law. The most common forms of behaviour which have been punished by forcible psychiatric confinement have been: expressing views critical of government practices, whether in written or in oral form; submitting to government authorities complaints against government officials; engaging in public demonstrations for purposes disapproved of by the authorities; belonging to unofficial groups informally labelled 'anti-Soviet' or 'illegal' by state security or other government officials; participating in religious activities; making persistent efforts to gain official permission to emigrate from the country; trying to leave the country without official permission. In many cases the forcible psychiatric confinement of the subject took place only after the authorities had tried by other means to deter him or her from engaging in such activities. In many cases it was exactly such exercise of human rights which officially-appointed psychiatrists labelled as symptomatic of mental illness.

(2) Neither the subject nor his or her relatives, friends and sympathizers believed the subject to be in need of forcible in-patient psychiatric treatment. Many prisoners of conscience have been permitted to emigrate after being released from psychiatric hospitals, and have been seen by psychiatrists and other individuals abroad who formed the view that their psychiatric confinement was not justified on medical grounds. Foreign psychiatrists have reached similar conclusions after examining former victims during visits to the USSR. During the period from 1977 to 1979 Dr Alexander Voloshanovich, a Moscow psychiatrist who lent his expert services to the unofficial Working Commission for the Investigation of the Use of Psychiatry for Political Purposes, gave in-depth psychiatric examinations to 36 dissenters who feared they might be forcibly confined to psychiatric hospitals. Most of the 36 had previously been forcibly confined to psychiatric hospitals. Dr Voloshanovich concluded that none of them required forcible hospitaliza-

tion on any grounds nor had they required this in the past.

(3) The subjects were not known to have any record of violence nor did the authorities or the psychiatrists involved demonstrate how they were dangerous to themselves or others.

Yet between mid-1975 and mid-1979 in more than 100 known such cases officially-appointed psychiatrists ruled that dissenters were mentally ill to such a degree that compulsory in-patient psychiatric treatment was necessary.

A simple indication of how psychiatric diagnoses have been used for political persecution is that often when Soviet citizens have associated together in activities, which, though not illegal, were not approved of by the authorities, several of the participants have been officially diagnosed as mentally ill and forcibly confined to psychiatric hospitals – as though the group's participants were mentally ill *en masse*. The following are cases in point.

In 1971 seven members of an unofficial group advocating Marxist-Leninist views different from those enforced by the Communist Party of the Soviet Union were arrested in Leningrad and charged with 'anti-Soviet agitation and propaganda'. Four of them were ruled mentally ill and confined to psychiatric hospitals: Vyacheslav Dzibalov, Sergei Purtov, Andrei Kozlov and Mariya Musiyenko…

During the mid-1970s two brothers, Alexander and Mikhail Shatravka, were arrested while trying to cross the border into Finland without permission from the Soviet authorities. Both were subsequently ruled mentally ill and ordered confined to special psychiatric hospitals.

In 1976 an entire family of religious believers (both parents and two daughters) were confined to a psychiatric hospital in Byelorussia on account of their religious faith, according to a prisoner of conscience who was himself held there at the time.

In 1974 a group of Russian Orthodox believers in Moscow organized a seminar to discuss religious and philosophical matters. Officials subsequently told participants that the seminar was 'anti-Soviet'. Of at least eight people who have been arrested since 1976 in connection with the seminar, four (Alexander Argentov, Edward Fedotov, Alexander Kuzkin and Alexander Pushkin) were confined to psychiatric hospitals under the civil procedure and another (Sergei Yermolayev) was confined to the Serbsky Institute for diagnosis under the criminal procedure, but subsequently ruled accountable.

A number of workers grouped together in Moscow in 1976 to protest collectively at violations of their labour rights. By early 1978 no less than five of the group's leading members had been confined to psychiatric hospitals: Vladimir Klebanov, Yevgeny Nikolayev, Gavriil Yankov, Gennady Tsvyrko and Varvara Kucherenko….

Since the early 1970s enough has been known about the nature of diagnoses by officially-appointed psychiatrists in cases of political and religious dissenters to identify a number of common features.

First, such diagnoses usually give only a vague,

generalized explanation of the mental illness from which the subject is purportedly suffering and the nature of the symptoms. Professor Andrei Snezhnevsky, Director of the Institute of Psychiatry of the USSR Academy of Medical Sciences and, through him, the Serbsky Institute of Forensic Psychiatry in Moscow have provided a strong lead for the country's psychiatrists in making such diagnoses. Snezhnevsky's most distinctive contribution to Soviet psychiatry has been his extremely broad definition of schizophrenia, an illness which in his interpretation need not be accompanied by external symptoms even when it is serious enough to justify forcible hospitalization. Schizophrenia, often in its 'sluggish' form, has been the diagnosis most commonly made of dissenters...

The following are examples of how officially-appointed psychiatrists have characterized the mental illness of dissenters: 'nervous exhaustion brought on by her search for justice' (Nadezhda Gaidar in 1976); 'psychopathic paranoia with overvalued ideas and tendencies to litigation' (Mikhail Zhikharev in 1974); 'schizophrenia with religious delirium' (Alexander Voloshchuk in 1977); 'reformist delusions' or 'reformist ideas' (Yevgeny Nikolayev in 1978); 'psychopathy with tendency to litigation' (Alexander Komarov in 1978); 'delusional ideas of reformism and struggle with the existing social political system in the USSR' (Vladimir Rozhdestvov, 1978); a 'mania for reconstructing society' (Mikhail Kukobaka, 1976).

Another common characteristic of official diagnoses of dissenters is that 'seemingly normal' people have often been labelled 'dangerously mentally ill'. The broad rejection of 'apparent normality' as an obstacle to forcible hospitalization derives authority both from the theories of Professor Snezhnevsky and the Serbsky Institute and from the 1971 directive governing civil commitment to psychiatric hospitals (summarized above)....

Another feature of official psychiatric diagnoses of dissenters is that they have commonly focused precisely on the subjects' exercise of their human rights as symptomatic of mental illness. When subjects have refused to accept that their behaviour was brought on by mental illness, psychiatrists have often described this as 'lack of criticism'. Typical of this was the case of Pyotr Starchik, who was diagnosed in 1973 as suffering from 'creeping schizophrenia' and confined to a special psychiatric hospital. The symptoms identified by an officially-appointed forensic psychiatric commission included his religious belief and his 'rudeness' to the investigators of his case. After his release in 1975 Starchik, an amateur composer, held concerts of his songs in his Moscow flat which were attended by large audiences. In the summer of 1976 state security officials warned him that if he continued to hold these concerts he would be confined to a psychiatric hospital again. In September 1976 he was forcibly committed to an ordinary psychiatric hospital in Moscow. Reportedly the hospital's admittance journal explained his forcible commitment thus:

S.D. [socially dangerous]. Was an in-patient in the psychiatric hospital in Kazan for compulsory treatment under Article 70. Recently he has been composing songs of anti-Soviet content and has been holding gatherings of 40 or 50 people in his flat. On examination he was well-orientated. There were no major disturbances of his consciousness. His contact was formal. He was suspicious. He answered questions monosyllabically. He does not deny having composed the songs, and said 'I have my own world views'. Lacks critical faculty...

Another characteristic of the diagnosis of dissenters by officially-appointed psychiatrists is that very often the state security authorities have played a direct role in the decision-making of the psychiatrists, often to the extent of deciding themselves what the diagnosis should be.

One of the many documented illustrations of this comes from the case of Anatoly Ponomaryov, a Leningrad engineer who has been repeatedly confined to psychiatric hospitals throughout the 1970s for his *samizdat* writings and his open protests to the authorities. When in October 1975 he was forcibly confined for the fourth time, another well-known dissenter, the historian Mikhail Bernstam, accidentally learned of it at once and went to see Dr L.D. Fedoseyeva, the deputy chief doctor of the psychiatric clinic where Ponomaryov had been diagnosed and ordered committed. The psychiatrist told Bernstam that the reason for Ponomaryov's hospitalization was his protest letters, which 'hindered the work of public bodies'. She added that the fact that Ponomaryov's behaviour was 'otherwise normal' did not indicate that he was mentally healthy. Their conversation then took the following turn:

Bernstam: 'What sort of letters were they?'

Dr Fedoseyeva: 'Neither I nor the doctor treating him has read the letters but we know their contents. They are the letters of an ill man. They aren't anti-Soviet but in them he expresses a low opinion of the Soviet government and in general writes cynically about our leaders.'

Bernstam: 'If you haven't read the letters how do you justify Ponomaryov's hospitalization?'

Dr Fedoseyeva: 'We possess the information and an evaluation from the competent authorities.'

Bernstam: 'Which authorities do you mean?'

Dr Fedoseyeva: 'Surely you understand...'

Bernstam: 'Nonetheless?'

Dr Fedoseyeva: 'Well, officials of the KGB.'

Bernstam: 'You said the letters were a symptom of an aggravation of the patient's illness. But are KGB officials really competent to make such judgments?'

Dr Fedoseyeva: 'They make a political judgment and phone us, advising us to intern Ponomaryov. For us to make a medical diagnosis it's enough simply to know of the existence of anti-government letters. There's no need to read them.'

Soviet psychiatrists have frequently told the subjects of their diagnoses: 'Nothing depends on us.'

Published April 1980

DIFFERENT FACES OF IMPRISONMENT

The theme of Prisoners of Conscience Week in 1980 was 'Different Faces of Imprisonment'.

Graciela Geuna and Jorge Cazorla, photographed on their wedding day in Argentina. Within a year the bride had 'disappeared' and the bridegroom was dead, shot in the back during a kidnap attack. Graciela Geuna, now living abroad, was a university student in Córdoba when, on 10 June 1976, she and her husband were abducted by 20 armed men in plain

clothes – she later identified them as military personnel. She said that after her husband had been killed she was taken to a military 'concentration camp', where, stripped naked and tied hand and foot to bedsprings, she was given electric shocks, kicked and clubbed during 10 days' interrogation. She said she was kept blindfolded for 10 months. After 22 months she was released without charge or trial.

An estimated 15,000 people 'disappear' in one country and, in another, 25,000 people are seized, 'disappear' or are killed...

In a third country, the wife of an imprisoned nationalist leader lives out another 24 hours of a 'banning' order, the latest of a series that has ruled every day of her life for the past 16 years...

In a fourth, a trade unionist is detained by the police for the 24th time in two years...

The vast majority of these people, political prisoners – the cases of thousands of them documented in detail by AI – have been subjected to some kind of imprisonment that falls outside the usual sense of the word – that is, confinement in some official place of detention for a specified period.

They are victims of different 'faces' of imprisonment; in these cases: 'disappearance'; 'banning'; house arrest; internal exile; repressive short-term detention.

These are three of the methods used by governments to stifle dissent without resorting to 'classic' imprisonment.

'Disappearance' has become a major tool of governments in several parts of the world – the practice is best documented in a number of Latin American countries, but AI has information about 'disappearances' in other parts as well, for instance in East Timor, in the Philippines and in Ethiopia.

This repressive tool is used not only against declared political opponents but also against ordinary men and women considered to be a threat of some kind.

In a typical case, the victim is seized, often at home, by armed men and dragged off to an unknown destination. When family or friends make inquiries, the police deny that there has been an arrest. If an attempt is made to have the victim produced before a court, the authorities will assure the judge that the person concerned is not in their custody. They will refuse to acknowledge that the victim has been seized officially – even though the abduction may have been carried out by uniformed military personnel.

(In cases where abductions are the work of unofficial agents acting in collusion with the authorities the police will refuse to investigate, or else they may fail to inform the family of the results of any inquiries.)

AI has gathered massive evidence on the fate of 'disappeared' people, indicating that the victims are usually tortured and often killed. For instance, it estimates that about 15,000 people have 'disappeared' in Argentina since 1975 (it has documented more than 4,000 cases). The figures for Guatemala are even more shocking: 25,000 people seized, killed or 'disappeared' since 1966 – more than 1,000 of them in the first six months of 1980.

Under 'banning' and house arrest orders, prisoners of conscience are confined to their own house or town for specified periods. In some countries a form of internal exile is operated, with people being sent to live in a certain part of their country.

Such restrictions are accompanied by other restraints, such as having to report regularly to the authorities and surveillance, searches and interrogations by the police.

In South Africa more than 150 people are now restricted by 'banning' orders under legislation empowering the Minister of Justice to impose a variety of restrictions on people said to be engaged in 'activities which endanger or are calculated to endanger the security of the State or the maintenance of public order'. No specific reasons are given by the Minister; the orders are usually imposed for terms of from two to five years and are often reimposed on expiry.

'Banned' people may not, among other restrictions, be quoted in public or private; they may not prepare material for publication or attend any political or social 'gathering' – defined as any meeting of more than two people for a common purpose; their movements are restricted, usually to the magisterial district in which they reside.

Many banned people have also been subjected to partial house arrest – usually from 6.00pm to 6.00am during the week, and from noon on Saturday to 6.00am the following Monday.

In recent years it has also been common for 'banned' people to be banished to remote areas: Winnie Mandela's present five-year 'banning' order was amended shortly after its imposition in 1976 to provide for her banishment to a small town more than 350 kilometres from her home in Soweto.

In Chile, a decree promulgated in February 1980 gave the Minister of the Interior powers to order people to be sent to live in remote areas of the country for terms of internal exile (*relegación*) of up to three months for disturbing or attempting to disturb public order.

In South Korea the police and the Korean Central Intelligence Agency use house arrest to restrict people who, the government believes, may take part in political activities aimed at expressing their political opinions.

Members of church groups are often house arrested for short periods and the measure is also applied against politicians and the relatives of political prisoners: Lee Hi-ho, wife of the opposition leader Kim Dae-jung – sentenced to death in September (see October 1980 *Newsletter*) – has been under house arrest since 27 May 1980.

Some governments apply executive powers or special legislation to detain opponents for short periods and thus avoid the need to justify their actions before the courts.

The authorities may use such short-term detention to keep dissenters out of circulation at certain 'sensitive' times, but it can also provide the opportunity to extract information under torture, or as part of a general policy of harassment. The victims may be arrested, freed for a short spell then rearrested, a process which can be repeated over a number of years, a continual shuttling in and out of prison.

In Colombia short-term detention has often been widely used during periods of social unrest. Normal judicial controls against arbitrary arrest are dispensed with and prisoners are often held in military centres of detention.

There have been numerous allegations of torture by such short-term prisoners.

Under Polish law, a person may be held in custody without formal charges for up to 48 hours. In recent years such short-term detention has been the most common method of intimidation in official attempts to silence human rights activists.

In Pakistan, detaining alleged political prisoners for periods of several weeks or months has been a recurrent practice; since 5 July 1977, it has been carried out under martial law provisions, for 'activities prejudicial to public order' – detainees can be held for an initial period of three months, followed by further three-month periods.

AI Newsletter November 1980

Kazimierz Switon, a founding member of the Committee of Free Trade Unions in Katowice, Poland. In the two years to February 1980 he was detained in police custody 24 times.

Albertina Sisulu, wife of the jailed African nationalist leader Walter Sisulu. She has spent years of her life resricted under 'banning' orders imposed by the South African authorities. A prominent member of the United Democratic Front (UDF), she and 15 other members were arrested in February 1985 and charged with treason. Albertina Sisulu was acquitted in December 1985.

POLITICAL KILLINGS IN GUATEMALA

In the years between 1978 and 1981 nearly 5,000 Guatemalans were seized without warrant and killed. Several hundred others were assassinated after being denounced as 'subversives'. Over 600 who had reportedly been seized by the security services 'disappeared'. The Guatemalan Government laid the blame for these murders and 'disappearances' on independent anti-communist 'death squads'. The 1981 Amnesty International report 'Guatemala: A Government Program of Political Murder' added new evidence that these abuses were in fact carried out by units of the army and the police. Reproduced here are the introduction and the transcript of an interview with a conscript soldier who had served as a member of a plainclothes army unit in Guatemala City.

The human rights issue that dominates all others in the Republic of Guatemala is that people who oppose or are imagined to oppose the government are systematically seized without warrant, tortured and murdered, and that these tortures and murders are part of a deliberate and long-standing program of the Guatemalan Government.

This report contains information, published for the first time, which shows how the selection of targets for detention and murder, and the deployment of official forces for extra-legal operations, can be pin-pointed to secret offices in an annex of Guatemala's National Palace, under the direct control of the President of the Republic.

The report also includes transcripts of two unique interviews; the first is with a peasant who, as far as Amnesty International knows, is the sole survivor of political imprisonment in Guatemala in 1980; the second is with a former conscript soldier who served as a member of a plainclothes army unit and who described the abduction of civilians who were later tortured and murdered.

Between January and November in 1980 alone some 3,000 people described by government representatives as 'subversives' and 'criminals' were either shot on the spot in political assassinations or seized and murdered later; at least 364 others seized in this period have not yet been accounted for.

The Government of Guatemala denies having made a single political arrest or holding a single political prisoner since President Romeo Lucas Garcia took office in July 1978. All abuses are attributed to 'independent' paramilitary groups beyond official control. This report adds to previously available evidence that these actions are carried out by units of the regular security services. No convincing evidence has been produced that the groups described by the authorities do in fact exist.

In the final section of the report, Amnesty International reproduces the interviews, transcribed from tape recordings, with two Guatemalans who have had personal experience with the torture and murder of political suspects by the Guatemalan army.

The former prisoner was abducted on 15 February 1980 by a plainclothes army squad in a village in northern Guatemala. He escaped from Huehuetenango army base in western Guatemala after being held for 11 days.

He gives details of his place of detention – in the base slaughterhouse – and of how he was interrogated under torture by Guatemalan army officers.

He describes the execution of three other prisoners in his presence, strangled with a garrotte – a technique cited as the cause of death in hundreds of killings in 1980, including those of 37 people found in a mass grave in San Juan Comalapa, near Guatemala City, in March 1980.

The former conscript soldier, of Kekchi Indian origin, gives an account of his second year of military service, when he served as a member of a plainclothes army unit in Guatemala City. He describes the surveillance of civilians under political suspicion, and the abduction of civilians for interrogation under torture, and then murder,

Guatemalan police arrest demonstrators. Guatemala City, March 1982.

at the Guatemalan army base of the *Brigada Militar Mariscal Zavala* on the outskirts of Guatemala City.

His testimony is of particular significance as a document of record. Political killings and 'disappearances' involving government forces are not new in Guatemala: in 1976 Amnesty International estimated that about 20,000 people had been victims of these abuses since 1966, when they first began to occur regularly. But although in the past other members of the security services have told of their participation in abductions and killings – for instance, Lauro Alvarado y Alvarado, a National Police officer, who was later killed in 1975 (see *Guatemala: Amnesty International Briefing*, 1976, page 15) – this former conscript's testimony is the most extensive and detailed of its kind and the first by a conscript soldier describing the routine extra-legal security measures of regular army units.

Although the two interviews transcribed in part here were not conducted directly by Amnesty International, they are published as illustrations of the nature of political imprisonment and murder in Guatemala.

The interviews were conducted in February 1980.

The transcripts have been edited for length and the names of those involved removed. Their publication was decided only after their authenticity and accuracy had been determined by exhaustive analysis of the two tapes and extensive cross-checking of information. Only indirect communication was possible with the interviewer of the escaped prisoner but the former soldier was interviewed by a journalist from Europe now in close contact with Amnesty International.

The interviewers agreed to the tape transcripts being published by Amnesty International provided that they were edited so that no one could be endangered by their release. Although the escaped prisoner, whose identity is known to the Government of Guatemala, and the former soldier are now reported to be safe outside Guatemala, there is still fear of reprisals by the Government of Guatemala if their identities are publicized.

○ A number of anti-government guerilla groups have been operating in Guatemala since 1966 and Amnesty International is aware that there continue to be armed confrontations between government and guerrilla forces, with lives lost on both sides. However, Amnesty International does not accept government assertions that all or most killings of the sort described in this report are the result of armed conflict or are the work of agents operating independently and out of the government's control.

Amnesty International opposes the torture and execution of prisoners in all cases, whether by government forces or opposition groups. It believes that confrontation between government and violent opposition groups cannot be held to justify these human rights violations.

Testimony of a conscript

How long did you serve in the army?

Well, when I joined, well they didn't tell us anything but, when they seized us, they just seized us without letting us, well, talk to our families – what did it matter to them? That's what they told us then, but when they got us there they said that it was three years, because that's the service that you have to do.

So you have been in the army three years?

Only two years; I was in the army two years.

*It is the military commissioners (*comisionados militares*), isn't it, men in plain clothes but armed, who hunt down the men for the army?*

Yes, well, here the commissioners are like that, civilians, they don't carry weapons, just their machetes, but actually clubs too – big ones.

Does this military commissioner do his work alone, or helped by other soldiers or civilians?

Yes, well before they used to seize people, well more peacefully. They didn't beat them, not a lot that is, but now they do.

Why now?

Because now, now they aren't the only ones who seize the young men for the barracks; the military police do too. They go around with a truck, and anyone they find ... they don't tell them even where they are being taken, if you are carrying some of your things, something like a pack or something, they don't care, if there is room in the truck then they take it in. If they don't like you, they throw it in the street...

So, now it isn't just the military commissioners but also the military itself?

Yes. What happens now is that the military commissioners are afraid because really the peasants now know what's going on and what they do now is get together in crowds and if the commissioner dares to seize one of their group, what they do is beat them up, so now this means the commissioners are afraid.

The boys attack the military commissioners?

Yes, this is happening, because as they already know – just as we do who have already left – we tell them that the army isn't any good because, because, well, because I've finally discovered the army is nothing, nothing but a school of murderers, so that's what you are dragged into, nothing better than that.

... [a long section concerning recruitment procedures and basic training methods has been eliminated from this transcript for reasons of space.]

... then after we'd gone through all this, we, as soldiers, then we became regular soldiers and we did our service, then they gave us arms, because we could use them, and we went to the firing range to shoot, and so on. By then they were sure that we wouldn't run away ... They sent us to watch banks, plantations, different zones in the capital, at night. Even if it was raining, we went out in the back of a pick-up truck with our machine-guns, we went out to keep an eye on everything, at midnight.

Weren't you afraid that one day an officer might have ordered you to kill someone?

I wasn't afraid. At that time I was full of the ideas they filled me with. I wasn't afraid they might tell me to kill someone. I used to do it because my mentality by then had changed completely – that's what had happened to me.

You could kill people without any problems?

Yes, without problems. Once they saw that I was really keen and understood the things they had taught me, they took me out of my unit with two others. Afterwards, we didn't stay in the same unit but were instructed separately. They didn't discipline us much then; we had already suffered enough, so they didn't discipline us so much, although the men in the unit did get disciplined.

Then they gave us a little black 'galil' that had only just arrived.

Is that a weapon?

Yes, 'galil'.

It's very sophisticated isn't it?

Yes, it's very new. They said Israel sent them to Guatemala, because it owed Guatemala something and other arms arrived. This one can fire a maximum of 350

shots a minute.

So they gave us this weapon and we were happier because we were better equipped. When these weapons arrived they gave us one each, then stopped giving us the M-1 rifles. They collected these and stored them. When they gave us this weapon, they took me out of the unit but the others stayed on.

Then they sent the three of us to the office of the S-2, where we met officers. They stopped cropping our hair, instead they let us look really good. They told us: 'Now you have been selected; you were chosen; you aren't just simple soldiers any more, like those in the unit. If you've got guts you might even become officers', they told us.

They told you that you were better than the others?

Yes, better than the others.

Then, they had already brainwashed you?

Yes, that's what I'm saying, they had already brainwashed me; they had already filled my head with their own ideology, so I felt superior to my fellow soldiers … What I thought then was that I was superior to everyone because I had managed to reach this position. They gave us separate training and each of us was given a .45 and left full of enthusiasm.

.45, what's that?

It's a weapon only officers use, with eight shots. They gave us one and we went out in civilian clothes. They told us: 'You are going to get orders. You are going out now.' They sent us out on the street in an army car.

That's how we used to go out, as civilians, but to keep an eye on things, especially to control the students, because there [in S-2] we went to different classes where they told us that the students could be guerrillas and that they were the people who cause the disorder on the streets, and that according to the law in the army's constitution, you've got to kill all of these people.

That's what they told us, then we went out in twos and threes to drive around the capital and control things.

Did you have permission to kill anyone?

Only suspicious characters. And they gave us orders of the day. And we also had classes – we were students just like the suspects! And we could kill them.

And they gave us special identity cards so that if there were any police around, even if there were more of them than us and we did certain things we could just show them these, so they wouldn't seize us and we could get away. That's what they told us. They gave us cards, so that if we made some great mistake – we could kill someone, just like that, and then escape, and the police wouldn't have the power to seize us; we could just show them the cards.

And the police don't do anything?

They don't do anything, nothing. So I realized that the army is a school for murderers, it's as simple as that. They said to me, if you discover your father is in subversive movements – I didn't understand the word – 'subversive', they said, is whatever is against the government and is what causes disorder in Guatemala – if your father is involved in groups like that, kill him, because if you don't he'll try and kill us …

Could you kill your father or your mother or your sister?

Anyone who turned up, if we were ordered to. I could

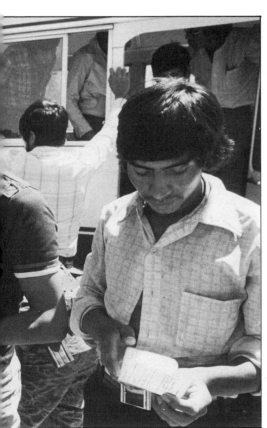

◄ *Army identity check of bus passengers on the Pan American Highway, Guatemala. Buses are frequently checked in this way and suspects taken away by the army.*

▲ *The National Palace in Guatemala City … Amnesty International's 1981 report published evidence showing that targets for political murder were selected in secret offices in an annex to the main building.*

have done it then, that's how I used to feel, I'd do anything the army told me to. I remember how, when I was in it and we set off to bring in two students – I say they were students – I didn't think of fighting, or anything; there was nothing in my mind. So we went to get these students, and we went to get another man who was also a student, at about two in the morning.

And there were others as well as us; there were others who got the job of seeing what time they left school, what time they got back, where they ate, how they dressed and so on. That's what other people did.

But aren't there officers who tell you to investigate what these people do? Do you get the names from officers?

Yes, the officers give us this information – the names and the places.

And you have to check them out?

Yes, that was my job. We went out to find things out; we even talked to a lot of people.

To learn more?

Actually, to watch them; see who they were, and where they were. That was the job we had to do in the streets. We would stay there, and there were always officers travelling around in private cars too, with radios. There might be one in the central park in zone 1, another could be in zone 6, or in zone 7, who were in contact – they could talk directly to each other.

And they wore the uniforms of judicial police? G-2? – all these people?

Well, they were in plain clothes; in civilian clothes or in actual army uniform. When they set out to attack that man I was telling you about, he said he was just out having a lemonade. I asked the boy about it; he was very young; they brought him in all tied up, they had him well and truly tied up and blindfolded. Only his mouth was uncovered so he could talk. His arms were tied. We were going to move him, they had him...

You had to transfer him – did you have to capture this boy?

We had our job to do, but there were other people who had to actually do that job. We just set out to move him from where they had him.

And where did you have to go to see these people?

We took him to the *Brigada Mariscal Zavala* to hand him over.

An army base [un cuartel]?

Yes, the base. But not actually the barracks; but in Guatemala City in the base there are cells; let's see, there's one cell they call 'the powder magazine' ['el polvorín'], there's another cell they call 'the olive' ['la aceituna'], that is where we put him in a locked room. We arrived about two in the morning. They had him all tied up then; his mouth was gagged, and he had a bullet wound here – he couldn't talk. Then they did whatever they wanted to with him, and later, when we arrived, we just picked him up as if he was an animal, then threw him into the car and that was that. We took him there, sat him down, untied his feet, sat him up again, and next day an officer arrived. He brought a tape-recorder and began to ask: 'What is your profession?'

'What work do you do?' 'Where do you work?' 'Where do you study?' and so on, questioning him.

Were you there all the time?

Yes, because it was my job to be. I was there and so I knew what they did.

Had they tortured this boy?

Well, yes.

Beaten him?

Yes, sure.

Was electrical apparatus also used?

Yes, it was.

You saw it?

Yes, I have seen it – some things the Model Platoon [*Pelotón Modelo*] carry about with them which they call 'canes' ['bastones'], with electric batteries – no, they're called 'batons' ['batones']. If they touch you with these things, you fall down, you're electrocuted, they, that's what they have.

I mean, I knew this man didn't want to say whether he belonged to a secret organization, or was 'subversive' as they put it, and they began to beat him savagely.

How did you feel then?

When I was there, I felt sorry when I watched them hitting him.

Did you think that boy was a guerrilla?

Yes, yes I did. But I felt sorry for him when they beat him, and he didn't want to say he was one. He said he was accused of being a guerrilla – but no, what he said was: 'They have accused me of being a guerrilla, but why should they? – if I was a guerrilla I wouldn't be here'. 'Talk', they said, and began to beat him.

Where did you have to beat this boy?

No, it wasn't me...

You just watched?

Yes, I watched. They were from G-2; they were the people who beat him, plainclothes army agents.

Are they from the secret service of the army?

Yes, they were. I stood back when they were beating him, because I didn't want to be drawn into it – I didn't want to join in beating him up. I kept out of the way when I saw they were beating him. Three more men arrived, all trussed up. They tape-recorded everything these men said and as there were a lot of names on that list – there were countless names on the 'black list', that's what we call it. The people on the list are – that's the order they gave us – wherever we find them we just ask their names and if it's them, we kill them.

Did they kill that boy too?

Yes, what they said to him was, if you don't talk, we'll kill you.

But was he killed?

No, I didn't kill him.

No, but did the others kill this boy?

Oh yes, definitely; he confessed: 'I confess everything, everything' – that he wasn't a guerrilla or anything, but, in any case, they began to beat him, that is to torture him, and they even tried to knock out one of his teeth like this, with a hammer. They hit him with a hammer like this. He screamed. They even smashed his finger. They put it on a piece of iron and hit it with the hammer to make him talk; but he didn't say anything; and so the next day, at about 12 o'clock at night – though I'm not sure of this – if it was the judicial police, or the G-2 who turned up – there is such a bunch of them, so you couldn't figure out who was who – who am I for example? If I'm from G-2, you wouldn't tell me anything and I wouldn't tell you anything because this is a security precaution to stop enemies getting control of us. They tell us not to identify ourselves but we have the same idea, the same work. Then at midnight they took those men who were there; they just went and grabbed them by the hair and feet and threw them into a car and took them away – took them who knows where.

They went off to kill them and then leave them somewhere?

Must have. That's how it's done. Because at that time of the night ... if they were going to set them free they would have done it in the daytime. Why drag them out at that hour of night? So they would have killed them on the road and left them just thrown down anywhere.

Do they always take the people they capture out at night-time?

Yes, they go out...

Always at night?

Yes.

Never in daylight?

No, only at night, at the quietest time of night.

In official or private cars?

Private ... what they use mostly are those cars – vans – like station-wagons, with darkened windows – cars you'd never imagine had killers in them – though they can be in any car.

But where do they capture and kill the people? In the countryside? In the towns?

In the towns. Like the students that 'disappear'. It's definitely them that do it and they come and take them away at night, they seize them at night and kill them just like that; then they turn up just dumped anywhere.

But what have you done in the little towns and in the countryside? Have you gone out in trucks? And did you have to do house-to-house searches, or what?

Yes, when we were there, it was pretty much like that. We'd go off in a truck; we'd get to the place we had to search, yes, search and so forth; I mean if there were any people there who were, well, suspicious characters. What we kept an eye on was mostly the organizations where a lot of people get together – and there are guerrillas there too. So that's what we would go off to deal with. They'd take us in a truck. In the villages which cars can't get to, we'd walk and then search the houses just like that. Simple.

You searched from house to house?

In ... where they killed ... where we went, about 20 of us went through all the houses to see if we couldn't find any papers, the ones they'd told us about.

When we found a paper in a house, we took the family out, and if there was just one person we killed him. And

that's what happened. We arrived in a car, left it far away then walked on. And they told us not to be afraid and if we found the papers to kill those people, and that's the way it was – but we didn't find any papers, so we didn't do anything...

You could have killed anyone?

Anyone who was a suspicious character.

And has your unit killed too?

Well, yes – the others did.

Yes, the people you find when you search like that you kill. And if they are not killed then, you just leave them and note things down. You get to know them really well, and in order not to commit these crimes at that moment, you jot down the name of the house and such like, so that they can secretly order another commission to 'bring them to justice', [*ajusticiar*]. That's what you do, that's what we all do – I mean, get the name of the young man, the father and so on; find out what work he does, where he works etc. The reports these commissions make are sent into the offices, such and such an office, circulated in such and such a way. The people there are in charge of finding a commission and secretly giving it its orders. Only they know where it's gone and what it's going to do. This is all done by Army G-2 – that's the way they work.

And the reason I'm telling you this is because I was there. These killers come from the actual army. They told us I wasn't guilty of anything, because they told us: 'You yourselves are going out to kill and because you've got your cards, you can kill the people on your list. If a policeman turns up, show him your gun like this and your card in this hand, then they won't seize you' – that's what they said.

So what I mean is, you kill, then you return; you get dressed. You've maybe committed these crimes in army uniform; if so, they tell you to get out of those clothes fast and put on civilian clothes or police clothes then go out and look for whoever killed the person.

But how are we supposed to find them if it was us that did it in the first place? How can we go out and find them? They have this fantastic idea [*idea mágica*] and – this is what's going on right now today in Guatemala.

They say 'unknown persons' killed the student and that today they are being sought by the police; but how can they find them if the people who did it are the people going out to do the searching? This is what the army is up to.

The soldiers can kill people when they have orders to, but can they kill people without orders, just because someone is a suspicious character?

Yes, certainly, any of us can be ordered to kill any man like that, who is a suspicious character. Yes, we have got the right to kill him, and even more so if we have been given strict orders to. Yes, we have the right to commit these offences.

What did the officers say?

Well, they say that if we don't carry out all the orders that they give us, if we disobey, instead of them dying, they will kill us, so you have to be very careful about all this.

Published February 1981

DOCTORS URGED TO SHUN EXECUTIONS

The professions, trade unions and other groups in the community with special interests, skills or influence are frequently approached by Amnesty International for support in its work. One such special sector is organized into medical groups. In some countries medical groups help organize campaigns on behalf of prisoners in poor health and examine and treat victims of torture and ex-prisoners in need of medical care. Their voice may carry particular weight in appeals directed at other medical personnel, as this news release urging United States doctors not to take part in execution by lethal injection shows.

Prominent doctors in several countries have appealed to Oklahoma doctors to refuse to take part in the proposed first-ever execution by lethal injection in the US, Amnesty International said today (Wednesday 23 September 1981).

Thomas 'Sonny' Hays, convicted of murder in 1977, has been condemned to die by the new method. He was granted a 30-day postponement on 9 September while legal argument on his case continues.

Two telegrams were sent to the Oklahoma Medical Association – one from 11 internationally renowned doctors in France, Ireland, Sweden, Switzerland and the United Kingdom, and the other from the Medical Advisory Board of Amnesty International, the worldwide human rights movement. Both declared that participation by doctors in executions would be a violation of medical ethics.

Of some 850 people under sentence of death in the US, nearly 180 face execution by lethal injection under new laws in four states: Oklahoma, Texas, Idaho and New Mexico.

Among the internationally known figures who signed one of the appeals were two Nobel Prize winners from France, Dr André Lwoff and Professor François Jacob; the former chairman of the British Medical Association's Ethics Committee, Dr R.E.W. Fisher; and the former president of the World Medical Association, Dr Justus Imfeld of Switzerland.

Their message emphasized that medical ethics 'enjoin doctors to practise for the good of their patients and never to do harm'.

The other appeal, from the Medical Advisory Board of Amnesty International, pointed out that the regulations laid out in Oklahoma for the new method require a doctor to determine that poison flows into the prisoner's veins and to decide when death has occurred so that the execution can stop. These tasks should not be undertaken by any doctor, the appeal said. The Board also noted that the American Medical Association had declared that doctors should not participate in executions. The Advisory Board is made up of doctors from Canada, Denmark, Sweden and France.

Amnesty International opposes the death penalty under all circumstances. A representative of the movement said today that there was a danger that execution by injection might be wrongly presented as 'humane', diverting attention from the agony suffered by prisoner and family.

Amnesty International, which has proposed that the US set up a commission to examine the effects of the death penalty, has repeatedly pointed out that the penalty has never been shown to have any special value as a deterrent to crime.

News release 23 September 1981

THE WRITER AND HUMAN RIGHTS

'The writer and human rights' was the theme of a four-day international writers' congress in Toronto, Canada, in October 1981. Two of its aims were to reaffirm the principle of universal respect for human rights and to draw attention to the plight of imprisoned writers – many of them adopted as prisoners of conscience – and campaign for their release. Amnesty International's Secretary General addressed writers who had gathered from all over the world.

Vaclav Havel, a Czechoslovak playwright sentenced to four and a half years' imprisonment in October 1979. He was one of a group of people belonging to the Committee for the Defence of the Unjustly Persecuted – known as VONS – arrested in May 1979 for preparing and circulating information about people they considered to be unjustly persecuted. Vaclav Havel was released from prison in February 1983 on health grounds, 10 months before the expiry of his sentence.

Writers have a specific role in the defence of human rights and the fact that so many of them are prisoners of conscience in countries around the world shows that they are willing to accept their responsibility to speak on behalf of those who cannot.

One of their tasks is to counter the systematic propaganda warfare waged by governments concerned about their image and disturbed by reports of torture in their countries that are flashed around the world.

The propaganda campaigns by such governments take many forms. For instance, the measures adopted by the South African Government have included taking over newspapers at home and abroad, bribing politicians and publishing a 'smear' book called *Amnesty for Terrorism* – this was after AI had published a report on political imprisonment in South Africa.

We know also that other governments are investing money to 'correct' their international reputation and there are international 'markets' where governments can trade principles for nuclear power plants, arms, wheat or oil.

The more such cynicism pervades the world the more important becomes the role of writers and journalists. It is not by chance that so many of the prisoners of conscience for whom AI works are writers and journalists: one single poem, one article or book can open eyes closed by millions of dollars' worth of propaganda.

Some of them are imprisoned because they tried to publish their works independently, defying state censorship. Some are in jail for their unpublished manuscripts, which have been confiscated or destroyed. Some have become victims because they tried to tell others of their prison experiences. Other writers have joined the struggle for human rights in their country and been arrested for that. There are those who have written about the fundamental social and political problems faced by their nations – and been convicted of conducting 'propaganda against the state'. Some have joined opposition political parties or banned organizations. Some have been in the forefront of the resistance to repression, continuing their struggle under successive regimes, and finally paying for their convictions with their lives.

The purpose of shackling the writer is to create silence. But words can be stronger than chains. When the Indonesian novelist Pramoedya Ananta Tur was sent to the isolated island of Buru in the late 1960s he was at first denied pen and paper. By the time he was eventually released some 12 years later in 1979 he had begun compiling the stories he had composed and related to his fellow prisoners in the evenings. Two volumes of these stories have now been published, but in May this year Indonesia's Attorney-General banned their further circulation.

When the Venezuelan poet Ali Lameda was released in 1974 after six years' imprisonment in North Korea, he told a journalist: 'They killed everything except my memory'. By this, he meant the more than 300 sonnets and 400 other poems he had composed mentally – without benefit of either pen or paper. It was an extraordinary feat, described by a Latin American critic as 'a gigantic creative effort in a world of horror and misery'.

These images of the poet in prison call to mind the words of the Russian imagist poet Akhmatova describing the 17 months she spent in the prison lines in Leningrad under Stalin: 'Once someone, somehow recognized me. Then a woman standing behind me, her lips blue with cold … woke from the stupor that enveloped us and asked me, whispering in my ear (for we spoke only in whispers): 'Could you describe this?' I said, 'I can.' Then something like a smile glided over what had once been her face.'

We deal with that world of whispers and desperate messages, where names and snatches of verse are scratched on prison walls, where lives are risked to pass on news to the outside world.

Out of Libertad Prison in Uruguay some time ago came a tiny collection of poems smuggled out on cigarette papers. Among them, this one:

> *You should see*
> *the contradictions*
> *in the army.*
> *You should have heard*
> *the arguments between*
> *the sub-lieutenant and the captain*
> *while they were torturing me.*

There were no names, no signatures on the poems. In a real sense, they were *prison poems*.

When AI was asked by the organizers of this conference if it could supply a list of all writers in prison throughout the world, the answer was that it could not. Secrecy and censorship make any complete tally impossible. AI did compile a small selection of cases that could stand as symbols for all others, both the known and the unknown. The range, even in this handful of examples, illustrates the fact that we are dealing with an issue that crosses the demarcations of ideology and government.

○ Ahmed Fu'ad Negm, of Egypt, well known throughout the Arab world for his colloquial poetry, is currently serving a sentence of one year's imprisonment in Cairo. His poems frequently describe social or political injustice and many are set to music and sung by the blind musician Sheikh Imam. Both have been imprisoned several times for their songs.

○ Jorge Mario Soza Egaña, a 55-year-old Chilean poet and short story writer, was sentenced in August 1980 to four years' internal exile in Freirina, a small town in the semi-desert region of northern Chile. He is unable to find work there and has had to build himself a small shack to live in. He is reported to have been tortured after his arrest in May 1980 and was charged under a law prohibiting 'Marxist' organizations.

○ Yang Ching-Chu, a writer from the Republic of China (Taiwan), is serving a prison sentence of four years and two months, imposed after he had taken part in a demonstration in December 1979 to mark the anniversary of the Universal Declaration of Human Rights. At the time he was on the editorial committee of the opposition magazine *Formosa*.

○ Haroldo Conti, the Argentinian novelist and short story writer, was dragged out of his home by a group of armed men on 5 May 1976 and then 'disappeared'. Although his detention was never officially acknowledged, a released prisoner has testified to seeing him in a secret detention centre in Argentina.

○ Don Mattera, the South African poet, is currently restricted under a second five-year banning order. Ebenezer Maqina, author of *The Trial*, is also banned and prevented from writing for publication.

○ Armando Valladares, the Cuban poet who has been paralysed in his legs for several years, is still serving a 30-year prison sentence. Earlier this year he is reported to have been attacked by guards and security officers in the prison hospital and beaten unconscious.

These imprisonments violate agreed international standards. The Universal Declaration of Human Rights states: 'Everyone has the right to freedom of opinion and expression. This right includes the freedom to hold opinions without interference and to seek, receive and impart information and ideas through any media and regardless of frontiers.' The same right is spelled out in Article 19:2 of the International Covenant on Civil and Political Rights.

This means that the right of freedom of expression is part of international law. But this has not prevented governments from arresting writers who have done no more than to speak up, or even from introducing laws which by themselves make a mockery of the right of expression. Criticism is branded as 'subversion' or 'anti-state propaganda', sympathy for a minority group as an 'attempt to divide the nation'.

Several prisoners of conscience have been incarcerated just for their attempts to discuss such hypocrisy, for their work for real human rights. In many cases they are not recognized as authors or journalists by the 'establishment' in their home countries.

The forces that threaten to stifle creativity and freedom of expression are real and are continually claiming their victims. We must have the courage to work through our differences and manifest our solidarity with those who are being silenced. There is a great deal we can do, confident that, in the words of the writer Georgi Vladimov, 'All attempts to control literature will inevitably be as unsuccessful as projects for perpetual motion machines'.

AI Newsletter 1981

URGENT ACTION amnesty international URGENT ACTION

International Secretariat, 10 Southampton Street, London WC2E 7HF, England

*Amnesty International opposes by all appropriate means the imposition
and infliction of death penalties and torture or other cruel, inhuman or
degrading treatment or punishment of prisoners or other detained or
restricted persons whether or not they have used or advocated violence.
(Amnesty International Statute, Article 1(c))*

EXTERNAL (for
general distribution)

AI Index: AFR 62/31/81
Distr: UA

UA 248/81

Fear of Torture/Legal Concern

13 October 1981

ZAIRE: Citizen KAPOKELA Sango
===============================

Kapokela Sango, probably aged 20-25, was resident in Abumbe
village in Zaire's eastern Kivu region (*collectivité de* Tanganyika,
zone de Fizi, *sous-région de* Sud-Kivu). He was arrested in Abumbe by
the security police (*Centre national de recherches et d'investigations - CNRI*) on 23 September 1981 and was taken to a detention centre
in Uvira. His uncle and aunt tried to visit him there but were also
arrested.

After being transferred to a cell in Mulimbi military camp in
Uvira, Kapokela Sango is reported to have been transferred to an
unknown destination. After being arrested and transferred in similar
circumstances last March, two young men were subsequently found dead
with bullets through their heads. Sud-Kivu sub-region is an
"operational zone", so it is possible that Kapokela may be held
without charge or trial for an indefinite period. There is a
serious likelihood that he is being tortured and a possibility that
he may be killed. He was apparently arrested because he was known to
be critical of the government and was consequently suspected of links
with armed rebels active in Sud-Kivu.

AI has been concerned about human rights violations in Zaire for
many years. The security forces in the country in general and in
Sud-Kivu sub-region in particular have extensive powers to arrest
suspects and to hold them incommunicado without charge. In these
circumstances detainees are frequently ill-treated and have in
several instances this year been killed while in detention.

RECOMMENDED ACTION:

Telegrams/express letters *in French if possible, otherwise in
English (or Dutch)* asking for an urgent assurance that Citoyen
Kapokela Sango is being treated in accordance with internationally
recognized standards and that he has not been subjected to ill-
treatment. Also inquire why he was arrested, whether he has been
charged and where he is held. In all letters explain that he was
arrested on 23 September at Abumbe village in Fizi zone in Kivu
region (*dans la zone de Fizi, région du Kivu*).

*LAWYERS are urged to write in their professional capacity to
Citoyen Yoka Mangono, who was until recently President of the
Kinshasa Bar Association.*

THE MISSING CHILDREN OF ARGENTINA

In December 1981 Amnesty International launched a worldwide campaign to expose and halt the use by governments of 'disappearances' as a means of eliminating suspected opponents. Many of the victims were feared dead, but the special mark of 'disappearance' as a tool of repression is that people remain unaccounted for, missing without trace, and that government officials claim to have no knowledge of them. Families are left in permanent uncertainty. As part of the campaign Amnesty International focussed on 67 missing children in Argentina – some 'disappeared' with their parents after raids by security forces, others borne by women in detention pregnant at the time of their abduction.

After searching for her two little granddaughters for two and a half years, Maria Laura Iribar de Jotar finally traced them during a visit to a juvenile court in the province of Buenos Aires – just as adoption formalities were being completed with the family who had been looking after them.

That was in March 1980. The grandmother had last seen the children – Tatiana, then aged four years, and Laura, then two months – together with their parents on 17 October 1977, the day they had 'disappeared', victims of the Argentine armed forces' policy of secret kidnappings.

A week after their parents' 'disappearance' Tatiana and Laura had apparently been found crying in the street. Although Tatiana was able to give her name, she and her sister were registered in separate orphanages as 'NN' – name unknown. No attempt was made to locate the family.

In 1978 the pair went to live with the married couple that eventually adopted them – but it was not until 19 March 1980 that their grandmother could be certain they were still alive.

Now she is allowed to visit her grandchildren. Their parents, Mirta Graciela Britos and Alberto Javier Jotar, are still on the lists of the 'disappeared'.

For other grandmothers in Argentina the search continues – for grandchildren whom they too last saw before the parents were abducted by the security forces, and for others they have never seen ... because the children were born in secret detention centres during their mothers' captivity.

At least 53 pregnant women are known to have been detained since the military coup of 1976 in Argentina – and at least 14 small children were seized with their parents.

According to AI's information, only one of the parents detained with their children has ever been seen again: Sara Mendez, an Uruguayan citizen, whose 20-day-old baby, Simon, was snatched from her soon after she was arrested at her flat in Buenos Aires on 13 July 1976. Transferred to Uruguay with over 60 other Uruguayans arrested that year in Argentina, she reappeared in the women's prison of Punta Rieles. When the then British Ambassador visited the prison in 1977, she appealed to him to find her baby. But, like other children, Simon had 'disappeared'. (AI learned in mid-October that Sara Méndez had been released in March 1981.)

Grandparents believe that most of these missing children have been placed for adoption, often with military families. In desperation, some relatives have placed newspaper advertisements appealing for news of missing babies.

The mothers of a young married couple, Roberto and Patricia Toranzo, placed this advertisement in the daily *La Nación*:

'It is over a year since our children failed to return home. Our denunciations have been shelved. Our court appeals refused. Our children are hardworking and studious. She is a teacher, he is a technician and engineering student.... Patricia was expecting a child ...

'We want to know where it is. What has been done

▲ Tatiana Ruarte Britos was four when she and her two-months-old half sister Laura were found crying in the street after being abducted with their parents in October 1977. Their grandmother's long search for them ended in March 1980 – just as they were being adopted. Tatiana and Laura are still with their adoptive parents but are in contact with their real family.

▲ Stella Maris Montesano was seven months' pregnant when she and her husband were abducted from their home in La Plata in October 1976. She reportedly gave birth in detention.

▼ Astrid Patino Caravelle was three when she and her mother Gabriella were abducted in Córdoba in April 1976. She was located in January 1984, and is now in touch with her real family.

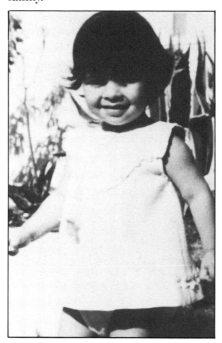

▼ Mariana Zaffaroni Islas was 18 months old when she 'disappeared' after security forces raided the Buenos Aires home of her parents, Uruguayan exiles, in September 1976. A child fitting Mariana's description was located in 1984 living with a member of the State Intelligence Service, who had registered her as his own child. In September 1984 a court order was issued prohibiting the family from leaving Argentina.

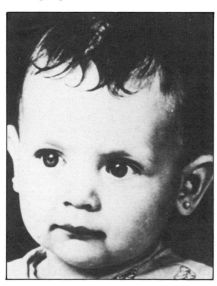

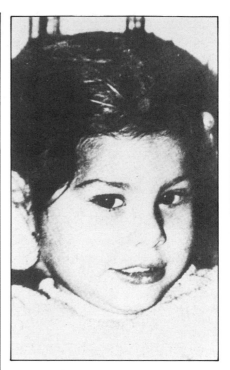

▲ Jorgelina Planas was three and a half when her mother Christina was abducted in May 1977. She was handed over to the children's court in Lomas de Zamora, Buenos Aires province, but later taken away by an air force officer and allegedly given to a family for adoption. A girl fitting Jorgelina's description has been located living with a member of the Air Force.

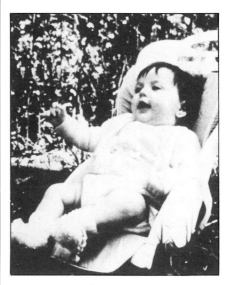

▲ Clara Anahi Mariani was three months old when she 'disappeared' after security forces raided her parents' home in La Plata in November 1976. Her mother was killed. A child fitting her description was located, and a judge has ordered blood tests.

▲ *Liliana Irma Ross de Rossetti was five months'
pregnant when she was abducted in the city of La
Plata on 10 December 1976. Her family has
established that she was taken to Olmos Prison
Hospital (for ordinary criminal prisoners), where she
gave birth to twins in April 1977. On 17 May she was
removed from Olmos in one car and the twins were
taken away in another. The family does not know
where any of them are. Twin boys fitting the Rossetti
brothers' description were located in 1985 living as
the natural sons of a federal police officer. Blood tests
were ordered by a judge but the police officer failed to
appear and the family has gone into hiding.*

▲ *The* **Escuela de Mecánica de la Armada (ESMA),** *the
principal naval training college in Buenos Aires,
which has been used as a detention centre for
abducted prisoners.*

with it? How is it being brought up? What future is reserved
for it?'

'The fact that a woman prisoner was pregnant never
led to her getting any sort of consideration under torture.
Those who did not lose their babies on the torture tables,
having survived the interrogation stage, were thrown into
the cells under the same conditions as the rest ... When
their pregnancy was very advanced, they were admitted to
the infirmary and were given a little more food. They were
given a layette for the baby, stolen in other operations.
When there were only a few days left before the delivery,
they said that they were taking them away to the Military
Hospital.' From testimony on secret detention camps given
to *AI* by two former prisoners.

'One day while I was washing plates, they took me to
wash diapers and rubber pants ... I realized that there were
children on the other side from where we were. At that time
I heard the voices of children of about four years of age,
asking why their parents had those things [hoods] on their
heads. I asked the guard how it was possible for children to
be there. He said ... they had been brought with their
parents because there was no place to leave them. However,
they were going to be taken away the next day.' From
testimony of Estela Cornalea de Falicoff to the Inter-
American Commission on Human Rights, published April
1980.

But the appeals, the pilgrimages to children's homes,
to hospitals, to the courts, to government offices, to the
military authorities, to the police stations, to the Church,
have all failed to find the lost children.

The Jotar-Britos children are among the exceptions.
Another case occurred in June 1979, when a Chilean social
worker visiting Venezuela recognized a magazine photograph of a missing Uruguayan brother and sister.

Nearly three years earlier, the boy, then aged four, and
his 18-month-old sister had been found abandoned in
Valparaiso, Chile, and taken into care. They were later
adopted by a dentist and his wife.

The childen are Anatole and Victoria Julien, who
'disappeared' with their parents when security forces
invaded their home in Buenos Aires on 26 September
1976. They had been taken across the border and left in
Chile. They have now been reunited with their grandparents.

The great majority of grandparents, uncles, aunts,
brothers and sisters, have searched in vain. They must
endure the agony of knowing that perhaps not far away, cut
off not only from their parents but from all their family
links, these children are being brought up with new
identities. Some may have been left in orphanages, either
official or clandestine. Others may have been adopted by
families who do not know their background, and many may
have been taken by military families who know very well
who their parents were.

AI Newsletter November 1981

HUMAN RIGHTS VIOLATIONS IN PAKISTAN

In July 1977 the military administration of General Zia ul-Haq took power in Pakistan and imposed martial law, suspending many fundamental human rights guaranteed in the Constitution. The former Prime Minister, Zulfikar Ali Bhutto, was executed in 1979 after a controversial trial and appeals process. Amnesty International noted a steady deterioration in the human rights situation and in early 1982 it published 'Pakistan: Human rights violations and the decline of the rule of law' from which this extract is taken.

Nearly all political prisoners are held under martial law provisions.

Detention without trial

The government has wide powers of preventive detention both under Martial Law Order 78 of 26 May 1980, and under the Maintenance of Public Order Ordinance. Martial Law Order 27 limits the period of detention to 12 months. The martial law orders allow detention without trial on vaguely defined grounds: 'for the purpose of preventing him from acting in a manner prejudicial to the purpose for which martial law has been proclaimed or to the security of Pakistan, or any part thereof, the maintenance of peaceful conditions in any part of Pakistan or the efficient conduct of martial law.'

Martial Law Order 78 incorporated Martial Law Order 12 of 1977, but removed the obligation to inform the detainee of the grounds for detention. Under Martial Law Order 78 the grounds for detention 'shall not be communicated to the detainee'. The civilian courts had previously set aside many political detention orders: for example on 11 December 1979 the Lahore High Court declared the detention of 13 people under Martial Law Order 12 'unlawful' and ordered their immediate release. The court found 'the material pertaining to the detention … insufficient', (*Dawn*, 12 December 1979). However such scrutiny of executive action is no longer allowed under the PCO [Provisional Constitution Order 1981].

Amnesty International believes the provisions of Martial Law Order 78 are used arbitrarily and on a large scale to detain non-violent critics of the government. Detention orders are usually renewed every three months, but Amnesty International knows of several people detained for far longer than the maximum of 12 months allowed by the legislation.

Many hundreds of political party members have been detained without trial in recent years for long periods. Among them are Begum Nusrat Bhutto, the wife of the late Prime Minister, who succeeded him as leader of the PPP [Pakistan People's Party]. By July 1981 she had spent 26 of the preceding 41 months in detention under martial law provisions; her daughter Benazir had been detained for 24 months during the same period. The leader of the *Tehrik-i-Istiqlal*, Air Marshal (Retired) Asghar Khan, has been detained a number of times under both the present and previous administrations. His period of detention since 29 May 1980 greatly exceeds the maximum 12 months officially allowed under Martial Law Order 27. All three are among the prisoners of conscience adopted by Amnesty International.

Political activities banned

Political prisoners are often tried by military courts, particularly under regulations banning ordinary political activity and criticism of the armed forces:

○ Martial Law Regulation 13 states: 'No person shall, by word, either spoken or written, or by signs or by

147

visible representation or otherwise, bring or attempt to bring into hatred or contempt or excite or attempt to excite disaffection towards the Armed Forces or any members thereof.' (Maximum punishment: five years' imprisonment and 10 lashes.)

○ Martial Law Regulation 33 states: 'No person shall in any manner whatsoever directly or indirectly indulge or participate in political activity', the definition of which includes: 'A. Organizing any political party, canvassing or campaigning in public or in private, or propagating the cause of any political party or any politicians by words, either spoken or written, or by sign or by visible representation or in any other manner or at any place whatsoever.'

'D. Arranging, attending or joining any procession of a political nature.'

'2. (e) making, printing, producing, publishing or distributing directly or indirectly any matter … connected with … furthering the cause of any political party, politician or candidate … or is likely to cause sensation or misunderstanding amongst the people or which is prejudicial to the precepts of Islam or the Ideology or integrity or security of Pakistan or public peace or the national interest or which tends or is likely to cause disaffection towards the Martial Law Administration …' (Maximum punishment: seven years' imprisonment, 20 lashes and a fine.)

Political prisoners are often tried for printing political literature, taking part in political processions or undertaking other peaceful political activity, under Martial Law Regulations 4, 5 and 18.

○ Martial Law Regulation 4 states:
'1. No person shall publish, print, circulate, or cause to be published, printed, or circulated or otherwise be in possession of any pamphlet, poster or publication or any type of literature calculated to promote or attempt to promote feeling or enmity or hatred between different provinces, classes, sects, or religious orders.' (Maximum punishment: 10 years' imprisonment and 30 lashes.)

○ Martial Law Regulation 5 states:
'1. No person shall organize or convene or attend any meeting, not being a religious congregation, in an open public place, or organize or take out a procession, not being a religious funeral or marriage procession, without the prior written permission of the Martial Law Administrator concerned.' (Maximum punishment: seven years' imprisonment, fine and 10 lashes.)

○ Martial Law Regulation 18 prohibits a wide spectrum of political activities. Article 3 reads:
'3. No political party or person shall, by words, either spoken or written, or by signs or by visible representation or otherwise, propagate any opinion, or act in a manner prejudicial to the ideology or the integrity or the security of Pakistan, or prejudicial to the purpose for which Martial Law has been proclaimed.' Maximum punishment: seven years' imprisonment, fine and 10 lashes.)

Although Martial Law Regulation 23 of 19 September 1977 states that trade union activity is allowed, the regulation bans all 'strikes and lock-outs'. Martial Law Regulation 51 of 14 June 1981 forbids 'agitational activity' by people 'in government service' and 'in corporation service' in widely defined terms: anyone engaging in activity 'which is intended or is likely to impair the normal functioning or efficiency of any department or office of the government' including 'causing or inciting of strikes or slow movements' may be dealt with 'in a summary way or his case may be referred to a military court for trial'. (Maximum punishment: five years' imprisonment and five lashes.) On 16 August 1981 the government banned all trade union activity in Pakistan International Airlines (PIA), and the penalty for disobeying was put at a maximum of five years' imprisonment and five lashes under Martial Law Regulation 52.

The terms of these martial law regulations are so wide that any form of political activity or criticism of the government can be punished by imprisonment and flogging after a summary trial. Most political prisoners are sentenced to imprisonment of up to 12 months, and some are also flogged. Longer terms of imprisonment have been imposed. For example, Aslam Saghir, the driver of Dr Zafar Niazi, (a prominent PPP member and former dentist to Zulfikar Ali Bhutto), was sentenced to three years' imprisonment on 29 January 1981 for helping deliver political pamphlets. He was sentenced under Martial Law Regulations 13 and 33 and has been adopted as a prisoner of conscience.

Military courts

With very few exceptions, political prisoners are tried by military courts. These courts are not only empowered to try military personnel, they may also try civilians for many martial law offences, including those banning political activity.

Since the promulgation of the Constitution (Second Amendment) Order 1979 they can also try offences under the Pakistan Penal Code, previously the exclusive jurisdiction of the civil courts. Martial law authorities decide whether a case is to be heard by a military tribunal or a civilian court. Only military courts try cases of treason, sedition, 'prejudicial activity' and 'seducing members of the Armed Forces', (Martial Law Order 77).

Summary Military Courts

Summary military courts consist of one member who need not be a member of the Bar. The accused can address the court and cross-examine witnesses, but only a summary of the evidence need be taken down. The defendant has no right to be represented by a lawyer, and although the accused may be assisted, this person cannot address the court directly. These courts can impose up to one year's imprisonment and 15 lashes. In most cases the maximum period of imprisonment is imposed. No appeal is allowed, but there is provision for review by the Zonal Martial Law Administrator.

Special Military Courts

Special military courts consist of three people, one a magistrate, the other two career army officers of the rank of Major or Lieutenant-Colonel. Amnesty International understands that the army officers do not need to have any legal training. The courts may try all martial law and penal code offences and impose all punishments, including the death penalty and amputation of a hand; executions or amputations have to be confirmed by the Chief Martial Law Administrator. Only a summary of the evidence need be recorded and, if necessary, 'may be dispensed with in a case and in lieu thereof an abstract of evidence may be recorded'. (Martial Law Order 5, 11 July 1977). Cross-examination of witnesses is allowed. Amnesty International has been told that decisions are recorded on printed forms under the heading 'guilty or not guilty', and that this is sufficient to constitute a judgment. There is no requirement to give a reasoned judgment in writing, even in cases involving the death penalty.

Any question relating to the jurisdiction of the military courts or the legality of their actions must be referred to the Chief Martial Law Administrator, whose decision is final. Under martial law there is no provision for judicial review of the legality of decisions taken by the martial law authorities by any court of law in Pakistan.

During a mission to Pakistan in January 1978 Amnesty International delegates were able to attend a hearing before a summary military court. In July 1980 the secretary of the Centre for the Independence of Judges and Lawyers, a unit of the International Commission of Jurists, requested permission to attend such a trial. Permission was refused by the provincial authorities even though proceedings are in principle open to the public (*CIJL Bulletin*, No. 6, October 1980).

Amnesty International has received disturbing accounts of the way these military tribunals try political prisoners. The Baluchistan High Court in a judgment of 2 July 1980 quoted the case of a student who was accused of having participated in an illegal procession, a case referred to it by former Attorney General Yahya Bakhtiar. At his trial no witness named the student, nor did any identify him. 'But the Presiding Officer was helpless. He told the accused student that although the evidence did not indicate his guilt he could not do anything as the higher authorities sent down direction that he was to be sentenced to one year's rigorous imprisonment' (imprisonment with hard labour). The Baluchistan High Court observed: 'This quality of justice is being tried to be provided in preference to the existing courts, and with such sanctity that the judgment of military courts and tribunals are being sought to be kept above the judicial scrutiny of the superior courts. Such a step is not likely to promote the good of the people.' (NLR 1980 Civil Quetta, page 889).

This case illustrates the miscarriages of justice which are likely to occur when basic legal safeguards are suspended. Of particular concern are

○ the summary recording of evidence,

○ the denial of the right to be represented by a lawyer,

○ the absence of the right to appeal to a court of law,

○ the fact that judges are career army officers who are part of the Executive,

○ the removal of the requirement to give a reasoned judgment in writing.

Trials before military courts therefore fall far short of international standards to ensure a fair and open trial. This is particularly disturbing as the military courts are widely used to punish peaceful dissent, and often hand down severe punishments, including the death penalty.

Published February 1982

This man was convicted by a military court in October 1979. He was sentenced to 15 lashes and one year's imprisonment for committing 'immoral acts'. A crowd estimated at 10,000 witnessed his punishment, in Rawalpindi, Pakistan.

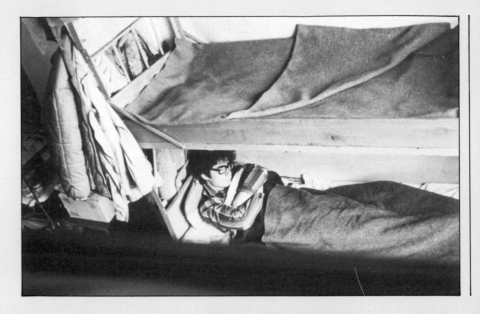

These clandestine photographs were smuggled out of the Bialoleka detention camp near Warsaw in late May 1982, some seven months after the declaration of martial law in Poland and the crackdown on the independent trade union Solidarity. Many Solidarity activists were detained here.

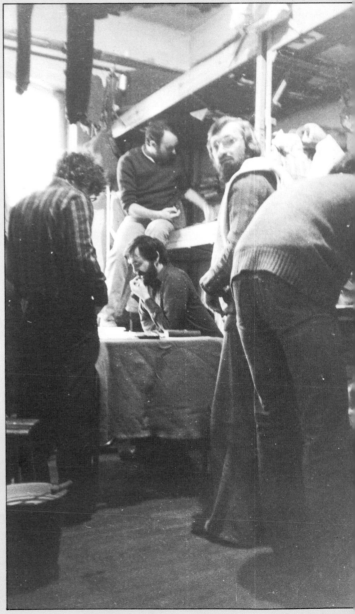

MARTIAL LAW IN POLAND

Martial law was declared in Poland on 13 December 1981. The independent trade union Solidarity was suspended, as were other independent trade union and student organizations, and thousands of Solidarity activists and others were interned. The following extracts come from the 'Amnesty International Report 1983' (which each year includes a country-by-country survey of human rights abuses of concern to Amnesty International) and from a paper entitled 'Internment in Poland' issued in 1982.

Internment, introduced with martial law, was most widely applied during the first month, when some 6,800 people were officially acknowledged to have been interned. Although some internees were released in December 1981 and there were releases throughout 1982, new internments continued to take place as late as November. According to official statements, internees were not suspected or accused of any crime; they were interned because their past conduct gave rise to 'justified suspicion that if they remained at liberty they would not observe legal order or would engage in activities endangering the interests of the security or defence of the State'. Internment was enforced by the militia with no court supervision. There was no fixed term for internment, which could, and in some cases did, last for the duration of martial law. Those interned included most members of the National Commission of the independent trade union Solidarity, Solidarity advisers, regional officials, members and supporters, members of independent farmers' and students' unions, members of civil and human rights groups and other people officially regarded as opponents of the government. Lech Walesa, Solidarity's leader, was placed under house arrest.

Internees were held in 'isolation centres' in prisons, reformatories and in worker and army holiday accommodation. With the exception of women detainees and well-known intellectuals held in holiday centres, most internees experienced conditions described as cold, unhygienic and overcrowded. Internees frequently reported that they were interrogated by the state security police and pressed to collaborate with police, to emigrate or to sign a statement that they would not engage in anti-state activity, as a condition for release. A number of internees complained that they had been denied medical treatment or that this had been delayed. There were also allegations that internees had been beaten by guards; such incidents, for instance, were reported to have taken place on 13 February at Wierzchowo Pomorskie, on 25 March at Ilawa and on 14 August at Kwidzyn. In the last case six internees were said to have been badly injured and hospitalized. Priests and delegates from the International Committee of the Red Cross were allowed to visit internees throughout the year.

The majority of people imprisoned for political offences during 1982 had expressed opposition to martial law by strikes, demonstrations, leaflets or clandestine trade union activity. Most were convicted of 'martial law offences', that is, of violating Articles 46-48 of the Martial Law Decree of 12 December 1981. This penalized participating in a suspended trade union or association, organizing strikes or protest actions and printing or disseminating 'false information liable to arouse public anxiety or riots'. Most such cases reported to Amnesty International were tried by special summary proceedings introduced under martial law. In these proceedings pre-trial detention was compulsory and most detainees did not have access to a lawyer during investigation; various procedural time limits were reduced and heavier penalties imposed: a minimum of three years' imprisonment and loss of civil rights for up to 10 years. The accused had no right of appeal. In some cases, however, sentences were increased after an 'extraordinary appeal' by the Procurator General. Certain martial law offences were tried by military courts, involving further restrictions, for example on public access to the court and on the accused's choice of lawyer. The majority of sentences imposed under summary proceedings for martial law offences in cases known to Amnesty International were for three to four years' imprisonment. Some lower sentences were imposed under normal proceedings, and there were also acquittals.

Amnesty International was also concerned about allegations that political prisoners had been severely beaten by prison guards. Prisoners in Gdansk prison, including some 15 prisoners of conscience, were reported to have been attacked and beaten by guards on 23 July after rumours had circulated within the prison that inmates were about to start a hunger-strike. Some 20 younger prisoners were forced to take a very hot shower and beaten again. Police dogs were alleged to have been set on certain prisoners.

Published 1984

Conditions of internment

Initial reports received by Amnesty International stated that many internees were held in harsh, cold and overcrowded conditions in internment centres located in evacuated prisons, investigation centres, barracks, reformatories (social rehabilitation centres) and worker and army holiday accommodation.

Several reports indicate that some of the worst hardships initially suffered by internees were due to the fact that local authorities had not made preparations for their reception. On 9 January, the army newspaper *Zolnierz Wolnosci* quoted an interview with the regional prison chief of Wroclaw who (referring to some 920 people locally interned) confirmed reports of internees being kept in a prison courtyard poorly clothed in sub-zero temperatures. 'Unfortunately such facts did take place ... we were simply not prepared for quickly receiving and accommodating such a number of people. We, too, were surprised by the proclamation of martial law. We did ... everything in our powers to alleviate the hardships of waiting.'

On 21 December an official government spokesman insisted that internees were held in 'bearable conditions and have the right to visits by close relatives, may receive food parcels, have access to religious practices, are receiving books and periodicals and are provided with means of personal hygiene and have medical care. Those who want to can work. Some of the internees are staying at holiday homes. All have the right to contact one another.'

While other reports indicate that by this date conditions in certain internment centres had somewhat improved, most reports agreed that conditions varied considerably from one centre to another and that prominent intellectuals generally had much better conditions than workers. This is also indicated by the experience of Teresa Bogucka, head of Solidarity's Cultural Committee in Warsaw, who was interned following the imposition of martial law but was released on New Year's Eve. Her account was published in the *Guardian* (London) on 20 January 1982:

'Q: What happened the night you were informed?

A: It was late at night. The bell of the door rang very loudly. (Police) explained the situation was 'special', and they would show me a paper in a moment. It was an order for internment in Bialoleka (camp) in connection with martial law ... They played an easy trick on my intelligence. They said 'You know, it is probably a misunderstanding. So after two hours you will come back' ... As a result I took almost nothing with me. At 12.30 I was at the police headquarters in Wilcza street. There was an incredible crowd ... At around 3 am we reached a prison. The staff were upset. They asked us what had happened. They let us into a cell where there were only mattresses. They said the store was closed so they couldn't get us anything. The cell was not heated. It had broken windows through which snow blew in ... In the morning a guard came, took pity on us and gave us blankets. It became clear that there was no water. During the whole time I was there – three days – not once was I brave enough to take off my coat or to undress. We asked to be able to wash our hands and faces at least. So they brought us snow, explaining that the water was cut off...'

After three days, she was transferred by helicopter to an army holiday house at Jaworzno, together with a group of other internees, mostly university professors and writers.

'As a vacation house it was poor, as a prison it was luxurious. We found ourselves in a camp, undoubtedly for the chosen few, where we could move between rooms ... Complete freedom in the rooms, ... excellent food, ... walks. It was served by the normal militia, I think, with police badges, and they treated us politely and even with embarrassment that such amazing people like scientists were here. And that's how it generally looked. We immediately became aware that the intelligentsia was separated from the workers who were left in Bialoleka and Olszynka.'

By contrast, a declaration by internees in Bialoleka, printed in an underground publication of Solidarity in early January, stated:

'We hereby declare that, despite the assurances issued by the so-called Military Council of National Salvation, our detention is not designed to keep us isolated from society, but most of all is an act of repression and revenge. There are among us gravely ill people. Our repeated demands that they be freed, or at least assured proper medical care, have been ignored. ... The conditions in which we are being held do not differ significantly from the conditions existing in the majority of Polish prisons. Our group, of almost 300 people, has been placed in twelve-person cells of 18 square metres each, in unsanitary conditions. There is no hot water or laundry detergents, except soap, which helps disease to spread. There is a flu

Bydgoszcz prison, Poland, September 1981. The banner on the left reads 'We will not give up' and on the right 'Solidarity is with us'.

epidemic in the camp. The prison rules read to us are more severe than those in the Nazi POW camps. We are deprived of the right to move freely within the camp, to maintain contact with prisoners in other cells, and to take part in educational and cultural activities or recreation. Daily collective prayer is also forbidden. The rules are set up so that the camp commandant has unlimited powers. Despite repeated requests, we have not been allowed to study the texts of the international conventions – especially the Hague and Geneva conventions, ratified by Poland, which regulate the procedures concerned with interned persons – in order to compare these texts with the prison rules. We have demanded contact with representatives of the authorities and of the International Red Cross – also to no avail.

'We were granted the opportunity to have our families visit us between Christmas and the New Year. Presently the camp commandant limited the number of family visits to one per month, and only on a weekday during normal working hours. Our families are being misinformed about the dates and possibility of visits. Letters sent by us do not reach their addresses. Letters mailed from outside do not come to us.

'Despite the fact that no criminal proceedings are pending against any of us, we are subject to informal interrogations by secret police. They threaten us with the prolongation of detention if we do not sign the loyalty oath.'

On 8 January the foreign press reported that prisoners in Bialoleka were taking turns to go on hunger strike in support of this protest. Nonetheless, according to some unofficial accounts, conditions in Bialoleka are good in comparison with certain other centres; those at a centre on Hel peninsula are described as particularly harsh.

There have been isolated reports of internees having been beaten on arrest or after their internment, but the limited information available at present to Amnesty International suggests that this has not been widespread or systematic.

Published February 1982

● 'THE WORD "FRIEND" GIVES US THE STRENGTH TO GO ON'

Batlle Oxandabarat Scarrone often took part in the marches of the sugarcane cutters from the north of Uruguay to the capital, Montevideo, to claim better working conditions and wages. During a long and distinguished history of trade union activity he became President of the regional branch of the main trade union confederation in the country, the *Confederación Nacional de Trabajadores* (CNT). As such, he was arrested on 20 June 1972, charged with 'Attack on the Constitution' and sentenced to 13 years' imprisonment. As part of a general clamp-down on left-wing organizations, the government banned the CNT itself in June 1973. He was left alone following the death of his brother in 1979 – his sister having fled into exile in Barcelona.

An Amnesty International group in the Federal Republic of Germany took up his case. Apart from the campaigning work they undertook to call for his release, they also offered their moral support to Batlle and his family, continuing to write to him regularly during the years he was incarcerated. When he was released, the group paid for his airline ticket from Montivideo to Barcelona so that they could be reunited.

Following his release on 10 March 1985, Batlle wrote to the group: 'To begin this letter . . . it has been shown that there is no distance, nor place or race which can stop human relationships being established and developed through the means of communication which are within our reach. All we have to do is to think and be aware that there are millions of others . . . and that one can be of use to a fellow human being from a distance. Through the means of a letter . . . to receive the word "friend" and "brother" comforts us and gives us strength to go on with our principles – to construct a more just and humane world. Today, happily, in freedom and in Spain with my family, censorship cannot prevent me from communicating my gratitude for everything you have done for me.'

PRISONERS OF CONSCIENCE IN EGYPT

Between 1971 and 1982 Amnesty International adopted as prisoners of conscience people of differing political persuasions and religious beliefs in Egypt. Many were accused of belonging to illegal communist organizations or of participating in their activities. In the following case, published in 'Egypt Violations of human rights', 176 people were charged in connection with 'food riots' that had taken place in January 1977.

On 18 and 19 January 1977 riots and demonstrations took place in Cairo and other major towns throughout Egypt in reaction to a government announcement that, contrary to earlier statements, subsidies on basic foodstuffs and commodities were to be cut in compliance with the terms laid down for a loan from the International Monetary Fund.

Many acts of violence took place during the two days and public and private buildings, as well as vehicles, were set on fire. Thousands of people were arrested and there were numerous trials for offences relating to the violence. Among those arrested and detained were several hundred who had not been involved in any violence and were detained solely because of their political beliefs. They were held for several months and it was later announced that 176 of them were to be formally charged and brought to trial.

Fifty-three of the 176 defendants were charged with 'instigation' of the events of 18 and 19 January (usually by means of written material – newspaper articles or messages on student notice-boards – produced in the previous years and months), (Articles 102 (bis) and 174 of the penal code). Another 86 were accused of membership of the banned Egyptian Workers Communist Party – principally under provisions of Article 98 of the penal code and, in several cases where individuals were arrested during February 1977, under Law 2 of 1977. The remaining 37 were accused of membership of the banned Egyptian Communist Party (principally under Article 98A of the penal code).

One hundred and thirty-one defendants were present when the trial began before the Supreme State Security Court in Cairo on 16 April 1978; all but six of them were granted provisional liberty. This session of the trial was attended by an Amnesty International observer.

The defence protested that only 15 copies of the case dossier existed and that the price was £500 (Egyptian) a copy. They called for an adequate number of copies to be prepared and made available to lawyers for the defence free of charge. They further requested a postponement of the trial to allow the defence adequate time in which to study the dossier, which then consisted of 11,000 pages. They also asked for the six defendants remaining in custody to be granted provisional liberty.

The court decided that the price of the dossier should be reduced to £200 (Egyptian) and that two free copies should be given to the Egyptian Bar Association. It decided also that the six defendants in question should remain in detention, and it adjourned proceedings for a month.

In response to defence requests, a second postponement of a month was declared on 16 May so that students among the defendants could study and sit for examinations and to allow further time for the defence to study the case dossier, of which 22 copies now existed.

Seven further sessions and postponements took place on 20 June, 18 October, 20 November, 18 and 26 December 1978, 1 January 1979 and 1 February 1979.

On 11 February 1979 the defence protested that another 1,100 pages had been added to the case dossier and that only three complete copies existed. The defence also submitted that the case should be tried in an ordinary court and not an exceptional court.

When the court announced that the trial should proceed, all defence lawyers withdrew in protest and were fined £50 (Egyptian) because of their conduct. The court ordered that these lawyers be replaced and adjourned proceedings to 1 March. Afterwards, the Chairman of the Bar Association intervened, assuring the court that the defence lawyers' sole objective had been to secure all standard defence rights for their clients. The fines were subsequently withdrawn and additional copies of the dossier were made available to all lawyers for the defence. The trial continued without incident for another year. Amnesty International sent delegates to observe part of the proceedings in November 1979.

The verdicts were announced by the Supreme State Security Court on 19 April 1980. Of the 176 defendants, 156 were acquitted; 11 were sentenced to three years' imprisonment and a fine of £100 (Egyptian); and nine received sentences of one year's imprisonment and a fine of £50 (Egyptian). Those convicted did not serve their sentences, however, as the court's decision was not considered final until it had been reviewed by the President of the Republic.

In 1981 the President vetoed the verdicts and ordered a retrial before a different court of the same standing. This began before the State Security Court on 17 April 1982. Further proceedings were adjourned to 23 October 1982, on which date they were postponed to 15 January 1983 – six years after the alleged offences took place.

Published 1983

Close-up of remains from a mass grave at Cheung Ek, Kampuchea, where over 8,000 bodies were discovered. This is one of 50 photographs documenting mass political killings by the Government of Democratic Kampuchea between 1975 and 1979. It comes from 'Cambodia Witness', an exhibition sponsored by the United States section of Amnesty International circulating in the United States and Europe as part of Amnesty International's campaign against political killings by governments.

POLITICAL KILLINGS BY GOVERNMENTS

Political killings by governments were documented in a special report published in 1983 which detailed evidence in over 20 countries and spearheaded a campaign launched to expose these killings and mobilize public opinion. These extracts are taken from the report and the April 1983 Newsletter.

MASS KILLINGS IN INDONESIA (1965 TO 1966) AND KAMPUCHEA (1975 TO 1979)

'In 1975 … we were made to change policy: the victory of the revolution had been too quick. If the population was not wiped out immediately, the revolution would be in danger because the republican forces, the forces of Sihanouk, the capitalist forces would unite against it. It was therefore necessary to eliminate all these forces and to spare only those of the Communist Party of Kampuchea. It was necessary to eliminate not only the officers but also the common soldiers as well as their wives and children. This was also based on revolutionary experience. In the past, Sihanouk had killed revolutionaries, but their wives, children and relatives had united against him and had joined us. That must not be repeated against us now. In the beginning, however, only officers' families were killed. At the beginning of 1976, however, the families of common soldiers were also killed. One day at Choeung Prey, I cried for a whole day on seeing women and children killed. I could no longer raise my arms. Comrade S— said to me: 'Get on with it.' I said: 'How can I? Who can kill women and children?' Three days later I was arrested, in June 1976.'
Testimony of a former Khmer Rouge *cadre to the International Commission of Jurists.*

The government-instigated killings in Indonesia in 1965 and 1966 and in Kampuchea in 1975 to 1979 rank among the most massive violations of human rights since the Second World War. A conservative estimate of the number of people killed in Indonesia is 500,000. In Kampuchea the number of victims was at least 300,000.

Both in Indonesia in 1965 and 1966 and in Kampuchea in 1975 to 1979 the governments decided to transform the political map within their countries through the physical liquidation of the political opposition. Elements of such a policy may exist elsewhere, for example in the killing of political leaders or selected members of political groups. The scale of the Indonesian and Kampuchean tragedies resulted from the governments concerned being intent on the permanent physical eradication of all opposition in the case of Kampuchea, and of left-wing opposition in the case of Indonesia.

In Indonesia the principal targets were members of the Indonesian Communist Party and its affiliated organizations – the trade unions, the women's organization (GERWANI) and the peasants' association (Barisan Tani Indonesia). Their families were killed too. In Kampuchea, the victims came from several categories including personnel of the former government, members of the bourgeoisie and intelligentsia and from currents *within* the revolutionary movement that were out of line with the leadership. In addition, many members of ethnic minorities were killed in both countries.

In both Indonesia and Kampuchea the killings were not committed in a period of armed conflict. Resistance was minimal in both cases.

The government-instigated killings of Communist party members and supporters in Indonesia in 1965 and 1966 rank among the most massive violations of human rights since the Second World War: a conservative estimate put the number of killings at 500,000. This photo shows people about to be massacred.

Indonesia (1965 to 1966)

At the beginning of 1965 the Indonesian Communist Party (PKI) was the largest political party in the country. It operated legally and had declared its commitment to peaceful social change.

On 30 September 1965 a group of nationalist army officers led by Lieutenant-Colonel Untung attempted to stage a coup against the government of President Sukarno. Six army generals were killed. The coup attempt was crushed by General Suharto in 24 hours.

During the next few weeks the army leadership under Generals Suharto and Nasution consolidated their control over the government. At the same time they linked the leadership of the PKI with the coup attempt and blamed the PKI for the killing of the six generals. As a result of these accusations PKI members were attacked by mobs and several thousand members were arrested in Jakarta. But it was in Central Java, a long-time PKI stronghold, that the killings of PKI members began.

The arrival in Central Java of two battalions of the Indonesian 'Red Berets', or Army Paracommandos (RPKAD), signalled an army decision to crush the PKI in Central Java before annihilating the party throughout the country. The RPKAD began killing PKI members in Central Java in mid-October 1965, when the PKI was already in disarray and was not offering armed resistance. An Indonesian Government White Paper later argued that the RPKAD had arrived in Central Java to prevent a large-scale insurgence, but there is little evidence that there was in fact a threat of insurrection.

There was no set pattern to the killings that then began and that claimed the lives of an estimated 500,000 Indonesians in the following nine months. However, certain features recurred. Everywhere local officials of the PKI and its affiliated organizations were rounded up and shot. In many cases whole families were killed; it was often said by the perpetrators that the liquidation of entire families would serve to eliminate the communist menace for all time.

The first killings in nearly every province were initiated by the army. In some areas the army was assisted by gangs of youths belonging to *Ansor*, an affiliate of the *Nahdatul Ulama*, a fundamentalist Muslim party. In Java, Bali and Sumatra, night after night for months, local army commanders loaded lorries with captured PKI members – their names checked off against hastily prepared lists – and drove them to isolated spots nearby for execution, usually by bullet or knife. In some cases the bodies were grotesquely mutilated before being buried in hurriedly dug mass graves.

In the town of Kediri in Central Java, a PKI stronghold, some 7,000 PKI supporters are estimated to have been killed. In Banjuwangi in East Java, 4,000 people were killed in a few days. In East Java most people were executed with long sugar-cane knives and sickles; the slaughter often assumed a ritualistic and ceremonial character. In several places the killers held feasts with their bound victims present. After the meal each guest was invited to decapitate a prisoner – apparently to involve as many as possible in the killings.

As the purge accelerated in November 1965 headless bodies covered with red flags were floated down rivers aboard rafts and heads placed upon bridges. Every day for several months riverside residents in Surabaya in East Java had to disentangle bodies that were caught on jetties. At one point so many bodies from Kediri filled the Brantas river that the downstream town of Jombang lodged a formal protest complaining that plague might break out. In the small mill town of Batu so many were executed within the narrow confines of a small police courtyard that it was decided that it would be simpler to cover the piles of bodies with layers of cement rather than bury the victims.

The killings in Bali began sporadically in the west of the island during November 1965. The arrival of RPKAD troops on the island soon ensured that the killings assumed a systematic character. Armed with machine-guns, commandos scoured villages in groups of 25, in some cases executing the entire male population. Hundreds of houses belonging to known communists, their relatives and friends were burned down within a week of the purge being launched. The occupants were slaughtered as they ran out of their dwellings.

A commonly accepted estimate of deaths resulting from the operation in Bali is 50,000, with women and children among the victims. All Chinese retail shops in Denpasar and Singaradja were destroyed and their owners executed after summary judgments were issued convicting them of financing the PKI. The killings of Chinese on Bali were soon followed by persecution elsewhere in Indonesia, claiming thousands of Chinese lives and leading to the exodus of many other Chinese from the country.

By early 1966 the killings had reached virtually all of Indonesia. From Java to Bali they had spread to Sumatra, Kalimantan (Borneo), Sulawesi, Lombok, Flores and Timor. In one incident alone in the city of Medan, North Sumatra, some 10,500 prisoners were reportedly killed in the space of a few days. On the island of Belitung, birthplace of D.N. Aidit, the PKI chairman, hundreds of victims were thrown down disused mineshafts and others towed out to open sea where their boats were sunk.

The responsibility for the killings in Indonesia rested unquestionably with the Indonesian Army which by then effectively controlled the government. Before the killings General Nasution had called for the extirpation of the PKI, and he was reported to have told an army staff conference as the RPKAD arrived in Central Java that 'all of their [PKI] followers and sympathizers should be eliminated'. During a visit to Surabaya he called for the PKI's extinction 'down to its very roots'. In mid-November, as the killings gathered momentum, General Suharto signed an order authorizing an 'absolutely essential clearing out' of the PKI and its sympathizers from the government. This directive, No. 22/KOTI/1965, set up 'special teams' to carry out the order and authorized the teams to request military assistance 'if necessary'.

During the first few months of the killings, President Sukarno and some of his ministers tried to bring them to a halt, but without success. On 11 March 1966 President Sukarno's government was formally replaced by the military government of General Suharto, still in power in 1982.

The precise number of people killed will probably never be known. An inquiry team set up by President Sukarno at the end of 1965 estimated that there had been 87,000 deaths. However, this figure referred only to the island of Java, and the inquiry took place at a time when the killings were just starting in many other places. In late 1966 an investigation commissioned by the army and conducted by the University of Indonesia estimated that one million people had perished since the start of the killings. There are some indications that this estimate may be too high. Admiral Sudomo, the head of the chief government security agency (KOPKAMTIB), later scaled the figure down to 500,000. In addition, some 750,000 people were arrested and detained without charge or trial. Several hundred were still in detention in 1982. In a period of less than a year all the leading figures of the PKI, Indonesia's largest political party, together with countless thousands of its members and supporters, had been killed.

Kampuchea (1975 to 1979)

On 17 April 1975 forces of the revolutionary communist movement known as the *Khmer Rouge* entered the capital of Cambodia, Phnom Penh, overthrowing the government of Lon Nol. This was the outcome of several years' civil war between the *Khmer Rouge* and the Lon Nol government, which was supported by the United States of America. Upon taking power the new government immediately set out to evacuate all cities and towns and to execute the leadership of the former government.

By 1975 the population of Phnom Penh had swollen to more than two million, roughly one third of the total population, as a result of the civil war and the US bombing and destruction of agriculture. On the morning of 17 April 1975 *Khmer Rouge* troops toured the city ordering the population to evacuate the city within three days on pain of death. In practice many residents were given less than an hour in which to leave. Those who refused, procrastinated or showed some opposition were beaten or shot dead. Old people, disabled, children, pregnant women and hospital patients were all forced to leave the city without distinction.

During the evacuation many people are known to have died. Some were killed by *Khmer Rouge* troops in order to keep the marchers moving or to maintain discipline. Refugees from Phnom Penh have spoken of people, particularly the young, dying on the roadside. One of the city's leading physicians, Dr Vann Hay, said that on his march from Phnom Penh he saw the body of a child about every 200 metres.

In the following days other cities and towns were evacuated including Battambang (200,000 inhabitants), Svay Rieng (130,000), Kompong Chhnang (60,000),

Kompong Speu (60,000) and Siem Reap (50,000). The loss of life from this gigantic shift of population is incalculable.

The population of the evacuated cities and towns, known as the 'new people' as distinct from the 'base people' (the peasantry), were moved to agricultural sites where they were forced to work long hours on irrigation works and the cultivation of rice under strict discipline. Slight infringements of discipline were frequently punished by execution.

The evacuation of Cambodia's cities was accompanied by the first of several purges – that of the officer corps and senior officials of the former Lon Nol government. Nearly all high-ranking officers, senior officials, police officers, customs officials and members of the military police appear to have been executed during the days immediately after 17 April 1975. Detailed and independent accounts have been obtained from the towns of Phnom Penh, Battambang, Siem Reap, Pailin and Kompong Speu. In some places all officers from lieutenant upwards were executed. Even this distinction of rank was often lost, and in the first few months after the revolution some local authorities were apparently given a free hand in deciding whom to execute. On the forced marches from Phnom Penh *Khmer Rouge* forces were permitted to pull out of the marching columns anyone they suspected of being associated with the former administration and kill them on the spot.

Many accounts of these killings are now available. For example: 'The chairman of Tuk Phok district, named Miec Vay, summoned 50 guerrillas from various villages of his district and gave them this oral order: "The former Lon Nol soldiers are our enemies. We must kill all enemies to celebrate the day of victory. This is the order of our leader Pol Pot. Anyone who refuses to kill is disobeying orders and must inflict on himself due punishment." We obeyed the district chairman's order and the 50 of us killed 2,005 Lon Nol soldiers.' (From evidence before a revolutionary tribunal in Phnom Penh in August 1979.)

It appears from such testimonies that the killings were not simply an act of revenge conducted in the heat of victory but were carried out in fulfilment of a central government policy.

Non-commissioned officers, army privates, minor officials and village headmen were treated differently from region to region. Some were executed in the days following the *Khmer Rouge* victory, others were sent to hard labour camps while others were allowed to return home. In late 1975, however, the policy towards lesser officials changed; systematic executions of this group then began and continued into 1976.

The killings of former Lon Nol officers and officials extended to their families. Wives and children were executed to prevent them becoming opponents of the new government.

The killings of former government personnel were soon followed by executions of members of the bourgeoisie and intelligentsia. The rationale behind this practice was

reflected in a document issued by the Executive Bureau of the Eastern Region Party Committee:

'We must heighten our revolutionary vigilance as regards those elements who have served in the administrative machinery of the former regime, such as technicians, professors, doctors, engineers and other technical personnel. The policy of our Party is not to employ them in any capacity. If we run after this technology, we will feel that they submit to us and we will use them, but this will create the opportunity for enemies to infiltrate our ranks more deeply with every passing year and this will be a dangerous process.'

In line with this policy intellectuals – often crudely identified as those who wore spectacles – were singled out for particularly harsh treatment and in many regions of the country were summarily executed. Many refugees report that from early 1976 intellectuals, teachers and students, often described by the *Khmer Rouge* as 'the worthless ones', disappeared from their places of work and were presumed to have been killed. A former *Khmer Rouge* cadre recalled that in Kompong Cham province it was decided 'to arrest the worthless ones', in other words, intellectuals, teachers, pupils beyond the seventh grade. The country had to be rid of them. That was the decision of the Central Committee, just as it had been its decision to wipe out the soldiers in 1975-1976.'

Besides the killing of political and social groups designated enemies of the revolution, many thousands of individuals were executed on such grounds as minor infringements of work discipline. Offences such as illicit sexual relationships, criticizing or challenging official instructions, resistance to the introduction of communal eating (after 1977), and even laziness were often punished by death.

From 1975 to 1977 there were regional variations in the pattern of repression. In the Eastern Zone, although former Lon Nol officers had been killed in 1975, conditions do not seem to have been as harsh as elsewhere. This resulted from political differences between regional authorities and the central government in Phnom Penh.

These differences came to a head in 1978 when the central government leadership under Pol Pot launched what was, in effect, an invasion of the Eastern Zone (which bordered on Viet Nam). The long-simmering conflict between the centre and the more moderate eastern communists exploded into open warfare in May 1978, and the following months saw one of the most massive purges of the entire *Khmer Rouge* period. Tens of thousands of people including officers and soldiers, together with their fathers, mothers, wives and children were executed. The victims included all Eastern Zone cadres who could be traced, people evacuated from the cities in 1975, and anyone with Vietnamese relatives and connections. It has been estimated that 100,000 people were killed in this purge because the party centre in Phnom Penh had decided that the Eastern Zone was led by '*Khmer* bodies with Vietnamese minds'. A former rubber plantation worker, one of many refugees

Interior of S-21 (Toul Sleng) detention and interrogation centre in Phnom Penh, Kampuchea, where between 1975 and 1979 nearly 20,000 people were executed, often after torture. Photographs of the prisoners were taken by Democratic Kampuchean officials. After 1979, the prisoners' photographs were displayed on the walls of the grond floor. In the foreground are the leg-irons used to shackle the prisoners.

interviewed, said:

'They killed all the Eastern Zone cadres, and ordinary people who committed the most minor offences, such as talking about one's family problems at night. Every day they would take away three to five families for execution. We would hear them screaming for help...'. (Kiernan, *Khmer Bodies with Vietnamese Minds: Kampuchea's Eastern Zone, 1975-1978*, Monash University, 1980.)

The local party leader So Phim and almost the entire Zone Committee, the local military hierarchy and all but two members of the regional committees were executed. Executions of cadres are reported to have occurred in almost all districts, sub-districts and villages. A number of villages, including So Phim's home village, are reported to have been entirely wiped out.

Members of ethnic minorities also were the victims of repeated massacres with thousands of Chinese, Vietnamese, Lao and Thai being killed. The Cham, a Muslim people, were singled out for especially harsh treatment. From the early days of the Democratic Kampuchean Government (*Khmer Rouge*) all religious activity was rigorously repressed and religious leaders executed. In the case of the Cham this was followed in early 1976 by a ban on the use of their native language, the suppression of their religious beliefs and forcing them to raise pigs and eat pork. Cham villages were dispersed and the Cham people told that they were a weak link in the nation. Cadres are reported to have told Cham leaders in 1977 in the south-west region: '...the Chams are hopeless. They abandoned their country to others. They just shouldered their fishing nets and walked off, letting the Vietnamese take over this country.'

Executions of Cham leaders and dignitaries and the populations of entire villages soon followed. In Stung Trang, lorries loaded with Chams were reportedly pushed down steep ravines. The district of Kompong Xiem, in the province of Kompong Cham, with five hamlets and a total population of 20,000, was reported to have been razed to the ground and all its inhabitants killed. In the district of Koong Neas, in the same province, out of an estimated 20,000 inhabitants there were reportedly only four survivors. It is now conservatively estimated that more than half of the total 1975 Cham population of 400,000 was killed between 1975 and 1978.

Of all the mass killings carried out during the *Khmer Rouge* rule of Kampuchea, the most clearly documented are those that took place at Tuol Sleng, also known as S21. Tuol Sleng was a former school in Phnom Penh used by the *Khmer Rouge* as a centre for torture and execution. Careful records were kept of prisoners and the prison archives, which have survived virtually intact, show that nearly 15,000 people were liquidated there. Some of the victims of Tuol Sleng were *Khmer Rouge* soldiers from the Eastern Zone; others were members of the government or other Kampuchean communists suspected of opposing the government.

At any one time the prison held an average of 1,000 to 1,500 prisoners. Most were held for a short time, tortured and forced into writing confessions before being killed. The names of alleged co-conspirators elicited through confessions were recorded and elaborate charts drawn up showing lines of 'contacts' in coloured inks.

The rate of executions increased after October 1977. On 15 October 1977 the prison record books show 418 killed; on 18 October, 179 were killed; on 20 October, 88 and on 23 October, 148. The highest single figure was 582 recorded executions on 27 May 1978. In many cases, as with the veteran communist Hu Nim, the cause of death was recorded as 'crushed to bits'.

In January 1979 the Government of Democratic Kampuchea was overthrown by the forces of the Kampuchean United Front for National Salvation, after an invasion by Vietnamese troops in December 1978. The country was renamed the People's Republic of Kampuchea. The new government established a special tribunal which in August 1979 tried *in absentia* Pol Pot and Ieng Sary, the Prime Minister and Foreign Minister in the Democratic Kampuchea Government. They were charged with genocide and both were sentenced to death. During the trial, witnesses testified to having participated in torture and killings committed on the orders of the authorities. Victims of imprisonment and torture also testified against the accused *Khmer Rouge* leaders. Documents on prisons and mass graves were presented to the court.

In August 1981 Democratic Kampuchea's Foreign Minister Ieng Sary, attending a United Nations conference on Kampuchea in New York, was confronted with some of the evidence of killings during a press interview. Ieng Sary admitted that the documents were genuine and confirmed the killing of Hu Nim and the existence of Tuol Sleng. He also acknowledged what no other *Khmer Rouge* leader had admitted before – that it was official policy to liquidate people accused of opposing the regime. He justified the policy by saying that 'the circumstance was proletarian dictatorship. We were in the middle of class struggle.'

Despite the magnitude of the killings in Indonesia and Kampuchea, the international community did little to try to stop them. The United Nations first took official note of the human rights situation in Kampuchea in March 1978 when there was considerable discussion at the UN Human Rights Commission. It asked the Sub-Commission on Prevention of Discrimination and Protection of Minorities to consider the matter in 1979. Several governments and non-governmental organizations submitted information and the sub-commission decided to investigate further. The Government of Kampuchea responded by calling it 'impudent interferences in internal affairs'. In January 1979 the commission received a report about human rights violations in Kampuchea, but by that time the *Khmer Rouge* government had been overthrown.

To some extent this inaction may have been caused by lack of information at an early date. The killings in Indonesia and Kampuchea took place in conditions of considerable secrecy and in some cases it was weeks and even months before any details became available outside the country. When information did emerge, there were accusations that it was exaggerated for political reasons. Prompt research by impartial external investigative bodies, using such techniques as interviews with refugees, might have led to earlier and more effective measures to counteract the killings.

In Indonesia the killings subsided only when the principal target, the communist party, had been destroyed. In Kampuchea they ended only when the government was overthrown.

Published March 1983

AMNESTY INTERNATIONAL SUPPLEMENT

Political killings by governments take place in different parts of the world and in countries of widely differing ideologies. They range from individual assassinations to the wholesale slaughter of mass opposition movements or entire ethnic groups. The scale of the crime is sometimes not known to the international community before it has reached proportions that will damage a whole society for generations to come.

Hundreds of thousands of people in the past 10 years have been killed by the political authorities in their countries. The killings continue. Day after day *AI* receives reports of deliberate political killings by the army and the police, by other regular security forces, by special units created to function outside normal supervision, by 'death squads' sanctioned by the authorities, by government assassins.

The killings take place outside any legal or judicial process; the victims are denied any protection from the law. Many are abducted, illegally detained, or tortured before they are killed.

Sometimes the killings are ordered at the highest level of government: in other cases the government deliberately does not investigate killings or take measures to prevent further deaths.

Governments often try to cover up the fact that they have committed political killings. They deny that the killings have taken place, they attribute them to opposition forces, or they try to pass them off as the result of armed encounters with government forces or of attempts by the victims to escape from custody.

The pattern of killings is often accompanied by the suspension of constitutional rights, intimidation of witnesses and relatives of victims, suppression of evidence and a weakening of the independence of the judiciary.

These political killings are crimes for which governments and their agents are responsible under national and international law. Their accountability is not diminished because opposition groups commit similar abhorrent acts. Nor does the difficulty of proving who is ultimately answerable for them lessen the government's responsibility to investigate unlawful killings and take steps to prevent them.

Official cover-up

The facts about political killings by governments are often hidden or distorted by those responsible. The official cover-up may take many forms: concealing the fact of the killing, for example by making prisoners 'disappear'; blaming killings on opposition forces or independent armed groups; or passing off unlawful killings of defenceless individuals as the result of armed encounters or escape attempts.

One means of covering up political killings by governments is to conceal the identity of the perpetrators, claiming that the killings were the work of clandestine

▲ *The graves of Teodoro Aligado and Epifanio Simbajon, arrested without warrant by members of the Philippines Constabulary on 25 June 1981 in Barrio Lourdes, Pagadian City, Zamboanga del Sur province. They were detained on suspicion of being members of the New People's Army, the armed wing of the Communist Party of the Philippines. The two were removed from Pagadian City Jail on 29 June for further interrogation – later that day they were shot dead. Police officers alleged that they had been killed while trying to escape, but friends and relatives of the dead men have disputed the official version of events.*

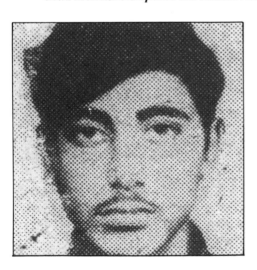

Student leader Peddi Shankar, aged 23, was shot dead in an alleged 'encounter' with the police on 2 November 1980 in Moinbinpetta village, Sironcha Taluka, Chandrapur district, Maharashtra state, India.

Villagers testified that Peddi Shankar was shot in the back in broad daylight from a distance of some 50 feet by a squad from the State Reserve Police of Maharashtra, and that neither he nor his four companions (who escaped) had fired a shot.

groups over whom the government has no control.

In the Philippines, the authorities have commonly responded to allegations of human rights violations by claiming that they are the result of armed conflict, particularly with the New People's Army (NPA), the armed wing of the Communist Party of the Philippines. People reported to have 'disappeared' are described as having 'gone underground'. Those killed by military personnel are said to have been killed in combat.

In India, in December 1980 the Minister of State for Home Affairs informed the lower house of the Indian parliament that 216 'Naxalites' – members of the Communist Party of India (Marxist-Leninist) – had been shot dead by police in Andhra Pradesh state since 1968. He added that the shootings were 'a sequel to armed attacks launched by Naxalites on police'.

Eye-witness accounts obtained by *AI* and other investigating bodies indicate that a number of the victims had been arrested and, in some cases, tortured before being shot.

Creating a cover-up can involve fabrication of evidence. For example, in Colombia, there have been a number of unexplained killings by official forces in rural 'militarized' zones, where the army has for some years had violent clashes with guerrillas.

On the morning of 26 April 1981 an army patrol entered the ranch of Ramón Cardona in Albania, Caqueta, dragged him and two others from the house and took them into the nearby hills. Screams were heard. The next day the three men were found dead, their bodies bearing signs of severe torture. According to reports of the incident, neighbours were ordered to transfer the bodies to a clearing, where soldiers placed a small quantity of food, an empty army knapsack and a camouflage shirt by the bodies. The soldiers then told local people and army officers who arrived to view the bodies that the supplies were evidence that the men had been guerrillas. An army press bulletin subsequently declared that the men had ambushed an army patrol and been killed in an exchange of fire.

'Disappeared' victims

Many political killings by governments have been concealed because the victims have 'disappeared' after being taken into custody: the authorities have tried to hide both the fact of the killing and their own responsibility. Sometimes the victims of 'disappearance' are later discovered in prison, or released; sometimes it is learned that they have been killed.

Since the March 1976 military coup the Argentine armed forces have killed many real or imagined opponents of the military government as part of a 'war' against subversion. It is impossible to know the precise number of victims. This is partly because of the secrecy surrounding the 'war' against subversion and partly because most of these killings have been linked to the practice of 'disappearances' carried out by the armed forces after the coup. Most of these 'disappearances' occurred between 1976 and 1978.

Libyan assassinated in London ... police activity around the body of Mahmoud Abdul Salam Nafi', shot dead in the doorway of the Arab Legal Centre on 25 April 1980. The two Libyan gunmen who shot him were captured, tried for murder, convicted and sentenced to life imprisonment. At their trial they said that their victim had been sentenced to death by a revolutionary committee and they had taken it upon themselves to execute the sentences. At least 14 Libyans have been killed or wounded in assassination attempts outside their country since February 1980 when the Third Congress of the Libyan Revolutionary Committees issued a declaration calling for the 'physical liquidation' of enemies of the 1969 revolution living abroad.

The Libyan leader, Colonel Gaddafi, has explicitly sanctioned the international assassination campaign against his opponents in a number of official statements and press interviews. On 17 February 1983 the General People's Congress (the body assigned to ratify official policy in Libya), adopted a resolution calling for the renewal of the assassination campaign against Libyans abroad, who were classified as 'hostile'. The resolution stated that 'every citizen is responsible for the liquidation of the enemies of the people and revolution'.

Typically, the victims were taken from their houses at night by men who identified themselves as agents of the police or armed forces. A few were subsequently released or acknowledged as official detainees. Usually the victims were taken to secret camps run by the armed forces or police, where almost all are believed to have been tortured. The majority of these 'disappeared' people have never been seen again.

Hundreds of people – including a number of 'disappeared' individuals – are believed to have been buried in unmarked graves discovered recently in at least nine cemeteries in the Buenos Aires area. Investigations carried out since October 1982 have revealed that up to four hundred bodies may have been buried in unmarked graves in the Gran Bourg cemetery alone.

In Guatemala, many victims of 'disappearances' have been killed – only extremely rarely has a 'disappeared' person later been found in custody or reappeared alive.

It has, however, often been difficult to verify the fact that an individual who has 'disappeared' has died. Bodies have been recovered from secret graveyards in such a state of decomposition that identification was impossible. Corpses have been found at roadsides far from where abductions took place, mutilated beyond recognition.

In Guinea, President Sekou Touré's government has failed to account for approximately 2,900 prisoners who 'disappeared' after being arrested for political reasons between 1969 and 1976. Many are believed to have died as a result of torture, execution, deliberate starvation or inhuman prison conditions.

In Afghanistan, thousands of people 'disappeared' after the People's Democratic Party (PDP) government came to power following a military coup in April 1978. The precise number of 'disappearances' and killings is not known.

In December 1979 the new government of President Babrak Karmal took power and declared a general amnesty. During an *AI* mission to Kabul in February 1980 delegates met relatives of some of the thousands of prisoners who were known to have been arrested but who had not been released under the general amnesty. The Karmal government has said that all those not released in December 1979 had been killed before it came to power. Government officials told *AI* that they had a list of 4,584 people who had been killed, but that they believed the number of killings and 'disappearances' was actually higher.

Since December 1979 *AI* has received reports of killings of civilians in areas of armed conflict in Afghanistan. The reports have alleged killings by both government forces and insurgents. Detailed and precise accounts have been difficult to obtain.

The killings

Political killings by governments have been committed in most, if not all, of the regions of the world. The cases in this report show that they are not confined to any one political system or ideology. Further examples are given here of political killings since 1980 believed to have been carried out by official forces or others linked to the government. The circumstances of the killings and the nature of government involvement vary from country to country. Some governments have been shown to be responsible by their wilful failure to investigate adequately or to prevent further killings.

The victims – individuals and entire families – have come from all walks of life and from many political persuasions and religious faiths. Politicians, government officials, judges, lawyers, military officers, trade unionists, journalists, teachers, students and schoolchildren, religious workers and peasants: all have lost their lives. In some cases well-known political figures have been publicly assassinated; in others whole villages have been wiped out, and the news has not reached the outside world for weeks or months. Often, the victims belonged to the political opposition – often they were simply members of a particular ethnic group or lived in an area targeted for security operations.

In El Salvador, thousands of people have been killed by the security forces since the military coup of October 1979. The victims have included not only people suspected of opposition to the authorities, but thousands of unarmed peasant farmers living in areas targeted for military operations in the government's counter-guerrilla campaign. People monitoring government abuses, such as journalists and human rights workers, as well as church activists, community workers, political militants and trade unionists, have been arrested and killed. Patients have been abducted from hospital beds by security forces and killed.

Testimonies received daily by *AI* implicate all branches of the Salvadorian security services in the killings. In addition to the regular armed forces El Salvador also relies on special security forces such as the National Guard, which combines police and military functions, the National Police and the Treasury Police. All these units have repeatedly been named in reports of political killings. So has a nominally civilian paramilitary unit called ORDEN (now renamed *Frente Democrático Nacionalista*, Democratic Nationalist Front), established in 1967 to carry out a clandestine 'counter-terror' campaign against government opponents. New 'civil defence brigades' set up under military control are also reported to have carried out killings in rural areas. Recently the Atlactl Brigade, one of the special new units trained by US military advisers, has been blamed repeatedly for killings of unarmed peasants.

The Salvadorian authorities continue to maintain that any abuses were perpetrated by security or armed forces personnel exceeding their authority. They have also on several occasions stated that officers or troops implicated in these abuses have been removed from duty, or assigned to non-combatant positions.

The authorities have also claimed that atrocities in rural areas were perpetrated by independent extremist groups or 'death squads' out of government control. Other reports, however, have indicated that the so-called 'death squads' are made up of members of ORDEN or other off-duty or plain-clothes security personnel acting in cooperation with the regular armed forces.

In Libya, the Third Congress of the Libyan Revolutionary Committees issued a declaration in February 1980 calling for the 'physical liquidation' of enemies of the 1969 revolution living abroad. Since then at least 14 Libyan citizens have been killed or wounded in assassination attempts outside Libya.

In Uganda, the widespread unlawful killings of the eight-year military government of President Idi Amin ended only with the overthrow of the regime in 1979.

In the aftermath of the armed conflict, a high level of criminal violence continued, with many unexplained but possibly politically motivated murders.

Opponents and supporters of the government and members of the security forces were killed under the successive governments of Yusuf Lule, Godfrey Binaisa, and the Military Commission.

Former President Milton Obote returned to power after elections in 1980. Instability continued, and early 1981 saw a series of guerrilla attacks. Many civilians – particularly alleged political opponents – were arrested by the army and there were reports of torture and killings in military custody. Unarmed civilians are also reported to have been killed by security forces operating against guerrillas in the countryside.

In Iran, in addition to the large number of officially announced executions which have taken place since the revolution of February 1979 (more than 4,500 by the end of March 1983), *AI* has received many reports of executions which have not been announced and may not have been preceded by a trial. In other cases it is clear from the circumstances of the killings that no legal proceedings took place.

Some months after the 1979 revolution, fighting broke out between government forces and members of the Turkoman ethnic group. Four Turkoman leaders were arrested and imprisoned in Evin Prison, Tehran, from where they were kidnapped and killed. The then President of Iran, Abolhassan Bani-Sadr, sent two missions to discover how the Turkoman leaders had died and the findings of both missions were that they had been kidnapped and killed by the Revolutionary Guards.

Members of the Baha'i religion have been killed in circumstances suggesting official involvement. *AI* knows of no case in which anyone has been prosecuted in connection with such a killing.

Kurds have also been killed in circumstances which suggest strongly that extrajudicial executions have taken place. One report described the killing of 18 workers on 14 September 1981 at a bricklaying factory near the village of Saroughamish. According to the report Revolutionary Guards arrested the workers, put them against a wall and machine-gunned them.

Fifty-one villagers are reported to have been killed by Revolutionary Guards in the village of Dehgaz in the

Caspian region between June and September 1981. Those killed were allegedly sympathizers of the opposition People's Mujahideen Organization of Iran.

In Chad, there have been reports of killings of civilians and soldiers no longer in combat by forces loyal to Hissein Habré (who was sworn in as President on 21 October 1982) after they occupied the capital, N'Djamena, in June 1982 and moved on to consolidate Habré's control of the country. Eye-witness accounts have described defeated soldiers of the opposing *Forces armées tchadiennes*, Chadian Armed Forces, and some of their civilian collaborators, being killed by the pro-Habré forces, the *Forces armées du nord*, Armed Forces of the North.

In Namibia, South African military forces are in conflict with nationalist guerrillas belonging to the South West Africa People's Organization (SWAPO). Church leaders and others have reported that civilians have been killed by South African soldiers because they were thought to support or sympathize with SWAPO.

In Bolivia, following the July 1980 military coup, *AI* received reports that security forces were involved in numerous 'disappearances' and political killings.

In the mining areas of Huanuni, Catavi and Siglo Veinte, where strikes against the coup had been organized, troops used tanks and heavy weapons to put down resistance to the military take-over.

In Chile, during the first few months after the 1973 military coup thousands of people were reported to have been summarily executed; between 1973 and 1977 hundreds – mainly political activists, trade unionists and peasants – 'disappeared' after being arrested by the security forces. The 'disappearances' and killings which took place between 1973 and 1977 remain officially unexplained.

Since 1977, a number of alleged members of banned political parties and organizations, such as the *Movimiento de Izquierda Revolucionaria* (MIR), Movement of the Revolutionary Left, have died in the custody of the Chilean secret police, the *Central Nacional de Informaciones* (CNI), in circumstances which indicate that they may have died after torture, or may have been deliberately killed by other methods. A number of other killings have been described officially as the result of 'confrontations' with members of the security forces, such as the CNI.

In some instances of alleged 'confrontations' and deaths in custody, official investigations have been started, but reports indicate that once the CNI or other security forces have been implicated the investigation has been passed from the civilian courts to the military courts. Military courts have consistently failed to bring those responsible to justice.

In Mexico, there have been reports of a number of killings in which regular army units have been involved or some other official link is known or suspected. On 25 July 1982, for example, a military detachment entered Coacoyult in the municipality of Ajuchitlán, Guerrero, and took 13 peasants away with them. Of the 13, five were later found dead.

In East Timor, which has been occupied by Indonesia since December 1975, there have been numerous reports of people being executed after surrendering to, or being captured by, Indonesian armed forces.

In the Republic of Korea (South Korea), at least 40 people were killed when army paratroopers dispersed a peaceful student demonstration in Kwangju on 18 May 1980. *AI* has received reports and eye-witness accounts alleging that paratroopers clubbed people on the head indiscriminately and bayoneted them; that many of the dead were shot in the face, and that others were stabbed to death.

At least 1,200 civilians are reported to have died in disturbances in the following nine days; the South Korean authorities said that 144 civilians, 22 soldiers and four police officers died.

Tens of thousands of Guatemalans have been killed for political reasons under successive governments since 1966. They have been killed by regular military and police units, both on and off duty, in uniform and in plain clothes; by official security guards assigned to government functionaries; by private security guards often led by former police or military personnel; and by 'death squads' – armed groups, often made up of off-duty military and security personnel, which *AI* believes are linked to the government.

The victims have come from all sectors of Guatemalan society: peasants and Indians, trade unionists, church activists, political leaders, journalists and members of the legal profession.

Peasants have been massacred in areas where guerrillas were believed to be active, apparently to prevent the guerrillas gaining supplies and support, and to intimidate the population.

In Syria, since 1980 there have been several reported incidents of killings by the security forces. On 27 July 1980 hundreds of prisoners – most of them believed to have been members of the outlawed Muslim Brotherhood – were reported to have been killed in Palmyra (Tadmur) desert prison by the *Saray al Difa'*, Special Defence Units, a special military force under the command of President Assad's brother, Rifa'at Assad. On the night of 23 April 1981 Syrian security forces reportedly sealed off parts of the town of Hama, carried out house-to-house searches, dragged people from their homes, lined them up in the streets and shot them. *AI* received the names of over 100 of those reported killed.

On 2 February 1982 violent clashes between security forces and Muslim Brotherhood fighters, following the discovery of a hidden cache of arms, developed into a near-insurrection in the town of Hama.

Syrian troops and security forces encircled the town and bombarded it from the air and the ground. A news blackout was imposed by the authorities but in early March, after the fighting had ended, reports of massacres and atrocities began to reach the outside world. Most reports indicated that at the start of the fighting government officials and their families in Hama were systematically sought out and killed by the rebels. Later, however, massacres were reported to have been committed by government forces, partly through aerial bombardment but also by troops on the ground as they regained control of the town.

In the aftermath of the Israeli invasion into the Lebanon, hundreds of Palestinian and Lebanese civilians in the refugee camps of Chatilla and Sabra in West Beirut were massacred between 16 and 18 September 1982, by armed Lebanese militia members. The Israeli armed forces were in military control of the area at the time.

An Israeli judicial commission was later established to determine whether the Israeli authorities had any responsibility for the killings. Headed by the Chief Justice of the Israeli Supreme Court, the commission met in open and closed sessions and took evidence from front-line commanders and high-ranking military officers and cabinet officials, including the Army Chief of Staff, the Minister of Defence and the Prime Minister.

The commission reported in February 1983. It concluded that Israeli forces had 'absolutely no direct responsibility' for the massacres but that Israeli officials, 'because of things that were well known to all', should have foreseen that the danger of a massacre existed if the militia members entered the camps without preventive measures being taken. The commission concluded also that Israeli officials did not take 'energetic and immediate' actions to restrain the Lebanese militiamen or to put a stop to their actions. The commission recommended that measures be taken against certain named officials, including the Israeli Minister of Defence.

In Iraq, several political suspects in custody were allegedly poisoned in 1980 shortly before they were released. Two of the cases involved Iraqis who were examined by doctors in the United Kingdom after they had left Iraq. Both were found to be suffering from thallium poisoning. (Thallium is a heavy metal used commercially in rat poison.) One of the two died; the other was said to have recovered.

Well over 20 Yugoslav political emigres have been assassinated since the early 1970s, including two in 1980, and emigre circles have frequently alleged that Yugoslav state security service (SDS) agents were responsible. The findings of courts outside Yugoslavia have in several cases supported such allegations.

In Ethiopia, thousands of people were unlawfully and deliberately killed by the security forces after the Provisional Military Government assumed power in 1974 – particularly during the government's 'Red Terror' campaign in 1977 and 1978. Between November 1977 and about February 1978, an estimated 5,000 political opponents of the government were killed in Addis Ababa alone.

In Burundi, at least 80,000 people are believed to have been killed in May and June 1972 after a rebellion inspired by the numerically larger Hutu ethnic group against the dominant Tutsi group.

AI Newsletter April 1983

The Chilean artist Hugo Eduardo Riveros Gómez, 29, found dead on the outskirts of Santiago on 8 July 1981 – his hands had been tied behind his back and he had been stabbed three times. A piece of cardboard had been left on his chest; written in blood on it was the letter 'R' – a symbol intended to represent the 'Resistance', a name used by left-wing opponents of the government. The day before, three men had blindfolded him and dragged him out of his home. He had been under surveillance by men in plain clothes for several days beforehand. He had recognized one of the men as a secret police agent who had reportedly tortured him in October 1980, when he had been detained incommunicado for more than a fortnight. After that spell of detention he was charged, on 5 November 1980, with belonging to a banned organization. In March 1981 he was released on bail. At the end of June the prosecution recommended that he be sentenced to 541 days' relegación, internal exile. He was murdered about a week later. His wife's request for an investigating judge to be appointed to inquire into the killing was refused by the Santiago Appeals Court in July 1981. Proceedings were in fact initiated by the 18th Criminal Court – but it closed the case without having found anyone responsible for Hugo Riveros' death. Amnesty International believes that the 'Resistance' symbol left on his body was put there to mislead investigations and that there are grounds to believe that the security forces were involved in Hugo Riveros' death: for example, the fact that he had been under surveillance and the way he was abducted are consistent with methods used by the secret police.

165

LIFE IN A SOVIET LABOUR CAMP

A detailed description of living conditions in a Soviet labour camp for political prisoners was published by Amnesty International in 1984.

Balys Gayauskas, a Lithuanian, pictured with his wife. He is one of at least 15 prisoners of conscience in special regime camp VS 389-36/1, in Perm region. Since 1948 he has been sentenced to a total of 40 years' imprisonment on political grounds.

Amnesty International has received a detailed first-hand description of living conditions in a special labour camp for political prisoners singled out by the Soviet authorities for particularly severe treatment. The document confirms previous information of harsh conditions in the camp.

The description by a prisoner of conscience held at the 'special regime' camp near Perm, some 1,200km east of Moscow, tells of men being confined to tiny, stinking cells in which flickering electric light burns night and day; living on poor rations and brackish water; having to fulfil excessive work norms; receiving inadequate medical treatment; and being denied many of the rights of most 'non-political' labour camp inmates.

'Special regime' camps are designated by the Soviet penal system for 'especially dangerous' prisoners. At least 15 of the men held in special camps VS 389-36/1, however, are known to be there after having been prosecuted repeatedly for non-violent attempts to express their beliefs. All 15 were convicted of 'anti-Soviet agitation and propaganda' and sentenced to at least 10 years' imprisonment.

The camp, set up in 1980 and attached to a larger 'strict regime' corrective labour colony in the Ural Mountains, held over 30 prisoners at last report. The description, which reached *AI* in October 1983, was written in April 1982. *AI* was not able to corroborate the details, but they are consistent with other information received by the organization. *AI* has decided to make the account public in the belief that it is authentic.

The material published below comes from the prisoner's description, which was sent abroad through unofficial channels. His account, about 1,000 words long, includes descriptions of the different types of cell in which the inmates are confined during the years of their imprisonment: living cells, work cells and exercise cells – the last being known as 'barrels', concrete rectangles half a dozen paces long and covered with a barbed wire grid; medical treatment, food, letters and infrequent visits are also dealt with. The following are excerpts translated from the original Russian.

'They take away from every prisoner the legal documents relating to his case. In other words, they remove the possibility of protesting about the case – a prisoner does not have the material he needs in order to struggle for his rights.

'Since our cases are shams – unsubstantiated fabricated claims made by the KGB – they do not want such material to find its way abroad.

'To all our complaints regarding our cases the authorities give a standard answer: the case has been examined thoroughly and the sentence of the court is correct: 10 years' [imprisonment] plus five years' [internal] exile. To other complaints the Procuracy usually answers: the facts have not been proved. Often complaints are sent for investigation to the very person about whom you are complaining.

'The regime in the camp is like that in a KGB

investigation and isolation cell. In particular they try to isolate us from society and from each other. Between two and five prisoners share a cell. Each is allotted two square metres of space in the cell, which is crammed with ... bunks and a table.

'We do not meet prisoners from other cells: we work in separate cells and only with those with whom we live. The exercise cells are arranged so that it is impossible to pass on notes – and to prevent us exchanging a few words a guard walks along a catwalk above. If we begin to talk we are taken away from the exercise cell.

'The living and work cells are equipped with toilets. Last year they put up a partition about 1.5m high in the living cells ... but all the same the toilet is not screened off from the rest of the cell. There is no ventilation and so it stinks. In the work cells there is not even this formal partition....

'The work cells are dark: electric light is necessary by day.... The light burns at night too.... In autumn and winter the electric light is very weak and flickers. It is very difficult to read; it ruins your eyes ... many prisoners have weak and aching eyes. The work is light but the work norms are high and few fulfil them; some are punished as a result. The privileges provided for by the labour code for the sick and disabled are not applied here. They must work to death.

'After lunch a few rays of sunlight fall into the exercise cells. But you are not allowed to take off your jacket – this must be buttoned right up. Some guards do not even let you take off your headgear.

'In all there are five exercise cells – known as *'bochki'* ('barrels'). Three of them are approximately 3m by 5m and 2.5m high. Two of these are made of concrete and are enclosed above by a barbed wire grid. The exercise period lasts one hour. The two other cells are 2m by 2m and 2.5m high. The sun never reaches them. This is where prisoners in solitary confinement may exercise – their exercise lasts half an hour.

'The food is bad ... Groats, meat (a piece of gristle, bone) which is often rotten. We hardly ever get vegetables – and when we do they are never fresh. In the [camp] shop you can spend up to four roubles a month on margarine, vegetable oil, sweets.... Sometimes there is tinned fish, occasionally processed cheese, and biscuits. The water is very bad. Sometimes they bring drinking water into the kitchen, but most frequently there is none – and then they boil stagnant water, which is very dirty ... it stinks, but you have to drink it.

'For two camps there is one doctor, who does not visit every day. The dentist and other specialists come very rarely. The medical treatment is merely first aid. There are not enough medicines. The hospital is at camp 35. People who have been there say it is better in the camp lock-up here than in the hospital. The hospital cells are like those in the lock-up: small and dark, and cold in winter. The medical treatment is a formality. There is nowhere [separate] to wash. The bath is in the toilet [section]. In winter it is very cold and it is better not to wash as you risk catching a chill. The exercise cells in the hospital are the same as our small one: "barrels". Prisoners on special regime in the hospital are kept in maximum isolation.

'Letters not written in Russian take six to eight weeks to reach us. [The home language of prisoners may be Ukrainian, Lithuanian or any one of the USSR's national languages.] We receive letters only from close relatives: those from other people do not in practice arrive. Apparently they are forbidden. Very often the authorities even confiscate letters from our wives, mothers and children – and even our own letters [to them]. Greetings on religious holidays are forbidden. All postcards are confiscated. They explain this by saying that they are ideologically and politically harmful, or that they contain conspiracies.

'If you begin to inquire why they are not handed over, or write to the Procurator about it, they answer that the letter has been rightfully confiscated and destroyed. They maintain that they have the right to destroy correspondence. The Procuracy always justifies the administration in advance. We do not receive any letters from abroad.

'Prisoners convicted of "anti-Soviet agitation and propaganda" are often deprived of meetings with visitors. And when anyone does receive a visit then it is usually for one or two days [instead of the three days allowed for by law]. Short visits take place here or else you are taken to camp 36. These visits are conducted through a double window and last for an hour or two. Since it is a very long way for friends and relatives to travel for a meeting, many prisoners refuse them.

'We are not allowed to keep anything we write down .... They take it away. Their explanation is: you have the right to write, but you do not have the right to keep what you have written. Therefore, as soon as you have written a sentence, the guard has the right to take it away. Recently they took away our books, journals and exercise books. They left us with only five books or journals each. It is therefore very difficult to study anything.

'Our conditions differ from those in other camps. They are considerably harsher than the conditions of special regime camps for criminal prisoners. The rules laid down by the code on the maintenance of prisoners are not applied to us. In many cases we are at the mercy of the local administration.'

'Wilful disobedience' by inmates now punishable by up to five years' further imprisonment

A new law providing for up to five years' further imprisonment for 'wilful disobedience' by inmates of corrective labour institutions has been introduced into the Russian Penal Code.

It was introduced under an *ukaz* (decree) issued on 13 September 1983 by the Supreme Soviet of the Russian Soviet Federated Socialist Republic (RSFSR). It came into effect on 1 October. Article 188-3 reads as follows:

'Wilful disobedience to the legitimate demands of the

administration of a corrective labour institution, or any other form of resistance to the administration in the carrying out of its duties by a person serving a term of imprisonment – if in the course of one year this person has been subjected to punishment for violating the requirements of the regime, by way of transfer to premises of the cell-type (solitary confinement) or by transfer to a prison … is punishable by imprisonment of up to three years.

'The same actions committed by an especially dangerous recidivist or a person convicted of a grave crime … is punishable by imprisonment for a period of one to five years.'

The terms of the new law are extremely vague. They do not specify what is meant by 'legitimate demands' on the part of the administration, nor what constitutes 'wilful disobedience' or 'any other form of resistance' on the part of the prisoner. The grounds for pressing charges against a prisoner under this article depend on the subjective assessment of the administration of the corrective labour institution.

Most Soviet prisoners of conscience known to *AI* are serving terms of imprisonment in corrective labour institutions. In the 10 months leading up to the introduction of the new law *AI* learned of 12 prisoners of conscience who had been sentenced to further imprisonment on fresh charges while they were completing their first term. In each case investigation has shown that the prisoner was re-imprisoned for continued peaceful exercise of his or her human rights.

Most of these prisoners were serving their first sentence alone in corrective labour institutions designated for criminal prisoners, and there are grounds for believing they may have been victimized.

Many of them were tried within the corrective labour institution itself, or with only criminal prisoners and members of the administration acting as witnesses. *AI* is concerned that internationally agreed standards of fair trial may not have been observed in their cases.

AI fears that the introduction of Article 188-3 into the RSFSR Criminal Code makes prisoners of conscience in corrective labour institutions in the Russian Republic increasingly vulnerable to lengthy reimprisonment on vague and arbitrary grounds.

AI Newsletter February 1984

● FREE AT LAST

Le Thi Som Mai, a Vietnamese prisoner of conscience, was finally released from prison in early 1983 and is now back home with her brothers and sisters. Le Thi Som Mai, aged 21, was arrested in December 1981 with a group of other young people after trying to escape illegally from Viet Nam. She was adopted as a prisoner of conscience by Amnesty International in July 1982. It campaigned for her immediate release on the grounds that her detention violated the Universal Declaration of Human Rights. Amnesty International had also been concerned that her health was deteriorating as a result of lack of food and medicine and having to undertake hard physical labour. In the camp where she was held, the duties consisted of clearing virgin land for cultivation. Several young people are reported to have died there of malaria and dysentery.

Le Thi Som Mai and her six brothers and sisters had been the targets of official harassment on a number of occasions because of their parents' prominence as non-Communist writers under the pre-1975 South Vietnamese Government. Her father, Tran Da Tu, was a well-known poet, broadcaster and journalist and her mother, Nha Ca, a distinguished novelist. Both were arrested in April 1976 during a government campaign against 'decadent' literature. Her mother was released in December 1976 but her father is still detained without charge or trial (his case is under investigation by Amnesty International).

CAMPAIGN FOR THE ABOLITION OF TORTURE

In 1984 a fresh drive to end torture was launched: the Campaign for the Abolition of Torture. 'Torture in the Eighties' chronicled reports from 98 countries and contained a 12-Point Program for the Prevention of Torture which formed the basis for the campaign.

While government representatives universally and collectively condemn torture, more than a third of the world's governments have used or tolerated torture or ill-treatment of prisoners in the 1980s. Political suspects and other prisoners face torture in police stations, secret detention centres, camps and military barracks.

In a major new report, 'Torture in the Eighties', Amnesty International cites allegations of torture and ill-treatment in some 98 countries – documenting complaints by victims in every region of the world, from security headquarters in Spain to prison cells in Iran, from secret police centres in Chile to special psychiatric hospitals in the Soviet Union.

The report cites cases involving systematic torture during interrogation – electric shocks, severe beatings and mock executions; harsh prison conditions; the participation of doctors in the process of torture; and punishments such as flogging and amputation.

The report is part of Amnesty International's continuing campaign against torture and it spells out a global program for the abolition of this abuse.

Thousands upon thousands of Amnesty International volunteers around the world are working together to eradicate torture and prevent cruel treatment of prisoners. In the next two years they will be taking part in a special drive to try to rid the world of these violations of human rights.

Torture as an institution

Torture does not occur simply because individual torturers are sadistic, even if testimonies verify that they often are. Torture is frequently part of the state-controlled machinery for suppressing dissent. Concentrated in the torturer's electrode or syringe is the power and responsibility of the state. However perverse the actions of individual torturers, torture itself has a rationale: isolation, humiliation, psychological pressure and physical pain are means of obtaining information, of breaking down the prisoner and of intimidating those close to him or her.

It is very often used as an integral part of a government's security strategy. If threatened by guerrillas, a government may condone torture as a means of extracting vital logistical information from captured insurgents. If the government broadens its definition of security, the number of people who appear to threaten it become larger.

The implication of others in banned activities or the intimidation of targeted social sectors like students, trade unionists or lawyers may become the rationale for torture in the new circumstances.

Emergency legislation may facilitate torture by giving extensive powers of detention to the security forces. This process may be accelerated if the military take over governmental, police and judicial functions.

The Uruguayan Government's fight against the urban guerrilla movement *Movimiento de Liberación Nacional* (or *Tupamaros*), Movement of National Liberation, is an example.

Torture began as a police method of interrogation in the 1960s. After the army entered the conflict in 1971, torture continued to be used mainly for the interrogation of suspected guerrillas, though on a much larger scale. The Law of State Security and Internal Order, granting broad powers to the security forces, came into effect in 1972, and a year later the military took effective control of government behind a civilian facade.

The result of these changes is that the emergency legislation introduced in 1972 has been the formal basis for the detention of hundreds of people suspected of non-violent political or trade union activities. Many have been tortured – long after the *Tupamaros* were defeated – by one of several security units of the armed forces and convicted by military courts to long-term sentences.

The illegal methods first applied to suspected *Tupamaros* became, by 1975, routine treatment for virtually any peaceful opponent of the Uruguayan Government who fell into the hands of military units.

A specific motive for using torture is often to intimidate the victim and other potential dissidents from further political activity. Students detained for demonstrating or leafleting in the Republic of Korea have been tortured and beaten routinely at police stations, then released without charge.

The intimidation of rural populations by means of torture and killings has been part of government strategies to bring the population or particular parts of the country under government control. Guatemalan counter-insurgency operations in the early 1980s, for example, included the terrorization of targeted rural populations in an effort to ensure that they did not provide support for guerrillas. Tortured, dying villagers were displayed to relatives and neighbours, who were prevented from helping them. Newspapers in urban areas during this period were allowed to publish photographs of mutilated bodies, ostensibly as an aid to families seeking their missing relatives, but also as a warning to all citizens not to oppose the government.

In specific instances the torturers may want to keep their practices hidden from the local populace. According to a secret Indonesian army manual used in East Timor and obtained by Amnesty International in July 1983, 'if the use of force is required [for interrogation], there should not be a member of the local population present … to witness it so that the antipathy of the people is not aroused'.

Armed conflict in Afghanistan has led to the involvement of the military and the state security police in torture to obtain intelligence information about guerrillas, to intimidate the population from supporting them, and to discourage strikes and demonstrations in the towns.

If detainees are charged and eventually tried, a confession may be the primary evidence against them. The increased number of assaults during interrogation during and after 1976 in Northern Ireland was partly a result of a governmental security strategy to obtain confessions that could be used in court. In Spain, torture and ill-treatment are still used in some police stations to obtain confessions from suspects charged under the anti-terrorist law.

Torture and ill-treatment are also used as punishments, sometimes in addition to prison sentences. In Pakistan since 1977 and Mozambique since 1983, prisoners have been flogged, sometimes in public, while serving sentences for political or criminal offences. Caning, flogging and, in a few countries, amputation are inflicted as judicially prescribed punishments.

Prisoners often face further ill-treatment after interrogation, sentencing or confinement. Prisoners on hunger-strike against harsh prison conditions or against their own torture have been severely beaten in the Republic of Korea. One is known to have died in 1982 following such a protest; others have needed hospital treatment. At least 15 military prisoners in Morocco are reported to have died in custody during the 1980s, in part as a result of diseases caused by appalling conditions and of a complete lack of medical care. In the USSR in the 1980s, medical personnel, in collaboration with the secret police, continued the practice of administering powerful pain-causing and disorienting drugs to prisoners of conscience who are forcibly confined to psychiatric hospitals for political rather than authentic medical reasons.

Isolated incidents of torture do occur without governmental approval – but it remains the government's duty to investigate them and discipline the offenders; failure to do so may well be taken as a signal that such abuses are officially tolerated.

Methods

The methods vary: for example, the long-used *falanga* (beating on the soles of the feet, also called *falaka*); the Syrians' 'black slave', an electrical apparatus that inserts a heated metal skewer into the bound victim's anus; the *cachots noirs* in Rwanda, black cells totally devoid of light in which prisoners have been held for as long as a year or more. Some methods can make the verification of torture and ill-treatment especially difficult – pain-causing drugs administered forcibly to prisoners of conscience in Soviet psychiatric hospitals, the forcible use of techniques of sensory deprivation, and the electrodes that have become an almost universal tool of the torturer's trade.

Victims

Victims include people of all social classes, age groups, trades, professions and political or religious views. Criminal suspects as well as political detainees are subject to torture in many countries, although the information available to Amnesty International deals mostly with political cases.

In El Salvador, children have reportedly been tortured, and in Iran under the government at the time of writing, children held with their mothers in the women's block of Evin Prison have been forced to witness the torture of their mothers. Women often face special degradation at the hands of their male torturers. Relatives of wanted people in Syria, including adolescents, have reportedly been held as hostages and tortured to force suspects to give themselves up. Foreign nationals seeking asylum in the Congo have allegedly been tortured to force them to confess to espionage. Victims in Ethiopia have allegedly included members of several ethnic and religious minorities suspected either of supporting armed groups fighting for territorial independence or of obstructing the revolution.

Agents

The agencies involved in torture give an indication of the degree of governmental responsibility for it. Frequently several military and police intelligence units as well as police forces and prison employees are implicated, thus demonstrating the widespread institutionalization of the practice.

The general picture that emerges of torture agencies is often one of groups specially trained to torture, who have an elevated view of their role in protecting state security against 'subversives'. State propaganda reinforces this view, as does any real violence perpetrated against the state or their colleagues by opposition groups. If they are aware that their acts are criminal, they also know that their superiors will protect them in the unlikely event that the state attempts to prosecute them.

Preconditions

Torture most often occurs during a detainee's first few days in custody. These critical hours are usually spent incommunicado, when the security forces maintain total control over the fate of the detainee, and deny access to relatives, lawyers or independent doctors. Some detainees are held in secret, and the authorities may deny that certain detainees are held, making it easier to torture or kill them or to make them 'disappear'.

The suspension of *habeas corpus* and other legal remedies, trials of political detainees in military courts and the lack of any independent means of examining and recording a prisoner's medical condition allow the security forces to conceal evidence of torture from lawyers, civilian magistrates, independent doctors and others who would be capable of taking action against their illegal activities.

Further incentives are trial procedures that do not exclude from evidence statements extracted under torture or during long periods of incommunicado detention, a government's refusal to investigate allegations of torture, its peremptory denial that torture occurs in the face of mounting evidence such as deaths in custody, its obstruction of independent domestic or international investigations, the censorship of published information about torture, and the immunity from criminal and civil prosecution given to alleged torturers.

A calculated assault on human dignity

Apologists for torture generally concentrate on the classical argument of expediency, which purports to justify undesirable but 'necessary' suffering inflicted on an individual only

▲ *Smolensk Special Psychiatric Hospital*

▲ *Chernyakhovsk Special Psychiatric Hospital*

▲ *Oryol Special Psychiatric Hospital*

Torture is often inflicted as part of government suppression of dissent. In the Soviet Union people who have been detained for criticizing the authorities have been confined in psychiatric institutions where some of them have been given pain-causing drugs.

171

for the purpose of protecting the greater good of the greater number.

This apology ignores the fact that the majority of torture victims, even in countries beset by widespread civil conflict, have no security information about violent opposition groups to give away.

They are tortured either to force confessions from them or as a savage message not to oppose the government.

Even if torture could be shown to be efficient in some cases, it is never permissible.

Torture is a calculated assault on human dignity and for that reason alone is to be condemned absolutely. Nothing denies our common humanity more than the purposeful infliction of unjustified and unjustifiable pain and humiliation on a helpless captive.

Once justified and allowed for the narrower purpose of combating political violence, torture will almost inevitably be used for a wider range of purposes against an increasing proportion of the population.

Those who torture once will go on using it, encouraged by its 'efficiency' in some cases in obtaining the confession or information they seek, whatever the quality of the material thus obtained. They will argue within the security apparatus for the extension of torture to other detention centres; they may form elite groups of interrogators to refine its practice; they may develop methods that hide its more obvious effects; they will find further reasons and needs for it if particular segments of society become restive.... What was to be done 'just once' will become an institutionalized practice.

The process of torture

No experience of torture is typical, but there are discernible patterns in the thousands of personal testimonies, affidavits and statements that have reached Amnesty International in the 1980s.

For the individual victim torture can mean being seized at night, violently, while family and neighbours are terrorized into helplessness; being blindfolded and beaten in the police van or the unmarked car; the vague reasons, if any, given for the detention; the threats of execution, of rape, of family members being killed in 'accidents'; the preliminary questions at the police station or army barracks about present health, medicines, past illnesses, so as not to go too far in the procedures that follow; the sometimes senseless questions ('Why were you born in Tunceli?') for which there are no answers – and throughout, the anticipation and the fact of brute force, without limit, without end, the feeling of being totally at the mercy of those whose job is to have no mercy.

Torture usually means isolation: abduction, secret detention, incommunicado detention beyond the reach of family, friends and legal assistance. Blindfolding during days of interrogation and torture serves to increase the sense of being alone and defenceless. Iranian political prisoners released in 1982 tell of how it is used at Evin Prison, the Revolutionary Court headquarters in Tehran:

'The worst thing in Evin is being held blindfolded for days on end waiting for someone to tell you why you are there. Some people are left blindfold for days, weeks or months. One man has spent 27 months like this. None of the prisoners appear to know what he is being held for. After 27 months, he sits, largely in total silence, wagging his head from one side to the other. Sometimes he just sits knocking his head on the wall.'

Essential to torture is the sense that the interrogator controls everything, even life itself.

'This is nothing but the introductory exercise,' a South Korean security agent told a prisoner in 1979 after beating and stamping on him and burning his back with cigarettes. 'You can test the limit of your spiritual and physical patience when you are taken to the basement, where there are all kinds of torture instruments from ancient times to the modern age.'

Torture means degradation: insults, sexual threats or assaults, forcible eating of one's excrement, humiliation of one's family.

Torture often means breaking down under extreme pressure and severe pain, whether the confession signed or information given is true or false.

'Eventually, I was forced to answer in the way they wanted me to since the pain became intolerable,' said Fernando Benjamin Reveco Soto, who was tortured in

Some prisoners are singled out for special treatment. Muteba Tshitenge, a former civil servant, was held incommunicado for 13 months in Kinshasa, the capital of Zaire. He was subjected to mock executions, and said: 'Special instructions were given on how I was to be treated: no contact with the outside world; no family visits; solitary confinement; lashings morning, noon and night; no food. This special treatment is expected to result in death by torture, starvation or sickness ... (they) also hope that the prisoner will go mad.'

1982 by the *Central Nacional de Informaciones* (CNI), the Chilean secret police.

'They applied intense electric current to my hands … For 21 days I was held in the CNI's hidden premises … On each of the first 14 days which followed my arrest I was subjected to both physical and psychological torture … I was seen by the doctor after nearly all the torture sessions … I was given a document to sign which stated that I had been well treated. It also contained statements which I had made under pressure, and included others which I had never made at all. When I refused to sign I was threatened with further torture. Under such circumstances, I had to sign.'

In the USSR psychiatrists administer drugs as a form of punishment to prisoners of conscience detained in psychiatric hospitals. The drugs may serve to compel the prisoner to renounce his or her religious or political beliefs, or they may be given as 'treatment' for a prisoner's continuing 'delusions'. In the summer of 1980, for example, Vladimir Tsurikov, a 35-year-old worker from Krasnoyarsk, was interned for the third time in the USSR in connection with his peaceful attempts to emigrate. He describes the effect of drugs forcibly given to him:

'The triftazin [stelazine] made me writhe, and my legs began to twist about in a ridiculous way. I lost the ability to walk, while simultaneously feeling very restive and also feeling sharp pains in my buttocks at any movement – a result of the sulfazin [a one per cent solution of elemental sulphur in oil]. Fainting fits began, recurring very often: I fell and hit my head on the floor and on the brick walls. The pain prevented me sleeping or eating. The sulfazin made my temperature rise, and it then stayed around 40 degrees centigrade. Sometimes I experienced slight shivering and my tongue hung out…'

Like at least nine other known dissenters who were forcibly confined to psychiatric hospitals shortly before foreign visitors arrived in Moscow to attend the Olympic Games in July 1980, Vladimir Tsurikov was released shortly after the Games ended.

Many victims remain in prison, their situation uncertain and vulnerable. International support for them remains vital. After an Amnesty International mission in 1981 to Morocco, where delegates visited Kenitra Central Prison, Amnesty International received this message from a prisoner currently held there who had previously been tortured and had campaigned together with other prisoners of conscience for improved conditions:

'It is incontestable that our situation has improved in prison, but our situation is very precarious, since it is based on no judicial text (the government does not recognize having political detainees, and we are officially considered common criminals). In other words, the 'privileges' we have obtained thanks to the struggles we have waged in prison and the support given to us at the international level by many organizations, above all Amnesty International, all these 'privileges' are constantly threatened.'

The prevention of torture

Amnesty International believes that any government that wishes to stop torture has the means to do so. It is a question of political will. In adopting the Universal Declaration of Human Rights, the United Nations Declaration against Torture and other instruments of international law and human rights, governments have accepted the illegality of torture and agreed to abolish it.

Two instruments currently being elaborated by UN bodies would give additional protection.

The first is the draft Convention Against Torture and other Cruel, Inhuman or Degrading Treatment or Punishment which could give legally binding force to the standards included in the Declaration against Torture for states which ratified the Convention. It would establish 'universal jurisdiction', meaning that an alleged torturer could be brought to justice wherever he or she might be and whatever the nationality of the perpetrators or victims. It would provide that no one should be forcibly returned to a country where they risked being tortured.

The second is the draft Body of Principles for the Protection of all Persons Under any Form of Detention or Imprisonment which could establish additional safeguards. It could provide, for example, that relatives should be promptly informed of the whereabouts of prisoners; that

Torture is a violation of human dignity and international law. In many countries human rights groups have organized protests against its continued use, but those in the front line of the effort to stop torture often take great personal risks. Here, demonstrators march against martial law in Kwangju, South Korea, in May 1980. Following such demonstrations, many protesters were arrested and interrogated under torture, and eight were beaten to death.

prisoners should be promptly informed of their rights; and that there should be inquests into deaths in custody.

These two instruments should be adopted as soon as possible, in a form which provides the strongest possible measures of protection against torture.

Also currently under discussion, both regionally and in connection with the draft Convention and the draft Body of Principles, are proposals for national and international systems of independent visits of inspection to places of detention, which would help to provide additional protection against torture.

Without waiting for these new international instruments to be adopted, however, governments should review the safeguards against torture available in their own countries in the light of the provisions of the Declaration against Torture. Among other measures to be taken, they should make the text of the UN Code of Conduct for Law Enforcement Officials available to all law enforcement officials in their own languages.

Amnesty International has compiled a list of some of the principal measures which governments should take to prevent torture. The following 12-point Program for the Prevention of Torture has been compiled from existing international standards and from the recommendations which Amnesty International itself has made over the years to governments of countries where torture is inflicted. The organization believes that the program and the standards on which it is based should be publicized widely. The various points in the program can be used as a test of a government's willingness to prevent torture.

Governments must act to fulfil their responsibility for the prevention of torture but efforts can also be made by non-governmental groups in combating torture by disseminating practical information to victims and potential victims on prisoners' rights, procedures to be followed in lodging complaints of torture, or on what medical, financial or legal aid is available.

Bar associations and individual lawyers and judges can press for the adoption of legal safeguards against torture; members of parliament can send appeals through international channels and seek to prevent torture through investigative missions and special reports or hearings; journalists can expose torture by locating torture centres, identifying individual torturers and obtaining testimonies and photographic evidence.

Once reports of torture are published, the news media should follow up the story to see whether the government conducts an impartial and effective investigation of the allegations and brings those responsible to justice.

Among other individuals and groups which can help to prevent torture are religious leaders, who can denounce torture as incompatible with religious teachings and encourage action against it; trade unionists, who can mobilize support for their colleagues and others who have been tortured at home or abroad; women's organizations, which can take action concerning the special degradation faced by women at the hands of male torturers; and teachers' organizations, which can ensure that the issue of torture is raised within schools and universities in the context of human rights education.

Medical organizations can investigate allegations that members of their profession had participated in the infliction of torture and can impose appropriate disciplinary sanctions where involvement is proved.

Organizations of military, police and prison officials can press for training programs which instil a personal conviction that torture must not be inflicted.

Elsewhere, individuals should raise their voices to appeal for an end to the illegal and shameful use of torture, either working on their own or through the various non-governmental organizations engaged in programs of education and action, of which Amnesty International is one.

'The torturer has become ... an enemy of all mankind'

In a case of international significance, the father and sister of Joelito Filártiga, a 17-year-old Paraguayan youth who died under torture in 1976, filed a civil action for damages in a US court against their compatriot Américo Pena Irala, who was Inspector General of Police of Asunción at the time of the alleged torture.

Although the initial ruling in the federal district court found that the US courts did not have jurisdiction to hear the case, in June 1980 the US Federal Court of Appeals for the Second Circuit ruled that torture, when officially condoned, is a violation of international law under the Alien Tort Statute (Title 28 of the *United States Code*, Section 1350).

This was a landmark decision that opened a new domestic remedy in international human rights law, and an important precedent in a world where the enforcement of human rights law remains principally at the national level.

In the words of the US Court of Appeal's judgment, 'the torturer has become, like the pirate and slave trader before him ... an enemy of all mankind'.

AI Newsletter April 1984

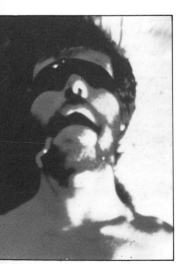

Blindfolding increases the feeling of being alone and defenceless. 'The worst thing is being held for days on end waiting for someone to tell you why you are there ... for days, weeks or months ... They keep people like that to add to the fear ... but when they suddenly whip off the folds to question you, you are almost blind, the light is painful and you can't concentrate on a single thought.' – An Iranian political prisoner released from Evin Prison in 1982.

AMNESTY INTERNATIONAL TWELVE-POINT PROGRAM FOR THE PREVENTION OF TORTURE

Torture is a fundamental violation of human rights, condemned by the General Assembly of the United Nations as an offence to human dignity and prohibited under national and international law.

Yet torture persists, daily and across the globe. In Amnesty International's experience, legislative prohibition is not enough. Immediate steps are needed to confront torture and other cruel, inhuman or degrading treatment or punishment wherever they occur and to eradicate them totally.

Amnesty International calls on all governments to implement the following 12-Point Program for the Prevention of Torture. It invites concerned individuals and organizations to join in promoting the program. Amnesty International believes that the implementation of these measures is a positive indication of a government's commitment to abolish torture and to work for its abolition worldwide.

1. Official condemnation of torture: The highest authorities of every country should demonstrate their total opposition to torture. They should make clear to all law enforcement personnel that torture will not be tolerated under any circumstances.

2. Limits on incommunicado detention: Torture often takes place while the victims are held incommunicado – unable to contact people outside who could help them or find out what is happening to them. Governments should adopt safeguards to ensure that incommunicado detention does not become an opportunity for torture. It is vital that all prisoners be brought before a judicial authority promptly after being taken into custody and that relatives, lawyers and doctors have prompt and regular access to them.

3. No secret detention: In some countries torture takes place in secret centres, often after the victims are made to 'disappear'. Governments should ensure that prisoners are held in publicly recognized places, and that accurate information about their whereabouts is made available to relatives and lawyers.

4. Safeguards during interrogation and custody: Governments should keep procedures for detention and interrogation under regular review. All prisoners should be promptly told of their rights, including the right to lodge complaints about their treatment. There should be regular independent visits of inspection to places of detention. An important safeguard against torture would be the separation of authorities responsible for detention from those in charge of interrogation.

5. Independent investigation of reports of torture: Governments should ensure that all complaints and reports of torture are impartially and effectively investigated. The methods and findings of such investigations should be made public. Complaints and witnesses should be protected from intimidation.

6. No use of statements extracted under torture: Governments should ensure that confessions or other evidence obtained through torture may never be invoked in legal proceedings.

7. Prohibition of torture in law: Governments should ensure that acts of torture are punishable offences under the criminal law. In accordance with international law, the prohibition of torture must not be suspended under any circumstances, including states of war or other public emergency.

8. Prosecution of alleged torturers: Those responsible for torture should be brought to justice. This principle should apply wherever they happen to be, wherever the crime was committed and whatever the nationality of the perpetrators or victims. There should be no 'safe haven' for torturers.

9. Training procedures: It should be made clear during the training of all officials involved in the custody, interrogation or treatment of prisoners that torture is a criminal act. They should be instructed that they are obliged to refuse to obey any order to torture.

10. Compensation and rehabilitation: Victims of torture and their dependants should be entitled to obtain financial compensation. Victims should be provided with appropriate medical care and rehabilitation.

11. International response: Governments should use all available channels to intercede with governments accused of torture. Intergovernmental mechanisms should be established and used to investigate reports of torture urgently and to take effective action against it. Governments should ensure that military, security or police transfers or training do not facilitate the practice of torture.

12. Ratification of international instruments: All governments should ratify international instruments containing safeguards and remedies against torture, including the International Covenant on Civil and Political Rights and its Optional Protocol which provides for individual complaints.

The 12-Point Program was adopted by Amnesty International in October 1983 as part of the organization's Campaign for the Abolition of Torture.

CHINESE 'DEMOCRACY MOVEMENT' ACTIVIST JAILED

The case of Wei Jingsheng from 'China: Violations of Human Rights'. Wei Jingsheng was one of the leaders of the 'democracy movement' that flourished in China in the late 1970s – his trial marked the end of a period of 'liberalization'.

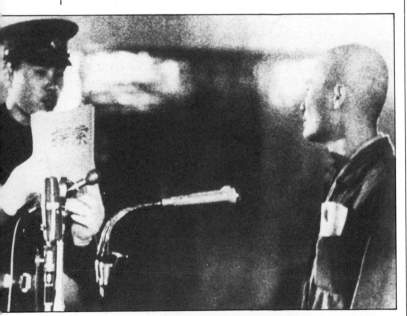

The trial of prisoner of conscience Wei Jingsheng: the trial that marked the end of the period of 'liberalization' that had begun in 1978 and that had seen the emergence of the 'democracy movement'. Prisoners usually have their heads shaved if they are convicted of a crime. Wei Jingsheng's head has already been shaved – before the outcome of his trial. He was sentenced to 15 years' imprisonment on 16 October 1979 for 'counter-revolutionary crimes'. In the photograph a public security agent shows Wei a copy of the unofficial journal Exploration, *in which he had published articles criticizing aspects of official policies.*

Wei Jingsheng, editor of one of the unofficial magazines banned in 1979, was tried in Beijing on 16 October 1979 for 'counter-revolutionary crimes' and sentenced to 15 years' imprisonment and an additional three years' deprivation of political rights.

Wei Jingsheng, a 29-year-old electrician and editor of *Exploration,* was arrested at the end of March 1979, two days after Beijing Municipality declared a ban on all wall-posters and publications 'opposed to socialism and to the leadership of the Chinese Communist Party'.

An unofficial movement calling for 'democracy and human rights' had developed in late 1978 after a relaxation in official policy had encouraged people to express their opinions and grievances. Wall-posters calling for democratic reforms and respect for human rights soon appeared in the main cities of China. Small unofficial magazines were started which often printed the texts of the wall-posters.

Between late 1978 and his arrest, Wei Jingsheng had published wall-posters and articles criticizing the political system in China and advocating democracy. In December 1978 he published an essay entitled 'The Fifth Modernisation' in which he argued that China needed not only to modernize its economy but also a political modernization: democracy.

Wei Jingsheng was tried by Beijing Intermediate People's Court in October 1979 and convicted of passing on 'military secrets' to a foreigner and conducting 'counter-revolutionary propaganda and agitation' through his writings. The first charge refers to information about the Sino-Vietnamese conflict of March 1979. Wei Jingsheng was accused of having given it to a foreigner while the fighting was still going on. According to unofficial sources, this information had in fact been published in *Reference News,* an official paper circulated to a large number of cadres in China although not available to the general public.

The trial was not open to the public or to foreign observers although a selected audience – 400 people according to official sources – was admitted into the courtroom. Those allowed in were given admission tickets in advance. Friends of Wei Jingsheng and others waiting outside the courtroom were refused entry.

Short extracts of the trial were shown on Chinese television. However, the official press did not publish any substantial report of the proceedings – only a summary of the prosecution case against Wei Jingsheng. The account of the trial published by the New China News Agency on 16 October 1979 did not mention any of the arguments put forward by Wei Jingsheng in his defence. This account revealed that the trial lasted just over seven hours and that the verdict was announced as follows:

'In order to consolidate the dictatorship of the proletariat, safeguard the socialist system, ensure the smooth progress of socialist modernization and punish counter-revolutionary criminals, the chief judge said, the court had sentenced Wei Jingsheng to 15 years' imprisonment, depriving him of political rights for an additional three years in accordance with the provisions of article 2, item 1, under article 6, items 2 and 3, under article 10, article 16 and article 17 of the Act for the Punishment of Counter-revolution.'

(New China News Agency, 16 October 1979)

Shortly after the trial, an unofficial transcript of the proceedings was circulated in Beijing. It was distributed at the 'democracy wall' by supporters of various unofficial magazines, some of whom were arrested after a large crowd had gathered to buy copies. The unofficial transcript was later published in Hong Kong and elsewhere. This was the first transcript of a Chinese dissenter's trial to become available outside China.

According to the unofficial transcript, three judges (one presiding judge and two assessors) conducted all the proceedings at the trial. This included the cross-examination of the defendant, Wei Jingsheng, and of the two prosecution witnesses. No defence witnesses were called in court. There was no defence lawyer, apparently because Wei Jingsheng had asked to conduct his own defence. The procurator read the charges against Wei Jingsheng at the beginning of the trial. The judge cross-examined the defendant and witnesses and the procurator then presented the indictment. Wei Jingsheng then read his defence statement and the procurator replied with a lengthy counter-argument. After an adjournment for a meeting of the 'judicial committee', the Chief Judge announced the verdict.

Several aspects of the trial proceedings are particularly interesting. For instance, the judge who cross-examined Wei Jingsheng on the first charge – 'passing on military secrets to a foreigner' – was mainly concerned with whether Wei Jingsheng knew he was doing something wrong when he gave information to a foreigner about China's conflict with Viet Nam. The question of whether or not this information was secret was not even mentioned in court, except by Wei Jingsheng. He said in his own defence that he never thought such information was secret as it was already circulating widely among Chinese citizens. The second charge – 'conducting counter-revolutionary agitation and propaganda' – was based only on articles written by Wei Jingsheng criticizing China's leadership and social system. Extracts of this and other articles were cited in court as incriminating evidence.

The two witnesses brought to court by the prosecution had formerly been involved with *Exploration*, the unofficial magazine edited by Wei Jingsheng. They confirmed that Wei was the author of articles cited by the prosecution and gave information on his past activities and contacts with foreigners. One of the two witnesses, Yang Guang, mentioned in his testimony that on 4 February 1979 he had borrowed a report by Amnesty International from a foreign journalist. It concerned political prisoners in China and extracts were later printed in issues two and three of *Exploration*.

After the trial, Wei Jingsheng appealed against the verdict and the case was heard by the Beijing High People's Court on 6 November 1979. According to an official account, Wei Jingsheng had asked a member of the Beijing Lawyers Association to act as his defence lawyer in this new hearing. The High Court confirmed the verdict and sentence against him. Chinese law allows only one appeal against a verdict and the judgment of the High Court was final.

During the weeks after the trial the official Chinese press published many articles about Wei Jingsheng. They appeared to be running a campaign aimed at justifying the sentence against him and denigrating his character, as well as acting as a warning to other young activists.

During this press campaign, several unofficial publications in Beijing published articles and wall-posters in defence of Wei Jingsheng. They pointed out that even if Wei could be considered to have made a mistake by revealing information on the military situation, this could not be treated as 'the crime of offering secret military intelligence to a foreigner'. They also said that Wei had taken no action that constituted an 'attempt to overthrow the dictatorship of the proletariat' and that, if no violence had been incited, it could not be said that a criminal act had occurred.

The large number of articles published in the official press justifying the verdict against Wei Jingsheng gives an indication of the significance of his case. As well as a warning to other activists, his trial marked the end of the period of liberalization which had started in 1978. During this period criticism of official policies, and unofficial publications, had been tolerated to a certain extent. According to unofficial Chinese sources, his trial was also meant to test reactions to the new laws and procedures due to come into force in January 1980.

Following his trial, Wei Jingsheng was reported to have been held for several years in solitary confinement in the detention centre adjacent to Beijing Prison No. 1. According to a former prisoner who was held in the Banbuqiao detention centre adjacent to the prison during 1980 and 1981, Wei Jingsheng was then detained in isolation in cell No. 11 of section 2 – a block reserved for 'major criminals'. He reported that Wei Jingsheng went on hunger-strike once during that period, and that in April 1981 he was suddenly moved from his cell because he was constantly 'making trouble' and it was feared that his rebellious spirit would influence the other prisoners.

In mid-1983 Wei Jingsheng was reported to be still confined in isolation in his cell, being allowed out for exercise only once a month and not allowed to meet other prisoners or to receive visits from his family. Amnesty International launched several appeals for his release and said it feared his health might be affected by the length of time he had spent in solitary confinement. The authorities, however, did not respond to these appeals. In May 1984 it was reported that Wei Jingsheng had twice been transferred to a hospital as his mental health had suffered, and he was reported to need treatment for schizophrenia.

Published 1984

POLITICAL KILLINGS COVER-UP IN EL SALVADOR

Most of the estimated 40,000 people killed in political violence in El Salvador between 1978 and 1983 were murdered by government forces which openly dumped mutilated corpses in an apparent effort to terrorize the population, concluded the report of a 1983 Amnesty International mission of inquiry. The mission studied official post-mortem investigative procedures in extrajudicial executions – political killings by military and security forces operating both in uniform and in plain clothes in the guise of so-called 'death squads'. The delegates concluded that Salvadorian medical, police and legal institutions were not fulfilling their forensic duties and that 'as a result, the existing system of certifying deaths seems … to facilitate the murder of individuals on a large scale.' The following case study is from the report 'Extrajudicial Executions in El Salvador, Report of an Amnesty International Mission to examine post-mortem and investigative procedures in political killings, 1-6 July 1983'.

US journalist John Sullivan 'disappeared' from his hotel room in San Salvador in December 1980, shortly after arrival in the country. His whereabouts were unknown until the trunk of his decapitated corpse was identified by a forensic pathologist in the United States in February 1983. The sequence of events in the Sullivan family's quest for information about the fate of their 'disappeared' son illustrates how the absence of a central, public record on violent deaths can hinder efforts to locate the missing and identify the dead. The case also indicates ways in which forensic evidence can be manipulated or concealed by the Salvadorian authorities, when related to extrajudicial executions by government forces.

John Sullivan was last seen at the Hotel Sheraton in San Salvador on 28 December 1980. His 'disappearance' followed in close succession upon the arrest and extrajudicial execution in November of six prominent Salvadorian opposition leaders, and the murder in December of three US nuns and a religious layworker. Some days after Sullivan's 'disappearance', two US labour advisors and the President of the Salvadorian Agrarian Reform Institute were killed in the coffee shop of his hotel by members of government security forces.

Items published in the Salvadorian press around the time of these events indicated disapproval in high-level government circles of foreign church and assistance agency personnel, particularly those associated with efforts to introduce agrarian reform or to seek conciliation with the armed opposition rather than military victory. Articles in the government-controlled press also attacked foreign journalists for allegedly advocating the guerrilla cause abroad.

US journalists who have studied the Sullivan case closely on behalf of his family have suggested that he may have been abducted by mistake for a Belgian priest associated with the 'popular' wing of the Roman Catholic church whom he superficially resembled. The priest had co-officiated at the funeral of the six prominent opposition leaders referred to above, who were detained and murdered the month before John Sullivan's 'disappearance'. The priest had later received death threats and went into hiding three days before Sullivan 'disappeared'. Alternatively, it has been suggested that Sullivan's attempts to contact Salvadorian guerrilla groups in order to interview them may have prompted his abduction.

It was later learned that the residents of Nuevo Cuscatlán, a small town south of the capital, heard explosions on the night of Sullivan's 'disappearance', and that next morning they found the mutilated corpse of what appeared to be a foreign caucasian male. The body was buried under the direction of security personnel in the presence of local civilian officials. Local people who assisted were paid in US coins from the pockets of the deceased. The Justice of the Peace and a local clerk prepared a burial report which stated that the corpse's hands had been amputated and the body dismembered, apparently by dynamite. Had the finding of the body been reported immediately to a centralised agency in El Salvador and the burial report inspected, it would have provided early indication, such as the size of the man's shoes, and the US labels in the clothing, that the body might have been that of John Sullivan. A hand found nearby that appeared to be from the same body could have been analysed for finger-prints at this stage and a positive identification probably made almost immediately. But evidently the hands were severed and the body mutilated in order to prevent identification. The failure of local security personnel and civil officials to take steps to either identify the body, or to make information on the finding of the body public, may also have been deliberate. It seems the local Justice of the Peace either did not inform civilian or military superiors that the body of an apparent foreigner had been buried in the area, or else tried to do so but the matter was not pursued.

The burial report itself was not uncovered by United States Embassy officials until after Sullivan's body had been identified in the United States more than two years later. The report had not been sent to any public records office in the nation's capital but was in a local government office in Santa Tecla, where it had not even been filed with other official documents but had simply been placed in a corner among a pile of miscellaneous papers.

On 30 December, two days after his 'disappearance', the maid at Sullivan's hotel in San Salvador realised that he was not using his room and notified the hotel manager of this each morning for the next five days. However, it was not until the morning of 4 January 1981, when the two American labour advisors were killed together with the President of the Salvadorian Agrarian Reform Institute in the coffee shop of Sullivan's hotel, that the hotel manager took action and notified a US military advisor, also resident in the hotel, of Sullivan's 'disappearance'.

Shortly after the US military advisor learned that Sullivan was missing, the Department of State was notified and the journalist's family learned the news. It was at this point, Salvadorian officials later maintained, that they issued a directive to all frontier posts and security services to conduct an 'urgent and exhaustive' search for John Sullivan. Whether or not the bulletin was ever actually issued, certainly no relevant information was released by the authorities in the ensuing months.

Sullivan's family first received specific information regarding his possible death when a major US newspaper received a letter from Nuevo Cuscatlán in October 1981. The writer claimed to be a Treasury Police agent with direct knowledge of Sullivan's arrest, torture and manner of

US journalist John Sullivan, who was killed in El Salvador in late 1980 after he 'disappeared'.

death. The letter advised the family that the corpse of a caucasian male foreigner which might be John Sullivan had been found at a spot near Nuevo Cuscatlán, which was often used by government security forces for dumping the victims of extrajudicial executions. The letter stated that the local authorities knew that a caucasian male had been buried there. It appeared to have been written in response to a series of advertisements which the Sullivan family had placed in Salvadorian newspapers asking for information as to the journalist's whereabouts.

A second letter delivered to the US Embassy in Honduras some months later claimed to be from the same writer and gave additional information regarding the alleged burial site. The writer suggested a way to confirm the letter's contents. The Embassy did not inform the Sullivan family of this second letter for some time. Later, Embassy officials claimed that this was because the letter appeared to be from an entirely different person than the first one, and that its writer appeared to be primarily interested in obtaining a financial reward.

The Sullivans also learned that neither the Salvadorian authorities or US Embassy staff had taken finger-prints from either of the letters, followed up on the information contained in them, or questioned a man who presented himself at the US Embassy in Honduras claiming he could act as intermediary between the Embassy or the family and the letter-writer. US officials said they lacked the authority to take such steps.

In the following months, the Sullivans received other letters concerning the case. Their writers repeatedly stated that the Treasury Police had been responsible for the 'disappearance' and death of a man believed to be John Sullivan. The family was unable to investigate these reports without assistance from the Salvadorian authorities.

In June 1982, yet another letter arrived, referring to unidentified bodies buried at Nuevo Cuscatlán, including one which might be John Sullivan. A map was enclosed showing the alleged burial site. The US Embassy in San Salvador sent an investigation team to the area. Local officials named in the letter as having been present at the burial of the as yet unidentified corpse first denied any knowledge of the matter, but then admitted that they were often asked to arrange and witness the burial of unidentified corpses in the area. It was only at this point that much of the information above regarding the discovery and burial of a white caucasian male on 29 December 1980 was obtained.

On 11 July 1982, after continued pressure by the Sullivan family and members of the US Congress who had become involved in the case, a body was exhumed at the point indicated on the map and the Salvadorian Government appointed a forensic pathologist to examine the corpse. He concluded that the remains were those of a man in his 40s (Sullivan was in his 20s) and of shorter stature than Sullivan.

By the time this examination took place, the mutilation the corpse had sustained, including the effects of the explosion which may have been the cause of death, as

Five victims of Salvadorian 'death squads'.

well as natural decomposition of the remains, made it impossible to use certain techniques, such as examination of the teeth or cranium in order to identify definitely the remains. US consular officials stated that the Salvadorian laboratory conditions under which the examination had been carried out would be considered sub-standard and unscientific in the United States. Sources in El Salvador suggested to Sullivan's family that the Salvadorian pathologist who had examined the remains at government request would have been in danger had he found the corpse to be that of Sullivan.

Given all of these reasons for doubt, the Sullivan family sent X-rays of the exhumed corpse to eight forensic specialists in the United States. All concluded that the X-rays were of a male in his mid to late 20s. A radiologist at the Smithsonian Institute in Washington, DC, stated that X-rays from Sullivan's records showed more similarity with the body in El Salvador than the Salvadorian report allowed. The Sullivans then began pressing to have the remains sent to the United States for further tests. The Salvadorian authorities refused to permit this, maintaining that according to Salvadorian law an unidentified body could not leave the country until it had been proved it was that of a foreigner – one of the issues in dispute.

A visit to El Salvador by a congressman from Sullivan's home state eventually provided the political impetus to move the Salvadorian authorities to release the body. The congressman managed to reach an *ad hoc* understanding with the President of the Salvadorian Supreme Court that the body could leave the country if the local magistrate in Cuscatlán signed the necessary release paper. Eventually, an official from another town signed the paper. Once the remains had been returned to the United States, a leading US professor of forensic pathology examined them, compared them with X-ray pictures in John Sullivan's medical records, and concluded in February 1983 that the corpse was that of John Sullivan, 'beyond all reasonable doubt'.

The US pathologist's post-mortem examination indicated that the body had been blown up, possibly by a stick of dynamite in the mouth. Because of the extensive damage which the corpse had sustained (the upper part of the body was destroyed, ribs were shattered, shoulder blades and the sternum missing) he was unable to determine whether the explosion had occurred before or after death.

Although John Sullivan's body was eventually found, identified and returned to his family for burial, many questions remain unanswered about deficiencies in the investigation of his death, in particular why the Salvadorian authorities have not even now questioned local officials who authorised and witnessed Sullivan's anonymous burial, or investigated allegations of the involvement of the Treasury Police and other named individuals in the killing.

Published May 1984

DEVELOPING AMNESTY INTERNATIONAL IN AFRICA

The challenge of developing Amnesty International as a truly worldwide movement, particularly in the developing countries, was recognized by Martin Ennals in his piece 'Amnesty International in the Eighties'. In November 1984 the movement held its first developmental conference in Africa.

Once a month a group of villagers from the coastal district of Lungi, near Freetown in Sierra Leone, meets to discuss human rights and to work on behalf of victims of abuses of these rights in different parts of the world.

The villagers include peasant farmers, workers at a small airport in Lungi, a couple of school teachers and several unemployed people. In order to meet they have to walk from their villages – some of them for miles – converging on the village of Kambia, which they must reach well before dusk because their meeting place that day may lack electricity.

These people are members of Amnesty International who have formed its first all-village group in Africa. This year, as part of worldwide campaigns by the movement, they have sent out appeals to government authorities urging the release of prisoners of conscience in Romania, Israel, Libya, Thailand, Mauritania and Viet Nam.

Nearly 5,000 miles from Kambia, on the other side of the continent, another Amnesty International group of teachers and post office workers on the tiny Indian Ocean island of Rodrigues, Mauritius, also meets monthly and sends off letters to government leaders worldwide, appealing for the release of prisoners of conscience, for fair trials for all political prisoners and for an end to torture and the death penalty.

Similar appeals are going out regularly from other Amnesty International groups in Africa, from members and sympathizers throughout the continent. They include people from all walks of life – among them farmers, trade unionists, students, judges, lawyers, community workers, doctors, nurses, labourers, technicians. All are participating in Amnesty International's global campaign against human rights violations – and together they have served to make Amnesty International a reality in Africa.

It is in this context that the movement is launching a developmental conference in Arusha, Tanzania – the Amnesty International Africa Regional Conference, 15 to 18 November – which will be attended by participants from 26 countries, 17 of them African: Cameroon, Ghana, Guinea, Ivory Coast, Kenya, Mauritius, Nigeria, Senegal, Sierra Leone, South Africa, Sudan, Tanzania, Togo, Tunisia, Zaire, Zambia and Zimbabwe.

Among the African participants will be representatives of nine non-governmental bodies working in the field of human rights; they include legal, church and student organizations.

Two of the principal speakers are former prisoners of conscience, the Rev. Simon Farisani, of South Africa, and Naby Moussa Touré, Guinea.

The conference will be addressed by Tanzania's Prime Minister Salim A. Salim.

The Arusha conference is a follow-up to Amnesty International's establishment in 1979 of an organized membership development program for Africa. In the five years since then it has been able to create and strengthen national sections, each consisting of several groups, in Ghana, Ivory Coast, Nigeria and Senegal, and also to set up groups in Mauritius, Sierra Leone, Tanzania and Tunisia.

In addition, the movement's publications – including its monthly newsletter and annual report – are now mailed to a wide range of subscribers and supporters all over the continent.

However, Amnesty International's Secretary General, Thomas Hammarberg, stresses that the movement's work in Africa to date is but a beginning.

'The need now is to expand the Amnesty International movement there; more members, more helpers, more people taking part in the battle against human rights abuses world-wide,' he says.

Analysis of Amnesty International's working methods and their application to Africa will form an important part of the Arusha conference. However, Secretary General Hammarberg is insistent that the organization will not meet in Arusha 'simply to teach what we have learned – but also to learn from others.'

'We will be calling in particular on the advice of representatives of African non-governmental organizations, such as the Arab Lawyers Union, the All-Africa Conference of Churches and the *Association des juristes africains*.'

He stresses that Amnesty International is not holding a conference in Africa to tell people what the problems are in Africa – but rather that it will 'draw attention again to the fact that human rights are under threat in every region of the world under governments of all persuasions – and the movement will try to enlist Africa's help to meet that continuing threat.'

AI Newsletter November 1984

Former prisoner of conscience the Reverend Simon Farisani, a principal speaker at the Amnesty International Africa Regional Conference, Tanzania, 1984.

● **WEST BENGAL**

The Amnesty International Jhargram group, West Bengal, India, organised a poster exhibition for its launch in 1983.

FILE ON TORTURE: AFGHANISTAN/ PHILIPPINES

As part of the continuing Campaign for the Abolition of Torture, the Amnesty International Newsletter regularly includes a supplement called the File on Torture. In December 1984 the countries highlighted were Afghanistan and the Philippines.

AFGHANISTAN

Amnesty International has received persistent reports of widespread and systematic torture of political suspects in Afghanistan under the government of President Babrak Karmal, who came to power in December 1979. Testimonies and other information received by the organization indicate that torture is inflicted in detention centres throughout the country which are administered by the State Information Services, *Khedamat-e Atla't Dawlati*, known as the *KHAD*.

Despite the release in early 1980 of many political prisoners held by former governments, and promises to improve the human rights situation in the country, opposition to the present government has been systematically suppressed and its opponents tortured.

Numerous reports have indicated that the treatment meted out to suspects by *KHAD* agents has followed a pattern: they are arrested and taken to one of many *KHAD* detention centres – Amnesty International knows of eight in Kabul alone – where they are first subjected to various forms of deprivation and then soon afterwards intensively tortured.

Suspects are reportedly deprived of all contact with family, lawyers or doctors, or even other prisoners, by being held incommunicado and in solitary confinement. During this period they may be continuously interrogated, threatened and deprived of sleep or rest; cases have also been reported of detainees having been deprived of food.

Former detainees have told Amnesty International that suspects who fail to cooperate with the *KHAD* are then tortured – the methods reported have included threats of execution, electric shocks, beatings, burning with cigarette ends and dousing with water.

Detainees are also known to have been kept in shackles or bound hand and foot for prolonged periods.

In some cases prisoners are reported to have been forced to watch their relatives being tortured.

Prisoners are reported to have suffered permanent injury as a result of torture and several are said to have died while they were being tortured.

Although Amnesty International has received reports of torture under all three governments since the 'Sawr' revolution of April 1978, when the People's Democratic Party of Afghanistan assumed power, it was only after the formation of the *KHAD* in late 1979 that the practice was reported to have become systematic.

The KHAD

The duties of the *KHAD* are widespread and include responsibility for supervising party members, the armed forces and ideological training for new party cadres. It is also charged with arresting and interrogating political suspects.

The *KHAD* is reported to have Soviet advisers attached to its main offices and there have been allegations of Soviet involvement in torture – several former prisoners have told Amnesty International of the presence of Soviet advisers in detention centres.

Each provincial capital has a *KHAD* office and detention centre.

○ In Kabul, the prisoners are reported to have been tortured in the following eight detention centres: (1) the *KHAD* headquarters in the Sheshdarak district; (2) the Internal Affairs Ministry building; (3) the Central Interrogation Office, known as the *Sedarat*; (4) the office of the military branch of the *KHAD*, known as *KHAD-e Nezami*; (5) *KHAD* 'Office Number Five', known as *KHAD-e Panj*; two private houses near the *Sedarat* building; (6) the Ahmad Shah Khan house; (7) the Wazir Akbar Khan house; and (8) the *KHAD* office in the Howzai Barikat district.

According to information received by Amnesty International, an internal *KHAD* report in late 1981 stated that four prisoners out of every 100 detained at the Sheshdarak detention centre in the preceding 12 months had died.

○ In the city of Kandahar, there are reported to be five *KHAD* detention centres: its headquarters in the former offices of the Morrison-Knudsen Construction Company in Manzal Bagh; the Vilayat, formerly the office of the central government in Kandahar; the detention centre of the *KHAD-e Nezami* (military *KHAD*) in the army base at Kandahar; and two private houses in the Shahr-e Nau district near the Musa Khan mosque.

○ In the city of Jalalabad, the main *KHAD* detention centre is situated behind the Nangarhar University Hospital.

○ Other detention centres where torture has been reported are in the towns of Faizabad (Badakhshan province) and Andkhoy (Faryab province).

In September 1982 the Afghan Government promulgated a 'Law on the Implementation of Sentences in the Prisons', Article 3 of which reinforces the prohibition of torture already contained in the constitution. At the same time the government stated that a number of police officers were being tried on charges of having tortured prisoners. No independent confirmation of this, however, was received.

Afghanistan acceded to the International Covenant on Civil and Political Rights and the International Covenant on Economic, Social and Cultural Rights on 24 January 1983.

In October 1983 Amnesty International wrote to President Karmal expressing grave concern at reports of ill-treatment and torture of detainees in the custody of the *KHAD*. The movement urged the government to establish an immediate inquiry into interrogation procedures used by the *KHAD* and that, if torture reports were found to be true, the responsible officials be charged and tried in conformity with Afghanistan's Penal Code. Amnesty International has received no reply or comment on these recommendations.

Arbitrary arrest of people alleged to be opposed to President Babrak Karmal's government appears to be widespread and it is rare for prisoners to be formally charged. To Amnesty International's knowledge, no laws relating to arrest and detention have been made public.

These arrests are carried out by the *KHAD* and detainees are then taken to one of the detention centres mentioned above. They are often held there incommunicado for many months and, in some cases, reportedly for years. Amnesty International was told of a man who was arrested by the *KHAD* in June 1981 and held in the Sheshdarak detention centre incommunicado until 1983.

No access to family or lawyers is allowed in these centres and it is extremely unusual for a prisoner to be allowed to see a doctor. After interrogation at these centres, some detainees may be released, but most are transferred to Pul-e Charkhi Prison in Kabul, where they are held indefinitely without charge or trial.

Although many of those tortured appear to have been involved in armed resistance to the government, other victims include civil servants, teachers and students who have been detained merely on suspicion of opposition to the authorities. Many of those arrested claim not to have been involved in politics at all but to have been detained as a deterrent to others or on the basis of false information from spies.

Testimonies

The following are extracts from testimonies of former prisoners interviewed by Amnesty International, or whose testimonies were sent to the organization, after they had left the country. Their names are withheld at their request because all have relatives remaining in the country.

A is a former senior civil servant in the Public Works Department in Kabul who was arrested in July 1982 for alleged involvement with a group organizing armed resistance to the government. His wife and three children were detained at the same time and held incommunicado in the *Sedarat* detention centre; they were not ill-treated. **A** was held at the *Sedarat* for three and a half months before being transferred to Pul-e Charkhi.

'For the first 12 days of my detention I was held in solitary confinement. Thereafter I shared a cell with nine others. I was taken for questioning on many occasions and each time I was beaten on the head and body and kicked in the lumbar region and in the legs. Once I was questioned by teams of interrogators and allowed no sleep for 48 hours. On three occasions I was subjected to electric shock treatment which was administered by electrodes being attached to my tongue and toes. I fainted each time and was doused with water; then the treatment began again.'

He was released uncharged from Pul-e Charkhi Prison in June 1983.

B, another senior civil servant at the time of his arrest in August 1982, was held by the *KHAD* for six weeks in a former private house near the *Sedarat* detention centre. In a message to his family after his release he wrote:

'Since I have been out of hospital my health has not been good ... [During detention] My nails were pulled out after nearly four-inch needles had been stuck into my finger tips. Sometimes at night 10 or 11 people assaulted me by jumping on me. I was given electric shocks and suffered [ill-treatment] for five and a half months continuously...'

C was a senior high school student at the time of his arrest in the city of Jalalabad in January 1983. Many members of his family are reported to be involved in the armed resistance to the government and this may have been the reason for his arrest.

'I was held in the *KHAD* detention centre in Jalalabad for over a month. I was questioned almost every evening, the interrogation beginning punctually at 10.00pm. I was beaten frequently with sticks and on six occasions electric shocks were administered to my fingers and toes. One of my cellmates had wires connected to his genitals.

'Each interrogation session lasted about four hours. Shouts of pain could be heard all through the night. Prisoners were brought back from the interrogation rooms with marks of beatings visible all over their bodies.

'One night a captured guerrilla was brought to the prison. He was wounded in the arm. During the interrogation the officials would extinguish their cigarettes on his body. One of them put a lighted cigarette into the wound. The man was shrieking.'

D, a 60-year-old businessman at the time of his arrest in April 1981, stated that he was detained on 25 April after two vehicles carrying *KHAD* personnel had drawn up outside his house.

'I was bundled into the first vehicle while men from the second came out and searched my house. I was never to set foot in my home again. I was taken to a large private house near the *Sedarat* ... known as the Ahmad Shah Khan house...

'At 2am the following day I was taken out ... to be interrogated by five Afghans all in civilian clothes. I was asked why my son-in-law had defected to the Americans and told that all my children had now defected to the imperialist west. I was warned that if I did not make a full confession I would be killed.

'When I denied all knowledge of my son-in-law defecting, which was completely true, they started beating me. I am an old man and my health had been poor for some time. They beat me until I fell to the floor and lost consciousness. When this happened they would throw water over me and try to bring me round. This process lasted for two hours. By the end I was not able to stand.

'For the next 18 days I was detained in the same room. Each alternate night, exactly at 2am, I was taken out ... for interrogation. The pattern was always the same: questions, then beatings and then more questions...

'I was never subjected to electric shock treatment. One evening, however, when I was brought to the interrogation room, on a table in a corner were several torture instruments, indeed they were referred to as such. They included a baton with wires attached and a cap to be placed over the head, and used for the administering of electric shocks.

'As the days went by my eyes became swollen and blurred. My body was bruised all over. My clothes were filthy with blood and I was allowed no change of clothing. My wife had no idea where I was or why I was being imprisoned.'

THE PHILIPPINES

Amnesty International has regularly received reports of systematic torture in the Philippines since the imposition of martial law there in September 1972. Despite the lifting of martial law in January 1981, members of the armed forces have retained extensive powers of arrest and detention in cases involving 'subversives' and other 'public order violators'.

Although an extensive legal framework exists to provide safeguards in cases of such arrests, suspects have commonly been abducted without warrant and detained incommunicado and in violation of other procedural safeguards.

In many cases, detainees have been taken to undisclosed and unauthorized interrogation centres, known as 'safehouses', where interrogation by members of the armed forces intelligence agencies has been accompanied by torture. Detainees have been held in 'safehouses' for periods ranging from a few days to several months. Amnesty International knows of instances where detainees held in such 'safehouses' have not been seen alive again and are presumed or, in some cases, known to have died as a result of ill-treatment.

Allegations range from 'man-handling' by police and armed forces personnel in rural areas and the regular use of intimidation during interrogation, to the infliction of electric shocks, cigarette burns, near suffocation by water or plastic bags, sexual abuse and rape, being forced to stand or squat for long periods, and threats of execution.

Most allegations of torture refer to intelligence personnel from the Philippines Constabulary and other branches of the armed forces.

The Philippines Government has been active in condemning torture in international fora, being a sponsor of the Declaration Against Torture adopted by the United Nations General Assembly in 1975 and making a Unilateral

Pul-e-Charki prison in Afghanistan, where hundreds of political prisoners are held.

Declaration in October 1979 stating its intention to comply with the Declaration and implement its measures in national legislation and other effective measures. Nevertheless detainees have had great difficulty in getting allegations of ill-treatment or torture impartially investigated.

An illustration of the difficulties faced is provided by the case of 25 people who were detained after a series of arrests in the Manila area between 26 February and 1 March 1982. They included eight active trade unionists and others alleged to have been members of the banned Communist Party of the Philippines. All 25 were held in detention centres, including 'safehouses', and were interrogated by intelligence personnel from different branches of the armed forces. During the interrogations, most of the detainees were kept incommunicado. Most of the men later testified that they had been intimidated, threatened, deprived of sleep and given beatings, which included being punched in the stomach, struck on the ears, and hit on the head with rifle butts.

Four detainees, Marco Palo, Danilo de la Fuente, Edwin López and Noel Etabag, said they had been tortured with electric shocks. Marco Palo subsequently received hospital treatment for over three weeks.

On 3 March writs of *habeas corpus* and detailed complaints of torture and ill-treatment were submitted by 17 of these detainees to the Supreme Court, which then ordered medical examinations of the detainees.

The medical reports on several mention tenderness of the head, neck, chest and stomach areas, and various scars. The report on Noel Etabag noted pairs of scars caused by punctures on his arms which, he claimed, were caused by electrodes used in his torture; that on Marco Palo noted multiple skin lesions with pairs of scars caused by punctures on his arms and legs.

On 17 April 1982 the 17 detained men individually filed complaints of ill-treatment with the Office of the Inspector General of the Armed Forces. To Amnesty International's knowledge, no public investigation into these complaints has been made nor have the findings of any government inquiry been made public.

On 29 July 1982 complaints of torture were submitted on behalf of 23 of the 25 arrested to the United Nations Sub-Commission on the Prevention of Discrimination and Protection of Minorities. The detainees have also filed a civil suit for 6.5 million pesos (almost $US 500,000) damages against various named military officers responsible for their arrest and detention. The submissions to the Supreme Court were dismissed in November 1983. The detainees have since filed a motion for a reconsideration of their petitions.

Torture alleged after arrest of 'subversives'

Amnesty International has received persistent reports of torture and ill-treatment of detainees who have been arrested after accusations of subversive activities, particularly detainees suspected of association with the New People's Army (NPA), the armed wing of the Communist Party of the Philippines.

In one case this year, three farmers from East Kahayagan in Aurora, Zamboanga del Sur, were reportedly tortured by members of the Civilian Home Defence Force and members of a military airborne division while undergoing interrogation about alleged NPA activities after their arrest on 20 March 1984. They are reported to have made sworn statements that they had been tortured while at Camp Dos in Aurora. According to the reports:

○ Pio Bercede said he was repeatedly beaten with a radio antenna, hit several times in the face and abdomen, hung by the neck from the ceiling and had several lighted matches put in his mouth.

○ Felipe Solon said he was made to eat coal and soil, and Pablo Ponce alleged that he was given electric shocks.

After their transfer later that day to the airborne division's headquarters in Molave, they were reportedly further ill-treated by being kicked, forced to eat rice mixed with hot pepper, and made to squat for long periods. They were released on 22 March, reportedly after having been made to sign statements that they had been humanely treated, and having agreed to kill other suspected members of the NPA.

According to church sources, they have since been subjected to intimidation by military personnel who have allegedly ordered them to withdraw their complaints.

Many of the people who have made allegations of torture to Amnesty International have been active in church-sponsored human rights work or trade unions.

○ Rolieto Trinidad, who works for the Justice and Peace Ecumenical Group and is a former director of the Social Action Centre in Tagum, Davao del Norte, was arrested with six others on 16 January 1982 apparently while they were preparing for a seminar on human rights the following day.

Rolieto Trinidad later testified to the following: they were taken to the Philippines Constabulary headquarters in Tagum, where he was beaten while naked and blindfolded, hot pepper was applied to his eyes, mouth and genitals, and his head was covered with a wet cloth which almost suffocated him. On 18 January he was transferred to the intelligence unit (R-2) attached to the Military Command, Region XI, in Davao City, where, amongst other tortures his fingernails were burned with cigarettes and he was repeatedly nearly suffocated by having a polythene bag put over his head. Eventually he made a statement which, after further torture on 21 January, he signed.

Rolieto Trinidad, who was adopted by Amnesty International as a prisoner of conscience, was later charged with subversion and detained for over two years until his acquittal on 20 February 1984. In dismissing the charges, his trial judge ruled that his confession had been extracted under torture and was therefore inadmissible as evidence.

○ Five trade unionists (Cesar Bristol, Romeo Castilla, Danilo Garcia, Herminia Ibarra and Fernando Reyes), all organizers with the independent trade union

A protester makes the peace sign while being hosed down with water during a rally in Manila, the Philippines, in December 1984. The rally was broken up by the police.

confederation *Kilusang Uno Mayo* (KMU), First of May Movement, or its affiliates, were arrested early on 22 July 1984 while taking part in a meeting the day before a planned mass rally in Manila. The detainees were reportedly held incommunicado and interrogated in the Military Intelligence and Security Group (MISG) station in Camp Bagong Diwa, Taguig, Metro Manila.

They later alleged that they were tortured by beatings, cigarette burns and electric shocks. At a court hearing for the preliminary investigation of their case before the City Fiscal (prosecutor) of Pasig, their defence lawyers are reported to have displayed to the court evidence of injuries suffered during their detention. The lawyers later wrote to the commander of Camp Bagong Diwa asking for a medical examination of the detainees. No reply had apparently been received by September 1984.

○ Ruben Alegre was arrested on 26 August 1984 by a military intelligence official at a house in Las Pinas, a suburb of Manila. A subsequent police statement alleged that he had been responsible for the killing in May 1984 of Brigadier General Tomas Karingal, commander of the Quezon City police, and that he was commander of an NPA liquidation squad. The NPA are reported to have claimed responsibility for the killing. Ruben Alegre himself claimed that he was solely a trader in pork and fish.

After arrest he was taken to the Military Intelligence Security Group (MISG) station at Camp Bagong Diwa, Taguig, Metro Manila, where he was reportedly held incommunicado. According to press reports, he told a Supreme Court *habeas corpus* hearing on 6 September that

he had been tortured for three days: given electric shocks to the genitals, tied up and struck on the chest and thighs. At this hearing lawyers acting for him were said to have submitted a medical report concluding that he had been kicked in the head, hit on the thighs with a hammer, struck on the nape of his head with an iron bar, and given electric shocks on his genitals.

Call for preventive measures

Amnesty International has consistently urged the Philippines Government to take steps to prevent torture by ensuring strict implementation of existing safeguards and taking firm disciplinary action against people found responsible for such practices. The *Report of an Amnesty International Mission to the Republic of the Philippines, 11-28 November 1981*, published in September 1982, included reports the mission had received of torture and ill-treatment and recommended various measures for the prevention of torture in the Philippines, such as the abolition of 'safehouses', the abolition of waivers of detention whereby detainees waive their right to be presented to a judicial authority, and stricter implementation of existing safeguards. Amnesty International also called for independent investigations into the allegations of torture published in its report.

In reply, the Philippines Government dismissed Amnesty International's recommendations, asserting that existing procedures were adequate and rejecting evidence that they had been systematically violated.

LABOUR CAMPS IN ALBANIA

Albania has been largely isolated from the rest of the world since it was established as a communist state at the end of the Second World War. Despite the difficulties of extracting and checking information about political imprisonment, in 1984 Amnesty International considered that the information it had gained concerning human rights violations in Albania merited publication. This extract, describing conditions in a labour camp, is from the report 'Albania: Political Imprisonment and the Law'.

Spac labour camp for political prisoners is in Mirdite district, a major copper-producing region, and prisoners in the camp are employed in the mining of pyrites, from which copper is extracted.

The mining area lies within the camp itself, which is surrounded by several rows of barbed-wire fencing 3m high, with watchtowers manned by armed guards at regular intervals. The camp's outer perimeter is patrolled by military guards with dogs. At night spotlights are trained on the fences.

The following information about conditions in Spac is based on the testimony of former prisoners.

Prisoners are housed in unheated concrete barracks with some 300-400 prisoners to each unit, divided among 12-15 rooms. They sleep on straw mattresses on three-tier wooden platforms along each side of the room and are provided with two to three blankets, and (since 1975) with sheets, which are changed once a month. There is a separate washroom with showers, but these are apparently frequently out of order and prisoners usually wash at cold taps in the washroom or in the mine galleries, where water is available. In an annexe to the washroom, prisoners can sometimes heat water for cooking or to wash themselves and their clothes. Work uniforms of heavy cotton are issued once a year, helmets every two years and boots every six months.

The daily food ration for prisoners who work is said to be as follows: bread (often made with maize flour) – 800-900g; potatoes – 245g; sugar – 10-25g; jam – 150g; oil – 15g; meat – 30-45g; beans – 150g; condensed milk – 15g. Prisoners who do not work receive much less. Without exception former prisoners have stated that the food was very poor and the diet seriously deficient in protein, fresh vegetables and fruit. Prisoners commonly suffer a severe loss of weight.

The main meal is usually bread and soup with beans and rice or macaroni. Prisoners supplement these rations with food sent by their families (they may receive up to 10kg a month, but it seems that few receive regular parcels) and with purchases of oil, macaroni, rice and biscuits at the prison canteen (which also sells cigarettes).

The prison has a small infirmary with some 10 beds; both the doctor and dentist are themselves prisoners and can only provide the most basic treatment (dental care is said to be limited to extractions). Prisoners have complained that unless they are running high fevers they are forced to work. Gravely ill prisoners are sent to Tirane prison hospital. Some former prisoners have referred to the problem of mental disturbance and illness among inmates. One prisoner who was detained in Spac in the late 1960s alleged that he had seen mentally ill prisoners throw themselves on the barbed-wire fence surrounding the camp, where they had been shot by guards.

Work

Prisoners work eight hours a day in the mines, six days a week. It is apparently not uncommon, however, for them to be required to work on the seventh day as well. The work consists primarily of opening up and securing galleries, drilling rock to lay charges (these are set off by civilian non-prisoners) and loading the broken rock onto wagons. Work norms are reported to be high and prisoners who fail to achieve them may be required to work extra hours, or be punished by deprivation of visits or solitary confinement. Those who achieve work norms are reportedly paid between two and a half and three leks a day, and most prisoners average about 60 leks a month (the average civilian wage for comparable work is about 480 leks a month). Industrial protection is said to be very poor. A prisoner who was released from Spac in November 1982 stated that towards the end of his time there cotton masks were not replaced when they wore out. Prisoners were told that new machinery using water would be introduced which would render the use of protective masks unnecessary; however, this did not materialize while he was there and thus some prisoners worked without the protection of masks. Lack of industrial safeguards has reportedly led to serious accidents. A former prisoner held in Ballsh in the late 1970s recalled the arrival there of four prisoners from Spac who had become partially paralysed after the collapse of a gallery.

Visits

Prisoners are allowed half-hour visits by relatives once, or sometimes twice, a month. In practice, comparatively few prisoners seem to receive regular visits, either because their families are intimidated or because they lack the necessary time or money to make long journeys.

Visits generally take place in a room outside the camp, in the presence of a guard. Prisoners and visitors are separated by bars. Members of the Greek minority have complained that they were forbidden to speak to their relatives in their mother tongue and were obliged to use Albanian.

Relatives may bring food and clothing for prisoners. The latter may receive any number of letters but may write only two a month. All correspondence is censored.

Education, recreation

Ex-prisoners have reported that they were given regular political lectures by the camp's Political Commissar but the frequency of this form of education appears to have varied considerably.

No vocational training is provided and prisoners are not allowed to study or teach each other foreign languages. There is a library which is said to be stocked almost exclusively with official texts by Party leaders, and prisoners may subscribe to the official daily press. In the evening radio programs are broadcast over a loudspeaker and prisoners may watch television for a few hours. A film is shown once a month. Prisoners are permitted to play dominoes or chess (not cards) and volley-ball. In the past there was reportedly a prisoners' orchestra, but this was banned after a prison riot in 1973.

Discipline and punishments

A prisoner who quarrels with other inmates or with guards, who breaks camp regulations or fails to achieve work norms may be punished in a variety of ways: by deprivation of the right to visits, correspondence or parcels, by being given reduced rations and by solitary confinement in a small, windowless cell known as a *biruce*. The prison authorities may impose the latter punishment for up to one month, which may be extended to three months with the approval of the district procurator. During confinement in the *biruce* prisoners do not work.

A former prisoner has alleged that he was punished by three months' solitary confinement in the early 1980s after he had tattooed an eagle (the Albanian national emblem) without an accompanying communist red star symbol on his body. He said the cell measured no more than 2m by 1.5m. He slept on a mattress and had only one blanket. (Other former prisoners have alleged that they were sometimes forced to sleep on the cell's bare cement floor or were at best given a blanket or board to sleep on.) While undergoing this punishment he was denied letters and visits, received reduced food rations and was allowed only three cigarettes a day, he said.

Another former prisoner detained during the 1970s in Spac alleged that on three occasions guards had stripped him to the waist, tied him to a post and beaten him with a length of rubber hose filled with gravel.

This plan of Spac labour camp 303 is based on sketches by former prisoners who were there between the mid-1970s and 1982. The camp is said to be ringed by several high barbed-wire fences.

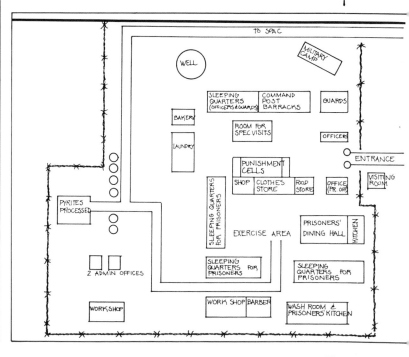

Strikes and violent protests by prisoners in Spac camp

The severity of conditions and treatment in Spac camp have provoked prisoners to engage in strikes and violent protest on at least two occasions, in 1973 and 1978. Both times the protests were ruthlessly suppressed by the authorities and the leaders were executed. The most detailed account received by Amnesty International concerns the events of 1973; it was given by a former prisoner who had participated in the Spac strike that year.

'At 6.30 am on 19 May, as we were about to begin the first shift, we heard guards beating our fellow-prisoners in the camp cells. We demanded that the camp and prison authorities should put an end to this. But our demand was met with threats and blows. We were isolated in a corridor leading out of the camp to where we worked. Soon other prisoners came to our aid and there followed clashes with the guards. After about 20 minutes we forced the guards to withdraw. We then organized a meeting in the camp dining-hall and came to a unanimous decision to seek the help of the United Nations with a view to getting their representatives to intervene on our behalf as soon as possible. We forwarded this request to government representatives in Tirane. This request was repeated in large letters on a cardboard placard...

'Large army and police forces arrived at the camp, together with senior government officials and the Camp Commandant, Muharrem Shehu; the Camp Commissar, Shahin Skura; the head of the Department of Internal Affairs of Mirdite district, Pandi Kita; the Chief Security Officer of Mirdite, Gjergj Zefi; the camp Security Officer, Fejzi Aliaj, and others. They appealed to us over the loudspeaker to end the strike and retract our demands. If we persisted [they said] they would use force and gas against us.

'Because we rejected this appeal, the authorities turned off the drinking water and stopped all food supplies at 12 noon on 19 May. Then at 9.00 am on 22 May, after we had been on strike and endured hunger and thirst for three days, we were suddenly attacked by large units equipped with truncheons. The camp army and guards were joined by 200 special riot police sent from Tirane.

'After clashes lasting an hour, we were too exhausted by hunger and thirst to carry on the fight. We were finally overwhelmed and handcuffed in pairs. On the prisoners' side no one was killed; the riot police suffered two casualties. We were immediately subjected to the most brutal tortures which went on for 24 hours.

'Then a special military tribunal sent from Tirane sentenced to death four prisoners aged from 24 to 32. They were Skender Demiri, from an orphanage in Tirane; Zef Pali, from Sukthi in Durres district; Hajri Pashai, from Llakatund in Vlore district, and Skender Shohollari, from Pogradec district. Our friends were executed near the camp at 3.40 pm on 24 May 1973. We all heard the shots. Besides this, 56 prisoners were given additional sentences ranging from 10 to 25 years.'

The same source stated that he had been informed that a similar strike took place in 1978, after which three political prisoners were executed: Vangjel Lezha and Fadil Kokomani, both previously correspondents for Albania's leading daily *Zeri i Popullit*, and Xhelal Koprencka, from Korce, who had worked as a surveyor in Shkoder before his arrest and imprisonment. On this occasion, too, many other prisoners were reportedly punished with additional sentences of up to 25 years' imprisonment. (A second source has independently informed Amnesty International of the execution of Xhelal Koprencka in 1978 after a strike by prisoners.)

Published December 1984

A forced labour camp in the Malt Valley, Albania. The photo was taken from a moving bus while the guide's attention was diverted by other passengers: there were strict orders against photos being taken during the bus ride.

HUMAN RIGHTS DEBATE IN PERU

The publication in January 1985 of Amnesty International's 'Briefing on Peru' received wide publicity within the country and intensified the national debate on human rights violations.

More than 1,000 men, women and children have 'disappeared' after being seized by troops or police since a remote area of Peru was placed under military rule two years ago. Hundreds of others are known to have been killed in custody, often after torture. In a new briefing on Peru, published on 23 January, *AI* points out that the true scale of the abuses by government forces in the mountainous southern area is not yet known.

The massive atrocities started after the launch of a military campaign against the *Sendero Luminoso* ('Shining Path') guerrilla movement, itself responsible for scores of execution-style killings and torture of civilians.

Since then, killings of captives by government forces have become so established that relatives of the 'disappeared' have learned to search roadside dumping grounds where bodies regularly turn up, often mutilated beyond recognition. The victims found in these dumps and in mass graves are usually naked, marked by torture, and with single gunshot wounds to the head.

Human rights violations on this scale are unprecedented in modern Peru. They have been inflicted mainly on peasants, local leaders and young people in the Emergency Zone, established at the end of 1982. The zone comprised 13 of Peru's more than 140 provinces at the time the report went to press.

Peru's Attorney-General, the Public Ministry he heads, and some judges have tried to protect the rights of the local people and have uncovered some of the abuses, but have been unable to halt them. Government prosecutors in the area have protested publicly against the armed forces' obstruction of their investigations.

AI has told the government that it condemns killing or torture of prisoners by the guerrillas, and recognizes the need to prevent and punish such crimes, but that government action must be within internationally accepted human rights standards.

The briefing on Peru includes basic information on some 1,000 reported 'disappearances' known to *AI*. It notes that the movement also knows of more than 400 cases of individuals named as having been detained and later found dead. All these are from the Emergency Zone; they have no parallel elsewhere in Peru.

Despite the remoteness of the area, *AI* – as well as local human rights groups and Peruvian officials – has amassed abundant evidence of the abuses and of the existence of unmarked mass graves and dumping grounds in areas under military control.

Local people provided the evidence, often by travelling to the main city in the Emergency Zone, Ayacucho, or the national capital, Lima. Documents and testimonies have come directly from families and community representatives, from church, professional, trade union and human rights organizations, and from lawyers. Hundreds of victims' relatives have filled out questionnaires based on a form prepared by the United Nations Working Group on Enforced or Involuntary Disappearances. In February 1984 Dr Zegarra Dongo, outgoing

Ayacucho chief prosecutor, told the press that his staff had received 1,500 formal complaints of prisoners' 'disappearances' in the previous 14 months.

The Interior Ministry has said that in the 18 months up to the middle of 1984, 2,000 alleged guerrillas were killed and more than 1,600 civilians were alleged to have been killed by guerrillas. There is evidence that both categories include many civilians detained and killed by government forces.

Security patrols have raided schools as well as villages and homes to take away victims. All young people appear to be suspect – and so liable to 'disappearance' – in areas where the guerrillas are active. *AI* has documentation on 76 children and teenagers under 18 who have 'disappeared'.

Relatives of the 'disappeared' report being threatened with death by soldiers when they look for their loved ones at known dumping grounds, which are always near main roads regularly patrolled by troops or police. Many of the bodies are blindfolded and bound.

AI Newsletter February 1985

The national debate on human rights violations in Peru is reported to have intensified since the publication on 23 January of AI's *Peru Briefing* (see February *Newsletter*).

Extensive reports on the briefing appeared in the

Amnesty International's **Peru Briefing,** *published in 1984, was read throughout the country by all sections of the population. This reader was part of a group of people gathered on the steps of the cathedral in Ayacucho, the main city in the Emergency Zone.*

A Peruvian television program 'Encuentros' (Encounters) gave the results of a survey on the briefing, using a sample of 1,000 people in the capital, Lima. They are reported to have shown that more than 70 per cent of the sample had heard of the report and that more than 47 per cent thought that 'a pluralist commission should be appointed to investigate Amnesty International's denunciations'.

country's major newspapers and magazines – one magazine printed the full 20-page Spanish-language version – and on the day of publication an hour-long prime-time television program was devoted to it. Copies of the briefing were on sale at news kiosks in 16 cities in Peru.

With some exceptions, the Peruvian Government's public reaction to the briefing appears to have been different in tone to harshly critical comments which followed the publication in September 1983 of an extensive memorandum to President Fernando Belaúnde Terry. President Belaúnde then said in a television interview that *AI* was 'a Communist organization', and that its letters to his government were 'thrown directly into the wastepaper basket'.

On 16 January, General Oscar Brush Noel, former Minister of Defence and now Minister of Interior, made a statement flatly rejecting *AI's* briefing. He claimed that the government respected the life and honour of Peru's citizens, and that Shining Path guerrillas alone were responsible for violating human rights in Peru.

On 20 January the general was questioned by international press agency correspondents on a news report published the day before; it contained evidence that nine people found that week in clandestine graves in Ayacucho had been previously detained by police and military forces and had 'disappeared'. He replied that 'only the Armed Forces Joint Command' was authorized to make statements concerning the situation in Ayacucho.

On 18 January, General César Praeli, head of the Armed Forces Joint Command, was quoted as stating that 'the Armed Forces of Peru reject the Amnesty International report'.

Asked about the ever more numerous clandestine graves and the dozens of corpses discovered, showing signs of torture and gunshot wounds, he reportedly said: 'I am convinced that they are not acts perpetrated by the Armed Forces but by members of the terrorist group,' and added that the Command responsible for the Emergency Zone would carry out an exhaustive investigation in this regard and would study *AI's* briefing.

A series of statements have been made to the Peruvian and international news media by the Peruvian Prime Minister, Luis Percovich. On 23 January he reportedly declared that the government would investigate *AI's* allegations and 'give precise and public reports of this'. Later that day he is reported to have said that 'isolated' excesses by the security forces had taken place and that those responsible had been handed over to 'the appropriate authorities'.

On 25 January, the Prime Minister told reporters in Lima that Peruvian officials with information from the police and military would answer *AI's* charges at the meeting of the United Nations Human Rights Commission in Geneva in February and March.

On 5 February the international news agency *Reuters* reported that the Prime Minister had told reporters that 'widespread errors' had been found in Amnesty International's briefing, affirming that:

'... 53 of the 1,005 people Amnesty alleged to have disappeared in a government anti-guerrilla crackdown before last October had applied for voter registration cards after that date.'

On 1 February, *AI* cabled the Prime Minister welcoming the promise of an investigation into unresolved 'disappearances' in Peru and requesting his intercession to ensure the safety of three young Peruvians reported detained and 'disappeared' on 25 and 28 January in the Ayacucho Emergency Zone.

In a second cable on 7 February, *AI* expressed great interest in the Prime Minister's statement affirming the reappearance of 53 people previously reported 'disappeared'.

AI's cable also stressed its hope that most or all of the individuals reported to have remained 'disappeared' after detention at the time the briefing was prepared would reappear alive.

○ *AI* has sent the Peruvian Government case outlines on another 70 people reported to have 'disappeared' in the Emergency Zone on whom it has received dossiers. It also sent the names of 16 people reported to have 'disappeared' whose bodies have since been found.

AI Newsletter March 1985

Peru's Attorney General, Alvaro Rey de Cástro, examining Amnesty International's Peru Briefing, which was published on 23 January 1984. He is reported to have said the briefing provided 'a call for reflection by the forces in charge of the suppression of terrorism', and by the government itself. The Attorney General heads Peru's Public Ministry, which has continued to make determined efforts to bring the facts of extrajudicial killings and the country's 1,000-plus 'disappearances' out into the open. Public Ministry representatives regularly and publicly protested about the obstruction of their work by police and military authorities in Peru's Emergency Zone.

● 'MY ONLY CRIME WAS MY CONCERN FOR HUMANITY'

When individuals expose the crimes of the state they are often punished as though they were criminals. A petition calling for the release of all political prisoners in Yugoslavia was sent to the Presidency in November 1980. One of those who had collected signatures for it was Dobroslav Paraga, a 19-year-old student of law and theology. The State Security Police arrested him without warrant on 21 November 1980 and at his trial in May 1981 he was found guilty of 'hostile propaganda' and 'participating in hostile activity'. His first sentence of three years' imprisonment was increased after more legal proceedings to four years. He was released on 21 November 1984, and wrote this letter to Amnesty International:

'During that time of persecution and suffering, I came to know your generous hearts, full of sympathy, full of solidarity, fraternal affection and ideal support. Your constant care for my fate and the efforts you took to publicize this ... did not permit injustice to triumph. My only crime was my concern for humanity.

'I passed 271 days in solitary confinement, often without the right to read or rest. Because of that my eyes have become weak. However for me that is all nothing in comparison with the great happiness of being able to feel authentic human solidarity and to gain, in you, such devoted friends. I pray that God enables you to feel my great gratitude and friendship. We are united by the same ideal: to do well for all people. You defend human rights, for me this is the greatest duty of every person. Unfortunately my rights are very limited, even annulled: I no longer have a passport and cannot travel outside Yugoslavia. This is why it is not possible for me to thank you in person and to make the direct acquaintance of those to whom I owe so much. However, I wish to remain your grateful brother who would like to give you more than possibilities and circumstances permit...'

TORTURE IN IRAQ

Allegations that political suspects were routinely tortured in the custody of Iraq's security forces to extract confessions for use in evidence in court or to force detainees to renounce their political affiliations and join the ruling Ba'th party have long reached Amnesty International. In 1979 and 1980, 15 Iraqis who alleged that they had been tortured were interviewed and medically examined by a panel of Amnesty International doctors: their case histories were published in 'Iraq: Evidence of Torture' in 1981. This extract is from the paper 'Torture in Iraq 1982 – 1984', published in 1985.

Ali Hama Salih, a 12-year-old Iraqi Kurd from the village of Ja'afevan in Sulaimanya Province. He was arrested on 25 February 1981 and detained for interrogation at Karadagh Security Headquarters. His corpse was subsequently handed back to his family badly marked by torture.

A former prisoner, aged 44, who was held in Baghdad's Abu Ghraib Central Prison between May 1982 and March 1984 submitted a testimony to Amnesty International in July 1984. He was one of 114 persons who had 'disappeared' since reportedly being arrested between 1979 and 1982 by Iraqi security forces. When approached by Amnesty International about these cases, the Iraqi Government had claimed that the names submitted by the organization were fictitious. However, the person concerned had apparently been arrested after refusing to collaborate with the secret service, and the report he submitted to Amnesty International regarding his places of detention, conditions of imprisonment and use of torture, was consistent with reports received by AI in the past.

The following details on prison conditions and torture methods are extracted from his testimony.

Description of prison conditions and alleged torture

In Baghdad Central Prison, 'the cells are 2×3.5 metres, very dark and completely covered in red/brown tiles. These cells were really intended for one person and for short periods of interrogation but in fact are used for long periods with up to 18 people at one time. In some of these small cells, people have been detained for several years ... a shower and open toilet are built in to each cell ... cold water is turned off and only turned on once a week for a couple of hours ... there are no visits from relatives, no correspondence and absolutely no information for the relatives of the whereabouts of the prisoners.

'There are some large cells with an area of approximately 50 square metres. One of these is specifically for female prisoners. With mass arrests or shortage of space the long corridors on both floors are also used. Steel poles are welded between the cell doors on both sides of the corridor at a height of about 20cm from the floor (this first happened in 1983) and the prisoners are handcuffed by one hand to this pole. In each of these large cells there are 80-130 prisoners, sometimes as many as 200. There is only one shower and an open lavatory for all of them. The air is foul and in order to sleep prisoners have to periodically swap places with one another.

'Medical treatment is very poor. Sick prisoners only receive medical treatment when they have reached a critical point. I have heard of many cases of death as a result of torture or appalling living conditions. In the large cell where I spent several months, we actually saw a man die in front of our eyes. It was the summer of 1983, there were approximately 130 people in the room, the air was very bad and extremely warm. An Iraqi prisoner fell unconscious, which often used to happen. We banged on the door to alert the guard. In the meantime, a prisoner (a doctor) tried to help him. When the guard and the doctor finally arrived it was far too late and he was already dead. He was about 30 years old, an electronics engineer, married with a small daughter.

'Approximately 50% of the prisoners were tortured. There are different methods of torture carried out in the torture chambers in the basement. At the entrance to the torture chamber there is a doormat with 'Welcome' written on it in English. Torture takes the form of: electric shocks, gas and cigarette burns; electric hot plates; hanging from the ceiling – handcuffed; being stretched on a special machine with hands and feet bound; beatings with a heavy cable or high pressure hose/tube. The tortured prisoners who are usually unconscious are then simply carried back to their cells and dumped on the floor in full view of their fellow prisoners.

'The prisoners are treated very badly by the prison officers ... anyone who does not completely submit, or protests about anything, eg by going on hunger-strike, gets severely beaten with cables by the guards in front of the other prisoners ... the guards consider all the prisoners to be spies, traitors and dangerous elements.

'Occasionally (approximately twice a month), the prisoners are taken to an area without a roof (approximately 80 square metres) for fresh air and sport. It lasts about half an hour. The guards give the orders, whip in hand. The prisoners have to endure unbearable 'sporting activities'; the whole 'sports time' turns into a series of beatings and insults.'

Abu Ghraib Khassa (Abu Ghraib Special) 'is an extension for the secret service of the main Abu Ghraib prison, with a separate entrance. Abu Ghraib Special is extremely closely guarded by the secret service personnel ... There are four lavatories in the hall which have cold, filthy water. Three times a day the cell door is unlocked and you are allowed to go to the lavatories for a few minutes during which time you have to wash the bowl and fill up the water container. There are no showers, if you want to wash, or wash your hair, you are only allowed 10 minutes extra twice a month and again only cold water. If there are more than four in a cell the prisoners have to go to the lavatory in pairs. If they stay too long they are whipped and beaten by the guards. They make no exceptions, if a person needs to go to the toilet in the night they have to use the water containers in the cell ... From 7am to 1pm sleeping and speaking to other prisoners is strictly forbidden; anyone who breaks this rule and gets caught is severely punished. It is unbearably hot in summer and extremely cold in winter, particularly at night. There is no heating whatsoever. A mercury lamp burns constantly in each cell (even at night)...'

Another case

An Iraqi doctor of medicine testified to Amnesty International in 1984 that he witnessed and was forced to participate in the taking of blood from prisoners which resulted in their death. According to his testimony, he was aware of approximately 1000 such operations having taken place during 1982 and 1983. The operations are reportedly directly controlled by Security Headquarters (Ri'asat al-Mukhabarat) in Baghdad, and carried out with the co-operation of a prison director and personnel of the Blood Bank Institute in Baghdad.

The following are extracts from his testimony:

'At Abu Ghraib prison in Baghdad ... where I was told there are ... donors who want to donate blood ... the prison doctor took me to the prison hospital. I found there two persons in a shock state, immobile and who exhibited air hunger with rapid thready pulse and cold clammy skin. The prison doctor told me that those two prisoners were criminals and that he bled them under the influence of hypnotic drugs in order to benefit from their blood before they are executed. This doctor also told me that he has directives from Security Headquarters to use this method with important political persons so as to give the reason for the subsequent death as 'heart failure'. The directive also applies to criminals sentenced to death.'

On another occasion at the same prison:

'The prison doctor ... told me that he will bleed three persons and asked me to help him. When I refused, he told me the Security Headquarters demanded that this operation must be done under my supervision and that if I refused, they will jail me.

'Whenever there was a 'blood shortage', especially during the war, Blood Bank Mobile Units collected blood from secondary schools, colleges, factories and prisons. The collection of blood during the past three years was non-voluntary on many occasions and without full medical examination, especially in the factories and prisons. In these cases, the normal quantity allowed by the regulations is collected, however.'

His medical opinion is:

'When a person is bled (usually in each of the cases 3-5 pints of blood):

1. he becomes acutely anaemic and loses consciousness, due to insufficient blood supply to the brain. The state of unconsciousness is treated by feeding the person with salt water in a quantity equal to the amount of blood taken. This procedure prevents the immediate death of the person.

2. despite the fact that the body is compensated for the loss of liquids, the amount of haemoglobin remains very low (2-4ml per 100mm), which is insufficient for the functioning of the vital organs.

3. As a result of this, and after 3-5 days, the heart fails and the person suffers from a sharp drop in the heart's activities, which leads to a heart attack and death. Diagnosis shows death by heart attack, and the families of the dead person are officially informed of his death due to this reason.'

Published 1985

● 'DO NOT FEAR THE STORM . . .'

In the Philippines, a group of church workers planning a symposium on human rights were arrested by the police in 1981 and charged with 'subversion'. Among them were Purificacion and Rolieto Trinidad, both involved in peaceful community development work. Purificacion was taken to a regional police headquarters. Her husband was taken to an unidentified place of detention known in the Philippines as a 'safehouse', where he was reportedly ill-treated during interrogation. Both were refused access to family and lawyers. They were charged with possessing subversive materials and held for months awaiting trial. Both were adopted by Amnesty International as prisoners of conscience.

In October 1983 Amnesty International issued a special medical appeal on behalf of Purificacion Trinidad after she had been transferred to hospital suffering from nervous depression and acute stomach pains. She was eventually released in December 1983 and reunited with her two young children. However, the Presidential Commitment Order which authorised her continued detention pending trial was not lifted. Rolieto was allowed to go home for Christmas and New Year.

However, he was not finally released until 28 February 1984, the day on which he and his wife were acquitted. In a card and poem from prison, sent to the Amnesty International members working on their behalf, the two prisoners wrote: 'Strong flexible bamboos do not fear the storm. They bend with the wind even as they stay firmly rooted to their grounds . . .'

CONSCIENTIOUS OBJECTORS TO MILITARY SERVICE

Amnesty International works for the release of people imprisoned because of their refusal, on conscientious grounds, to perform military service. The following extract is from a paper issued in 1985 on the imprisonment of conscientious objectors to military service which included details and cases from 14 countries: Cyprus, Finland, France, Federal Republic of Germany, German Democratic Republic, Greece, Hungary, Israel, Italy, Norway, South Africa, Switzerland, Turkey and the USSR.

1985 has been designated by the United Nations as International Youth Year. Its themes are: participation, development and peace. It seems appropriate, in this context, to draw attention to the plight of imprisoned conscientious objectors to military service. Hundreds of young people, in more than a dozen countries, are currently in prison because of their refusal on grounds of conscience to perform military service.

During the past decade, there has been a marked increase in tolerance towards conscientious objectors to military service. It has been many years since the last conscientious objector was sentenced to death. While legislation in some countries still prescribes severe sentences, imposition of such sentences is now rare. Many governments have liberalized their laws by broadening the grounds on which conscientious objection may be accepted, by simplifying recognition procedures and by increasing the possibilities for alternative service.

The present paper contains details on Amnesty International's concerns in 14 countries in which persons nevertheless continue to be imprisoned because of their conscientious objection to military service: Cyprus, Finland, France, Democratic Republic of Germany, Federal Republic of Germany, Greece, Hungary, Israel, Italy, Norway, South Africa, Switzerland, Turkey and the USSR. This is not an exhaustive list of countries where conscientious objectors are imprisoned but it is intended to illustrate Amnesty International's concerns in this area.

In some of these countries, there is no legal provision at all for conscientious objection to military service: persons objecting to military service on whatever grounds are routinely imprisoned. In other countries, only certain grounds for refusal (e.g. religious motives) are considered acceptable. All others lead to imprisonment. Prison sentences imposed on conscientious objectors vary from several weeks to four or five years in some cases. In some countries, conscientious objectors are again imprisoned if, after having served their sentence, they persist in refusing to perform military service. This may lead to several consecutive sentences for the same offence. Amnesty International is also concerned that in some countries the alternative service which recognized conscientious objectors are required to perform may be up to twice as long as ordinary military service. The organization opposes periods of alternative service which must be considered as a punishment for a person's conscientiously held convictions.

The right to refuse military service for reasons of conscience is founded on the Universal Declaration of Human Rights (Article 18) which provides for freedom of thought, conscience and religion. The International Covenant on Civil and Political Rights (Article 18), the European Convention on Human Rights and Fundamental Freedoms (Article 9), the American Declaration on the Rights and Duties of Man (Article 3), the American Convention on Human Rights (Article 12) and the African Charter on Human and Peoples' Rights (Article 8) each provide for freedom of thought, conscience and religion.

Limitations on the right to act in conformity with one's conscience can, under Article 29, paragraph 2 of the Universal Declaration of Human Rights, only be imposed 'for the purpose of securing due recognition and respect for the rights and freedom of others and of meeting the just requirements of morality, public order and the general welfare in a democratic society.'

With a few exceptions, however, inter-governmental organizations have so far been reluctant explicitly to proclaim the right to refuse military service on conscientious grounds. On 26 January 1967 the Consultative Assembly of the Council of Europe – an advisory body composed of members of parliament – adopted Resolution 337 (1967) which sets out the basic principles of the right to conscientious objection to military service. The Council of Europe's Committee of Ministers, however, has repeatedly refused to urge member-states to bring their legislation into line with these principles and to introduce the right of conscientious objection to military service into the European Convention on Human Rights. Nevertheless, the Council of Europe's Steering Committee for Human Rights is now elaborating a draft-recommendation on conscientious objection to military service for adoption by the Committee of Ministers.

At UN level, even less progress has been made. The question has been on the agenda of the UN Commission on Human Rights since 1971. Several questionnaires have been sent to member-states and several reports have been prepared, but no UN body has ever adopted a comprehensive resolution proclaiming the right to conscientious objection to military service. On 20 December 1978 the UN General Assembly adopted Resolution 33/165 by which it recognized 'the right of all persons to refuse military service in military or police forces which are used to enforce *apartheid*'. However, in March 1985 the UN Commission on Human Rights decided to defer until 1986 a draft-resolution which would have stated that 'conscientious objection to military service is a legitimate exercise of the right to freedom of thought, conscience and religion.' The resolution would have appealed to states 'to take measures aimed at recognizing the right to be exempted from military service on the basis of a genuinely held conscientious objection to armed service.'

Amnesty International hopes that International Youth Year will provide an occasion for states to review their laws and practices and for inter-governmental organizations to make further progress with a view to ensuring respect for the right to refuse military service for reasons of conscience or profound conviction.

Published March 1985

REPRESSION IN EAST TIMOR

In December 1975 Indonesian troops invaded East Timor. They have since systematically and persistently violated human rights in the territory. Amnesty International drew attention to this with its 1985 report 'East Timor, Violations of Human Rights, Extrajudicial Executions, 'Disappearances', Torture and Political Imprisonment' from which the following extracts come.

'No one who had links with Fretilin is safe; at any time people can be taken without their family knowing and put somewhere else; put in prison camp; or sometimes they just 'disappear'.' Father Leoneto Rego, a Portuguese priest who left East Timor in June 1979, describing the situation at the time of his departure. Maria Gorete Joaquim 'disappeared' in early 1979.

Since the invasion of December 1975 Indonesian troops have systematically and persistently violated human rights in East Timor. Amnesty International has received reports from a variety of sources of the 'disappearance' and arbitrary killing of non-combatants; of the torture and ill-treatment of people taken into the custody of Indonesian forces, including their detention in cruel and inhuman conditions; and of the imprisonment without charge or trial of people most often held on suspicion of opposing the Indonesian occupation. Since December 1983, when a number of East Timorese charged with political offences began to be brought to trial, Amnesty International has been concerned about the lack of fairness of these trials.

○ The reports received by the organization have included accounts of hundreds of killings of non-combatant civilians during and shortly after the invasion itself; the systematic execution of hundreds of people who had surrendered to or been captured by Indonesian forces in 1978 and 1979; the 'disappearance' or killing of more than 80 men and women in 1980; the reprisal killing of some 200 villagers in 1983; and the killing of about 100 men in one incident in 1984.

○ Prisoners are reported to have 'disappeared' after arrest on suspicion of links with Fretilin [*Frente Revolucionaria de Timor Leste*, Revolutionary Front of East Timor] forces; after interrogation in centres in Dili; after being taken out of temporary detention centres or official prisons. The fate of many of these 'disappeared' remains unknown.

○ Prisoners are reported to have been tortured in 'resettlement villages' all over the territory and in interrogation centres in the capital. Tortures reported have included the use of electric shocks, beatings and the near-drowning of prisoners. A number of the alleged victims are feared to have died as a result of their ill-treatment.

○ Arbitrary arrests and detentions are reported to have been carried out on a scale massive by any standard but particularly in relation to the territory's relatively small population: in one operation in 1981 up to 3,000 people are said to have been rounded up and deported to the island of Atauro, to live in conditions of squalor, disease and malnutrition.

○ The reported victims of all these abuses have come from virtually the whole spectrum of East Timorese society, although most have been villagers living in small highland settlements.

Access to information

Amnesty International's information on East Timor cannot be regarded as complete and it is not possible to assess the full scale of violations. The strict controls imposed by the Indonesian forces have limited access to the territory and the flow of information out of it. The violations described in this report have occurred in a situation in which the fundamental freedoms of expression, assembly, association and movement have not existed and in the absence of the constraints of legality. People have been detained and ill-treated for asserting their right to these freedoms. Movement and communication within and beyond East Timor have been tightly controlled. East Timorese permitted to leave the territory to be reunited with their families abroad have been routinely warned by Indonesian intelligence officers before leaving not to reveal information which might discredit the Indonesian occupation and have been threatened with reprisals against themselves and their relatives still in East Timor if they do so. Amnesty International has not been able to visit East Timor. In March 1984 it wrote to the Indonesian Minister of Justice asking to attend trials of political detainees then in progress in Dili. This request was refused on the grounds that the trials were a matter of domestic jursidiction and were being conducted in accordance with international norms.

Despite these circumstances, Amnesty International has accumulated a large body of information on its concerns in East Timor. Some of this information has been documentary, comprising published reports, accounts written and passed on to Amnesty International in confidence and other confidential material, including copies of interrogation reports by the Indonesian author-ities. Among these documents are official interrogation reports on prisoners taken into the custody of Indonesian forces.

Military manuals

In July 1983 Amnesty International received a set of military manuals issued to Indonesian troops serving in East Timor. These manuals, among other things, contain guidelines which appear to permit the use of torture and the issuing of threats on the lives of prisoners being interrogated. Although Indonesian officials have repeatedly tried to cast doubt on the authenticity of these documents, neither they nor anyone else has produced any evidence that might indicate that they are false. Indonesian officials have correctly stated that the Ministry of Defence and Security (HANKAM) never published the manuals, but Amnesty International is not aware of any claims that the Ministry did so. The manuals appear to have been written by officers of the Command for East Timor for local use and to have no application beyond East Timor.

Experts on Indonesia asked by Amnesty International to examine the documents were satisfied that they were genuine on the basis of the military terminology used, the nature of the charts and diagrams included, the format and style, the official stamps and their detailed comprehension of military organizational structure and tactics.

Indonesian officials have argued against the authen-ticity of the manuals largely on the grounds that it would, in the words of the country's Foreign Minister, Dr Mochtar Kusumaatmadja, be 'fantastic' that a manual prescribing the use of torture should have been issued. But the documents do not deal exclusively with torture. They are not 'torture manuals' and Amnesty International has never referred to them as such.

There are nine manuals in all covering a wide range of strategic problems, such as how to break up Fretilin support networks, the system of security in towns and resettlement villages, how to provide comprehensive guidance for villages, and procedures for interrogating captives. The reference to – and clear acceptance of the use of – torture is contained in a subsection of the manual on interrogation methods. Guidelines in the manuals on breaking up the Fretilin support networks and on the system of security in towns and 'resettlement villages' appear to permit interrogators to threaten the lives of prisoners.

First-hand evidence from other sources that military personnel have persistently resorted to torture and that people taken into custody by Indonesian troops have been arbitrarily executed tends to confirm Amnesty Internation-al's belief that the manuals are authentic. In any event, these manuals are only one part of the extensive evidence available on torture and other human rights violations in East Timor.

Other information has come from people interviewed by Amnesty International – they were generally unwilling to be identified by name. They included people who, because of work, position or family relationship, claimed to have knowledge of particular violations. Amnesty International also interviewed people who said they themselves had been the victims of human rights violations; they included former prisoners, people who said they had been tortured and others who gave accounts of how they had survived mass executions. Some of these informants have been affiliated with one or another East Timorese political grouping. However, Amnesty International has not relied exclusively on sources identified with any one political party or social or religious grouping in East Timor ...

Offensives against Fretilin

After the Indonesian attack on Dili on 7 December 1975, Fretilin forces withdrew south to Aileu and, when that town fell, to Ainaro in the mountains. Official Indonesian sources reported in January 1976 that Indonesian forces controlled a third of the territory, although in April 1976 Fretilin claimed that its forces still controlled 80 per cent of East Timor. The available information suggests that Indonesian forces were slow to consolidate their position outside the main towns. A series of localized campaigns from September 1977 until early 1979, involving massive aerial bombardment of areas thought to be under Fretilin control, led to the capture and surrender of many thousands of East Timorese, who were often driven out of the bush by hunger. A delegation of diplomats and journalists which visited East Timor in September 1978 at the invitation of the Indonesian Government reported that captured and surrendered East Timorese whom they had seen in 'resettlement camps' were evidently suffering from serious malnutrition.

By November 1979 the Indonesian Foreign Minister acknowledged that the food situation might be worse than that 'in Biafra or Cambodia'.

In March 1979 Indonesian authorities proclaimed the end of *Operasi Seroya* (Operation Lotus), launched at the time of the invasion, and announced that thenceforth East Timor would be fully under civilian administration. However, resistance to the Indonesian occupation persisted, with continuing reports of attacks by Fretilin on Indonesian outposts. In an effort to eliminate this resistance, Indonesian forces launched dry-season offensives, involving the conscription of large numbers of the population.

The ofensives included the April to September 1981 *Operasi Keamanan* (Operation Security), in which many thousands of civilians aged between 15 and 55 (according to the Indonesian authorities) are reported to have been deployed in human 'fences' to converge on remaining Fretilin positions. Hundreds of East Timorese reportedly died as a result of sickness or were killed during this operation.

A ceasefire between the two sides was agreed in March 1983 but later broke down and in August 1983 large numbers of additional Indonesian troops were brought to East Timor in yet another operation *Operasi Sapu Bersih* (Operation Clean-Sweep) aimed at eliminating Fretilin. An Australian parliamentary delegation which visited East Timor in July 1983 was informed by the Indonesian military commander of East Timor that Fretilin had about 300 members under arms and a total strength of between 1,000 and 2,000, including members' relatives.

In late 1984 and early 1985 Fretilin was still reported to be launching attacks on administrative posts. The Commander-in-Chief of the Indonesian armed forces, General Benyamin Moerdani, stated in December 1984 that 7,000 Indonesian troops were in the territory and that Fretilin had an estimated 700 members under arms, 1,000 'active members' and 3,000 to 5,000 'sympathizers'.

Estimates from a wide range of sources of the number of people who have died in East Timor since the invasion directly as a result of the armed conflict are as high as 200,000, about a third of the pre-invasion population. In April 1977 the then Indonesian Foreign Minister, Adam Malik, said between 50,000 and 80,000 people had died – this was before the worst of the bombardment and famine had begun. Those who had died included people killed during Indonesian bombardments, in armed encounters, as a result of famine and disease – both in the bush and after surrender or capture – as well as many hundreds reportedly executed after surrender or capture.

Published July 1985

● SUDAN

All political prisoners were released in Sudan in April 1985 when the army overthrew President Gaafar Mohamed Nimeiri's government after several days of non-violent demonstrations and a general strike.

Crowds of people went to prisons which held political detainees who were freed at their demand. The new Transitional Military Council subsequently decreed a formal amnesty for all political prisoners. Many prisoners of conscience adopted by Amnesty International were among those freed, together with several hundred political opponents detained without trial over the past six years, and large numbers of others arrested in the recent demonstrations, including officials of organizations of lawyers, doctors, engineers, academics and students.

In Khartoum some of the prisoners released from Kober prison celebrated in the streets, holding aloft the chains with which condemned prisoners were shackled for execution. A crowd gathered at the prison gallows, where Mahmoud Mohamed Taha, the 72-year-old leader of the Republican Brothers movement, had been hanged four months earlier after being summarily convicted of subversion and apostasy. The crowd destroyed the platform and chairs in the prison where over 100 prisoners convicted of theft during the previous 16 months had had either a hand or a hand and foot amputated.

SOUTH AFRICA: THE STATE OF EMERGENCY

Widespread civil unrest affected black townships in many parts of South Africa during 1984 and 1985. On 20 July 1985 the South African Government imposed a state of emergency throughout large areas of the country, which extended the powers of the security forces and granted them immunity in advance for any acts committed under those new powers. The following paper on detentions under the state of emergency was issued by Amnesty International to its members on 6 August 1985.

More than 1100 critics and opponents of the South African Government's *apartheid* policies, including former prisoners of conscience, were detained by security police in the first week following the imposition of a state of emergency throughout large areas of South Africa from midnight on 20 July 1985. Those detained are held incommunicado and are believed to be in solitary confinement. Their places of detention have not been disclosed and they may be held for unlimited periods. The security police are not required to bring charges against the detainees nor to provide reasons for their imprisonment without trial. Amnesty International fears that some detainees may be tortured or ill-treated: they are liable to interrogation by security police who have been granted immunity in advance against prosecution for any acts committed in connection with their use of emergency powers.

The state of emergency was imposed by State President P.W. Botha under provisions of the Public Security Act, No. 3 of 1953. This empowers the State President to declare an emergency either nationally or in specific localities if, in his opinion, 'the safety of the public, or the maintenance of public order is seriously threatened' and 'the ordinary law of the land is inadequate to enable the Government to ensure the safety of the public, or to maintain public order'. In all, 36 magisterial districts were placed under a state of emergency. Eighteen of these are located in the Transvaal, incorporating Johannesburg and Soweto and areas to the south – the 'Vaal Triangle' – and the east – the East Rand. In the Eastern Cape, some 17 districts, comprising Port Elizabeth and the surrounding area, were placed under the emergency. In Orange Free State province, one district only – Sasolburg – was placed under the state of emergency. Emergency powers were not invoked in the Western Cape or Natal. However, in imposing the emergency, the government made it clear that it might be extended to further districts which might be affected by black civil unrest.

Once a state of emergency is declared, the government is empowered under the Public Security Act to issue special regulations which remain in force throughout the duration of the state of emergency. This was done by the State President on 21 July 1985 by proclamation R.121 of 1985. The regulations so issued extended police powers of stop and search and conferred on the police and other law enforcement personnel, including the military, wide powers of arbitrary arrest and detention without trial. Section 3 of the regulations empowers the police or other law enforcement personnel, of whatever rank, to arrest any person within the emergency area without warrant and detain them without charges for 14 days. Further detention on an unlimited basis may then be authorized at the end of this initial two week period by the Minister of Law and Order, at his discretion. Detainees are held incommunicado and are not permitted contact with other categories of prisoners or anyone other than state officials. The police are not required to charge them or produce evidence against them in court, nor do the detainees have any means of appeal against their detention. The authorities need not give any reasons for individual detentions, nor are detainees' places of imprisonment disclosed. Under the emergency regulations, it was also made an offence punishable by up to 10 years' imprisonment for any person to disclose the name of any detainee without prior written authorization from the Minister of Law and Order or his representative.

The emergency regulations also confer on the police the power arbitrarily to impose curfews, control the dissemination of news, close any public or private place, control entry to and departure from particular areas, and remove from any area any person or section of the public in the interests of 'public order'. In addition, the Commissioner of Police and officers acting on his authority were empowered to take any action which they might consider 'necessary or expedient' in connection with the safety of the public or the maintenance of public order. At the same time, the government granted immunity in advance to all members of the police and other law enforcement personnel, government ministers and state officials for any acts committed 'in good faith' in connection with their use of emergency powers. In the case of any dispute, the onus of proof lies with the complainant to show that a particular act was not committed 'in good faith'.

A disturbing feature, given these immunity provisions and the past record of the security police with respect to physical and psychological abuse of detainees, is that all those detained under the emergency are liable to interrogation and may therefore be at grave risk of torture or other forms of ill-treatment.

Security police raids on the homes of critics and political opponents of the government commenced shortly after the emergency took effect on Sunday, 21 July. More than 100 people were detained during the first day that the emergency was in force: by the end of July the total number of detainees had risen to more than 1300. Those arrested included many members of black student organizations, in particular the Congress of South African Students (COSAS), and community organizations in black townships throughout the Johannesburg and Eastern Cape areas. Many of these organizations are affiliated to the anti-*apartheid* United Democratic Front (UDF). This was formed in 1983 to campaign against government racial policies, in particular the constitutional changes which were effected in 1984 and which extended the vote to the 'Coloured' (i.e. mixed race) and Indian minorities but perpetuated the exclusion of the black majority population from any voice in central government. By the time of the declaration of the emergency, many UDF leaders had already been imprisoned for political reasons or were awaiting trial on treason charges. They include a number of prisoners of conscience adopted by Amnesty International.

Others detained during the first week of the emergency included at least 11 black church ministers, several of whom had previously been active in attempting to calm the situation in the black townships and to reduce the level of confrontation between the black population and the police. Officials and members of predominantly black trade unions were also among those detained. For example, those detained in the Port Elizabeth area included most of the leadership of the locally-based Motor Assemblers and Component Workers Union of South Africa (MACWUSA), an unregistered black trade union deriving its support from black motor industry workers.

Political detainees held under the emergency powers have virtually no rights and may be subjected to a variety of punishments for what are termed 'disciplinary contraventions'. The contraventions, and the general conditions under which emergency detainees are to be held, were defined in a series of 'Rules' issued by the Minister of Justice on 21 July. They provided that detainees may be held either in prisons or police cells and required that they should be searched on committal. The Rules stipulate that the detainees should be held incommunicado and are to have no contact with other categories of prisoners. However, provision was made for individual visits to detainees if approved by the Minister of Law and Order or the Commissioner of Police. During such visits, no physical contact between the detainee and visitor is permitted and they must communicate in either English or Afrikaans, the official South African languages, neither of which is the mother tongue of most of those detained, or else have a police or prisons officer act as interpreter. There is no requirement that emergency detainees be visited on a regular basis by magistrates or the specially appointed inspectors of detainees who are required to visit other political detainees held under Section 29 of the Internal Security Act. However, the Rules imply that there may be some inspection of detainees' conditions and they do require that all detainees should be medically examined by a district surgeon, a government-employed doctor, on admission to their place of detention who should thereafter visit them 'regularly'. Provision is also made for ministers of religion to have access to detainees but the police may deny access to specific ministers.

Detainees held under the emergency are not permitted to communicate with the outside world through correspondence. They may not receive or send out letters, except with the express permission of the officer in charge of their place of imprisonment and the Commissioner of Police. Nor are they permitted reading matter other than the Bible or other holy books such as the Koran. They are not permitted to study in detention and they may not use radios or record players, though 'they may be allowed to listen' where internal broadcasts of music or radio programs are arranged by the staff in charge of the place of detention. The Rules regulating detention conditions provide that detainees be permitted to exercise in the open air for at least one hour per day and permit them to wear civilian clothing. They are not allowed to receive food parcels, cigarettes or other articles sent in from outside, but small amounts of money may be received and credited to them, for use within the place of imprisonment for purchasing cigarettes and toiletries. There is no require-

▲ *Police disperse students demonstrating against the state of emergency. Cape Town, South Africa, August 1985.*

▶ *Mourners on their way to a funeral in Port Elizabeth, South Africa, April 1985.*

ment that detainees work, except that they must keep clean their own place of detention, including the ablution facilities. To fail to do so would be to incur punishment for committing one of the 'disciplinary contraventions' as they are officially termed. In all, there are no less than 20 such contraventions listed in the Rules, infringement of which may led to detainees being subjected by the authorities in charge of the place of detention to a range of punishments including up to 30 days' solitary confinement in an isolation cell and corporal punishment.

The disciplinary contraventions include deliberately replying falsely to a member of the detaining staff, disobeying 'a lawful command or order' and being 'insolent or disrespectful' towards a police officer or other official. Detainees are prohibited also from communicating with any other detainee or other person when held 'at a place where it is not permissible for him to do so' or from leaving their 'allocated sleeping or eating place' without permission. A detainee who 'sings, whistles or makes unnecessary noise' or is 'a nuisance', is also liable to punishment under the disciplinary code, as is any detainee who 'disfigures or damages' any part of the place in which he is being detained or any other state property. Other provisions suggest that anyone who goes on hunger strike will be punished: it is a disciplinary contravention to act in any manner 'contrary to good order and discipline' or to cause 'discontent, agitation or insubordination' and participate 'in any conspiracy'. Those detainees who make complaints may also jeopardize their own situation further if the complaints are regarded by the authorities as 'false, frivolous or malicious'. Likewise, detainees who are considered 'idle, careless or negligent' or who refuse to clean the place where they are detained, including its sanitary facilities, are liable to punishment.

Punishments under the disciplinary code may be imposed either by a prison officer or the magistrate responsible for the district in which the place of detention is situated. The penalties for disciplinary contraventions include the requirement that the detainee should undertake 'certain specific work' in the prison for up to 14 days; solitary confinement with full diet for up to 30 days; corporal punishment up to a maximum of six strokes with a cane, but only when the victim is a man 'apparently under the age of 40 years' and when no other punishment has been imposed in respect of the same contravention. Detainees may also be sentenced to imprisonment in solitary confinement for periods up to 30 days during which they receive what is termed 'spare diet' on not less than 18 days, 'reduced diet' on six days and the full prison diet on the remaining six days.

The imposition of the state of emergency follows widespread civil unrest affecting black townships in many parts of South Africa. The government asserts that this unrest has been provoked by political agitators but others maintain that its real cause is the sense of grievance many black people have over issues such as local rent increases, the poor standard of facilities available to black school students under the racially-segregated educational system and the constitutional changes put into effect in 1984. After simmering unrest in many black townships during the early part of 1984, serious unrest broke out in early September 1984 in the area south of Johannesburg generally known as the 'Vaal Triangle', in particular in the townships known as Sharpeville, Sebokeng and Evaton. They appear to have been sparked off by local rent increases and the arrest of black community leaders who had opposed the constitutional changes, which were in the process of implementation in August and September. There were attacks by township residents on local black town councillors and black police officers, who were identified popularly as representatives of the authorities. Substantial police contingents, and subsequently army units, were deployed in the area and there was a further escalation of violence which extended in late 1984 and early 1985 into the Eastern Cape and East Rand, in particular, and parts of Orange Free State province. Large numbers of black township residents were shot by police and many were killed. The most serious single incident of this nature occurred in the Eastern Cape on 21 March 1985, the 25th anniversary of the Sharpeville killings, when police opened fire on a funeral procession near Uitenhage. This incident was subsequently the subject of a judicial commission of inquiry which found that 20 black people, including several children, had been killed and others wounded. The police, who had been equipped with firearms and lethal ammunition but no other means of crowd dispersal on orders from above, were exonerated by the inquiry although at least 15 of those killed were found to have been shot in the back. There have been many further police shootings of civilians since the Uitenhage killings on 21 March 1985, particularly in the Eastern Cape area, and many people have been killed as a result. Since early September 1984, the total number of deaths associated with the unrest is reported to number around 500. Most are as a result of shootings by the police.

Amnesty International has expressed great concern to the South African Government about the imposition of the state of emergency and the arrest and detention of large numbers of critics and opponents of *apartheid*, many of whom are believed to be prisoners of conscience. In particular, the organization has stressed its fear that those held may be tortured in detention or may 'disappear'. It is especially disturbing that detainees are being held incommunicado at secret locations by security police who are known to use torture on an extensive scale and who have been granted immunity in advance for any acts they commit. Amnesty International has urged the South African Government to withdraw immediately police powers of arbitrary arrest and detention without trial, remove the shield of immunity which has been extended to the police and other officials, and guarantee that all detainees are safeguarded against torture or other forms of ill-treatment. The organization has called also for the release of all prisoners of conscience and to bring to trial promptly or release all other detainees.

Published August 1985

Lilian Celiberti was sent to prison in 1981 by a military court in Uruguay. She had been abducted from her home in exile in Brazil and, after being brought across the border illegally by security agents, was falsely charged with trying to enter Uruguay surreptitiously with 'subversive' literature. Her two small children, Camilo aged eight and Francesca aged three, were abducted with her. Tortured, and told she would never see them again, she signed a false confession in order to secure their release.

Amnesty International adopted Lilian Celiberti as a prisoner of conscience. Her case was allocated to an Amnesty International group in Italy. For five years the group worked ceaselessly on her behalf, sending around 600 letters and appeals to the Uruguayan authorities, to which they received not a single reply. They succeeded in contacting 66 Italian members of parliament to obtain their help in the case; having a question raised in the Italian and European parliaments; contacting an Italian delegation going to Uruguay; asking numerous Italian lawyers to intervene with the President of the Uruguayan Supreme Military Tribunal; having news of her case broadcast on Italian television.

The group also entered into regular correspondence with Lilian's parents. This enabled the group to keep track of the little children and to raise money for clothing and travel assistance so that the children could visit their mother in prison. On 17 November 1983 Lilian Celiberti was released after completing her sentence.

A month later she wrote to the Amnesty International group in Italy: 'You have been present during all these years with a constancy and dedication which has accompanied me in the worst moments, giving me strength and joy. I remember clearly the emotion I felt on returning to my cell after one of the fortnightly visits, the only time I talked to anyone, having learned about your letters. The solidarity that is expressed over oceans of distance gives strength and faith in one's solitude, and helps one confront the repressive apparatus by keeping one's human integrity and its essential values intact...'.

If you are interested in learning more about the work of Amnesty International, you can contact the local section or group in your area, or write to the International Secretariat, 1 Easton Street, London WC1X 8DJ, United Kingdom.

PHOTOGRAPHIC CREDITS

Front Cover: Brian Smith
Back Cover: Jean Claude Francolon/Gamma
Alfred/Gamma: page 55
Associated Press: pages 24, 25 (bottom), 51, 73, 77, 88 (two), 93 (bottom), 97, 107 (bottom), 190, 203 (bottom)
Camera Press: pages 34, 40, 43, 44, 82, 89, 119
Deutsche Presse-Agentur: page 35
Gamma: pages 70, 150 (three), 176
Chas Gerretsen: page 79
David Hawk, 1981: pages 155, 159
Tim Jarvis: page 203 (top)
Keystone: pages 32, 64
Magnum: page 116
Susan Meiselas/Magnum: page 161
Ghislaine Morel/Gamma: page 59
Network: pages 135, 136
Judah Passow/Network: page 38 (left)
Press Association: page 162
Popperfoto: pages 21, 22 (two), 25 (top), 28, 29, 53, 54, 101, 111, 149, 153 (top), 187
R. Sharma: page 14
Chris Steele-Perkins: page 180
Tass/Popperfoto: page 185
The Guardian: page 66

INDEX

Figures in italies refer to photo captions. Note that countries mentioned in captions are only indexed if the photograph appears outside a chapter devoted to that country.